Estimating How the
Macroeconomy Works

Estimating How the Macroeconomy Works

Ray C. Fair

Harvard University Press
Cambridge, Massachusetts
London, England
2004

Copyright © 2004 by the President and Fellows of Harvard College

All right reserved

Printed in the United States of America

Library of Congress Cataloging-in-Publication Data

Fair, Ray C.
    Estimating how the macroeconomy works / Ray C. Fair.
      p. cm.
    Includes bibliographical references and index.
    ISBN 0-674-01546-0 (alk. paper)
    1. Macroeconomics.   I. Title.

  HB172.5.F345 2004
  339—dc22   2004047522

Contents

Tables

Figures

Preface

This book presents my work in macroeconomics from 1994 to the present. It is an extension of the work in Fair (1984, 1994). The period since 1994 contains the U.S. stock market boom and what some consider to be a "new age" of high productivity growth and low inflation. It is also the period that includes the introduction of the euro. A number of chapters are directly concerned with these issues. This period is also one of continuing large advances in computer speeds, which allows much more to be done in Chapters 9–14 than could have been done earlier.

The macro theory that underlies this work is briefly outlined in section 1.3 and discussed in more detail in Chapter 2. It was first presented in Fair (1974). The theory stresses microfoundations, and in this sense it is consistent with modern macro theory. It does not, however, assume that expectations are rational, which is contrary to much current practice. It makes a big difference whether or not one assumes that expectations are rational. If they are not rational, the Lucas critique is not likely to be a problem, and one can follow the Cowles Commission methodology outlined in section 1.2.

The rational expectations (RE) assumption is hard to test and work with empirically. The widespread use of this assumption has moved macroeconomics away from standard econometric estimation toward calibration and matching moments. The work in this book follows the Cowles Commission methodology and is thus more empirical than much recent macro research: the data play a larger role here in influencing the specification of the model. The empirical results in this book do not support some current practices. The tests of the RE assumption in Chapter 2 are generally not supportive of it. The results discussed in Chapter 7 do not support some of the key properties of what is called the "modern-view" model. The results in Chapter 4 do not support the dynamics of the NAIRU model.

Advances in computer speeds have greatly expanded the feasibility of using stochastic simulation and bootstrapping. Chapter 9 provides an integration of stochastic simulation in macroeconomics and bootstrapping in statistics. The availability of these techniques allows a way of dealing with possible nonstationarity problems. If some variables are not stationary, the standard asymptotic formulas may be poor approximations of the actual distributions, and in many cases the exact distributions can be estimated. Chapter 4 contains an example of this. The working hypothesis in this book is that variables are stationary around a deterministic trend. This assumption is not tested, but, as just noted, exact distributions are sometimes estimated. Regarding the RE assumption, the increase in computer speeds has made it computationally feasible to analyze even large-scale RE models using stochastic simulation and optimal control techniques. This is discussed in Chapter 13, where a large-scale RE model is analyzed.

I am indebted to many people for helpful comments on the research covered in this book. These include Don Andrews, Michael Binder, William Brainard, Don Brown, Gregory Chow, Joel Horowitz, Lutz Kilian, Andrew Levin, William Nordhaus, Adrian Pagan, David Reifschneider, Robert Shiller, and James Stock. Sigridur Benediktsdottir, Daniel Mulino, Emi Nakamura, and Jon Steinsson read the entire manuscript and made many useful suggestions.

New Haven
March 2004

Abbreviations

AC model	United States autoregressive components model
CE	Certainty equivalence
DFP	Davidon-Fletcher-Powell nonlinear optimization algorithm
DM	Deutsche mark
Fed	Federal Reserve Bank of the United States
FFA	Flow of funds accounts
FS method	Fair-Shiller comparison method
FSR	First-stage regressor
MC model	Multicountry econometric model
NIPA	National income and product accounts
RE	Rational expectations
RMSE	Root mean squared error
ROW model	Non–United States part of the MC model
2SLS	Two-stage least squares
US model	United States part of the MC model
US+ model	US model with added autoregressive equations for the exogenous variables
US(EX,PIM) model	US model with added equations for EX and PIM
VAR model	United States vector autoregressive model

Estimating How the Macroeconomy Works

1

Introduction

1.1 Outline of the Book

This book analyzes a number of macroeconomic issues using a multicountry econometric model, denoted the MC model. The methodology followed in the construction of the model is discussed in the next section, and the theory behind the model is discussed in section 1.3. The rest of the chapter then presents the notation that is employed throughout the book and discusses the main estimation and testing techniques that are used.

Chapter 2 is a reference chapter: it and Appendixes A and B present the complete MC model. Each stochastic equation in the MC model is tested in a number of ways, and the test results are presented in the tables in the appendixes and discussed in Chapter 2. One should get a sense from the test results how much confidence to place on the various equations.

Section 2.3 presents an overview of the model without details and notation. One can read this section and skip the rest of Chapter 2 on first reading. The rest of the chapter can be used for reference purposes as the rest of the book is read. Some of the key test results, however, are presented in Chapter 2, and one may want to look these over on first reading. The results show, for example, little support for the RE assumption. Another important result in this chapter concerns the estimated interest rate rule of the Fed. The test results discussed in section 2.4.10 show that the equation is stable over the entire 1954:1–2002:3 period except for 1979:4–1982:3, when the Fed announced that it was targeting monetary aggregates.

Chapter 3 tests the use of nominal versus real interest rates in consumption and investment equations. The results strongly support the use of nominal over real interest rates in most expenditure equations. These results have implications for the analysis of inflation shocks in Chapter 7.

Chapter 4 tests the dynamics of the NAIRU model. The price and wage equations in the MC model have quite different dynamic properties from those of the

1

NAIRU model, and so it is of interest to test the dynamics. The NAIRU dynamics are generally rejected. An alternative way of thinking about the relationship between the price level and the unemployment rate is also proposed in Chapter 4, one in which there is a highly nonlinear relationship at low values of the unemployment rate.

Chapter 5 estimates the size of the wealth effect for the United States. The size of the wealth effect is important in Chapter 6 in analyzing the effects of the stock market boom in the last half of the 1990s on the economy.

Chapter 6 uses the MC model to examine the question of whether there were important structural changes in the U.S. economy in the last half of the 1990s. One of the hypotheses tested in Chapter 2 for each stochastic equation is that the coefficients have not changed near the end of the sample period. For the United States the end of the sample period is from the first quarter of 1995 on, and the only main equation for which the hypothesis is rejected is the equation explaining the change in stock prices. In other words, the only major structural change in the U.S. economy in the last half of the 1990s appears to be in the determination of stock prices. An experiment in Chapter 6 shows that had there not been a stock market boom in the last half of the 1990s (and thus no large wealth effect), the U.S. economy would not have looked unusual relative to historical experience. All the unusual features appear to be caused by the wealth effect from the stock market boom.

Chapter 7 examines a currently popular model in macroeconomics, called here the "modern-view" model. In this model a positive inflation shock with the nominal interest rate held constant is expansionary. In order for this model to be stable, the coefficient on inflation in the nominal interest rate rule must be greater than one. The experiment in Chapter 7 shows that a positive inflation shock in the MC model with the nominal interest rate held constant is contractionary, not expansionary. The MC model is stable even if the coefficient on inflation in the nominal interest rate rule is zero! The modern-view and MC models thus have quite different monetary policy implications. The use of nominal over real interest rates in the MC model, which is discussed in Chapter 3, is one reason for the different responses of the two models to an inflation shock. The other reasons concern real income and real wealth effects that are in the MC model but not the modern-view model.

Chapter 8 estimates what inflation would have been in Europe in the 1980s had the Bundesbank followed a more expansionary monetary policy. Although this is not an interesting exercise under the dynamics of the NAIRU model, it is of interest under the dynamics of the price and wage equations in the MC model. (Remember that the dynamics of the NAIRU model are generally rejected in Chapter 4.) The results show, for example, that a one-percentage-point fall in the German unemployment rate is associated with a less than one-percentage-point increase in the German inflation rate.

The rest of the book requires extensive numerical calculations. Chapter 9 discusses stochastic simulation and bootstrapping. It integrates for the general model in this book the bootstrapping approach to evaluating estimators, initiated by Efron

(1979), and the stochastic simulation approach to evaluating models' properties, initiated by Adelman and Adelman (1959). A Monte Carlo experiment in Chapter 9 shows that the bootstrap works well for the U.S. part of the MC model regarding coverage accuracy.

Chapter 10 is concerned with the solution of optimal control problems. The standard approach to solving optimal control problems for the general model in this book, outlined in section 1.7, assumes certainty equivalence (CE). Although this assumption is strictly valid only for the case of a linear model and a quadratic objective function, the results in Chapter 10 show that the errors introduced by using the CE assumption for nonlinear models seem small. This is encouraging because the CE assumption allows optimal control problems to be solved that would not be computationally feasible otherwise.

Chapter 11 examines the use of policy rules and the solving of optimal control problems for their ability to dampen economic fluctuations caused by random shocks. Contrary to what would be the case using a modern-view model, even nominal interest rate rules with a small or zero coefficient on inflation are stabilizing in the MC model. Increasing the coefficient on inflation lowers price variability at a cost of increasing interest rate variability. The optimal control procedure with a high weight on inflation relative to output in the loss function gives results that are similar to the use of the estimated Fed rule mentioned above. The results also show that a tax rate rule could help stabilize the economy.

Chapter 12 uses stochastic simulation to examine the stabilization costs to Germany, France, Italy, and the Netherlands from joining the European Monetary Union (EMU). The estimated costs are conditional on the use of a particular interest rate rule for each country before the EMU and a common rule thereafter. Using the estimated rules in the MC model, the results show that Germany is hurt the most. France is actually helped by joining the EMU because the estimated rule for France is not very stabilizing (the Bank of France is estimated to have mostly just followed what the Bundesbank did), whereas the EMU rule is partly stabilizing for France. There is a substantial stabilization cost to the United Kingdom when it is added to the EMU, and the stabilization cost to Germany is even larger if the United Kingdom joins.

Chapter 13 shows that the stochastic simulation and optimal control calculations in Chapter 11 that were performed to examine policy questions are computationally feasible for models with rational expectations, even when the models are large and nonlinear. Most of the experiments in this book thus do not require that the model be a non-RE model like the MC model in order to be computationally feasible. The model analyzed in Chapter 13 is one with rational expectations in the bond market and where households have rational expectations with respect to future values of income.

Chapter 14 compares the accuracy of the U.S. part of the MC model to that of simpler, time-series models. The results show that considerable predictive power is lost using simpler models.

Chapter 15 summarizes the main conclusions of this study.

1.2   Methodology

The methodology followed in the construction of the MC model is what is called here the "Cowles Commission approach."[1] Theory is used to guide the choice of left-hand-side and right-hand-side variables for the stochastic equations in the model, and the resulting equations are estimated using a consistent estimation technique—two-stage least squares (2SLS). In a few cases a restriction is imposed on the coefficients in an equation, and the equation is estimated with the restriction imposed. It is never the case that all the coefficients in a stochastic equation are chosen ahead of time and thus no estimation done: every stochastic equation is estimated. In this sense the data rule.

The theory is that households form expectations of their relevant future variable values and maximize expected utility. The main choice variables are expenditures and labor supply. Similarly, firms form expectations and maximize expected profits. The main choice variables are prices, wages, production, investment, employment, and dividends. Firms are assumed to behave in a monopolistically competitive environment.

It is assumed that expectations are *not* rational. Agents are assumed to be forward looking in that they form expectations of future values that in turn affect their current decisions, but these expectations are not assumed to be rational (model consistent). Agents are not assumed to know the complete model. This is not to say, however, that expectations of future values are unaffected by current and past values; they are just not obtained using predictions from the model. As noted in the previous section, this book contains tests of the rational expectations (RE) hypothesis, and in most cases the hypothesis is rejected. If expectations are not rational, then the Lucas (1976) critique is not likely to be a problem.[2]

The econometric assumption is made that all variables are stationary around a deterministic trend. If this assumption is wrong, the estimated asymptotic standard errors may be poor approximations to the true standard errors. One way to examine the accuracy of asymptotic distributions is to use a bootstrap procedure, which is discussed in Chapter 9.

Much of the literature in macroeconomics in the last thirty years has used the RE assumption, and much of the literature in time-series econometrics has been concerned with nonstationary variables. The previous two paragraphs have thus assumed away a huge body of work, and some may want to stop reading here. There is, however, no strong evidence in favor of the RE assumption (and some against), and I don't find it plausible that enough people are sophisticated enough for the rational expectations assumption to be a good approximation. Regarding the stationarity assumption, it is well known that it is difficult to test whether a variable is nonstationary versus stationary

---

1. See section 1.2 in Fair (1994) for a more detailed discussion of this approach.

2. Evans and Ramey (2003) have shown that in some cases the Lucas critique is a problem even if expectations are not rational. These cases are specific to the Evans and Ramey framework, and it is unclear how much they can be generalized.

around a deterministic trend, and I don't see a problem with taking the easier road. At worst the estimated standard errors are poor approximations, and the bootstrap procedure can help examine this question.

In using theory as it is used in this book, there is much back-and-forth movement between specification and estimation. If, for example, a variable or set of variables is not significant or a coefficient estimate is of the wrong expected sign, one goes back to the specification for possible changes. Because of this, there is always a danger of data mining—of finding a statistically significant relationship that is in fact spurious. Testing is thus important, and much of this book is concerned with testing.

The methodology here is more empirically driven than the use of calibration, which is currently popular in macroeconomics. The aim here is to explain the data well within the restriction of a fairly broad theoretical framework. In the calibration literature the stress is more on examining the implications of very specific theoretical restrictions; there is only a limited amount of empirical discipline in the specification choices. The aim in the calibration literature is not to find the model that best explains, say, the quarterly paths of real GDP and inflation, which is the aim of this book.

The transition from theory as it is used here to empirical specifications is not always straightforward. The quality of the data is never as good as one might like, so compromises have to be made. Also, extra assumptions usually have to be made for the empirical specifications, in particular about unobserved variables like expectations and about dynamics. There usually is, in other words, considerable "theorizing" involved in this transition process. There are many examples of this in Chapter 2.

1.3   Macro Theory

The "broad theoretical framework" mentioned above that has been used to guide the specification of the MC model was first presented in Fair (1974a). It is summarized in Fair (1984), Chapter 3, and Fair (1994), Chapter 2. This work stresses three ideas: (1) basing macroeconomics on solid microeconomic foundations, (2) allowing for the possibility of disequilibrium in some markets, and (3) accounting for all balance-sheet and flow of funds constraints. Households and firms make decisions by solving maximization problems. Households' decision variables include consumption, labor supply, and the demand for money. Firms' decision variables include production, investment, employment, and the demand for money. Firms are assumed to behave in a monopolistically competitive environment, and prices and wages are also decision variables of firms. The values of prices and wages that firms set are not necessarily market clearing. Disequilibrium in the goods markets takes the form of unintended changes in inventories. Disequilibrium in the labor market takes the form of unemployment, where households are constrained by firms from working as much as the solutions of their unconstrained maximization problems say they want to.

Disequilibrium comes about because of expectation errors. In order for a firm to form correct (rational)[3] expectations, it would have to know the maximization problems of all the other firms and of the households. Firms are not assumed to have this much knowledge (that is, they do not know the complete model), and so they can make expectation errors.

Tax rates and most government spending variables are exogenous in the model. Regarding monetary policy, in the early specification of the theoretical model—Fair (1974a)—the amount of government securities outstanding was taken as exogenous, that is, as a policy variable of the monetary authority. In 1978 an estimated interest rate rule was added to the empirical version of the model—Fair (1978)—which was then added to the discussion of the theoretical model in Fair (1984), Chapter 3. The rule is one in which the Fed "leans against the wind," where the nominal interest rate depends positively on the rate of inflation and on output or the unemployment rate.

Interest rate rules are currently quite popular in macroeconomics. They are usually referred to as "Taylor rules" from Taylor (1993), although they have a long history. The first rule is in Dewald and Johnson (1963), who regressed the Treasury bill rate on the constant, the Treasury bill rate lagged once, real GNP, the unemployment rate, the balance-of-payments deficit, and the consumer price index. The next example can be found in Christian (1968), followed by many others. These rules should thus probably be called Dewald-Johnson rules, since Dewald and Johnson preceded Taylor by about 30 years!

Because the model accounts for all flow-of-fund and balance-sheet constraints, there is no natural distinction between stock market and flow market determination of exchange rates. This distinction played an important role in exchange rate modeling in the 1970s. In the model an exchange rate is merely one endogenous variable out of many, and in no rigorous sense can it be said to be *the* variable that clears a particular market.

Various properties of the theoretical model are referred to in the specification discussion of the empirical model in the next chapter. The reader is referred to the earlier references for a detailed discussion of the theoretical model. This discussion is not repeated in this book.

1.4   Notation and 2SLS Estimation

The general model considered in this book is dynamic, nonlinear, and simultaneous:

$$f_i(y_t, y_{t-1}, \ldots, y_{t-p}, x_t, \alpha_i) = u_{it}, \quad i = 1, \ldots, n, \quad t = 1, \ldots, T, \quad (1.1)$$

where y_t is an n-dimensional vector of endogenous variables, x_t is a vector of exogenous variables, and α_i is a vector of coefficients. The first m equations are assumed to be

---

3. The simulation model that has been used to analyze the properties of the theoretical model is deterministic, and so rational expectations in this context are perfect foresight expectations.

stochastic, with the remaining equations identities. The vector of error terms, $u_t = (u_{1t}, \ldots, u_{mt})'$, is assumed to be *iid*. The function f_i may be nonlinear in variables and coefficients. The T-dimensional vector $(u_{i1}, \ldots, u_{iT})'$ will be denoted u_i.

This specification is fairly general. It includes as a special case the VAR model. It also incorporates autoregressive errors. If the original error term in equation i follows an rth-order autoregressive process, say $w_{it} = \rho_{1i} w_{it-1} + \cdots + \rho_{ri} w_{it-r} + u_{it}$, then equation i in model 1.1 can be assumed to have been transformed into one with u_{it} on the right-hand side. The autoregressive coefficients $\rho_{1i}, \ldots, \rho_{ri}$ are incorporated into the α_i coefficient vector, and additional lagged variable values are introduced. This transformation makes the equation nonlinear in coefficients if it were not otherwise, but this adds no further complications because the model is already allowed to be nonlinear. The assumption that u_t is *iid* is thus not as restrictive as it would be if the model were required to be linear in coefficients.

Although it is not assumed that expectations are rational in the MC model, some of the work in this book uses the RE assumption. For a model with rational expectations, the notation is:[4]

$$f_i(y_t, y_{t-1}, \ldots, y_{t-p}, E_{t-1}y_t, E_{t-1}y_{t+1}, \ldots, E_{t-1}y_{t+h}, x_t, \alpha_i) = u_{it}$$
$$i = 1, \ldots, n, \quad t = 1, \ldots, T, \tag{1.2}$$

where E_{t-1} is the conditional expectations operator based on the model and on information through period $t - 1$. The function f_i may be nonlinear in variables, parameters, and expectations.

For the non-RE model 1.1, the 2SLS estimate of α_i is obtained by minimizing

$$S_i = u_i' Z_i (Z_i' Z_i)^{-1} Z_i' u_i \tag{1.3}$$

with respect to α_i, where Z_i is a $T \times K_i$ matrix of first-stage regressors. When a stochastic equation for a country is estimated by 2SLS in this book, the first-stage regressors are the main predetermined variables for the country. The predetermined variables are assumed to be correlated with the right-hand-side endogenous variables in the equation but not with the error term.

The estimation of RE models is discussed in the next section under the discussion of *leads*. The solution of RE models is discussed in section 13.3. Although RE models are considerably more costly to solve in terms of computer time, Chapter 13 shows that both optimal control and stochastic simulation are computationally feasible for such models.

1.5   Testing Single Equations

Each of the stochastic equations of the MC model has been tested in a number of ways. The following is a brief outline of these tests.

---

4. The treatment of autoregressive errors is more complicated in the RE model because it introduces more than one viewpoint date. This is discussed in Fair and Taylor (1983, 1990).

1.5.1   Chi-Square Tests

Many single-equation tests are simply of the form of adding a variable or a set of variables to an equation and testing whether the addition is statistically significant. Let S_i^{**} denote the value of the minimand before the addition, let S_i^* denote the value after the addition, and let $\hat{\sigma}_{ii}$ denote the estimated variance of the error term after the addition. Under fairly general conditions, as discussed in Andrews and Fair (1988), $(S_i^{**} - S_i^*)/\hat{\sigma}_{ii}$ is distributed as χ^2 with k degrees of freedom, where k is the number of variables added. For the 2SLS estimator the minimand is defined in equation 1.3. Possible applications of the χ^2 test are the following.

Dynamic Specification

Many macroeconomic equations include the lagged dependent variable and other lagged endogenous variables among the explanatory variables. A test of the dynamic specification of a particular equation is to add *further* lagged values to the equation and see if they are significant. If, for example, in an equation y_{1t} is explained by y_{2t}, y_{3t-1}, and x_{1t-2}, then the variables added are y_{1t-1}, y_{2t-1}, y_{3t-2}, and x_{1t-3}. If in addition y_{1t-1} is an explanatory variable, then y_{1t-2} is added. Hendry, Pagan, and Sargan (1984) show that adding these lagged values is quite general in that it encompasses many different types of dynamic specifications. Therefore, adding the lagged values and testing for their significance is a test against a fairly general dynamic specification. This test is called the "lags" test in Chapter 2.

The lags test also concerns the acceleration principle.[5] If, for example, the level of income is specified as an explanatory variable in an expenditure equation, but the correct specification is the change in income, then when lagged income is added as an explanatory variable with the current level of income included, the lagged value should be significant. If the lagged value is not significant, this is evidence against the use of the change in income.

Time Trend

Long before unit roots and cointegration became popular, model builders worried about picking up spurious correlation from common trending variables. One check on whether the correlation might be spurious is to add the time trend to the equation. If adding the time trend to the equation substantially changes some of the coefficient estimates, this is cause for concern. A simple test is to add the time trend to the equation and test if this addition is significant. This test is called the "T" test in Chapter 2.

Serial Correlation of the Error Term

As noted in section 1.4, if the error term in an equation follows an autoregressive process, the equation can be transformed and the coefficients of the autoregressive

---

5. See Chow (1968) for an early analysis of the acceleration principle.

process can be estimated along with the structural coefficients. Even if, say, a first-order process has been assumed and the first-order coefficient estimated, it is still of interest to see if there is serial correlation of the (transformed) error term. This can be done by assuming a more general process for the error term and testing its significance. If, for example, the addition of a second-order process over a first-order process results in a significant increase in explanatory power, this is evidence that the serial correlation properties of the error term have not been properly accounted for. This test is called the "RHO" test in Chapter 2.

Leads (Rational Expectations)

Adding values *led* one or more periods and using Hansen's (1982) method for the estimation is a way of testing the hypothesis that expectations are rational. The test of the RE hypothesis is to add variable values led one or more periods to an equation and estimate the resulting equation using Hansen's method. If the led values are not significant, this is evidence against the RE hypothesis.

For example, say that $E_{t-1}y_{2t+1}$ and $E_{t-1}y_{2t+2}$ are postulated to be explanatory variables in the first equation in model 1.2, where the expectations are assumed to be rational. If it is assumed that variables in a matrix Z_i are used in part by agents in forming their (rational) expectations, then Hansen's method in this context is simply 2SLS with adjustment for the moving-average process of the error term. The expectations variables are replaced by the actual values y_{2t+1} and y_{2t+2}, and the first-stage regressors are the variables in Z_i. Consistent estimation does not require that Z_i include all the variables used by agents in forming their expectations. The requirement for consistency is that Z_i be uncorrelated with the expectation errors, which is true if expectations are rational and Z_i is at least a subset of the variables used by the agents.[6]

If the coefficient estimates of y_{2t+1} and y_{2t+2} are insignificant, this is evidence against the RE hypothesis. For the "leads" tests in Chapter 2, three sets of led values are tried per equation. For the first set the values of the relevant variables led once are added; for the second set the values led one through four quarters are added; and for the third set the values led one through eight quarters are added, where the coefficients for each variable are constrained to lie on a second-degree polynomial with an end-point constraint of zero. The test in each case is a χ^2 test that the additional variables are significant. The three tests are called "Leads +1," "Leads +4," and "Leads +8."

1.5.2   AP Stability Test

A useful stability test is the Andrews and Ploberger (AP) (1994) test. It does not require that the date of the structural change be chosen a priori. If the overall sample period is 1 through T, the hypothesis tested is that a structural change occurred between

---

6. For more details, including the case in which u_{it} in model 1.2 is serially correlated, see Fair (1993b) or Fair (1994), pp. 65–70.

observations T_1 and T_2, where T_1 is an observation close to 1 and T_2 is an observation close to T.

The particular AP test used in this book is as follows.

1. Compute the χ^2 value for the hypothesis that the change occurred at observation T_1. This requires estimating the equation three times—once each for the estimation periods 1 through $T_1 - 1$, T_1 through T, and 1 through T. Denote this value as $\chi^{2(1)}$.[7]

2. Repeat step 1 for the hypothesis that the change occurred at observation $T_1 + 1$. Denote this χ^2 value as $\chi^{2(2)}$. Keep doing this through the hypothesis that the change occurred at observation T_2. This results in $N = T_2 - T_1 + 1$ χ^2 values being computed—$\chi^{2(1)}, \ldots, \chi^{2(N)}$.

3. The Andrews-Ploberger test statistic (denoted AP) is

$$AP = \log[(e^{\frac{1}{2}\chi^{2(1)}} + \cdots + e^{\frac{1}{2}\chi^{2(N)}})/N]. \tag{1.4}$$

In words, the AP statistic is a weighted average of the χ^2 values, where there is one χ^2 value for each possible split in the sample period between observations T_1 and T_2.

Asymptotic critical values for AP are presented in Tables I and II in Andrews and Ploberger (1994). The critical values depend on the number of coefficients in the equation and on a parameter λ, where in the present context $\lambda = [\pi_2(1 - \pi_1)]/[\pi_1(1 - \pi_2)]$, where $\pi_1 = (T_1 - .5)/T$ and $\pi_2 = (T_2 - .5)/T$.

If the AP value is significant, it may be of interest to examine the individual χ^2 values to see where the maximum value occurred. This is likely to give one a general idea of where the structural change occurred even though the AP test does not reveal this in any rigorous way.

In Chapter 2 three AP tests are computed for each stochastic equation for the United States corresponding to three different pairs of T_1, T_2 values: 1970.1, 1979.4; 1975.1, 1984.4; and 1980.1, 1989.4. One AP test is computed for each of the other stochastic equations (for the other countries), with T_1 40 quarters or 10 years after the first observation and T_2 40 quarters or 10 years before the last observation. A * is put before the AP value if the value is significant at the 99 percent confidence level. The null hypothesis is that there is no structural change.

---

7. When the 2SLS estimator is used, this χ^2 value is computed as follows. Let $S_i^{(1)}$ be the value of the minimand in equation 1.3 for the first estimation period, and let $S_i^{(2)}$ be the value for the second estimation period. Define $S_i^* = S_i^{(1)} + S_i^{(2)}$. Let S_i^{**} be the value of the minimand in 1.3 when the equation is estimated over the full estimation period. When estimating over the full period, the Z_i matrix used for the full period must be the union of the matrices used for the two subperiods in order to make S_i^{**} comparable to S_i^*. This means that for each first-stage regressor z_{it} two variables must be used in Z_i for the full estimation period, one that is equal to z_{it} for the first subperiod and zero otherwise and one that is equal to z_{it} for the second subperiod and zero otherwise. The χ^2 value is then $(S_i^{**} - S_i^*)/\hat{\sigma}_{ii}$, where $\hat{\sigma}_{ii}$ is equal to the sum of the sums of squared residuals from the first and second estimation periods divided by $T - 2k_i$, where k_i is the number of estimated coefficients in the equation.

Dummy variables that take on a value of 1.0 during certain quarters or years and 0.0 otherwise appear in a few of the stochastic equations of the MC model. For example, there are four dummy variables in the U.S. import equation that are, respectively, 1.0 in 1969:1, 1969:2, 1971:4, and 1972:1 and 0.0 otherwise. These are meant to pick up effects of two dock strikes. A dummy variable coefficient obviously cannot be estimated for sample periods in which the dummy variable is always zero. This rules out the use of the AP test if some of the sample periods that are used in the test have all zero values for at least one dummy variable. To get around this problem when performing the test, all dummy variable coefficients were taken to be fixed and equal to their estimates based on the entire sample period. This was also done for the end-of-sample stability test discussed next.

1.5.3   End-of-Sample Stability Test

As mentioned above, some consider that the U.S. economy entered a new age in the 1990s. An interesting test of this is to test the hypothesis that the coefficients in the U.S. stochastic equations differ, say, beginning about 1995. Consider the null hypothesis that the coefficients in an equation are the same over the entire 1954:1–2002:3 period. The alternative hypothesis is that the coefficients are different before and after 1995:1. There are 195 total observations and 31 observations from 1995:1 on. If the potential break point were earlier in the sample period, the methods in Andrews and Fair (1988) could be used to test the hypothesis. These methods cover the 2SLS estimator. However, given that there are only 31 observations after the potential break point, these methods are not practical because the number of first-stage regressors is close to the number of observations. In other words, it is not practical to estimate the equations using only observations for the 1995:1–2002:3 period, which the methods require.

The end-of-sample stability test developed in Andrews (2003) can be used when there are fewer observations after the potential break point than regressors. The test used in this book is what Andrews calls the P_b test. In the present context this test is as follows (again, the estimation method is 2SLS):

1. Estimate the equation to be tested over the whole period 1954:1–2002:3 (195 observations). Let d denote the sum of squared residuals from this regression for the 1995:1–2002:3 period (31 observations).

2. Consider 134 different subsets of the basic 1954:1–1994:4 sample period. For the first subset estimate the equation using observations 16–164, and use these coefficient estimates to compute the sum of squared residuals for the 1–31 period. Let d_1 denote this sum of squared residuals. For the second subset estimate the equation using observations 1 and 17–164, and use these coefficient estimates to compute the sum of squared residuals for the 2–32 period. Let d_2 denote this sum of squared residuals. For the last (134th) subset estimate the equation using observations 1–133 and 149–164, and use these coefficient estimates to compute the sum of squared residuals for the 134–164 period. Let d_{134} denote this sum of squared residuals. Then sort d_i by size ($i = 1, \ldots, 134$).

3. Observe where d falls within the distribution of d_i. If, say, d exceeds 95 percent of the d_i values and a 95 percent confidence level is being used, then the hypothesis of stability is rejected. The p-value is simply the percentage of the d_i values that lie above d.

Note in step 2 that each of the 134 sample periods used to estimate the coefficients includes half (rounded up) of the observations for which the sum of squared residuals is computed. This choice is ad hoc, but a fairly natural finite sample adjustment. The adjustment works well in Andrews's simulations.

In Chapter 2 one end-of-sample test is computed for each stochastic equation. For the United States the end period is 1995.1–2002.3. For the other countries the end period usually begins twelve quarters or three years before the last observation. In Chapter 6 the end-of-sample test is also computed for each stochastic equation for the United States for the end period 1995:1–2000:4.

1.5.4   Test of Overidentifying Restrictions

A common test of overidentifying restrictions when using 2SLS is to regress the 2SLS residuals, denoted $\hat{u}_i$, on Z_i and compute the R^2. Then $T \cdot R^2$ is distributed as χ_q^2, where q is the number of variables in Z_i minus the number of explanatory variables in the equation being estimated.[8] The null hypothesis is that all the first-stage regressors are uncorrelated with u_i. If $T \cdot R^2$ exceeds the specified critical value, the null hypothesis is rejected, and one would conclude that at least some of the first-stage regressors are not predetermined. This test is denoted "overid" in the tables discussed in Chapter 2.

1.5.5   Confidence Levels and Response to Rejections

Unless stated otherwise, a hypothesis will be said to be rejected if the p-value for the test is less than .01. If a hypothesis is not rejected, the test will be said to have been "passed." For example, if a leads test is passed, this means that the led values are not significant, which is a rejection of the RE hypothesis. A coefficient estimate will be said to be significant if its t-statistic is greater than 2.0 in absolute value. A variable will be said to be significant if its coefficient estimate is significant.

It will be seen in Chapter 2 that a number of tests are not passed. If an equation does not pass a test, it is not always clear what should be done. If, for example, the hypothesis of structural stability is rejected, one possibility is to divide the sample period into two parts and estimate two separate equations. If this is done, however, the resulting coefficient estimates are not always sensible in terms of what one would expect from theory. Similarly, when the additional lagged values are significant, the equation with the additional lagged values does not always have what one would consider sensible dynamic properties. In other words, when an equation fails a test, the change in the equation that the test results suggest may not produce what seem

---

8. See Wooldridge (2000), pp. 484–485, for a clear discussion of this.

to be sensible results. In many cases, the best choice seems to be to stay with the original equation even though it failed the test. Some of this difficulty may be due to small-sample problems, which will lessen over time as sample sizes increase. This is an important area for future work and is what makes macroeconomics interesting. Obviously less confidence should be placed on equations that fail a number of the tests than on those that do not.

1.6 Testing Complete Models

Once the α_i coefficients in model 1.1 have been estimated, the model can be solved. For a deterministic simulation the error terms u_{it} are set to zero. A dynamic simulation is one in which the predicted values of the endogenous variables for past periods are used as values for the lagged endogenous variables when solving for the current period. The solution technique for nonlinear models is usually the Gauss-Seidel technique.[9]

One widely used measure of fit is root mean squared error (RMSE). Let $\hat{y}_{it}$ denote the predicted value of endogenous variable i for period t. If the solution period is 1 through S, the RMSE is:

$$RMSE_i = \sqrt{\frac{1}{S}\sum_{t=1}^{S}(\hat{y}_{it} - y_{it})^2}. \qquad (1.5)$$

There are a number of potential problems in using the RMSE criterion to compare different models. One potential problem is data mining, where much specification searching may have been done to obtain good fits. In this case RMSEs may be low because of the searching and may not be an adequate reflection of how well the model has approximated the economy. One answer to this is to compute RMSEs for periods outside the estimation period, where less searching is likely to have been done. An even better answer is, data permitting, to compute RMSEs for periods that were not known at the time of the specification and estimation of the model.

Another potential problem is that models may be based on different sets of exogenous variables. One model may have lower RMSEs than another simply because it takes more variables to be exogenous. One answer to this is to estimate autoregressive equations for the exogenous variables and add these equations to the model, which produces a model with no exogenous variables. RMSEs from the expanded models can then be compared.

It may be that one model has lower RMSEs than another but that the predictions from both models have independent information. The procedure in Fair and Shiller (1990), denoted the "FS method" in this book, can be used to examine this question. The procedure is to regress (over the prediction period) the actual value of a variable on

---

9. See Fair (1984), Chapter 7, for a discussion of the use of the Gauss-Seidel technique in the present context.

the constant term and predictions from two or more models. If one model's predic-tion has all the information in it that the other predictions have plus some, then its coefficient estimate should be significant and the others not. If, on the other hand, all the predictions have independent information, all the coefficient estimates should be significant.

Coming back to RMSEs, they are not in general estimates of prediction error vari-ances, because these variances generally vary across time. Prediction error variances vary across time because of nonlinearities in the model, because of variation in the ex-ogenous variables, and because of variation in the initial conditions. This problem can be handled by using stochastic simulation to estimate variances. A stochastic simula-tion requires many solutions of the model, where each solution is based on a particular draw of the u_{it} error terms in model 1.1. Stochastic simulation is used in this book beginning with Chapter 9. Chapter 14 is concerned with comparing different mod-els using RMSEs and the FS method and with estimating variation using stochastic simulation.

1.7   Solving Optimal Control Problems

For some of the work in this book optimal control problems need to be solved using model 1.1. Under the assumption of certainty equivalence, a useful technique is as follows.

Assume that the period of interest is s through S and that the objective is to maximize the expected value of W subject to the model 1.1, where W is

$$W = \sum_{t=s}^{S} g_t(y_t, x_t). \tag{1.6}$$

Let z_t be the vector of control variables, where z_t is a subset of x_t, and let z be the vector of all the control values: $z = (z_s, \ldots, z_S)$. Under the CE assumption, the control problem is solved at the beginning of period s by setting the errors for period s and beyond equal to zero. If this is done, then for each value of z one can compute a value of W by first solving the model for $y_s, \ldots, y_S$ and then using these values along with the values for $x_s, \ldots, x_S$ to compute W in equation 1.6. Stated this way, the optimal control problem is choosing variables (the elements of z) to maximize an *unconstrained* nonlinear function. By substitution, the constrained maximization problem is transformed into the problem of maximizing an unconstrained function of the control variables:

$$W = \Phi(z), \tag{1.7}$$

where Φ stands for the mapping $z \longrightarrow y_s, \ldots, y_S, x_s, \ldots, x_S \longrightarrow W$. Given this setup, the problem can be turned over to a nonlinear optimization algorithm like Davidon-Fletcher-Powell (DFP). For each iteration of the algorithm, the derivatives of Φ with respect to the elements of z, which are needed by the algorithm, can be computed numerically. An algorithm like DFP is generally quite good at finding the optimum for a typical control problem.[10]

Let z_s^* be the computed optimal value of z_s. This is the value that would be implemented for period s by the control authority. Although the control problem also calculates the optimal values for periods $s + 1$ through S, in practice these would never have to be implemented because a new problem could be solved at the beginning of period $s + 1$ after period s was realized. This is the "open-loop feedback" approach. Chapter 10 examines the sensitivity of optimal control results to the use of the CE assumption.

1.8 The FP Program and the Website

All the calculations in this book have been done using the Fair-Parke (FP) program (2003). The first version of this program was available in 1980, and it has been expanded over time. See Fair (1984), Appendix C, for a discussion of the logic of the program. One of the advantages of the program is that it allows the user to move easily from the estimation of individual equations to the solution and analysis of the entire model.

The Fair-Parke program can be downloaded from the website *http://fairmodel.econ .yale.edu*. The datasets for the US model and for the overall MC model that are used by the FP program can also be downloaded. With these datasets and the FP program, all the calculations in this book can be duplicated. One can also work with the US and MC models online. Although estimation and stochastic simulation cannot be done online, many of the experiments in this book can be duplicated online.

---

10. See Fair (1974b) for various applications of this procedure. See also Fair (1984), section 2.5, for a discussion of the DFP algorithm.

2

The MC Model

2.1 The Model in Tables

This is a reference chapter for the MC model. This section outlines the presentation of the model in tables, and the next section discusses the treatment of expectations. Section 2.3 then gives a general overview of the model. Sections 2.4 and 2.5 discuss the model in detail and can be skipped on first reading.

There are 39 countries in the MC model for which stochastic equations are estimated. The countries are listed in Table B.1 in Appendix B. There are 31 stochastic equations for the United States and up to 15 each for the other countries. The total number of stochastic equations is 362, and the total number of estimated coefficients is 1,646. In addition, there are 1,111 estimated trade share equations. The total number of endogenous and exogenous variables, not counting various transformations of the variables and the trade share variables, is about 2,000. Trade share data were collected for 59 countries, and so the trade share matrix is 59 × 59.

The estimation periods begin in 1954 for the United States and as soon after 1960 as data permit for the other countries. They end between 1998 and 2002. The estimation technique is 2SLS except when there are too few observations to make the technique practical, where ordinary least squares is used. The estimation accounts for possible serial correlation of the error terms. The variables used for the first-stage regressors for a country are the main predetermined variables in the model for the country.

There is a mixture of quarterly and annual data in the model. Quarterly equations are estimated for 14 countries, and annual equations are estimated for the remaining 25. However, all the trade share equations are quarterly. There are quarterly data on all the variables that feed into the trade share equations, namely the exchange rate, the local currency price of exports, and the total value of imports per country. When the model is solved, the predicted annual values of these variables for the annual countries are converted to predicted quarterly values using a simple distribution assumption. The quarterly predicted values from the trade share equations are converted to annual values by summation or averaging when this is needed. The solution of the MC model is explained in section B.6 in Appendix B.

For ease of reference the United States part of the overall MC model is denoted the "US" model and the remaining part is denoted the "ROW" model. The ROW model consists of the individual models of all the other countries. Also, all the equations that pertain to the links among countries, such as the trade share equations, are put in the ROW model. There are 30 stochastic equations for the US model alone and 1 additional equation when the US model is imbedded in the overall MC model.

The discussion of the model in sections 2.4 and 2.5 relies heavily on the tables in Appendixes A and B. All the variables and equations in the US model are presented in Appendix A. Table A.1 lists the six sectors of the model, and Table A.2 lists all the variables in alphabetical order. All the equations, both the stochastic equations and the identities, are listed in Table A.3, but not the coefficient estimates. The coefficient estimates and test results are presented in Table A.4 for the 30 stochastic equations. Within Table A.4, Table A1 refers to equation 1, Table A2 refers to equation 2, and so on through Table A30.

The remaining tables in Appendix A are for completeness. They allow the model to be reproduced by someone else. These tables can be skipped if desired. Table A.5 lists the "raw data" variables, that is, the variables for which data were collected. Table A.6 shows the links using the raw data variables between the national income and product accounts (NIPA) and the flow of funds accounts (FFA). Table A.7 shows how the variables in the model were constructed from the raw data variables. Table A.8 shows how the model is solved under alternative assumptions about monetary policy. Table A.9 lists the first-stage regressors used for each equation for the 2SLS estimator. Finally, Table A.10 shows which variables appear in which equations. It is useful for tracking the effects of various variables.

Appendix B does for the ROW model what Appendix A does for the US model. Table B.1 lists the countries in the model, and Table B.2 lists all the variables for a given country in alphabetical order Table B.2 also shows how each variable in the model is constructed from the data. All the equations, both the stochastic equations and the identities, are listed in Table B.3, but not the coefficient estimates. The coefficient estimates and test results are presented in Table B.4 for the stochastic equations. There are up to 15 equations per country, and within Table B.4, Table B1 refers to equation 1, Table B2 refers to equation 2, and so on through Table B15. Table B.5 shows the links between the US and ROW models, and Table B.6 shows how the balance-of-payments data were used. There are a few other versions of the US model from the one presented in Appendix A, and these versions are discussed as they are used.

In presenting the stochastic equations in this chapter, ϵ_t is used to denote the error term in the equation. Sometimes μ_t is also used. The t subscript is sometimes dropped when there is no confusion about the time period.

2.2   Treatment of Expectations

It will be seen that lagged dependent variables are used as explanatory variables in many of the equations. They are generally highly significant even after accounting for any autoregressive properties of the error terms. It is well known that lagged dependent variables can be accounting for either partial adjustment effects or expectational effects and that it is difficult to identify the two effects separately.[1] For the most part no attempt is made in the empirical work in this book to separate the two effects. The rational expectations assumption is, however, tested in the manner discussed in section 1.5. Since most of the equations are estimated by 2SLS, one can also think of the predicted values from the first-stage regressions as representing the predictions of the agents if it is assumed that agents know the values of the first-stage regressors at the time they make their decisions.

For some of the tests specific measures of expectations are used. For example, two measures of inflationary expectations that are used are $\dot{p}^e_{4t} = (P_t/P_{t-4}) - 1$ and $\dot{p}^e_{8t} = (P_t/P_{t-8})^{.5} - 1$, where P_t is the price level in quarter t.

2.3   An Overview of the Model

Because of the MC model's size, it is difficult to get a big picture of how it works. In this section an attempt is made to give an overview of the model for a given country without getting bogged down in details and notation. The model for the United States is more detailed than the models for the other countries, and the discussion in this section pertains only to the models for the other countries. Table 2.1 is used as a framework for discussion. The table outlines for a given country how thirteen variables are determined. The first seven (consumption, investment, imports, domestic price level, short-term interest rate, exchange rate, and export price level) are determined by estimated equations; the next two (import price level and exports) are determined when all the countries are linked together; and the last four (output, current account, net assets, and world price level) are determined by identities.

Unless otherwise stated, the price levels are prices in local currency. Consumption, investment, imports, exports, and output are in real (local currency) terms. The exchange rate is local currency per U.S. dollar, so an increase in the exchange rate is a depreciation of the currency relative to the dollar.

The following discussion ignores dynamic issues. In most estimated equations there is a lagged dependent variable among the explanatory variables to pick up partial adjustment and/or expectational effects, but these variables are not listed in the table. Inventory investment is not discussed; the labor sector is not discussed; the interaction between prices and wages is not discussed; and the relationship between the short-term and long-term interest rate is not discussed. Finally, in terms of what is not discussed, it should be kept in mind that not every effect exists for every country.

---

1. See Fair (1984), section 2.2.2, for a discussion of this.

Table 2.1

Determination of Some Variables per Country in the ROW Model

	Explanatory Variables					
	Output or Income	Interest Rates Short & Long	Net Assets (Wealth)	Domestic Price Level	Import Price Level	World Price Level
Estimated Equations						
1 Consumption	+	−	+			
2 Investment	+	−				
3 Imports	+[a]	−		+	−	
4 Domestic Price Level	+				+	
5 Interest Rate (Short)	+			+[b]		
6 Exchange Rate[c]	−	−		+		
7 Export Price Level				+		+

	Export Price Level	Exchange Rate[c]	Export Prices Other Countries
When Countries Are Linked Together			
8 Import Price Level		+	+
9 Exports	−	+	+

Identities

10 Output = Consumption + Investment + Government Spending + Exports − Imports
11 Current Account = Export Price Level × Exports − Import Price Level × Imports
12 Net Assets = Net Assets previous period + Current Account
13 World Price Level = Weighted average of all countries' Export Prices

Notes:
a. Explanatory variable is consumption plus investment plus government spending.
b. Rate of inflation.
c. Exchange rate is local currency per dollar, so an increase is a depreciation.

The seven variables determined by estimated equations in Table 2.1 are:

1. **Consumption** depends on income, an interest rate, and wealth. Wealth is the net assets of the country vis-à-vis the rest of the world. The interest rate is either the short rate or the long rate. Monetary policy thus has a direct effect on consumption through the interest rate variables.

2. **Investment** depends on output and an interest rate. As with consumption, monetary policy has a direct effect on investment through the interest rate variables.

3. The level of **imports** depends on consumption plus investment plus government spending, on the domestic price level, and on the import price level. The price variables are important in this equation. If, for example, the import price level rises relative to the domestic price level, this has a negative effect on import demand. A depreciation of the country's currency thus lowers the demand for imports because it increases the import price level.

4. The **domestic price level** depends on output and the import price level, where output is meant to represent some measure of demand pressure. The import price level is a key variable in this equation. It is significant for almost all countries. When the import price level rises, this has a positive effect on the prices of domestically produced goods. This is the main channel through which a depreciation of the country's currency affects the domestic price level.

5. The **short-term interest rate** depends on output and the rate of inflation. The estimated equation for the interest rate is interpreted as an interest rate rule of the monetary authority. The estimated interest rate rules for the various countries are "leaning against the wind" equations. Other things being equal, an increase in output or an increase in the rate of inflation leads to an increase in the interest rate.

6. The **exchange rate** depends on the short-term interest rate and the domestic price level. All the explanatory variables are relative to the respective U.S. variables if the exchange rate is relative to the dollar and are relative to the respective German variables if the exchange rate is relative to the DM. A depreciation of a country's currency occurs if there is a relative decrease in the country's interest rate or a relative increase in the country's price level.

7. The **export price level** in local currency is determined as a weighted average of the domestic price level and a world price level converted to local currency, where the weight is estimated. If the weight on the world price level converted to local currency is one (and thus the weight on the domestic price level is zero), the country is a complete price taker on world markets. In this case, if the world price level in dollars is little affected by the individual country, then a depreciation of a country's currency of a given percentage increases the export price level in local currency by roughly the same percentage (since the world price level converted to local currency increases by roughly the same percentage), leaving the export price level in dollars roughly unchanged. Otherwise, the export price level in dollars falls with a depreciation, where the size of the fall depends on the estimated weight in the equation.

The next two variables in Table 2.1 are determined when the countries are linked together.

8. The **import price level** in local currency for a given country i depends on its dollar exchange rate and other countries' export prices in dollars. The import price level is a weighted average of all other countries' export prices converted to local currency, with a weight for a particular country j being the amount imported by i from j as a

fraction of i's total imports. If there is a depreciation of i's currency and no change in the other countries' export prices in their own local currency, then the import price level in local currency will rise by the full percentage of the depreciation.

9. The total level of **exports** for a given country i is the sum of its exports to all the other countries. The amount that country i exports to country j is determined by the trade share equations. The share of j's total imports imported from i depends on i's export price level in dollars relative to a weighted average of all the other countries' export price levels in dollars. The higher is i's relative export price level, the lower is i's share of j's total imports. There are 1,111 estimated trade share equations. Many estimated equations are thus involved in determining the response of a country's total exports to a change in its export price level.

The four identities in Table 2.1 are straightforward. They determine, respectively, **output**, the **current account**, **net assets**, and the **world price level**.

2.3.1   Effects of a Depreciation

Table 2.1 can be used to trace through the effects of a depreciation of a country's currency. This will be useful for understanding the experiment in Chapter 8. Assume that there is an exogenous depreciation of a country's currency. The depreciation raises the import price level in local currency. The increase in the import price level then has two main effects, other things being equal. The first is that the demand for imports falls (equation 3), and the second is that the domestic price level rises (equation 4). (All the equation references in the rest of this section are to the equations in Table 2.1.) The depreciation also reduces the price of exports in dollars unless the country is a complete price taker (equation 7). The decrease in the price of exports in dollars leads to an increase in the demand for the country's exports (equation 9). The depreciation is thus expansionary and inflationary: the level of imports falls, the level of exports rises, and the domestic price level increases. The effect on the current account is ambiguous because of the usual "J-curve" reasons.

2.3.2   Effects of an Interest Rate Decrease

Table 2.1 can also be used to trace through the effects of a decrease in a country's interest rate. Assume that there is an exogenous decrease in a country's interest rate. This leads, other things being equal, to an increase in consumption and investment (equations 1 and 2). It also leads to a depreciation of the country's currency (equation 6), which has the effects discussed above. In particular, exports increase (equation 9). The effect on aggregate demand in the country from the interest rate decrease is thus positive from the increase in consumption, investment, and exports.

There are two main effects on imports, one positive and one negative (equation 3). The positive effect is that consumption and investment are higher, some of which is imported. The negative effect is that the price of imports is higher because of the depreciation, which has a negative effect on the demand for imports. The net effect on imports can thus go either way.

There is also a positive effect on the price level. As noted above, the depreciation leads to an increase in the price of imports (equation 8). This in turn has a positive effect on the domestic price level (equation 4). In addition, if aggregate demand increases, this increases demand pressure, which has a positive effect on the domestic price level (also equation 4).

There are other effects that follow from these, including effects back on the short-term interest rate itself through the interest rate rule (equation 5), but these are typically second order in nature, especially in the short run. The main effects are as just described. The decrease in a country's interest rate should thus stimulate the economy, depreciate the currency, and lead to a rise in its price level.

This completes the general overview. The next two sections discuss the exact specifications.

2.4   The US Stochastic Equations

2.4.1   Introduction

The methodology that was followed in the specification and estimation of the stochastic equations is discussed in section 1.2. The estimates that are presented in Tables A1 through A30 (within Table A.4 in Appendix A) are those of the "final" specifications. Lagged dependent variables are generally used as explanatory variables to account for expectational and/or partial adjustment effects. Explanatory variables were dropped if they had highly insignificant coefficient estimates or estimates of the wrong expected sign. Most of the equations are estimated by 2SLS. The equations were first estimated under the assumption of a first-order autoregressive error term, and the assumption was retained if the estimate of the autoregressive coefficient was significant. In a few cases higher-order processes are used.

The χ^2 tests per equation are (1) adding lagged values of all the variables in the equation, (2) estimating the equation under the assumption of a *fourth*-order autoregressive process for the error term, (3) adding the time trend, and (4) adding values *led* one or more quarters. The other tests are (5) testing for structural stability using the AP test, (6) testing for structural stability using the end-of-sample test, and (7) testing the overidentifying restrictions. The basic estimation period is 1954:1–2002:3, for a total of 195 observations.

In the discussion of the US stochastic equations in this section, no mention will be made of the results in the tables regarding the overidentifying tests. For all the equations the p-values are greater than .01, and so the null hypothesis that the first-stage regressors are uncorrelated with the error term in the equation is never rejected. Nor is any mention made of the results of the end-of-sample tests. These tests are discussed in Chapter 6. For only 3 of the 30 equations in Tables A1–A30 is the p-value for the end-of-sample test less than .01.

The "broad theoretical framework" that is used to guide the specification of the stochastic equations was discussed in section 1.3. This framework will be called the "theoretical model."

The notation for the six sectors in the US model is presented in Table A.1. It is h for households, f for firms, b for financial, r for foreign, g for federal government, and s for state and local governments.

2.4.2 Household Expenditure and Labor Supply Equations

The two main decision variables of a household in the theoretical model are consumption and labor supply. The determinants of these variables include the initial value of wealth and the current and expected future values of the wage rate, the price level, the interest rate, the tax rate, the level of transfer payments, and a possible labor constraint.

In the econometric model the expenditures of the household sector are disaggregated into four types: consumption of services, CS; consumption of nondurable goods, CN; consumption of durable goods, CD; and residential investment, IHH. Four labor supply variables are used: the labor force of men aged 25–54, $L1$; the labor force of women aged 25–54, $L2$; the labor force of all others aged 16+, $L3$; and the number of people holding more than one job, called "moonlighters," LM. These eight variables are determined by eight estimated equations.

Real after-tax income, YD/PH, is used as an explanatory variable in the expenditure equations, which implicitly assumes that the labor constraint is always binding on the household sector. In an earlier version of the model—Fair (1984)—a real wage rate variable and a labor constraint variable were used instead of YD/PH. The labor constraint variable was constructed to be zero or nearly zero in tight labor markets and to increase as labor markets loosen. The "classical" case is when the labor constraint is zero, where expenditures depend on the real wage rate. The "Keynesian" case is when labor markets are loose and the labor constraint variable is not zero. In this case the labor constraint variable is correlated with hours paid for, and so having both the real wage rate and the labor constraint variable in the equation is similar to having a real labor income variable in the equation. Tests of these two specifications generally support the use of YD/PH over the real wage rate and the labor constraint variable, and so YD/PH has been used. This does not necessarily mean, however, that the classical case never holds in practice. It may be that the use of the labor constraint variable is not an adequate way to try to account for the classical case. This is an area for future research.

The household real wealth variable is AA. The household after-tax interest rate variables in the model are RSA, a short-term rate, and RMA, a long-term rate. These interest rates are nominal rates. Chapter 3 is concerned with testing for nominal versus real interest rate effects, and it will be seen that in most cases the data support the use of nominal over real interest rates.

Age distribution variables, $AG1$, $AG2$, and $AG3$, were tried in the four expenditure equations, and they were jointly significant at the 5 percent level in three of the four, the insignificant results occurring for the *IHH* equation. They were retained in the three equations in which they were significant.[2]

Table A1: Equation 1. *CS*, consumer expenditures: services

Equation 1 is in real, per capita terms and is in log form. The explanatory variables include income, an interest rate, wealth, the time trend, and the age variables.

The age variables are highly jointly significant (*p*-value zero to four places), and all the other variables are significant. The significance of the time trend suggests that there is a trend in the relationship not captured in any of the other variables. For the leads tests income is the variable for which led values were tried—in the form $\log[YD/(POP \cdot PH)]$. For the lags test the lagged values of the age variables were not included. The equation passes the lags, RHO, and leads tests, but it fails the AP stability tests. The AP results suggest that there is a break in the late 1970s.

Table A2: Equation 2. *CN*, consumer expenditures: nondurables

Equation 2 is also in real, per capita, and log terms. The explanatory variables include income, an interest rate, wealth, and the age variables.

The age variables are jointly significant at the 5 percent level (*p*-value of .0417). The other variables are also significant. Both the level and the change of the lagged dependent variable are significant in the equation, and so the dynamic specification is more complicated than that of equation 1. Again income is the variable for which led values were tried, and for the lags test the lagged values of the age variables were not included. The equation fails the lags and RHO tests, and it passes the *T* and leads tests. It also fails the AP stability tests, with the break point probably in the mid- to late 1970s. The failure of the lags and RHO tests suggests that the dynamics have not been completely captured.

Table A3: Equation 3. *CD*, consumer expenditures: durables

Equation 3 is in real, per capita terms. The explanatory variables include income, an interest rate, wealth, the age variables, $DELD(KD/POP)_{-1} - (CD/POP)_{-1}$, and $(KD/POP)_{-1}$. *KD* is the stock of durable goods, and *DELD* is the depreciation rate of the stock. The construction of these two variables is explained in Appendix A.

The justification for including the stock variable in the equation is as follows. Let KD^{**} denote the stock of durable goods that would be desired if there were no adjustment costs of any kind. If durable consumption is proportional to the stock of durables, then the determinants of consumption can be assumed to be the determinants of KD^{**}:

$$KD^{**} = f(\ldots), \tag{2.1}$$

---

2. The age distribution variables are explained in Fair (1994), section 4.7. They are meant to pick up the effects of the changing age distribution of the U.S. population on aggregate household expenditures.

where the arguments of f are the determinants of consumption. Two types of partial adjustments are then postulated. The first is an adjustment of the durable stock:

$$KD^* - KD_{-1} = \lambda(KD^{**} - KD_{-1}), \tag{2.2}$$

where KD^* is the stock of durable goods that would be desired if there were no costs of changing durable expenditures. Given KD^*, desired durable expenditures, CD^*, is postulated to be

$$CD^* = KD^* - (1 - DELD)KD_{-1}, \tag{2.3}$$

where $DELD$ is the depreciation rate. By definition $CD = KD - (1 - DELD)KD_{-1}$, and equation 2.3 is merely the same equation for the desired values. The second type of adjustment is an adjustment of durable expenditures, CD, to its desired value:

$$CD - CD_{-1} = \gamma(CD^* - CD_{-1}) + \epsilon. \tag{2.4}$$

This equation is assumed to reflect costs of changing durable expenditures. Combining equations 2.1–2.4 yields:

$$\begin{aligned} CD - CD_{-1} = \gamma(DELD \cdot KD_{-1} - CD_{-1}) + \gamma\lambda KD_{-1} \\ + \gamma\lambda f(\ldots) + \epsilon. \end{aligned} \tag{2.5}$$

This specification of the two types of adjustment is a way of adding to the durable expenditure equation both the lagged dependent variable and the lagged stock of durables. Otherwise, the explanatory variables are the same as they are in the other expenditure equations.[3]

The interest rate used in equation 3, RMA, is multiplied by a scale variable, CDA. CDA is exogenous in the model. It is constructed from a peak to peak interpolation of CD/POP.

All the variables in equation 3 are significant except the wealth variable, which has a t-statistic of 1.53. The estimate of γ, the coefficient of $DELD(KD/POP)_{-1} - (CD/POP)_{-1}$, is 0.329. This is the partial adjustment coefficient for CD. The estimate of $\gamma\lambda$, the coefficient of $(KD/POP)_{-1}$, is 0.024, which gives an implied value of λ, the partial adjustment coefficient for KD^*, of 0.073. KD^* is thus estimated to adjust to KD^{**} at a rate of 0.073 per quarter. Income is the variable for which led values were tried, and for the lags test the lagged values of the age variables were not included. The equation passes the lags, RHO, and T tests. It passes two of the three leads tests. It fails the AP tests, where the break is probably in the mid- to late 1970s.

---

3. Note in Table A3 that CD is divided by POP, and CD_{-1} and KD_{-1} are divided by POP_{-1}, where POP is population. If equations 2.1–2.4 are defined in per capita terms, where the current values are divided by POP and the lagged values are divided by POP_{-1}, then the present per capita treatment of equation 2.5 follows. The only problem with this is that the definition used to justify equation 2.3 does not hold if the lagged stock is divided by POP_{-1}. All variables must be divided by the same population variable for the definition to hold. This is, however, a minor problem, and it has been ignored here. The same holds for equation 4.

Table A4: Equation 4. *IHH*, residential investment—h

The same partial adjustment model is used for residential investment that was used above for durable expenditures, which adds $DELH(KH/POP)_{-1} - (IHH/POP)_{-1}$, and $(KH/POP)_{-1}$ to the residential investment equation. KH is the stock of housing, and $DELH$ is the depreciation rate of the stock. The construction of these two variables is explained in Appendix A. Equation 4 does not include the wealth variable because the variable was not significant. Likewise, it does not include the age variables because they were not significant. It is estimated under the assumption of a second-order autoregressive process for the error term. The interest rate used in equation 4, RMA_{-1}, is multiplied by a scale variable, $IHHA$. $IHHA$ is exogenous in the model. It is constructed from a peak-to-peak interpolation of IHH/POP.

Income is the variable for which led values were tried. All the variables in equation 4 are significant, and it passes all the tests, including the stability tests. The estimate of γ, the partial adjustment coefficient for IHH, is 0.538. The estimate of $\gamma\lambda$ is 0.033, which gives an implied value of λ, the partial adjustment coefficient for KH^*, of 0.061.

Table A5: Equation 5. $L1$, labor force—men 25–54

Equation 5 explains the labor force participation rate of men aged 25–54. It is in log form and includes as explanatory variables the wealth variable and the unemployment rate. The unemployment rate is meant to pick up the effect of the labor constraint on labor supply (a discouraged worker effect).

The wealth variable has a negative coefficient estimate, as expected. The unemployment rate also has a negative coefficient estimate, as expected, although it only has a t-statistic of -1.69. The equation passes the lags and T tests, but it fails the RHO test. It passes two of the three AP tests.

Table A6: Equation 6. $L2$, labor force—women 25–54

Equation 6 explains the labor force participation rate of women aged 25–54. It is in log form and includes as explanatory variables the real wage and the wealth variable.

Again, the wealth variable has a negative coefficient estimate. The real wage variable has a positive coefficient estimate, implying that the substitution effect dominates the income effect. The variable for which led values were tried is the real wage, $\log(WA/PH)$. The equation passes all the tests. One of the χ^2 tests has $\log PH$ added as an explanatory variable. This is a test of the use of the real wage in the equation. If $\log PH$ is significant, this is a rejection of the hypothesis that the coefficient of $\log WA$ is equal to the negative of the coefficient of $\log PH$, which is implied by the use of the real wage. As can be seen, $\log PH$ is not significant.

Table A7: Equation 7. $L3$, labor force—all others 16+

Equation 7 explains the labor force participation rate of all others aged 16+. It is also in log form and includes as explanatory variables the real wage, the wealth variable, and the unemployment rate.

The coefficient estimate of the real wage is positive and the coefficient estimate of the wealth variable is negative, although neither is significant. The unemployment rate has a significantly negative coefficient estimate. The variable for which led values were tried is the real wage.[4] The equation passes all the tests except one of the three AP tests.

Table A8: Equation 8. *LM*, number of moonlighters

Equation 8 determines the number of moonlighters. It is in log form and includes as explanatory variables the real wage and the unemployment rate.

The coefficient estimate of the real wage is positive and significant, suggesting that the substitution effect dominates for moonlighters. The coefficient estimate of the unemployment rate is negative and significant, which is the discouraged worker effect applied to moonlighters. The variable for which led values were tried is the real wage. The equation passes the lags, RHO, and leads tests. It fails the T test. It also fails the test of adding log PH (log PH is significant), which is evidence against the real wage constraint. It fails the three AP tests.

This completes the discussion of the household expenditure and labor supply equations. A summary of some of the general results across the equations is in Section 2.4.11.

2.4.3 The Main Firm Sector Equations

In the maximization problem of a firm in the theoretical model there are five main decision variables: the firm's price, production, investment, demand for employment, and wage rate. These five decision variables are determined jointly in that they are the result of solving one maximization problem. The variables that affect this solution include (1) the initial stocks of excess capital, excess labor, and inventories, (2) the current and expected future values of the interest rate, (3) the current and expected future demand schedules for the firm's output, (4) the current and expected future supply schedules of labor facing the firm, and (5) the firm's expectations of other firms' future price and wage decisions.

In the econometric model seven variables are chosen to represent the five decisions: (1) the price level for the firm sector, *PF*; (2) production, *Y*; (3) investment in nonresidential plant and equipment, *IKF*; (4) the number of jobs in the firm sector, *JF*; (5) the average number of hours paid per job, *HF*; (6) the average number of overtime hours paid per job, *HO*; and (7) the wage rate of the firm sector, *WF*. Each of these variables is determined by a stochastic equation, and these are the main stochastic equations of the firm sector.

Moving from the theoretical model of firm behavior to the econometric specifications is not straightforward, and a number of approximations have been made. One of the key approximations is to assume that the five decisions of a firm are made sequentially rather than jointly. The sequence is from the price decision, to the production

---

4. Collinearity problems prevented the Leads +4 test from being performed for equation 7.

decision, to the investment and employment decisions, to the wage rate decision. In this way of looking at the problem, the firm first chooses its optimal price path. This path implies a certain expected sales path, from which the optimal production path is chosen. Given the optimal production path, the optimal paths of investment and employment are chosen. Finally, given the optimal employment path, the optimal wage path is chosen.

Table A10: Equation 10. *PF*, price deflator for $X - FA$

Equation 10 is the key price equation in the model. The equation is in log form. The price level is a function of the lagged price level, the wage rate inclusive of the employer social security tax rate, the price of imports, the unemployment rate, and the time trend. The unemployment rate is taken as a measure of demand pressure. The lagged price level is meant to pick up expectational effects, and the wage rate and import price variables are meant to pick up cost effects. The log of the wage rate variable has subtracted from it log *LAM*, where *LAM* is a measure of potential labor productivity. The construction of *LAM* is explained in Appendix A; it is computed from a peak to peak interpolation of measured productivity. *LAM* is also discussed in section 6.4 in the analysis of long-run productivity movements.

An important feature of the price equation is that the price *level* is explained by the equation, not the price *change*. This treatment is contrary to the standard Phillips-curve treatment, where the price (or wage) change is explained by the equation. It is also contrary to the standard NAIRU specification, where the change in the change in the price level (that is, the change in the inflation rate) is explained. In the theoretical model the natural decision variables of a firm are the levels of prices and wages. For example, the market share equations in the theoretical model have a firm's market share as a function of the ratio of the firm's price to the average price of other firms. These are price levels, and the objective of the firm is to choose the price-level path (along with the paths of the other decision variables) that maximizes the multiperiod objective function. A firm decides what its price *level* should be relative to the price *levels* of other firms. This thus argues for a specification in levels, which is used here. The issue of the best functional form for the price equation is the subject matter of Chapter 4, where the NAIRU model is tested.

The time trend in equation 10 is meant to pick up any trend effects on the price level not captured by the other variables. Adding the time trend to an equation like 10 is similar to adding the constant term to an equation specified in terms of changes rather than levels. The time trend will also pick up any trend mistakes made in constructing *LAM*. If, for example, $LAM_t = LAM_t^a + \alpha_1 t$, where LAM_t^a is the correct variable to subtract from the wage rate variable to adjust for potential productivity, then the time trend will absorb this error.

All the variables in equation 10 are significant. The variable for which led values were tried is the wage rate variable. All the χ^2 tests are passed. The last two tests have output gap variables added. When each of these variables is added, it is not significant and (not shown) the unemployment rate retains its significance. The unemployment rate thus dominates the output gap variables. The equation passes two of the three AP tests.

Table A11: Equation 11. Y, production—f

The specification of the production equation is where the assumption that a firm's decisions are made sequentially begins to be used. The equation is based on the assumption that the firm sector first sets its price, then knows what its sales for the current period will be, and from this latter information decides on what its production for the current period will be.

In the theoretical model production is smoothed relative to sales. The reason for this is various costs of adjustment, which include costs of changing employment, costs of changing the capital stock, and costs of having the stock of inventories deviate from some proportion of sales. If a firm were only interested in minimizing inventory costs, it would produce according to the following equation (assuming that sales for the current period are known):

$$Y = X + \beta X - V_{-1}, \tag{2.6}$$

where Y is the level of production, X is the level of sales, V_{-1} is the stock of inventories at the end of the previous period, and β is the inventory-sales ratio that minimizes inventory costs. The construction of V is explained in Appendix A. Since by definition $V - V_{-1} = Y - X$, producing according to equation 2.6 would ensure that $V = \beta X$. Because of the other adjustment costs, it is generally not optimal for a firm to produce according to equation 2.6. In the theoretical model there was no need to postulate explicitly how a firm's production plan deviated from equation 2.6 because its optimal production plan just resulted, along with the other optimal paths, from the direct solution of its maximization problem. For the empirical work, however, it is necessary to make further assumptions.

The estimated production equation is based on the following three assumptions:

$$\log V^* = \beta \log X, \tag{2.7}$$

$$\log Y^* = \log X + \alpha(\log V^* - \log V_{-1}), \tag{2.8}$$

$$\log Y - \log Y_{-1} = \lambda(\log Y^* - \log Y_{-1}) + \epsilon, \tag{2.9}$$

where $*$ denotes a desired value. (In the following discussion all variables are assumed to be in logs.) Equation 2.7 states that the desired stock of inventories is proportional to current sales. Equation 2.8 states that the desired level of production is equal to sales plus some fraction of the difference between the desired stock of inventories and the stock on hand at the end of the previous period. Equation 2.9 states that actual production partially adjusts to desired production each period.

Combining equations 2.7–2.9 yields

$$\log Y = (1 - \lambda) \log Y_{-1} + \lambda(1 + \alpha\beta) \log X - \lambda\alpha \log V_{-1} + \epsilon. \tag{2.10}$$

Equation 11 is the estimated version of equation 2.10. The equation is estimated under the assumption of a third-order autoregressive process of the error term, and three dummy variables are added to account for the effects of a steel strike in the last half of 1959.

The estimate of $1 - \lambda$ is 0.317, and so the implied value of λ is 0.683, which means that actual production adjusts 68.3 percent of the way to desired production in the current quarter. The estimate of $\lambda\alpha$ is 0.241, and so the implied value of α is 0.353. This means that (in logs) desired production is equal to sales plus 35.3 percent of the desired change in inventories. The estimate of $\lambda(1 + \alpha\beta)$ is 0.880, and so the implied value of β is 1.197. The variable for which led values were used is the log level of sales, log X. Equation 11 passes all the tests. The passing of the leads tests, which means that the led values are not significant, is evidence against the hypothesis that firms have rational expectations regarding future values of sales.

The estimates of equation 11 are consistent with the view that firms smooth production relative to sales. The view that production is smoothed relative to sales was challenged by Blinder (1981) and others. This work was in turn challenged in Fair (1989) as being based on faulty data. The results in Fair (1989), which use data in physical units, suggest that production is smoothed relative to sales. The results using the physical units data thus provide some support for the current aggregate estimates.

Table A12: Equation 12. KK, stock of capital—f

Equation 12 explains the stock of capital of the firm sector, KK. Given KK, the nonresidential fixed investment of the firm sector, IKF, is determined by identity 92:

$$IKF = KK - (1 - DELK)KK_{-1}, \tag{92}$$

where $DELK$ is the depreciation rate. The construction of KK and $DELK$ is explained in Appendix A. Equation 12 will sometimes be referred to as an "investment" equation, since IKF is determined once KK is.

Equation 12 is based on the assumption that the production decision has already been made. In the theoretical model, because of costs of changing the capital stock, it may sometimes be optimal for a firm to hold excess capital. If there were no such costs, investment each period would merely be the amount needed to have enough capital to produce the output of the period. In the theoretical model there was no need to postulate explicitly how investment deviates from this amount, but for the empirical work this must be done.

The estimated equation for KK is based on the following two equations:

$$\begin{aligned}
\log(KK^*/KK_{-1}) = {} & \alpha_0 \log(KK_{-1}/KKMIN_{-1}) + \alpha_1 \Delta \log Y \\
& + \alpha_2 \Delta \log Y_{-1} + \alpha_3 \Delta \log Y_{-2} + \alpha_4 \Delta \log Y_{-3} \\
& + \alpha_5 \Delta \log Y_{-4} + \alpha_6 r,
\end{aligned} \tag{2.11}$$

$$\begin{aligned}
& \log(KK/KK_{-1}) - \log(KK_{-1}/KK_{-2}) = \\
& \lambda[\log(KK^*/KK_{-1}) - \log(KK_{-1}/KK_{-2})] + \epsilon,
\end{aligned} \tag{2.12}$$

where r is some measure of the cost of capital, α_0 and α_6 are negative, and the other coefficients are positive. The construction of *KKMIN* is explained in Appendix A. It is, under the assumption of a putty-clay technology, an estimate of the minimum amount of capital required to produce the current level of output, Y. $KK_{-1}/KKMIN_{-1}$ is thus the ratio of the actual capital stock on hand at the end of the previous period to the minimum required to produce the output of that period. The variable $\log(KK_{-1}/KKMIN_{-1})$ will be referred to as the amount of "excess capital" on hand.

KK^* in equation 2.11 is the value of the capital stock the firm would desire to have on hand in the current period if there were no costs of changing the capital stock. The desired change, $\log(KK^*/KK_{-1})$, depends on (1) the amount of excess capital on hand, (2) five change-in-output terms, and (3) the cost of capital. The lagged output changes are meant to be proxies for expected future output changes. Other things equal, the firm desires to increase the capital stock if the output changes are positive. Equation 2.12 is a partial adjustment equation of the actual capital stock to the desired stock. It states that the actual percentage change in the capital stock is a fraction of the desired percentage change.

Ignoring the cost-of-capital term in equation 2.11, the equation says that the desired capital stock approaches *KKMIN* in the long run if output is not changing. How can the cost of capital term be justified? In the theoretical model the cost of capital affects the capital stock by affecting the kinds of machines that are purchased. If the cost of capital falls, machines with lower labor requirements are purchased, other things being equal. For the empirical work, data are not available by types of machines, and approximations have to be made. The key approximation that is made in Appendix A is the postulation of a putty-clay technology in the construction of *KKMIN*. If there is in fact some substitution of capital for labor in the short run, the cost of capital is likely to affect the firm's desired capital stock, and this is the reason for including a cost-of-capital term in equation 2.11.

Combining equations 2.11 and 2.12 yields:

$$\Delta \log KK = \lambda\alpha_0 \log(KK_{-1}/KKMIN_{-1}) + (1 - \lambda)\Delta \log KK_{-1}$$
$$+ \lambda\alpha_1\Delta \log Y + \lambda\alpha_2\Delta \log Y_{-1} + \lambda\alpha_3\Delta \log Y_{-2} \qquad (2.13)$$
$$+ \lambda\alpha_4\Delta \log Y_{-3} + \lambda\alpha_5\Delta \log Y_{-4} + \lambda\alpha_6 r + \epsilon.$$

Equation 12 is the estimated version of equation 2.13.

The estimate of $1 - \lambda$ is 0.938, and so the implied value of λ is 0.062. The estimate of $\lambda\alpha_0$ is -0.0068, and so the implied value of α_0 is -0.110. This is the estimate of the size of the effect of excess capital on the desired stock of capital. The variable for which led values were tried is the log change in output. Equation 12 passes all the tests. The passing of the leads tests is evidence against the hypothesis that firms have rational expectations with respect to future values of output.

There are two cost-of-capital variables in equation 12. Both are lagged two quarters. One is an estimate of the real AAA bond rate, which is the nominal AAA bond rate, RB, less the four-quarter rate of inflation. The other is a function of stock price changes. It is the ratio of capital gains or losses on the financial assets of the household sector (mostly from corporate stocks) over three quarters to nominal potential output. This ratio is a measure of how well or poorly the stock market is doing. If the stock market is doing well, for example, the ratio is high, which should in general lower the cost of capital to firms. Both cost-of-capital variables are significant in Table A12, with t-statistics of -2.45 and 2.19.

One might think that the second cost-of-capital variable in equation 12 is simply picking up the boom in the stock market and in investment since 1995. However, when equation 12 is estimated only through 1994.4, this cost-of-capital variable has even a larger coefficient estimate than in Table A12 (0.00062 versus 0.00048) and is still significant (t-statistic of 2.08).

Table A13: Equation 13. *JF*, number of jobs—f

The employment equation 13 and the hours equation 14 are similar in spirit to the capital stock equation 12. They are also based on the assumption that the production decision is made first. Because of adjustment costs, it is sometimes optimal in the theoretical model for firms to hold excess labor. Were it not for the costs of changing employment, the optimal level of employment would merely be the amount needed to produce the output of the period. In the theoretical model there was no need to postulate explicitly how employment deviates from this amount, but this must be done for the empirical work.

The estimated employment equation is based on the following two equations:

$$\log(JF^*/JF_{-1}) = \alpha_0 \log[JF_{-1}/(JHMIN_{-1}/HFS_{-1})] \\ + \alpha_1 \Delta \log Y, \tag{2.14}$$

$$\log(JF/JF_{-1}) - \log(JF_{-1}/JF_{-2}) = \\ \lambda[\log(JF^*/JF_{-1}) - \log(JF_{-1}/JF_{-2})] + \epsilon, \tag{2.15}$$

where α_0 is negative and the other coefficients are positive. The construction of *JHMIN* and *HFS* is explained in Appendix A. *JHMIN* is, under the assumption of a putty-clay technology, an estimate of the minimum number of worker hours required to produce the current level of output, Y. *HFS* is an estimate of the desired number of hours worked per worker. $JF_{-1}/(JHMIN_{-1}/HFS_{-1})$ is the ratio of the actual number of workers on hand at the end of the previous period to the minimum number required to produce the output of that period if the average number of hours worked were HFS_{-1}. The variable $\log[JF_{-1}/JHMIN_{-1}/HFS_{-1})]$ will be referred to as the amount of "excess labor" on hand.

JF^* in equation 2.14 is the number of workers the firm would desire to have on hand in the current period if there were no costs of changing employment. The desired change, $\log(JF^*/JF_{-1})$, depends on the amount of excess labor on hand and the change in output. This equation says that the desired number of workers approaches *JHMIN/HFS* in the long run if output is not changing. Equation 2.15 is a partial adjustment equation of the actual number of workers to the desired number.

Combining equations 2.14 and 2.15 yields:

$$\Delta \log JF = \lambda\alpha_0 \log[JF_{-1}/(JHMIN_{-1}/HFS_{-1})] + (1-\lambda)\Delta \log JF_{-1}$$
$$+ \lambda\alpha_1 \Delta \log Y + \epsilon. \tag{2.16}$$

Equation 13 is the estimated version of equation 2.16. It has a dummy variable, $D593$, added to pick up the effects of a steel strike.

The estimate of $1-\lambda$ is 0.455, and so the implied value of λ is 0.545. The estimate of $\lambda\alpha_0$ is -0.105, and so the implied value of α_0 is -0.193. This is the estimate of the size of the effect of excess labor on the desired number of workers. The variable for which led values were tried is the change in the log of output. The equation passes all the tests. Again, the passing of the leads tests is evidence against the hypothesis that firms have rational expectations with respect to future values of output.

Table A14: Equation 14. *HF*, average number of hours paid per job—f

The estimated hours equation is:

$$\Delta \log HF = \lambda \log(HF_{-1}/HFS_{-1})$$
$$+ \alpha_0 \log[JF_{-1}/(JHMIN-1/HFS_{-1})] + \alpha_1 \Delta \log Y + \epsilon. \tag{2.17}$$

The first term on the right-hand side of equation 2.17 is the (logarithmic) difference between the actual number of hours paid for in the previous period and the desired number. The reason for the inclusion of this term in the hours equation but not in the employment equation is that, unlike JF, HF fluctuates around a slowly trending level of hours. This restriction is captured by the first term in 2.17. The other two terms are the amount of excess labor on hand and the current change in output. Both of these terms affect the employment decision, and they should also affect the hours decision since the two are closely related. Equation 14 is the estimated version of equation 2.17.

The estimate of λ is -0.216, and the estimate of α_0 is -0.041. All the coefficient estimates are significant in the equation. The variable for which led values were tried is the change in the log of output. The equation passes all the χ^2 tests. It fails the three AP tests.

Table A15: Equation 15. *HO*, average number of overtime hours paid per job—f

Equation 15 explains overtime hours, HO. Let $HFF = HF - HFS$, which is the deviation of actual hours per worker from desired hours. One would expect HO to be close to zero for low values of HFF (that is, when actual hours are much below desired hours), and to increase roughly one for one for high values of HFF. An approximation to this relationship is

$$HO = e^{\alpha_1 + \alpha_2 HFF + \epsilon}, \tag{2.18}$$

which in log form is

$$\log HO = \alpha_1 + \alpha_2 HFF + \epsilon. \tag{2.19}$$

Equation 15 is the estimated version of equation 2.19. Both *HFF* and *HFF*$_{-1}$ are included in the equation, which appears to capture the dynamics better. The equation is estimated under the assumption of a first-order autoregressive error term.

All the coefficient estimates in equation 15 are significant, and the equation passes all but the *T* test.

Table A16: Equation 16. *WF*, average hourly earnings excluding overtime—f

Equation 16 is the wage rate equation. It is in log form. In the final specification, the wage rate was simply taken to be a function of the constant term, the time trend, the current value of the price level, the lagged value of the price level, and the lagged value of the wage rate. Labor market tightness variables like the unemployment rate were not significant in the equation. The time trend is added to account for trend changes in the wage rate relative to the price level. The potential productivity variable, *LAM*, is subtracted from the wage rate in equation 16. The price equation, equation 10, is identified because the wage rate equation includes the lagged wage rate, which the price equation does not. The wage rate equation is identified because the price equation includes the price of imports and the unemployment rate, which the wage rate equation does not.

A constraint was imposed on the coefficients in the wage equation to ensure that the determination of the real wage implied by equations 10 and 16 is sensible. Let $p = \log PF$ and $w = \log WF$. The relevant parts of the price and wage equations regarding the constraints are

$$p = \beta_1 p_{-1} + \beta_2 w + \ldots, \tag{2.20}$$

$$w = \gamma_1 w_{-1} + \gamma_2 p + \gamma_3 p_{-1} + \ldots. \tag{2.21}$$

The implied real wage equation from these two equations should not have $w - p$ as a function of either w or p separately, since one does not expect the real wage to grow simply because the levels of w and p are growing. The desired form of the real wage equation is thus

$$w - p = \delta_1 (w_{-1} - p_{-1}) + \ldots, \tag{2.22}$$

which says that the real wage is a function of its own lagged value plus other terms. The real wage in equation 2.22 is *not* a function of the level of w or p separately. The constraint on the coefficients in equations 2.20 and 2.21 that imposes this restriction is:

$$\gamma_3 = [\beta_1/(1 - \beta_2)](1 - \gamma_2) - \gamma_1. \tag{2.23}$$

This constraint is imposed in the estimation by first estimating the price equation to get estimates of β_1 and β_2 and then using these estimates to impose the constraint on γ_3 in the wage equation.

The coefficient estimates in equation 16 are significant, and the equation passes all the tests. One of the χ^2 tests is a test of the real wage restriction, and this restriction is not rejected by the data. The final χ^2 test in the table has the unemployment rate added as an explanatory variable, and it is not significant. As noted above, no demand pressure variables were found to be significant in the wage equation.

2.4.4 Other Firm Sector Equations

There are three other, fairly minor, equations of the firm sector, explaining dividends paid, inventory valuation adjustment, and capital consumption.

Table A18: Equation 18. *DF*, dividends paid—f

Let Π denote after-tax profits. If in the long run firms desire to pay out all of their after-tax profits in dividends, one can write $DF^* = \Pi$, where DF^* is the long-run desired value of dividends for profit level Π. If it is assumed that actual dividends are partially adjusted to desired dividends each period as

$$DF/DF_{-1} = (DF^*/DF_{-1})^\lambda e^\epsilon, \tag{2.24}$$

then the equation to be estimated is

$$\Delta \log DF = \lambda \log(\Pi/DF_{-1}) + \epsilon. \tag{2.25}$$

Equation 18 is the estimated version of equation 2.25. The level of after-tax profits in the notation of the model is $PIEF - TFG - TFS$.

The estimate of λ is 0.027, which implies a slow adjustment of actual to desired dividends. The equation passes the lags and T tests, but it fails the RHO test. The last χ^2 test in Table A18 shows that the constant term is not significant. The above specification does not call for the constant term, and this is supported by the data. Regarding the first χ^2 test in the table, because of the assumption that $DF^* = \Pi$, the coefficient of $\log(PIEF - TFG - TFS)$ is restricted to be the negative of the coefficient of $\log DF_{-1}$. If instead $DF^* = \Pi^\gamma$, where γ is not equal to one, then the restriction does not hold. The first test in the table is a test of the restriction (that is, a test that $\gamma = 1$), and the hypothesis that $\gamma = 1$ is not rejected. The equation fails the AP tests.

Table A20: Equation 20. *IVA*, inventory valuation adjustment

In theory $IVA = -(P - P_{-1})V_{-1}$, where P is the price of the good and V is the stock of inventories of the good. Equation 20 is meant to approximate this. *IVA* is regressed on $(PX - PX_{-1})V_{-1}$, where PX is the price deflator for the sales of the firm sector. The equation is estimated under the assumption of a first-order autoregressive error term.

The coefficient estimate of $(PX - PX_{-1})V_{-1}$ is negative, as expected, and significant. The equation passes the χ^2 tests and one of the three AP tests.

Table A20: Equation 21. *CCF*, capital consumption—f

In practice capital consumption allowances of a firm depend on tax laws and on current and past values of its investment. Equation 21 is an attempt to approximate this for the firm sector. *PIK · IKF* is the current value of investment. The use of the lagged dependent variable in the equation is meant to approximate the dependence of capital consumption allowances on past values of investment. This specification implies that the lag structure is geometrically declining. The restriction is also imposed that the sum of the lag coefficients is one, which means that capital consumption allowances are assumed to be taken on all investment in the long run. Nine dummy variables are included in the equation, which are meant to pick up tax law changes. The equation is estimated under the assumption of a first-order autoregressive process for the error term.

The coefficient estimate of the investment term is significant. The first χ^2 test is a test of the restriction that the sum of the lag coefficients is one. This is done by adding $\log CCF_{-1}$ to the equation. This restriction is not rejected by the data. The equation passes all the other tests.

2.4.5 Money Demand Equations

In the theoretical model a household's demand for money depends on the level of transactions, the interest rate, and the household's wage rate. High wage rate households spend less time taking care of money holdings than do low wage rate households and thus on average hold more money. With aggregate data it is not possible to estimate this wage rate effect on the demand for money, and in the empirical work the demand for money has simply been taken to be a function of the interest rate and a transactions variable.

The model contains three demand-for-money equations: one for the household sector, one for the firm sector, and a demand for currency equation. Before presenting these equations it will be useful to discuss how the dynamics were handled. The key question about the dynamics is whether the adjustment of actual to desired values is in nominal or real terms.

Let M_t^*/P_t denote the desired level of real money balances, let y_t denote a measure of real transactions, and let r_t denote a short-term interest rate. Assume that the equation determining desired money balances is in log form and write

$$\log(M_t^*/P_t) = \alpha + \beta \log y_t + \gamma r_t. \tag{2.26}$$

Note that the log form has not been used for the interest rate. Interest rates can at times be quite low, and it may not be sensible to take the log of the interest rate. If, for example, the interest rate rises from 0.02 to 0.03, the log of the rate rises from -3.91 to -3.51, a change of 0.40. If, on the other hand, the interest rate rises from 0.10 to 0.11, the log of the rate rises from -2.30 to -2.21, a change of only 0.09. One does not necessarily expect a one-percentage-point rise in the interest rate to have four times the effect on the log of desired money holdings when the change is from a base of 0.02 rather than 0.10. In practice the results of estimating money demand equations do not seem to be very sensitive to whether the level or the log of the interest rate is used. For the work in this book the level of the interest rate has been used.

If the adjustment of actual to desired money holdings is in real terms, the adjustment equation is

$$\log(M_t/P_t) - \log(M_{t-1}/P_{t-1}) = \lambda[\log(M_t^*/P_t) - \log(M_{t-1}/P_{t-1})] + \epsilon. \quad (2.27)$$

If the adjustment is in nominal terms, the adjustment equation is

$$\log M_t - \log M_{t-1} = \lambda(\log M_t^* - \log M_{t-1}) + \mu. \quad (2.28)$$

Combining 2.26 and 2.27 yields

$$\log(M_t/P_t) = \lambda\alpha + \lambda\beta \log y_t + \lambda\gamma r_t + (1 - \lambda) \log(M_{t-1}/P_{t-1}) + \epsilon. \quad (2.29)$$

Combining 2.26 and 2.28 yields

$$\log(M_t/P_t) = \lambda\alpha + \lambda\beta \log y_t + \lambda\gamma r_t + (1 - \lambda) \log(M_{t-1}/P_t) + \mu. \quad (2.30)$$

Equations 2.29 and 2.30 differ in the lagged money term. In 2.29, which is the real adjustment specification, M_{t-1} is divided by P_{t-1}, whereas in 2.30, which is the nominal adjustment specification, M_{t-1} is divided by P_t.

A test of the two hypotheses is simply to put both lagged money variables in the equation and see which one dominates. If the real adjustment specification is correct, $\log(M_{t-1}/P_{t-1})$ should be significant and $\log(M_{t-1}/P_t)$ should not, and vice versa if the nominal adjustment specification is correct. This test may, of course, be inconclusive in that both terms may be significant or insignificant, but I have found that this is rarely the case. This test was performed on the three demand-for-money equations, and in each case the nominal adjustment specification won. The nominal adjustment specification has thus been used for the three equations.

It should be noted that the demand-for-money equations are not important in the model because of the use of the interest rate rule (equation 30 below). They are included more for completeness than anything else. When the interest rate rule is used, the short-term interest rate is determined by the rule and the overall money supply is whatever is needed to have the demand-for-money equations be met.

Table A9: Equation 9. *MH*, demand deposits and currency—h

Equation 9 is the demand-for-money equation of the household sector. It is in per capita terms and is in log form. Disposable income is used as the transactions variable, and the after-tax three-month Treasury bill rate, *RSA*, is used as the interest rate. The equation also includes the time trend. A dummy variable is added, which is 1 in 1998:1 and 0 otherwise. In the data for 1998:1 there is a huge decrease in *MH* and a huge decrease in *MF*, demand deposits and currency of the firm sector. This may be a data error or definitional change, and it was accounted for by the use of the dummy variable. The equation is estimated under the assumption of a fourth-order autoregressive process of the error term.

The test results show that the lagged dependent variable that pertains to the real adjustment specification, $\log[MH/(POP \cdot PH)]_{-1}$, is insignificant. This thus supports the nominal adjustment hypothesis. The interest rate is highly significant in the equation, but the income variable has a t-statistic of only 1.55. Equation 9 passes the lags test, but it fails the three AP tests. For another test, the age distribution variables were added to the equation to see if possible differences in the demand for money by age could be picked up. The "χ^2 (AGE)" value in Table A9 shows that the age distribution variables are not jointly significant (p-value of 0.2971). They were thus not included in the final specification.

The sum of the four autoregressive coefficients is 0.98339. For the preliminary bootstrap work in Chapter 9 some of the estimates of the equation had sums greater than 1.0, which sometimes led to solution failures. For the final results in Chapter 9, equation 9 was dropped from the model and *MH* was taken to be exogenous. As noted above, equation 9 is not important in the model, and so little is lost by dropping it.

Table A17: Equation 17. *MF*, demand deposits and currency—f

Equation 17 is the demand-for-money equation of the firm sector. The equation is in log form. The transactions variable is the level of nonfarm firm sales, $X - FA$, and the interest rate variable is the after-tax three-month Treasury bill rate. The tax rates used in this equation are the corporate tax rates, *D2G* and *D2S*, not the personal tax rates used for *RSA* in equation 9. The dummy variable for 1998:1 mentioned above is included in the equation.

All the variables are significant in the equation. The test results show that the lagged dependent variable that pertains to the real adjustment specification, $\log(MF/PF)_{-1}$, is insignificant. The equation passes all the tests.

Table A26: Equation 26. *CUR*, currency held outside banks

Equation 26 is the demand-for-currency equation. It is in per capita terms and is in log form. The transactions variable that is used is the level of nonfarm firm sales. The interest rate variable used is *RSA*, and the equation is estimated under the assumption of a first-order autoregressive error term.

All the variables in the equation are significant. The test results show that the lagged dependent variable that pertains to the real adjustment specification, $\log[CUR/(POP \cdot PF)]_{-1}$, is not significant, which supports the nominal adjustment specification. The equation passes all the tests except one of the three AP tests.

2.4.6   Other Financial Equations

The stochastic equations for the financial sector consist of an equation explaining member bank borrowing from the Federal Reserve, two term structure equations, and an equation explaining the change in stock prices.

Table A22: Equation 22. *BO*, bank borrowing from the Fed

The variable *BO/BR* is the ratio of borrowed reserves to total reserves. This ratio is assumed to be a positive function of the three-month Treasury bill rate, *RS*, and a negative function of the discount rate, *RD*. The estimated equation also includes the constant term and the lagged dependent variable.

The coefficient estimates of *RS* and *RD* in Table A22 are positive and negative, respectively, as expected, but they are not significant. The equation passes the lags and *T* tests, and it fails the RHO and AP tests.

As is the case for the demand-for-money equations, equation 22 is not important in the model because of the use of the interest rate rule (equation 30 below). It is again included for completeness. When the interest rate rule is used, the short-term interest rate is determined by the rule and *BO* is whatever is needed to have equation 22 be met.

Table A23: Equation 23. *RB*, bond rate
Table A24: Equation 24. *RM*, mortgage rate

The expectations theory of the term structure of interest rates states that long-term rates are a function of the current and expected future short-term rates. The two long-term interest rates in the model are the bond rate, *RB*, and the mortgage rate, *RM*. These rates are assumed to be determined according to the expectations theory, where the current and past values of the short-term interest rate (the three-month Treasury bill rate, *RS*) are used as proxies for expected future values. Equations 23 and 24 are the two estimated equations. The lagged dependent variable is used in each of these equations, which implies a fairly complicated lag structure relating each long-term rate to the past values of the short-term rate. In addition, a constraint has been imposed on the coefficient estimates. The sum of the coefficients of the current and lagged values of the short-term rate has been constrained to be equal to one minus the coefficient of the lagged long-term rate. This means that, for example, a sustained one-percentage-point increase in the short-term rate eventually results in a one-percentage-point increase in the long-term rate. (This restriction is imposed by subtracting RS_{-2} from each of the other interest rates in the equations.) Equation 23 (but not 24) is estimated under the assumption of a first-order autoregressive error term.

The overall results for the two equations are quite good. The short-term interest rates are significant in the two estimated equations except for RS_{-1} in equation 24. The first test result for each equation shows that the coefficient restriction is not rejected for either equation. Both equations pass the lags, RHO, and *T* tests. Equation 23 passes the three AP tests, and equation 24 passes one of the three. The variable for which led values were tried is the short-term interest rate, *RS*, and the χ^2 tests show that the led values are not significant. Two inflation expectations variables, $\dot{p}^e_{4t}$ and $\dot{p}^e_{8t}$, were added to the equations, and the test results also show that these variables are not significant.[5]

---

5. The restriction regarding the sum of the coefficients was not imposed for the lags, leads, and inflation expectations tests. Collinearity problems prevented the Leads +4 test from being performed for equation 23.

Table A25: Equation 25. *CG*, capital gains or losses on the financial assets of h

The variable *CG* is the change in the market value of financial assets held by the household sector, almost all of which is the change in the market value of corporate stocks held by the household sector. In the theoretical model the aggregate value of stocks is determined as the present discounted value of expected future after-tax cash flow, the discount rates being the current and expected future short-term interest rates. The theoretical model thus implies that *CG* should be a function of changes in expected future after-tax cash flow and of changes in the current and expected future interest rates. In the empirical work the change in the bond rate, ΔRB, is used as a proxy for changes in expected future interest rates, and the change in after-tax profits, $\Delta(PIEF - TFG - TFS + PIEB - TBG - TBS)$, is used as a proxy for changes in expected future after-tax cash flow. In the estimated equation, *CG* and the change in after-tax profits are normalized by $PX_{-1}YS_{-1}$, which is a measure of potential output in nominal terms. Equation 25 is the estimated equation, where $CG/(PX_{-1}YS_{-1})$ is regressed on the constant term, ΔRB, and $\Delta[(PIEF - TFG - TFS + PIEB - TBG - TBS)]/(PX_{-1}YS_{-1})$.

The fit of equation 25 is poor. The coefficient estimates have the right sign but are not significant. The equation passes the lags, RHO, T, and AP tests. The variables for which led values were tried are the change in the bond rate and the change in after-tax profits. The led values are not significant. For the final χ^2 test ΔRS, the change in the short-term rate, was added under the view that it might also be a proxy for expected future interest rate changes, and it is not significant.

Chapters 5 and 6 discuss the effects of *CG* on the economy. It will be seen that these effects are large; they account for most of the unusual features of the U.S. economy in the last half of the 1990s. Although fluctuations in *CG* have large effects, the results of estimating equation 25 show that most of these fluctuations are not explained.

2.4.7 Interest Payments Equations

Table A19: Equation 19. *INTF*, interest payments—f
Table A29: Equation 29. *INTG*, interest payments—g

INTF is the level of net interest payments of the firm sector, and *INTG* is the same for the federal government. Data on both of these variables are NIPA data. *AF* is the level of net financial assets of the firm sector, and *AG* is the same for the federal government. Data on both of these variables are FFA data. *AF* and *AG* are negative because the firm sector and the federal government are net debtors, and they consist of both short-term and long-term securities.

The current level of interest payments depends on the amount of existing securities issued at each date in the past and on the relevant interest rate prevailing at each date. The link from *AF* to *INTF* (and from *AG* to *INTG*) is thus complicated. It depends on past issues and the interest rates paid on these issues. A number of approximations have to be made in trying to model this link, and the procedure used here is as follows.

Let RQ denote a weighted average of the current value of the short-term interest rate, RS, and current and past values of the long-term rate, RB, with weights of .3 and .7:[6]

$$RQ = [.3RS + .7(RB + RB_{-1} + RB_{-2} + RB_{-3} + RB_{-4} + RB_{-5} \\ + RB_{-6} + RB_{-7})/8]/400. \tag{2.31}$$

The variable $INTF/(-AF)$ is the ratio of interest payments of the firm sector to the net financial debt of the firm sector. This ratio is a function of current and past interest rates, among other things. After some experimentation, the interest rate $.75RQ$ was chosen as the relevant interest rate for $INTF/(-AF)$. (The weighted average in equation 2.31 is divided by 400 to put RQ at a quarterly rate in percentage units.) In the empirical specification $INTF/(-AF + 40)$ is taken to depend on the constant term, $.75RQ$, and $INTF_{-1}/(-AF_{-1} + 40)$, where the coefficients on the latter two variables are constrained to sum to one.[7] This results in the estimation of the following equation:

$$\Delta[INTF/(-AF + 40)] = \alpha_1 + \alpha_2[.75RQ \\ - INTF_{-1}/(-AF_{-1} + 40)] + \epsilon. \tag{2.32}$$

This equation, which is equation 19, is estimated under the assumption of a first-order autoregressive error term. At the beginning of the sample period AF is close to zero, and 40 is added to it in the estimation work to lessen the sensitivity of the results to small values of AF.

The coefficient estimate for the interest rate variable is of the expected positive sign, but it is not significant. The first χ^2 test is of the hypothesis that the two coefficients sum to one, and the hypothesis is not rejected. The equation passes the RHO test, but it fails the lags, T, and two of the three AP tests.

Equation 2.32 was also estimated for the federal government, where $INTG$ replaces $INTF$ and AG replaces AF. (AG is large enough at the beginning of the sample period to make it unnecessary to add anything to it.) This is equation 29 in the model. In this case the equation was not estimated under the assumption of an autoregressive error term, although the restriction that the two coefficients sum to one was retained.

For equation 29 the interest rate variable is significant. The restriction is rejected, and the equation passes only the T test.

Equations 19 and 29 are important in the model because when interest rates change, interest payments change, which changes household income. As discussed above, it is difficult to model this link. Although the overall results for equations 19 and 29 are not strong, the equations are at least rough approximations of the links.

---

6. These weights were chosen after some experimentation. The results are not sensitive to this particular choice.

7. The reason for the summation constraint is as follows. If $0.75RQ$ is the interest rate that pertains to $INTF/(-AF + 40)$ in the long run, then a one-unit change in $0.75RQ$ should result in the long run in a one-unit change in $INTF/(-AF + 40)$, which is what the summation constraint imposes.

2.4.8   The Import Equation

Table A27: Equation 27. *IM*, imports

The import equation is in per capita terms and is in log form. The explanatory variables include per capita expenditures on consumption and investment, a price deflator for domestically produced goods, *PF*, relative to the import price deflator, *PIM*, and four dummy variables to account for two dock strikes. The equation is estimated under the assumption of a second-order autoregressive property of the error term.

The coefficient estimates are significant except for the estimate for the lagged dependent variable, which has a t-statistic of 1.90. The equation passes the lags, RHO, T, and AP tests. The variable for which led values were tried is the per capita expenditure variable, and the led values are not significant. The last χ^2 test in Table A27 adds log *PF* to the equation, which is a test of the restriction that the coefficient of log *PF* is equal to the negative of the coefficient of log *PIM*. The log *PF* variable is not significant, and so the restriction is not rejected.

2.4.9   Unemployment Benefits

Table A28: Equation 28. *UB*, unemployment insurance benefits

Equation 28 explains unemployment insurance benefits, *UB*. It is in log form and contains as explanatory variables the level of unemployment, the nominal wage rate, and the lagged dependent variable. The inclusion of the nominal wage rate is designed to pick up the effects of increases in wages and prices on legislated benefits per unemployed worker. The equation is estimated under the assumption of a first-order autoregressive error term.

All the coefficient estimates are significant. The equation passes the lags and RHO tests, and it fails the T and AP tests.

2.4.10   Interest Rate Rule

Table A30: Equation 30. *RS*, three-month Treasury bill rate

A key question in any macro model is what one assumes about monetary policy. In the theoretical model monetary policy is determined by an interest rate reaction function or rule, and in the empirical work an equation like this is estimated. This equation is interpreted as an equation explaining the behavior of the Federal Reserve (Fed).

In one respect trying to explain Fed behavior is more difficult than, say, trying to explain the behavior of the household or firm sectors. Since the Fed is run by a relatively small number of people, there can be fairly abrupt changes in behavior if the people with influence change their minds or are replaced by others with different views. Abrupt changes are less likely to happen for the household and firm sectors because of the large number of decision makers in each sector. This said, however, only one abrupt change in behavior appears evident in the data, which is between 1979:4 and 1982:3. This period,

1979:4–1982:3, will be called the "early Volcker" period.[8] The stated policy of the Fed during this period was that it was focusing more on monetary aggregates than it had done before.

Equation 30 is the estimated interest rate reaction function. It has on the left-hand side *RS*. This treatment is based on the assumption that the Fed has a target bill rate each quarter and achieves this target through manipulation of its policy instruments. Although in practice the Fed controls the federal funds rate, the quarterly average of the federal funds rate and the quarterly average of the three-month Treasury bill rate are so highly correlated that it makes little difference which rate is used in estimated interest rate rules using quarterly data. The right-hand-side variables in the equation are variables that seem likely to affect the target rate. The variables that were chosen are (1) the rate of inflation, (2) the unemployment rate, (3) the change in the unemployment rate, and (4) the percentage change in the money supply lagged one quarter. The break between 1979:4 and 1982:3 was modeled by adding the variable $D794823 \cdot PCM1_{-1}$ to the equation, where $D794823$ is a dummy variable that is 1 between 1979:4 and 1982:3 and 0 otherwise. The estimated equation also includes the lagged dependent variable and two lagged bill rate changes to pick up the dynamics.

The coefficient estimates in equation 30 are significant except for the estimate for the lagged money supply variable in the non–early Volcker period, which has a t-statistic of 1.88. Equation 30 is a "leaning against the wind" equation. *RS* is estimated to depend positively on the inflation rate and the lagged growth of the money supply and negatively on the unemployment rate and the change in the unemployment rate Adjustment and smoothing effects are captured by the lagged values of *RS*. The coefficient on lagged money supply growth is nearly 20 times larger for the early Volcker period than either before or after, which is consistent with the Fed's stated policy of focusing more on monetary aggregates during this period. This way of accounting for the Fed policy shift does not, of course, capture the richness of the change in behavior, but at least it seems to capture some of the change.

Equation 30 does very well in the tests. It passes the lags, RHO, and *T* tests. The variables for which led values were tried are inflation and the unemployment rate, and the led values are not significant. The inflation expectations variables, $\dot{p}^e_{4t}$ and $\dot{p}^e_{8t}$, were added to the equation, and these variables are not significant. Regarding the leads tests, these are tests of whether the Fed's expectations of future values of inflation and the unemployment rate are rational. The fact that the led values are not significant is evidence against the Fed's having rational expectations.

Regarding stability tests for equation 30, any interesting test must exclude the early Volcker period since any hypothesis of stability that includes it is likely to be rejected. The Fed announced that its behavior was different during this period. One obvious hypothesis to test is that the equation's coefficients are the same before 1979:4 as they

---

8. Paul Volcker was chair of the Fed between 1979:3 and 1987:2, but the period in question is only 1979:4–1982:3.

are after 1982:3. This was done using a Wald test. The Wald statistic is presented in equation 3.6 in Andrews and Fair (1988). It has the advantage that it works under very general assumptions about the properties of the error terms and can be used when the estimator is 2SLS, which it is here. The Wald statistic is distributed as χ^2 with (in the present case) 8 degrees of freedom. The hypothesis of stability is not rejected. As reported in Table A30, the Wald statistic is 15.32, which has a p-value of .0532.

As noted in section 1.2, the first example of an estimated interest rate rule is in Dewald and Johnson (1963), followed by Christian (1968). An equation like equation 30 was first estimated in Fair (1978). After this, McNees (1986, 1992) estimated rules in which some of the explanatory variables were the Fed's internal forecasts of various variables. Khoury (1990) provides an extensive list of estimated rules through 1986. Two recent studies are Judd and Rudebusch (1998), where rules are estimated for various subsets of the 1970–1997 period, and Clarida, Galí, and Gertler (2000), where rules are estimated for the different Fed chairmen.

There seems to be a general view in the recent literature that estimated interest rate rules do not have stable coefficient estimates over time. For example, Judd and Rudebusch (1998, p. 3) state, "Overall, it appears that there have not been any great successes in modeling Fed behavior with a single, stable reaction function." The passing of the stability test for equation 30 is thus contrary this view. One likely reason that the stability hypothesis has generally been rejected in the literature is that most tests have included the early Volcker period, which is clearly different from the periods both before and after. The tests in Judd and Rudebusch (1998), for example, include the early Volcker period.

2.4.11 Additional Comments

The following are general comments about the results in Tables A1–A30, usually pertaining to groups of equations.

Lags, RHO, T, and Stability Tests

For the χ^2 tests, 27 of 30 equations pass the lags test, 24 of 29 pass the *RHO* test, and 22 of 26 pass the T test. Of the 87 AP stability tests, 48 are passed. For the end-of-sample stability test, 27 of 30 are passed. All the overidentifying restrictions tests are passed. The overall results thus suggest that the specifications of the equations are fairly accurate regarding dynamic and trend effects. The results are less strong for the AP test, where for some of the equations there are signs of a changed structure in the 1970s. It may be useful in future work to break some of the estimation periods in parts, but in general it seems that more observations are needed before this might be a sensible strategy. Also, it will be seen in Chapter 9 that the AP test may reject too often, and so the AP results in Tables A1–A30 may be too pessimistic.

Rational Expectations Tests

The led values are significant at the 1 percent level in only one case: Leads +8 for equation 3. They are significant at the 5 percent level in only four cases: (1) Leads +1 and Leads +8 in equation 1, (2) Leads +1 in equation 2, and (3) Leads +1 in equation 3. Overall, the data thus strongly reject the hypothesis that expectations are rational.

The present negative results about the RE hypothesis are consistent with Chow's (1989) results, where he finds that the use of adaptive expectations performs much better than the use of rational expectations in explaining present value models.

Age Distribution Effects

The age variables, $AG1$, $AG2$, and $AG3$, are jointly significant at the 5 percent level in three of the four household expenditure equations, and the sign patterns are generally as expected. This is thus evidence that the U.S. age distribution has an effect on U.S. macroeconomic equations.[9]

Excess Labor, Excess Capital, and Other Stock Effects

The excess capital variable is significant in the investment equation, 12, and the excess labor variable is significant in the employment and hours equations, 13 and 14. Regarding other stock effects, the stock of inventories has a negative effect on production (equation 11), the stock of durable goods has a negative effect on durable expenditures (equation 3), and the stock of housing has a negative effect on residential investment (equation 4).

Stock Market Effects

The real wealth variable, AA, appears in three of the four household expenditure equations. AA is affected by CG, which is mostly the change in the value of stocks held by the household sector, and so changes in stock prices affect expenditures in the model through their effect on household wealth. The size of this effect is discussed in Chapter 5. The wealth variable also appears in three of the four labor supply equations, where the estimated effect is negative, and so changes in stock prices also affect labor supply. Finally, one of the cost of capital variables in the investment equation 12 is a function of lagged values of CG, and so stock prices have an effect on plant and equipment investment through this variable.

Interest Rate Effects

Either the short-term or long-term interest rate is significant in the four household expenditure equations. Also, interest income is part of disposable personal income, YD, which is significant in the four equations. Therefore an increase in interest rates has a negative effect on household expenditures through the interest rate variables and a positive effect through the disposable personal income variable. In addition, the change in a long-term interest rate has a negative effect on the change in the value of stocks

---

9. This same conclusion was also reached in Fair and Dominguez (1991). In this earlier study, contrary to the case here, the age variables were also significant in the equation explaining IHH.

(equation 25), and so interest rates have a negative effect on household expenditures through their effect on household wealth. A long-term interest rate is significant in the investment equation 12, and so interest rates have a negative effect on plant and equipment investment through this variable. The short-term interest rate also appears in the three demand-for-money equations.

Money Demand Adjustment

In all three money demand equations the nominal adjustment specification dominates the real adjustment specification. The nominal adjustment specification is equation 2.28.

Unemployment Rate

The unemployment rate is significant in two of the four labor supply equations and nearly significant in one of the other two. There is thus some evidence that a discouraged worker effect is in operation. The unemployment rate is the demand pressure variable in the price equation 10 and is highly significant. The unemployment rate and the change in the unemployment rate are significant in equation 30, the estimated interest rate rule.

Price of Imports

The price of imports, *PIM*, is an explanatory variable in the price equation 10, where it has a positive effect on the domestic price level. It also appears in the import equation 27, where it has a negative effect on imports, other things being equal.

Potential Productivity

Potential productivity, *LAM*, is exogenous in the model. It is constructed from a peak-to-peak interpolation of measured productivity. It appears in the price and wage equations 10 and 16. It is also used in the definition of *JHMIN*, which appears in the employment and hours equations 13 and 14, and it is in the definition of potential output, *YS*.

Dummy Variables

A dummy variable appears in equations 9 and 17 to account for a possible data error. Three dummy variables appear in equation 11 to account for a steel strike; one dummy variable appears in equation 13 to account for the same steel strike; and four dummy variables appear in equation 27 to account for two dock strikes. A dummy variable appears in equation 30 to account for the announced change in Fed behavior in the early Volcker period. Finally, nine dummy variables appear in equation 21 to account for depreciation tax law changes.

2.5   The ROW Stochastic Equations

2.5.1   Introduction

Stochastic equations are estimated for 38 countries aside from the United States, with up to 15 equations estimated per country. The estimates and test results are presented in Tables B1 through B15 in Table B.4 in Appendix B. The 2SLS technique was used for the quarterly countries and for equations 1, 2, and 3 for the annual countries. Ordinary least squares was used for the other equations for the annual countries. The 2SLS technique had to be used sparingly for the annual countries because of the limited number of observations. The first-stage regressors for each equation are listed on the website mentioned in section 1.8.

The estimation periods were chosen on the basis of data availability. With three exceptions, the periods were chosen to use all the available data. The three exceptions are the interest rate, exchange rate, and forward rate equations, where the estimation periods were chosen to begin after the advent of floating exchange rates. The earliest starting quarter (year) for these periods was 1972:2 (1972). For the EMU countries the estimation periods for the interest rate, exchange rate, and forward rate equations end in 1998:4. Because the EMU countries have had a common monetary policy since 1999:1, there are no longer individual interest rate, exchange rate, and forward rate equations for these countries. The end-of-sample stability test was not performed for these equations for the EMU countries.

No dummy variables are used for the ROW model except for Germany. Four dummy variables were added to the estimated equations for Germany except for equations 7–10. The first dummy variable is 1 in 1990:3 and 0 otherwise; the second is 1 in 1990:4 and 0 otherwise; the third is 1 in 1991:1 and 0 otherwise; and the fourth is 1 in 1991:2 and 0 otherwise. These were added to pick up any effects of the German reunification. To save space, the coefficient estimates of the dummy variables are not presented in the tables. As noted in section 1.5, the coefficient estimates of the dummy variables were taken as fixed when performing the AP and end-of-sample stability tests.

The tests per equation are similar to those done for the US equations. Remember from section 1.5 that for the AP test T_1 is taken to be 40 quarters or 10 years after the first observation and T_2 is taken to be 40 quarters or 10 years before the last observation. For the end-of-sample stability test the end period begins 12 quarters or 3 years before the last observation. For the serial correlation test the order of the autoregressive process was two for the quarterly countries and one for the annual countries. (For the test for the United States the order was four.) The led values were one-quarter-ahead values for the quarterly countries and one-year-ahead values for the annual countries. Subject to data limitations, the specification of the ROW equations follows fairly closely the specification of the US equations. Data limitations prevented all 15 equations from being estimated for all 38 countries. In addition, some equations for some countries were initially estimated and then rejected for giving what seemed to be poor results.

One important difference between the US and ROW models is that the asset variable A for each country in the ROW model measures only the net asset position of the country vis-à-vis the rest of the world; it does not include the domestic wealth of the country. Also, the asset variable is divided by $PY \cdot YS$ before it is entered as an explanatory variable in the equations. (PY is the GDP price deflator and YS is an estimate of potential real GDP.) This was done even for equations that were otherwise in log form. As discussed in Appendix B, the asset variable is off by a constant amount, and so taking logs of the variable is not appropriate. Entering the variable in ratio form in the equations allows the error to be approximately absorbed in the estimate of the constant term.[10] This procedure is, of course, crude, but at least it responds somewhat to the problem caused by the level error in A.

Because much of the specification of the ROW equations is close to that of the US equations, the specification discussion in this section is brief. Only the differences are emphasized.

A dagger (†) after a coefficient estimate in Tables B1–B15 indicates that the variable is lagged one period. To save space, only the p-values are presented for each test in the tables except for the AP stability test. As for the US equations, an equation will be said to pass a test if the p-value is greater than 01. For the AP stability test the AP value is presented along with the degrees of freedom and the value of lambda. The AP value has an asterisk (*) in front of it if it is significant at the 1 percent level, which means that the equation fails the stability test. No tests are performed for countries AR, BR, and PE because of very short estimation periods (for country abbreviations, see Table B.1). Also, stability tests are not performed for countries with very short estimation periods.

There are obviously many estimates and test results in the tables, and it is not feasible to discuss each estimate and test result in detail. The following discussion tries to give a general idea of the results.

2.5.2   The Equations and Tests

Table B1: Equation 1. *IM*, total imports

Equation 1 explains the total real per capita imports of the country. The explanatory variables include the price of domestic goods relative to the price of imports, per capital expenditures on consumption plus investment plus government spending, and the lagged dependent variable. The variables are in logs. Equation 1 is similar to equation 27 in the US model. The main difference is that the expenditure variable includes government spending, which it does not in equation 27.

The coefficient estimate for the expenditure variable is of the expected sign for all countries, and many of the estimates of the coefficient of the relative price variable are

---

10. Let $[A_{t-1}/(PY_{t-1} \cdot YS_{t-1})]^a$ denote the correct variable for period $t-1$, and let $[A_{t-1}/(PY_{t-1} \cdot YS_{t-1})]$ denote the measured variable. Under the assumption that $\delta = [A_{t-1}/(PY_{t-1} \cdot YS_{t-1})]^a - [A_{t-1}/(PY_{t-1} \cdot YS_{t-1})]$ is constant for all t, the measurement error is absorbed in the constant term.

significant. Equation 1 does fairly well for the lags test, where there are 6 failures out of 31, and for the end-of-sample stability test, where there is only 1 failure out of 28. However, for the RHO test there are 16 failures out of 31, for the T test there are 14 failures out of 31, for the AP stability test there are 23 failures out of 30, and for the overid test there are 10 failures out of 15. There is one other test in Table B1. For the countries in which the relative price variable was used, the log of the domestic price level was added to test the relative price constraint. The constraint was rejected (that is, log PY was significant) in 6 of the 24 cases.

Table B2: Equation 2. C, consumption

Equation 2 explains real per capita consumption. The explanatory variables include the short-term or long-term interest rate, per capita income, the lagged value of real per capita assets, and the lagged dependent variable. The variables are in logs except for the interest rates and the asset variable. Equation 2 is similar to the consumption equations in the US model. The two main differences are (1) there is only one category of consumption in the ROW model compared with three in the US model and (2) the income variable is total GDP instead of disposable personal income.

The income variable is significant for almost all countries, and the interest rate and asset variables are significant for many countries. The interest rates in these equations provide a key link from monetary policy changes to changes in real demand. Regarding the tests, 4 of 34 fail the lags test, 10 of 34 fail the RHO test, 12 of 34 fail the T test, 17 of 33 fail the AP test, 2 of 31 fail the end-of-sample test, and 9 of 20 fail the overid test. The led value of the income variable was used for the leads test, and it is significant in only 3 of 34 cases.

Table B3: Equation 3. I, fixed investment

Equation 3 explains real fixed investment. It includes as explanatory variables the lagged value of investment, the current value of output, and the short-term or long-term interest rate. The variables are in logs except for the interest rates. Equation 3 differs from the investment equation 12 for the US, which uses a capital stock series. Sufficient data are not available to allow good capital stock series to be constructed for most of the other countries, and so no capital stock series were constructed for the ROW model. The simpler equation just mentioned was estimated for each country.

The output variable is significant for most countries, and an interest rate variable is significant for many. Again, the interest rates in these equations provide a key link from monetary policy changes to changes in real demand, in this case investment demand. Regarding the tests, 17 of 33 fail the lags test, 20 of 33 fail the RHO test, 17 of 33 fail the T test, 19 of 31 fail the AP test, 3 of 30 fail the end-of-sample test, and 5 of 17 fail the overid test. The dynamic and trend properties are thus not well captured in a number of cases. The led value of output was used for the leads test, and in only 2 of 33 cases is the led value significant.

Table B4: Equation 4. Y, production

Equation 4 explains the level of production. It is the same as equation 11 for the US model—see equation 2.10. It includes as explanatory variables the lagged level of production, the current level of sales, and the lagged stock of inventories.

The value of λ presented in Table B4 is one minus the coefficient estimate of lagged production. Also presented in the table are the implied values of α and β in equation 2.10. For the quarterly countries λ ranges from 0.331 to 0.853 and α ranges from 0.056 to 0.421. For the annual countries λ ranges from 0.534 to 0.974 and α ranges from 0.023 to 0.094. For the United States λ was 0.683 and α was 0.353.

Equation 4 does well in the tests except for the AP test. Two of 10 equations fail the lags test, 2 of 10 fail the RHO test, none of 10 fail the T test, 7 of 10 fail the AP test, and none of 10 fail the end-of-sample test. The led value of sales was used for the leads test, and in only 2 of 10 cases is the led value significant.

As was the case for equation 11 in the US model, the coefficient estimates of equation 4 are consistent with the view that firms smooth production relative to sales, and so these results add support to the production smoothing hypothesis.

Table B5: Equation 5. PY, price deflator

Equation 5 explains the GDP price deflator. It is the same as equation 10 for the US model except for the use of different demand pressure variables. It includes as explanatory variables the lagged price level, the price of imports, the nominal wage rate (when available), a demand pressure variable, and the time trend.

Three demand pressure variables were tried per country. The first is the output gap variable, ZZ, which equals $(YS - Y)/YS$, where Y is actual output and YS is a measure of potential output. The construction of YS is discussed in Appendix B. For the second variable, $\log Y_t$ was regressed on the constant term and t, and $\widehat{\log Y_t} - \log Y_t$ was taken as the demand pressure variable, where $\widehat{\log Y_t}$ is the predicted value from the regression. The third variable is the unemployment rate when data for it are available. The demand pressure variable whose coefficient estimate was of the expected sign and had the largest t-statistic in absolute value was chosen per country.

The estimates of the final specification of equation 5 are presented in Table B5. A demand pressure variable (denoted DP in the table) appears in 27 of the 32 cases. (The note to Table B5 indicates which demand pressure variable was chosen for each equation.) The price of imports appears in all but 3 cases, and in most cases it is significant. Import prices thus appear to have important effects on domestic prices for most countries.

The results of two lags tests are reported in Table B5. The first is the usual test, and the second is one in which an extra lag is added for each variable. Equation 5 does fairly well in the tests except for the AP test. Seven of 32 equations fail the first lags test, 11 of 32 fail the second lags test, 9 of 32 fail the RHO test, 20 of 30 fail the AP test, 1 of 29 fails the end-of-sample test, and 5 of 13 fail the overid test. The led value of the wage rate was used for the leads test, and in 3 of 7 cases the led value is significant.

Table B6: Equation 6. $M1$, money

Equation 6 explains the per capita demand for money. It is the same as equation 9 for the US model. The same nominal versus real adjustment specifications were tested here as were tested for US equation 9 (and for the US equations 17 and 26). Equation 6 includes as explanatory variables one of the two lagged money variables, depending on which adjustment specification won, the short-term interest rate, and income.

The estimates in Table B6 show that the nominal adjustment specification was chosen in 12 of the 20 cases. The equation does well in the tests except for the AP test. One of 20 equations fails the lags test, 4 of 20 fail the RHO test, 5 of 20 fail the T test, 11 of 20 fail the AP test, 1 of 19 fails the end-of-sample test, and 1 of 9 fails the overid test. The first test in the table (N versus R) adds the other lagged money variable (that is, the lagged money variable not chosen for the final specification). Only for the United Kingdom is the variable significant. For the United Kingdom both variables are significant when included together.

As was the case for the United States, the demand-for-money equations for the other countries are presented for sake of completeness only. The short-term interest rate in a country is determined by the interest rate rule (equation 7 next), and the money supply is whatever is needed to have the money demand equation met.

Table B7: Equation 7. RS, short-term interest rate

Equation 7 explains the short-term (three-month) interest rate. It is interpreted as the interest rate rule of each country's monetary authority, and it is similar to equation 30 in the US model. For the EMU countries the equation is only relevant for the period through 1998:4. The explanatory variables that were tried (as possibly influencing the monetary authority's interest rate decision) are (1) the rate of inflation, (2) the output gap variable ZZ, (3) the German short-term interest rate (for the European countries only), and (4) the U.S. short-term interest rate. The U.S. interest rate was included on the view that some monetary authorities' decisions may be influenced by the Fed's decisions. Similarly, the German interest rate was included in the (non-German) European equations on the view that the (non-German) European monetary authorities' decisions may be influenced by the decisions of the German central bank.

Table B7 shows that the inflation rate is included in 16 of the 24 cases, ZZ in 12 cases, the German rate in 7 cases, and the U.S. rate in 17 cases. There is thus evidence that monetary authorities are influenced by inflation and demand pressure. Equation 7 does well in the tests. One of the 24 equations fails the lags test, 2 of 24 fail the RHO test, 2 of 24 fail the T test, 6 of 24 fail the AP test, none of 14 fail the end-of-sample test, and 5 of 13 fail the overid test.

Three important countries in the MC model are Japan, Germany, and the United Kingdom. The inflation rate and ZZ appear in each of the estimated rules for these countries. The equations pass all the tests except the T test for the United Kingdom. Also, the U.S. rate affects each of the three rates, and in this sense the United States is the monetary policy leader.

Equation 7 for EU is explained at the end of this section. It is only relevant from 1999:1 on.

Table B8: Equation 8. *RB*, long-term interest rate

Equation 8 explains the long-term interest rate. It is the same as equations 23 and 24 in the US model. For the EMU countries the equation is only relevant for the period through 1998:4. For the quarterly countries the explanatory variables include the lagged dependent variable and the current and two lagged short rates. For the annual countries the explanatory variables include the lagged dependent variable and the current and one lagged short rates. The same restriction was imposed on equation 8 as was imposed on equations 23 and 24, namely that the coefficients on the short rate sum to one in the long run.

The first test in Table B8 shows that the restriction that the coefficients sum to one is only rejected in 2 of the 20 cases. The equation does well in the other tests. Three of the 20 equations fail the lags test, 1 of 20 fails the RHO test, 5 of 20 fail the *T* test, 5 of 20 fail the AP test, none of 13 fail the end-of-sample test, and 1 of 12 fails the overid test. The led value of the short-term interest rate was used for the leads test, and it is not significant in any of the 19 cases.[11]

Equation 8 for EU is explained at the end of this section. It is only relevant from 1999:1 on.

Table B9: Equation 9. *E* or *H*, exchange rate

Equation 9 explains the country's exchange rate: *E* for the non-European countries plus Germany and *H* for the non-German European countries. *E* is a country's exchange rate relative to the U.S. dollar, and *H* is a country's exchange rate relative to the Deutsche mark (DM). An increase in *E* is a *depreciation* of the country's currency relative to the dollar, and an increase in *H* is a *depreciation* of the country's currency relative to the DM. For the EMU countries the equation is only relevant for the period through 1998:4.

The theory behind the specification of equation 9 is discussed in Fair (1994), Chapter 2. Equation 9 is interpreted as an exchange rate reaction function. The equations for *E* and *H* have the same general specification except that U.S. variables are the base variables for the *E* equations and German variables are the base variables for the *H* equations. The following discussion will focus on *E*.

It will first be useful to define two variables:

$$r = [(1 + RS/100)/(1 + RS_{US}/100)]^{.25}, \tag{2.33}$$

$$p = PY/PY_{US}. \tag{2.34}$$

The variable *r* is a relative interest rate measure. *RS* is the country's short-term interest rate, and RS_{US} is the U.S. short-term interest rate (denoted simply *RS* in the US model).

---

11. Collinearity problems prevented the leads test form being performed for Korea.

RS and RS_{US} are divided by 100 in the definition of r because they are in percentage points rather than in percents. Also, the interest rates are at annual rates, and so the term in brackets in the definition of r is raised to the 0.25 power to put r at a quarterly rate. For the annual countries 0.25 is not used. The variable p is the relative price level, where PY is the country's GDP price deflator and PY_{US} is the U.S. GDP price deflator (denoted $GDPD$ in the US model).[12]

The equation for E is based on the following two equations.

$$E^* = \alpha p r^\beta, \tag{2.35}$$

$$E/E_{-1} = (E^*/E_{-1})^\lambda e^\epsilon. \tag{2.36}$$

Equation 2.35 states that the long-run exchange rate, E^*, depends on the relative price level, p, and the relative interest rate, r. The coefficient on the relative price level is constrained to be one, which means that in the long run the real exchange rate is assumed merely to fluctuate as the relative interest rate fluctuates. Equation 2.36 is a partial adjustment equation, which says that the actual exchange rate adjusts λ percent of the way to the long-run exchange rate each period.

Equations 2.35 and 2.36 imply that

$$\log(E/E_{-1}) = \lambda \log \alpha + \lambda(\log p - \log E_{-1}) + \lambda\beta \log r + \epsilon. \tag{2.37}$$

The restriction that the coefficient of the relative price term is one can be tested by adding $\log E_{-1}$ to equation 2.37. If the coefficient is other than one, this variable should have a nonzero coefficient. This is one of the tests performed in Table B9.

The equations for the European countries (except Germany) are the same as above with H replacing E, RS_{GE} replacing RS_{US}, and PY_{GE} replacing PY_{US}.

Exchange rate equations were estimated for 25 countries. For a number of countries the estimate of the coefficient of the relative interest rate variable was of the wrong expected sign, and in these cases the relative interest rate variable was dropped from the equation. Also, for 7 countries—CA, JA, AU, IT, NE, UK, SO—the estimate of λ in equation 2.37 was very small ("very small" defined to be less than 0.025), and for these countries the equation was reestimated with λ constrained to be 0.050.

The unconstrained estimates of λ in the equation vary from 0.053 to 0.233 for the quarterly countries and from 0.071 to 0.489 for the annual countries. A small value for λ means that it takes considerable time for the exchange rate to adjust to a relative price level change. The relative interest rate variable appears in 7 equations. It is only significant in 2 (CA and NE), however, so there is only limited support for the hypothesis that relative interest rates affect exchange rates.

The first test in Table B9 is of the restriction discussed above. The restriction is tested by adding $\log E_{-1}$ or $\log H_{-1}$ to the equation. It is rejected in 8 of the 25 cases. For the other tests, 7 of the 25 equations fail the lags test, 9 of 25 fail the RHO test, 10

---

12. The relative interest rate is defined the way it is so that logs can be used in the specification below. This treatment relies on the fact that the log of $1 + x$ is approximately x for small values of x.

of 25 fail the T test, 8 of 24 fail the AP test, none of 13 fail the end-of-sample test, and 3 of 12 fail the overid test.

Since equation 9 is in log form, the standard errors are roughly in percentage terms. The standard errors for a number of the European countries are quite low, but remember that these are standard errors for H, not E. The variance of H is much smaller than the variance of E for the European countries.

The relative interest rate variable appears in the equations for Japan, Germany, and the United Kingdom, and so relative interest rates have an effect on the exchange rates of these three key countries in the model. As noted above, however, they are not significant, and so the relative interest rate effects are at best weak.

Equation 9 for EU is explained at the end of this section. It is only relevant from 1999:1 on.

Table B10: Equation 10. F, forward rate

Equation 10 explains the country's forward exchange rate, F. This equation is the estimated arbitrage condition, and although it plays no role in the model, it is of interest to see how closely the quarterly data on EE, F, RS, and RS_{US} match the arbitrage condition. (EE differs from E in that it is the exchange rate at the end of the period, not the average for the period.) The arbitrage condition in this notation is

$$F/EE = [(1 + RS/100)/(1 + RS_{US}/100)]^{.25}e^\epsilon. \tag{2.38}$$

In equation 10, $\log F$ is regressed on $\log EE$ and $.25 \log(1 + RS/100)/(1 + RS_{US}/100)$. If the arbitrage condition were met exactly, the coefficient estimates for both explanatory variables would be one and the fit would be perfect.

The results in Table B10 show that the data are generally consistent with the arbitrage condition, especially considering that some of the interest rate data are not exactly the right data to use. Note the t-statistic for Switzerland of 14,732.73! Equation 10 plays no role in the model because F does not appear in any other equation.

Table B11: Equation 11. PX, export price index

Equation 11 explains the export price index, PX. It provides a link from the GDP price deflator, PY, to the export price index. Export prices are needed when the countries are linked together. If a country produced only one good, then the export price would be the domestic price and only one price equation would be needed. In practice, of course, a country produces many goods, only some of which are exported. If a country is a price taker with respect to its exports, then its export prices would just be the world prices of the export goods. To try to capture the in-between case where a country has some effect on its export prices but not complete control over every price, the following equation is postulated:

$$PX = PY^\lambda[PW\$(E/E95)]^{1-\lambda}e^\epsilon. \tag{2.39}$$

$PW\$$ is the world price index in dollars, and so $PW\$(E/E95)$ is the world price index in local currency. Equation 2.39 thus takes PX to be a weighted average of PY and the world price index in local currency, where the weights sum to one. Equation 11 was not estimated for any of the major oil exporting countries, and so $PW\$$ was constructed to be net of oil prices. (See equations L-5 in Table B.3.)

Equation 2.39 was estimated in the following form:

$$\log PX - \log[PW\$(E/E95)] = \lambda[\log PY - \log[PW\$(E/E95)] + \epsilon. \quad (2.40)$$

The restriction that the weights sum to one and that $PW\$$ and E have the same coefficient (that is, that their product enters the equation) can be tested by adding $\log PY$ and $\log E$ to equation 2.40. If this restriction is not met, these variables should be significant. This is one of the tests performed in Table B11.

Equation 11 was estimated for 32 countries. For 2 of the countries—SY and MA— the estimate of λ was greater than 1, and for these cases the equation was reestimated with λ constrained to be 1. When λ is 1, there is a one-to-one link between PX and PY. For 7 of the countries—GR, PO, CH, AR, CE, ME, and PE—the estimate of λ was less than 0, and for these countries the equation was reestimated with only the constant term as an explanatory variable. When this is done, there is a one-to-one link between PX and $PW\$(E/E95)$. Equation 11 was estimated under the assumption of a second-order autoregressive error term.

The results in Table B11 show that the estimates of the autoregressive parameters are generally large. The estimates of λ vary from 0.274 to 0.854 for the quarterly countries and from 0.076 to 0.870 for the annual countries. The first test in Table B11 is of the restriction discussed above. The restriction is rejected in 14 of the 32 cases. The equation fails the AP test in 9 of 30 cases. It fails the end-of-sample test in 1 of 28 cases.

It should be kept in mind that equation 11 is meant only as a rough approximation. If more disaggregated data were available, one would want to estimate separate price equations for each good, where some goods' prices would be strongly influenced by world prices and others would not. This type of disaggregation is beyond the scope of the model.

Table B12: Equation 12. W, wage rate

Equation 12 explains the wage rate. It is similar to equation 16 for the US model. It includes as explanatory variables the lagged wage rate, the current price level, the lagged price level, a demand pressure variable, and the time trend. The same restriction imposed on the price and wage equations in the US model is also imposed here. Given the coefficient estimates of equation 5, the restriction is imposed on the coefficients in equation 12 so that the implied real wage equation does not have the real wage depend on either the nominal wage rate or the price level separately. The same searching for the best demand pressure variable was done for the wage equation as was done for the price equation.

The estimates of equation 12 show only mild support for the demand pressure variables having an effect on the wage rate. A demand pressure variable (denoted DW in the table) appears in 5 of the 7 equations, but it is significant in only 2 of them. The test results show that the real wage restriction is rejected in 2 of the 7 cases. None of the 7 equations fail the lags test, none of 7 fail the *RHO* test, 6 of 7 fail the AP test, 1 of 7 fails the end-of-sample test, and 1 of 5 fails the overid test. The test results are thus good except for the AP results, which are poor.

Table B13: Equation 13. *J*, employment

Equation 13 explains the change in employment. It is in log form, and it is similar to equation 13 for the US model. It includes as explanatory variables the amount of excess labor on hand, the change in output, and the time trend. It also includes the lagged change in output for CA. It does not include the lagged change in employment, which US equation 13 does.

Most of the coefficient estimates for the excess labor variable are significant in Table B13, which is support for the theory that firms at times hold excess labor and that the amount of excess labor on hand affects current employment decisions. Most of the change in output terms is also significant. Regarding the tests, 6 of the 14 equations fail the lags test, 5 of 14 fail the RHO test, 7 of 14 fail the AP test, none of 14 fail the end-of-sample test, and 6 of 9 fail the overid test. The led value of the change in output was used for the leads tests, and it is significant in only one case.

Table B14: Equation 14. *L*1, labor force–men
Table B15: Equation 15. *L*2, labor force–women

Equations 14 and 15 explain the labor force participation rates of men and women, respectively. They are in log form and are similar to equations 5, 6, and 7 in the US model. The explanatory variables include the real wage; the labor constraint variable, *Z*; the time trend; and the lagged dependent variable. The construction of *Z* is explained in Appendix B. *Z* is used instead of *UR* in the ROW model to try to pick up discouraged worker effects.

Z is significant in a number of cases for equations 14 and 15, which provides some support for the discouraged worker effect. The real wage appears in 2 cases for equation 14 and in 3 cases for equation 15. When the real wage appeared in the equation, the log of the price level, log *PY*, was added to the equation for one of the tests to test the real wage restriction. Tables B14 and B15 show that log *PY* is significant (and thus the restriction rejected) in 2 of the 5 cases.

In Table B14, 5 of the 14 equations fail the lags test, 2 of 14 fail the RHO test, 7 of 14 fail the AP test, none of 14 fail the end-of-sample test, and 3 of 9 fail the overid test. In Table B15, 2 of the 12 equations fail the lags test, 2 of 12 fail the RHO test, 7 of 12 fail the AP test, none of 12 fail the end-of-sample test, and 4 of 8 fail the overid test.

Tables B7, B8, B9: EU Specifications

The 11 countries that make up the EU in the model are listed at the bottom of Table B.1 in Appendix B. The EU variables that are used in the model are listed near the bottom of Table B.2. The EU variables that are needed are *RS*, *RB*, *E*, *Y*, *YS*, and *PY*. Any other EU variables that are used are functions of these six variables. Data on the first three variables are available from the IFS (IMF international financial statistics). Y for EU is taken to be the sum of Y for the six quarterly EU countries: GE, AU, FR, IT, NE, and FI. The annual countries that are excluded are BE, IR, PO, SP, and GR. Similarly, YS for EU is taken to be the sum of YS for the six quarterly EU countries. PY for EU is the ratio of nominal output to real output for the six countries.

There are three estimated EU equations, explaining RS, RB, and E. These are equations 7, 8, and 9. The estimates are presented at the top of Tables B7, B8, and B9. The estimation period is 1972:2–2001:3 for equation 7, 1970:1–2001:4 for equation 8, and 1972:2–2001:4 for equation 9. German data are used prior to 1999:1, and a dummy variable that is 1 in 1999:1 and 0 otherwise is added to each equation to pick up any transition effects. The coefficient estimates of the dummy variable are not presented in the tables. PY for EU appears in equations 7 and 9. The EU output gap variable, ZZ, appears in equation 7. It is equal to $(YS - Y)/YS$, where Y and YS are the EU variables discussed above.

Remember that equation 7 for Germany is the estimated interest rate rule of the Bundesbank when it determined German monetary policy (through 1998:4). The use of German data prior to 1999:1 to estimate equation 7 for the EU means that the behavior of the European Central Bank (ECB) is assumed to be the same as the behavior of the Bundesbank except that the right-hand-side variables are EU variables rather than German ones. Likewise, the structure of the EU exchange rate equation 9 is assumed to be the same as the German equation except that the right-hand-side variables are changed from German ones to EU ones. The same is also true of the long-run interest rate equation 8.

Using only the six quarterly EU countries to construct Y, YS, and PY means that implicit in equation 7 is the assumption that the ECB only takes these six countries into account when setting its monetary policy. Although most of EU output is from the six quarterly countries, in future work the other countries should be included. This was not done here because of the lack of good quarterly data for the other countries.

The estimates in the three tables show that the estimates for EU are close to the estimates for Germany alone. This is, of course, not surprising since the EU equations have only 11 or 12 additional observations. These three equations are relevant from 1999:1 on; they play no role in the model prior to this time. When these three equations are relevant, equations 7, 8, and 9 for the individual EU countries are not part of the model. See Table B.3 for more detail.

The Trade Share Equations

The variable a_{ijt} is the fraction of country i's exports imported by j in period t, where i runs from 1 to 58 and j runs from 1 to 59. The data on a_{ij} are quarterly, with observations for most i, j pairs beginning in 1960:1.

One would expect a_{ijt} to depend on country i's export price relative to an index of export prices of all the other countries. The empirical work consisted of trying to estimate the effects of relative prices on a_{ijt}. A separate equation was estimated for each i, j pair. The equation is the following:

$$a_{ijt} = \beta_{ij1} + \beta_{ij2}a_{ijt-1} + \beta_{ij3}(PX\$_{it}/(\sum_{k=1}^{58} a_{kjt}PX\$_{kt}) + u_{ijt}, \tag{2.41}$$

$$t = 1, \ldots, T.$$

$PX\$_{it}$ is the price index of country i's exports, and $\sum_{k=1}^{58} a_{kjt}PX\$_{kt}$ is an index of all countries' export prices, where the weight for a given country k is the share of k's exports to j in the total imports of j. (In this summation $k = i$ is skipped.)

With i running from 1 to 58, j running from 1 to 59, and not counting $i = j$, there are 3,364 ($= 58 \times 58$) i, j pairs. There are thus 3,364 potential trade share equations to estimate. In fact, only 1,488 trade share equations were estimated. Data did not exist for all pairs and all quarters, and if fewer than 26 observations were available for a given pair, the equation was not estimated for that pair. A few other pairs were excluded because at least some of the observations seemed extreme and likely suffering from measurement error. Almost all of these cases were for the smaller countries.

Each of the 1,488 equations was estimated by ordinary least squares. The main coefficient of interest is β_{ij3}, the coefficient of the relative price variable. Of the 1,488 estimates of this coefficient, 74.7 percent (1,111) were of the expected negative sign. A total of 33.3 percent had the correct sign and a t-statistic greater than two in absolute value, and 56.2 percent had the correct sign and a t-statistic greater than one in absolute value. A total of 5.8 percent had the wrong sign and a t-statistic greater than two, and 12.8 percent had the wrong sign and a t-statistic greater than one. The overall results are thus quite supportive of the view that relative prices affect trade shares.

The average of the 1,111 estimates of β_{ij3} that were of the right sign is -0.0136. β_{ij3} measures the short-run effect of a relative price change on the trade share. The long-run effect is $\beta_{ij3}/(1 - \beta_{ij2})$, and the average of the 1,111 values of this is -0.0716.

The trade share equations with the wrong sign for β_{ij3} were not used in the solution of the model. The trade shares for these i, j pairs were taken to be exogenous.

In the solution of the model the predicted values of α_{ijt}, say, $\hat{\alpha}_{ijt}$, do not obey the property that $\sum_{i=1}^{58} \hat{\alpha}_{ijt} = 1$. Unless this property is obeyed, the sum of total world exports will not equal the sum of total world imports. For solution purposes each $\hat{\alpha}_{ijt}$ was divided by $\sum_{i=1}^{58} \hat{\alpha}_{ijt}$, and this adjusted figure was used as the predicted trade share. In other words, the values predicted by the equations in 2.41 were adjusted to satisfy the requirement that the trade shares sum to one.

2.5.3   Additional Comments

Lags, RHO, T, Stability Tests

The equations do moderately well for the lags, RHO, and T tests. For the lags test there are 65 failures out of 276 cases (23.6 percent); for the RHO test there are 84 failures out of 256 (32.8 percent); and for the T test there are 73 failures out of 229 (31.9 percent). These results suggest that the dynamic specifications of the equations are reasonably good. The results are not strong for the AP stability test, where there are 151 failures out of 299 (50.5 percent). More observations are probably needed before much can be done about this problem. The end-of-sample stability test results, on the other hand, are quite good, with only 10 failures out of 261 (3.8 percent). For the overid test there are 53 failures out of 142 (37.3 percent).

Rational Expectations Tests

There is little support for the use of the led values and thus little support for the rational expectations hypothesis. The led values are significant in only 11 out of 117 cases (9.4 percent).

Excess Labor and Other Stock Effects

The excess labor variable is significant in most of the employment equations 13. The stock of inventories is significant in most of the production equations 4.

Wealth Effects

The wealth variable, A, which is the country's net stock of foreign security and reserve holdings, appears in 8 of the consumption equations 2.

Interest Rate Effects

Either the short-term or long-term interest rate appears in most of the consumption and investment equations 2 and 3. The short-term interest rate also appears in the demand for money equations 6. The relative interest rate appears in 7 of the exchange rate equations 9. The U.S. short-term interest rate appears in 17 of the interest rate rules 7, and the German short-term interest rate appears in 7 of the rules.

Money Demand Adjustment

The nominal adjustment specification dominates the real adjustment specification in 12 of the 20 cases for the money demand equations 6.

Demand Pressure Variables

A demand pressure variable appears in nearly all the price equations 5 and the wage equations 12. The gap variable, ZZ, appears in many of the interest rate rules 7. The labor constraint variable, Z, appears in most of the labor supply equations 14 and 15.

Price of Imports

The price of imports, PM, appears in all but one of the price equations 10. It also appears in all but four of the import equations 1.

Potential Productivity

Potential productivity, *LAM*, is exogenous in the model. It is constructed from a peak-to-peak interpolation of measured productivity, Y/J. It appears in the price and wage equations 5 and 12. It is also used in the definition of *JMIN*, which appears in the employment equations 13, and it is in the definition of potential output, *YS*.

Dummy Variables

Dummy variables appear only in some of the German equations and in the three EU equations.

3

Interest Rate Effects

3.1 Introduction

This is a short chapter, but it contains an important set of empirical results.[1] It will be seen that the data rather strongly support the use of nominal over real interest rates in most expenditure equations. This chapter uses the consumption and investment equations of the MC model to test for nominal versus real interest rate effects. The aim of the tests is to see if the interest rates that households and firms use in their decision-making processes are better approximated by nominal or real rates.

3.2 The Test

The test is as follows. For period t, let i_t denote the nominal interest rate, r_t the real interest rate, and $\dot{p}_t^e$ the expected future rate of inflation, where the horizon for $\dot{p}_t^e$ matches the horizon for i_t. By definition $r_t = i_t - \dot{p}_t^e$. Consider the specification of a consumption or investment equation in which the following appears on the right-hand side:

$$\alpha i_t + \beta \dot{p}_t^e.$$

For the real interest rate specification $\alpha = -\beta$, and for the nominal interest rate specification $\beta = 0$. The real interest rate specification can be tested by adding $\dot{p}_t^e$ to an equation with $i_t - \dot{p}_t^e$ included, and the nominal interest rate specification can be tested by adding $\dot{p}_t^e$ to an equation with i_t included. The added variable should have a coefficient of zero if the specification is correct, and one can test for this.

Four measures of $\dot{p}_t^e$ were tried for countries with quarterly data (all at annual rates). Two of these have already been used for the tests in Chapter 2, namely $\dot{p}_{4t}^e$, which is $P_t/P_{t-4} - 1$, and $\dot{p}_{8t}^e$, which is $(P_t/P_{t-8})^{.5} - 1$, where P_t denotes the price level

---

1. The results in this chapter are updates of those in Fair (2002).

Table 3.1
Nominal versus Real Interest Rates: $\alpha i_t + \beta \dot{p}_t^e$

Variable	Real Test ($\alpha = -\beta$) p-value				Nominal Test ($\beta = 0$) p-value				Sample Period
	a	b	c	d	a	b	c	d	
Countries with quarterly data									
1 US: CS	.000	.000	.000	.000	.184	.045	.010	.181	1954:1–2002:3
2 US: CN	.000	.000	.000	.000	.005	.001	.002	.004	1954:1–2002:3
3 US: CD	.004	.000	.002	.032	.512	.129	.494	.686	1954:1–2002:3
4 US: IHH	.000	.000	.000	.000	.760	.032	.071	.464	1954:1–2002:3
5 US: IKF	.451	.369	.424	.484	.037	.039	.015	.034	1954:1–2002:3
6 CA: C	.008	.009	.017	.005	.991	.879	.569	.771	1966:1–2001:4
7 JA: C	.001	.003	.010	.000	.008	.116	.307	.007	1966:1–2001:3
8 JA: I	.007	.002	.000	.004	.341	.006	.020	.107	1966:1–2001:3
9 AU: C	.000	.000	.000	.000	.000	.000	.001	.000	1970:1–2001:3
10 AU: I	.306	.453	.189	.440	.253	.008	.012	.326	1970:1–2001:3
11 FR: I	.000	.000	.000	.000	.241	.043	.173	.349	1971:1–2001:3
12 GE: C	.000	.007	.241	.000	.030	.521	.278	.002	1970:1–2001:4
13 IT: C	.006	.002	.006	.008	.772	.955	.444	.892	1971:1–2001:3
14 IT: I	.000	.000	.000	.000	.057	.284	.813	.512	1971:1–2001:3
15 NE: C	.006	.004	.036	.016	.044	.788	.822	.018	1978:1–2001:4
16 NE: I	.004	.001	.000	.001	.095	.929	.999	.252	1978:1–2001:4
17 ST: C	.005	.002	.010	.011	.036	.008	.046	.079	1983:1–2000:4
18 UK: C	.002	.000	.000	.002	.159	.966	.620	.171	1966:1–2001:3
19 UK: I	.000	.000	.000	.000	.134	.779	.844	.034	1966:1–2001:3
20 AS: I	.003	.001	.001	.001	.100	.008	.027	.067	1966:1–2001:2
21 SO: C	.000	.001	.001	.003	.030	.061	.061	.054	1961:1–2001:3
22 SO: I	.000	.000	.000	.000	.546	.079	.131	.158	1961:1–2001:3
23 KO: C	.087	.047	.090	.080	.115	.180	.005	.104	1974:1–2001:4

for quarter t. The other two measures used in this chapter are the one-quarter change, $(P_t/P_{t-1})^4 - 1$, and the two-quarter change led once, $(P_{t+1}/P_{t-1})^2 - 1$. Three measures were tried for countries with only annual data: the one-year change, $P_t/P_{t-1} - 1$, the two-year change, $(P_t/P_{t-2})^{.5} - 1$, and the two-year change led once, $(P_{t+1}/P_{t-1})^{.5} - 1$, where P_t denotes the price level for year t.

The results of the tests are presented in Tables 3.1 and 3.2. The equations that are tested are the ones in Tables A1, A2, A3, A4, A12, B2, and B3. An equation was tested if the absolute value of the t-statistic of the coefficient estimate of the nominal interest rate variable was greater than 1.5. Except for US investment equation 12, nominal interest rates are used in the equations.[2] In Table 3.1 the p-value is presented for each equation

2. There is a potential bias from starting with equations chosen using nominal rather than real interest rates. Some experimentation was done to see if other equations would be added if real interest rates were used first, but no further equations were found.

Table 3.1
(*continued*)

		Real Test ($\alpha = -\beta$) p-value				Nominal Test ($\beta = 0$) p-value				Sample
	Variable	a	b	c	d	a	b	c	d	Period
Countries with annual data										
24	BE: I	.000	.000	.000		.185	.205	.114		1962–1998
25	DE: I	.016	.060	.164		.465	.031	.051		1967–2000
26	GR: C	.031	.046	.407		.008	.011	.010		1963–2000
27	GR: I	.000	.000	.000		.551	.449	.779		1963–2000
28	IR: C	.056	.105	.022		.029	.052	.009		1968–2000
29	PO: C	.019	.024	.032		.067	.246	.056		1962–1998
30	PO: I	.000	.000	.001		.892	.767	.758		1962–1998
31	SP: C	.547	.403	.706		.313	.381	.186		1962–2000
32	SP: I	.000	.000	.001		.245	.147	.441		1962–2000
33	NZ: C	.009	.009	.010		.998	.852	.764		1962–2000
34	VE: I	.001	.003	.001		.002	.057	.008		1962–2000
35	CO: C	.017	.046	.043		.124	.359	.454		1971–2000
36	PH: C	.065	.046	.028		.015	.026	.038		1962–2001
37	PH: I	.002	.002	.004		.539	.476	.158		1962–2001
38	CH: C	.112	.203	.036		.265	.949	.758		1984–1999

Notes:
- Quarterly countries: P_t = price level for quarter t.
  a: $\dot{p}_t^e = (P_t/P_{t-1})^4 - 1$; b: $\dot{p}_t^e = P_t/P_{t-4} - 1$; c: $\dot{p}_t^e = (P_t/P_{t-8})^{.5} - 1$; d: $\dot{p}_t^e = (P_{t+1}/P_{t-1})^2 - 1$.
- Annual countries: P_t = price level for year t.
  b: $\dot{p}_t^e = P_t/P_{t-1} - 1$; c: $\dot{p}_t^e = (P_t/P_{t-2})^{.5} - 1$; d: $\dot{p}_t^e = (P_{t+1}/P_{t-1})^{.5} - 1$.
- Variables: CS = Consumption of Services; CN = Consumption of Nondurables; CD = Consumption of Durables; IHH = Residential Investment; IKF = Nonresidential Fixed Investment; C = Total Consumption; I = Total Investment.

and each measure of $\dot{p}_t^e$. Columns a, b, c, and d correspond to the four measures of $\dot{p}_t^e$. Table 3.2 presents estimates of both α and β for each case. It also presents the estimate of α when no measure of $\dot{p}_t^e$ is included, which is the specification used in the MC model except for the U.S. investment equation.

As noted in Section 2.2, when the 2SLS estimator is used, which it is in most cases, the predicted values from the first-stage regressions can be interpreted as predictions of the agents in the economy under the assumption that agents know the values of the first-stage regressors at the time they form their expectations. Since both i_t and $\dot{p}_t^e$ are treated as endogenous in the 2SLS estimation, agents can be assumed to have used the first-stage regressions for i_t and $\dot{p}_t^e$ for their predictions. These predictions use the information in the predetermined variables in the model. This interpretation is important when considering the use of P_{t+1} in one of the measures of $\dot{p}_t^e$. Agents in effect are assumed to form predictions of P_{t+1} by running first-stage regressions.

Table 3.2

Estimates of α and β: $\alpha i_t + \beta \dot{p}_t^e$

	Variable	a $\hat{\alpha}$	a $\hat{\beta}$	b $\hat{\alpha}$	b $\hat{\beta}$	c $\hat{\alpha}$	c $\hat{\beta}$	d $\hat{\alpha}$	d $\hat{\beta}$	$\beta = 0$ $\hat{\alpha}$
Countries with quarterly data										
1	US: CS	−0.101	−0.037	−0.082	−0.056	−0.071	−0.093	−0.108	−0.038	−0.123
		(−3.79)	(−1.36)	(−3.02)	(−2.06)	(−2.66)	(−2.66)	(−4.14)	(−1.37)	(−5.75)
2	US: CN	−0.155	−0.100	−0.124	−0.117	−0.102	−0.132	−0.164	−0.105	−0.174
		(−3.84)	(−2.91)	(−2.96)	(−3.48)	(−2.21)	(−3.22)	(−4.06)	(−2.94)	(−4.24)
3	US: CD	−0.471	−0.123	−0.381	−0.302	−0.479	−0.219	−0.393	−0.079	−0.514
		(−2.75)	(−0.67)	(−2.11)	(−1.56)	(−2.06)	(−0.70)	(−2.29)	(−0.42)	(−3.23)
4	US: IHH	−2.781	0.047	−2.650	−0.777	−2.786	−1.129	−2.862	−0.244	−2.955
		(−5.84)	(0.31)	(−5.06)	(−2.22)	(−5.05)	(−2.01)	(−5.53)	(−0.75)	(−6.17)
5	US: IKF	−0.0049	0.0035	−0.0051	0.0036	−0.0061	0.0046	−0.0049	0.0037	−0.0025
		(−2.47)	(2.15)	(−2.51)	(2.12)	(−2.69)	(2.50)	(−2.50)	(2.19)	(−1.54)
6	CA: C	−0.096	−0.000	−0.095	−0.005	−0.119	0.023	−0.093	−0.009	−0.096
		(−2.89)	(−0.01)	(−2.75)	(−0.15)	(−3.23)	(0.57)	(−2.73)	(−0.30)	(−2.98)
7	JA: C	−0.063	−0.065	−0.079	−0.038	−0.078	−0.032	−0.073	−0.069	−0.117
		(−1.48)	(−2.69)	(−1.74)	(−1.59)	(−1.56)	(−1.03)	(−1.70)	(−2.69)	(−2.91)
8	JA: I	−0.242	−0.048	−0.147	−0.183	−0.180	−0.177	−0.219	−0.096	−0.264
		(−2.26)	(−0.95)	(−1.33)	(−2.75)	(−1.59)	(−2.33)	(−2.04)	(−1.61)	(−2.52)
9	AU: C	−0.032	−0.396	−0.026	−0.414	−0.119	−0.376	0.006	−0.506	−0.175
		(−0.32)	(−3.72)	(−0.32)	(−3.76)	(−1.60)	(−3.46)	(0.07)	(−4.59)	(−2.24)
10	AU: I	−0.908	0.477	−1.521	1.270	−1.548	1.089	−1.092	0.715	−0.735
		(−2.52)	(1.14)	(−3.71)	(2.66)	(−4.11)	(2.51)	(−2.30)	(0.98)	(−2.60)
11	FR: I	−0.207	−0.063	−0.156	−0.146	−0.163	−0.121	−0.189	−0.091	−0.249
		(−3.25)	(−1.17)	(−2.21)	(−2.02)	(−2.20)	(−1.36)	(−2.29)	(−0.94)	(−4.76)
12	GE: C	−0.121	−0.206	−0.259	0.057	−0.323	0.186	−0.030	−0.370	−0.231
		(−1.52)	(−2.04)	(−3.77)	(0.64)	(−3.45)	(1.09)	(−0.35)	(−3.02)	(−4.26)
13	IT: C	−0.033	−0.008	−0.042	0.001	−0.062	0.020	−0.039	−0.004	−0.042
		(−1.43)	(−0.29)	(−1.73)	(0.06)	(−2.36)	(0.76)	(−1.68)	(−0.14)	(−3.22)
14	IT: I	−0.213	0.050	−0.210	0.044	−0.189	0.014	−0.198	0.034	−0.169
		(−4.77)	(1.90)	(−3.78)	(1.07)	(−2.83)	(0.24)	(−3.36)	(0.66)	(−4.31)
15	NE: C	−0.493	0.262	−0.254	0.028	−0.187	0.022	−0.567	0.361	−0.229
		(−3.18)	(2.02)	(−2.09)	(0.27)	(−1.68)	(0.23)	(−3.44)	(2.37)	(−2.94)
16	NE: I	−1.585	0.711	−0.876	0.019	−0.884	−0.000	−1.103	0.228	−0.863
		(−3.00)	(1.67)	(−2.70)	(0.09)	(−2.64)	(−0.00)	(−3.30)	(1.15)	(−3.32)
17	ST: C	−0.490	0.193	−0.452	0.167	−0.704	0.337	−0.445	0.163	−0.307
		(−3.38)	(2.29)	(−4.63)	(2.98)	(−2.63)	(1.94)	(−3.90)	(2.48)	(−2.14)
18	UK: C	−0.078	−0.046	−0.149	0.001	−0.178	0.017	−0.083	−0.043	−0.148
		(−1.26)	(−1.41)	(−2.60)	(0.04)	(−2.66)	(0.50)	(−1.39)	(−1.37)	(−3.94)
19	UK: I	−0.572	0.077	−0.454	0.020	−0.455	−0.016	−0.819	0.162	−0.418
		(−3.92)	(1.50)	(−2.72)	(0.28)	(−2.53)	(−0.20)	(−4.23)	(2.12)	(−4.06)
20	AS: I	−0.179	−0.102	−0.113	−0.189	−0.118	−0.183	−0.160	−0.147	−0.237
		(−1.86)	(−1.64)	(−1.15)	(−2.64)	(−1.16)	(−2.21)	(−1.60)	(−1.83)	(−2.69)
21	SO: C	−0.106	−0.076	−0.103	−0.105	−0.100	−0.106	−0.096	−0.110	−0.127
		(−2.36)	(−2.18)	(−2.26)	(−1.87)	(−2.20)	(−1.88)	(−2.05)	(−1.93)	(−2.83)
22	SO:I	−0.761	0.045	−0.911	0.206	−0.827	0.188	−0.874	0.168	−0.726
		(−4.17)	(0.60)	(−4.56)	(1.76)	(−4.00)	(1.51)	(−4.37)	(1.41)	(−4.33)
23	KO: C	−0.182	0.071	−0.188	0.070	−0.277	0.179	−0.186	0.077	−0.124
		(−2.45)	(1.57)	(−2.43)	(1.34)	(−3.36)	(2.82)	(−2.56)	(1.63)	(−2.05)

Table 3.2
(continued)

	Variable	b $\hat{\alpha}$	b $\hat{\beta}$	c $\hat{\alpha}$	c $\hat{\beta}$	d $\hat{\alpha}$	d $\hat{\beta}$	$\beta = 0$ $\hat{\alpha}$
Countries with annual data								
24	BE: I	−2.611	0.594	−2.562	0.510	−2.780	0.666	−2.168
		(−4.58)	(1.33)	(−4.63)	(1.27)	(−4.86)	(1.58)	(−4.79)
25	DE: I	−1.936	0.734	−2.673	1.807	−2.703	1.986	−1.422
		(−2.39)	(0.73)	(−3.77)	(2.15)	(−3.44)	(1.95)	(−3.55)
26	GR: C	−0.063	−0.182	−0.033	−0.200	0.094	−0.198	−0.331
		(−0.43)	(−2.66)	(−0.20)	(−2.53)	(0.57)	(−2.58)	(−2.81)
27	GR: I	−1.970	0.214	−1.479	−0.242	−2.153	0.090	−1.690
		(−2.96)	(0.60)	(−2.24)	(−0.76)	(−3.36)	(0.28)	(−3.69)
28	IR: C	−0.050	−0.360	−0.016	−0.303	0.033	−0.594	−0.342
		(−0.20)	(−2.19)	(−0.06)	(−1.94)	(0.13)	(−2.62)	(−1.73)
29	PO: C	−0.592	0.274	−0.488	0.182	−0.625	0.277	−0.222
		(−2.49)	(1.83)	(−1.96)	(1.16)	(−2.41)	(1.91)	(−1.83)
30	PO: I	−1.018	−0.036	−0.974	−0.084	−0.940	−0.075	−1.060
		(−2.40)	(−0.14)	(−2.07)	(−0.30)	(−2.19)	(−0.31)	(−3.73)
31	SP: C	−0.223	0.124	−0.247	0.117	−0.202	0.141	−0.240
		(−2.48)	(1.01)	(−2.71)	(0.88)	(−2.17)	(1.32)	(−2.39)
32	SP: I	−0.588	−0.323	−0.459	−0.402	−0.693	−0.204	−0.864
		(−1.69)	(−1.16)	(−1.26)	(−1.45)	(−2.01)	(−0.77)	(−3.31)
33	NZ: C	−0.274	0.000	−0.295	0.017	−0.253	−0.022	−0.274
		(−1.97)	(0.00)	(−1.90)	(0.19)	(−1.95)	(−0.30)	(−2.68)
34	VE: I	−0.266	−0.385	−0.356	−0.376	−0.296	−0.464	−0.502
		(−1.26)	(−3.13)	(−1.57)	(−1.90)	(−1.33)	(−2.64)	(−2.28)
35	CO: C	−0.066	−0.109	−0.086	−0.089	−0.136	−0.068	−0.124
		(−0.88)	(−1.54)	(−1.10)	(−0.92)	(−1.60)	(−0.75)	(−1.85)
36	PH: C	−0.050	−0.137	−0.018	−0.186	−0.066	−0.170	−0.205
		(−0.42)	(−2.44)	(−0.14)	(−2.22)	(−0.53)	(−2.07)	(−1.91)
37	PH: I	−1.265	−0.154	−1.186	−0.253	−1.794	0.438	−1.413
		(−2.40)	(−0.61)	(−2.09)	(−0.71)	(−3.61)	(1.41)	(−3.04)
38	CH: C	0.303	−0.336	0.715	−0.478	0.501	−0.363	−0.624
		(0.44)	(−1.59)	(0.64)	(−1.27)	(0.90)	(−2.09)	(−1.65)

Note:
• See notes to Table 3.1. *t*-statistics are in parentheses.

3.3 The Results

The results for the real interest rate specification are in the left half of Table 3.1. A low *p*-value is evidence against the real interest rate hypothesis that $\alpha = -\beta$. With a few exceptions, the main one being the US investment equation, the results are not supportive of the real interest rate hypothesis. For the U.S. household expenditure equations (rows 1–4), 15 of the 16 *p*-values are less than .01. For the other quarterly countries, 57 of 72 are less than 01 and 64 of 72 are less than .05. For the annual countries 20 of 45 are less than .01 and 34 of 45 are less than .05.

The results for the nominal interest rate specification are in the right half of Table 3.1. A low *p*-value is evidence against the nominal interest rate hypothesis that $\beta = 0$. The results are generally supportive of the nominal interest rate hypothesis, again with the main exception being the U.S. nonresidential investment equation. For the U.S. household expenditure equations only 4 of 16 *p*-values are less than .01 and only 6 of 16 are less than .05. For the other quarterly countries 12 of 72 are less than 01 and 23 of 72 are less than .05. For the annual countries 4 of 45 are less than .01 and 11 of 45 are less than .05.

Table 3.2 presents the estimates of α and β. It also presents in the last column the estimate of α when $\dot{p}_t^e$ is not included (that is, when β is constrained to be zero). An interesting question is whether most of the estimates of β are positive. The right half of Table 3.1 shows that most estimates are not significant, but if most estimates are positive, this would be some evidence in favor of a real interest rate effect (or at least of expected inflation having a positive effect on demand).

Table 3.2 shows that for the U.S. household expenditure equations only 1 of the 16 estimates of β is positive. For the other quarterly countries 37 of 72 are positive, and for the annual countries 17 of 45 are positive. Of the positive coefficients, 10 have *t*-statistics greater than 2.0, and of the negative coefficients, 25 have *t*-statistics less than -2.0. There is thus more or less an even mix of positive and negative estimates of β except for the United States, where the negative estimates dominate. Many of the negative coefficient estimates of β are significant, which is completely at odds with the real interest rate hypothesis.

Overall, the nominal interest rate specification clearly dominates the real interest rate specification. Why this is the case is an interesting question. One possibility is that $\dot{p}_t^e$ is simply a constant, so that the nominal interest rate specification is also the real interest rate specification (with the constant absorbed in the constant term of the equation). If, for example, agents think the monetary authority is targeting a fixed inflation rate, this might be a reason for $\dot{p}_t^e$ being constant. Whatever the case, the empirical results do not favor the use of $i_t - \dot{p}_t^e$ in aggregate expenditure equations when $\dot{p}_t^e$ depends on current and recent values of inflation.[3] The main exception to this conclusion is US equation 12, which explains the capital stock (and thus, through identity 92, nonresidential fixed investment) of the firm sector. The real interest rate specification is not rejected for this equation. The nominal interest rate specification is rejected at the 95 percent confidence level, although not at the 99 percent confidence level.

---

3. It may be the case, of course, that some more complicated measure of $\dot{p}_t^e$ leads to the domination of the real interest rate specification. The present conclusion is conditional on measures of $\dot{p}_t^e$ that depend either on current and past values of inflation or, in case *d*, on the one-period-ahead future value of inflation.

4

Testing the NAIRU Model

4.1 Introduction

The price and wage equations in the MC model—equations 10 and 16 in the US model and equations 5 and 12 in the ROW model—have quite different dynamic properties from those of the NAIRU model, and the purpose of this chapter is to test the NAIRU dynamics.[1] It will be seen that the NAIRU dynamics are generally rejected.

Section 4.6 presents an alternative way of thinking about the relationship between the price level and the unemployment rate, one in which there is a highly nonlinear relationship at low values of the unemployment rate. Unfortunately, it is hard to test this view because there are so few observations of very low values of the unemployment rate.

4.2 The NAIRU Model

The NAIRU view of the relationship between inflation and the unemployment rate is that there is a value of the unemployment rate (the non-accelerating inflation rate of unemployment, or NAIRU) below which the price level forever accelerates and above which the price level forever decelerates. The simplest version of the NAIRU equation is

$$\pi_t - \pi_{t-1} = \beta(u_t - u^*) + \gamma s_t + \epsilon_t, \quad \beta < 0, \quad \gamma > 0, \tag{4.1}$$

where t is the time period, π_t is the rate of inflation, u_t is the unemployment rate, s_t is a cost shock variable, ϵ_t is an error term, and u^* is the NAIRU. If u_t equals u^* for all t, the rate of inflation will not change over time aside from the short-run effects of s_t and ϵ_t (assuming s_t and ϵ_t have zero means). Otherwise, the rate of inflation will

---

1. The results for the United States in this chapter are updates of those in Fair (2000). The results for the other countries are new.

67

increase over time (the price level will accelerate) if u_t is less than u^* for all t and will decrease over time (the price level will decelerate) if u_t is greater than u^* for all t.

A more general version of the NAIRU specification is

$$\pi_t = \alpha + \sum_{i=1}^{n} \delta_i \pi_{t-i} + \sum_{i=0}^{m} \beta_i u_{t-i} + \sum_{i=0}^{q} \gamma_i s_{t-i} + \epsilon_t, \quad \sum_{i=1}^{n} \delta_i = 1. \tag{4.2}$$

For this specification the NAIRU is $-\alpha / \sum_{i=0}^{m} \beta_i$. If the unemployment rate is always equal to this value, the inflation rate will be constant in the long run aside from the short-run effects of s_t and ϵ_t.

A key restriction in equation 4.2 is that the δ_i coefficients sum to one (or in equation 4.1 that the coefficient of π_{t-1} is one). This restriction is used in much of the literature. See, for example, the equations in Akerlof, Dickens, and Perry (1996, p. 38), Fuhrer (1995, p. 46), Gordon (1997, p. 14), Layard, Nickell, and Jackman (1991, p. 379), and Staiger, Stock, and Watson (1997a, p. 35). The specification has even entered the macro textbook literature—see, for example, Mankiw (1994, p. 305). There also seems to be considerable support for the NAIRU view in the policy literature. For example, Krugman (1996, p. 37), in an article in the *New York Times Magazine*, writes, "The theory of the Nairu has been highly successful in tracking inflation over the last 20 years. Alan Blinder, the departing vice chairman of the Fed, has described this as the 'clean little secret of macroeconomics.'"

An important question is thus whether equations like 4.2 with the summation restriction imposed are good approximations of the actual dynamics of the inflation process. The basic test that is performed in this chapter is the following. Let p_t be the log of the price level for period t, and let π_t be measured as $p_t - p_{t-1}$. Using this notation, equations 4.1 and 4.2 can be written in terms of p rather than π. Equation 4.1, for example, becomes

$$p_t = 2p_{t-1} - p_{t-2} + \beta(u_t - u^*) + \gamma s_t + \epsilon_t. \tag{4.3}$$

In other words, equation 4.1 can be written in terms of the current and past two price levels,[2] with restrictions on the coefficients of the past two price levels. Similarly, if in equation 4.2 n is, say, 4, the equation can be written in terms of the current and past five price levels, with two restrictions on the coefficients of the five past price levels. (If the coefficients on the past five price levels are denoted a_1 through a_5, the two restrictions are $a_4 = 5 - 4a_1 - 3a_2 - 2a_3$ and $a_5 = -4 + 3a_1 + 2a_2 + a_3$.) The main test in this chapter is of these two restrictions. The restrictions are easy to test by simply adding p_{t-1} and p_{t-2} to the NAIRU equation and testing whether they are jointly significant.

An equivalent test is to add π_{t-1} (that is, $p_{t-1} - p_{t-2}$) and p_{t-1} to equation 4.2. Adding π_{t-1} breaks the restriction that the δ_i coefficients sum to one, and adding both π_{t-1} and p_{t-1} breaks the summation restriction and the restriction that each price

---

2. "Price level" will be used to describe p even though p is actually the log of the price level.

level is subtracted from the previous price level before entering the equation. This latter restriction can be thought of as a first-derivative restriction, and the summation restriction can be thought of as a second-derivative restriction.

Equation 4.2 was used for the tests, where s_t in the equation is postulated to be $pm_t - \tau_0 - \tau_1 t$, the deviation of pm from a trend line. The variable pm is the log of the price of imports, which is taken here to be the cost shock variable. In the empirical work for the United States n is taken to be 12 and m and q are taken to be 2. For the other quarterly countries n is taken to be 8, with m and q taken to be 2. For the annual countries n is taken to be 3, with m and q taken to be 1. This fairly general specification regarding the number of lagged values is used to lessen the chances of the results being due to a particular choice of lags.

Equation 4.2 was estimated in the following form:

$$\Delta \pi_t = \lambda_0 + \lambda_1 t + \sum_{i=1}^{n-1} \theta_i \Delta \pi_{t-i} + \sum_{i=0}^{m} \beta_i u_{t-i} + \sum_{i=0}^{q} \gamma_i pm_{t-i} + \epsilon_t, \qquad (4.4)$$

where $\lambda_0 = \alpha + (\gamma_0 + \gamma_1 + \gamma_2)\tau_0 + (\gamma_0 + 2\gamma_1 + 3\gamma_2)\tau_1$ and $\lambda_1 = (\gamma_0 + \gamma_1 + \gamma_2)\tau_1$. The coefficients α and τ_0 are not identified in equation 4.4, but for purposes of the tests this does not matter. If, however, one wanted to compute the NAIRU (that is, $-\alpha / \sum_{i=1}^{m} \beta_i$), one would need a separate estimate of τ_0 in order to estimate α.[3]

For reference it will be useful to write equation 4.4 with π_{t-1} and p_{t-1} added:

$$\Delta \pi_t = \lambda_0 + \lambda_1 t + \sum_{i=1}^{n-1} \theta_i \Delta \pi_{t-i} + \sum_{i=0}^{m} \beta_i u_{t-i} + \sum_{i=0}^{q} \gamma_i pm_{t-i}$$
$$+ \phi_1 \pi_{t-1} + \phi_2 p_{t-1} + \epsilon_t. \qquad (4.5)$$

4.3 Tests for the United States

χ^2 Tests

The estimation period for the tests for the United States is 1955:3–2002:3. The results of estimating equations 4.4 and 4.5 are presented in Table 4.1. In terms of the variables in the US model, $p = \log PF$, $u = UR$, and $pm = \log PIM$. Regarding the estimation technique, the possible endogeneity of u_t and pm_t is ignored and ordinary least squares is used. Ordinary least squares is the standard technique used for estimating NAIRU models.

Table 4.1 shows that when π_{t-1} and p_{t-1} are added, the standard error of the equation falls from 0.00363 to 0.00334. The t-statistics for the two variables are -5.59 and

---

3. The present specification assumes that the NAIRU is constant, although if the NAIRU had a trend, this would be absorbed in the estimate of the coefficient of the time trend in equation 4.4 (and would change the interpretation of λ_1). Gordon (1997) has argued that the NAIRU may be time varying.

Table 4.1

Estimates of Equations 4.4 and 4.5 for the United States

Variable	Equation 4.4		Equation 4.5	
	Estimate	t-stat.	Estimate	t-stat.
cnst	0.0057	1.23	−0.0321	−3.51
t	−0.000005	−0.26	0.000221	4.36
u_t	−0.186	−1.75	−0.127	−1.28
u_{t-1}	−0.061	−0.33	−0.053	−0.31
u_{t-2}	0.151	1.35	0.018	0.17
pm_t	0.027	1.62	0.035	2.29
pm_{t-1}	0.046	1.50	0.039	1.36
pm_{t-2}	−0.073	−4.09	−0.042	−2.27
$\Delta\pi_{t-1}$	−0.787	−10.91	−0.305	−2.78
$\Delta\pi_{t-2}$	−0.662	−7.80	−0.306	−2.97
$\Delta\pi_{t-3}$	−0.489	−5.41	−0.255	−2.62
$\Delta\pi_{t-4}$	−0.334	−3.58	−0.190	−2.00
$\Delta\pi_{t-5}$	−0.365	−4.05	−0.269	−2.95
$\Delta\pi_{t-6}$	−0.256	−2.94	−0.187	−2.14
$\Delta\pi_{t-7}$	−0.159	−1.94	−0.108	−1.31
$\Delta\pi_{t-8}$	−0.135	−1.72	−0.087	−1.12
$\Delta\pi_{t-9}$	−0.130	−1.69	−0.086	−1.15
$\Delta\pi_{t-10}$	−0.246	−3.42	−0.206	−2.98
$\Delta\pi_{t-11}$	−0.096	−1.63	−0.080	−1.45
π_{t-1}			−0.621	−5.59
p_{t-1}			−0.055	−5.09
SE	0.00363		0.00334	
χ^2			32.20	

Notes:
- p_t = log of price level; $\pi_t = p_t - p_{t-1}$; u_t = unemployment rate; pm_t = log of the price of imports.
- Estimation method: ordinary least squares.
- Estimation period: 1955:3–2002:3.
- When p_{t-1} and p_{t-2} are added in place of π_{t-1} and p_{t-1}, the respective coefficient estimates are −0.676 and 0.621 with t-statistics of −5.63 and 5.59. All else is the same.
- Five percent χ^2 critical value = 5.99; 1 percent χ^2 critical value = 9.21.

−5.09, respectively, and the χ^2 value for the hypothesis that the coefficients of both variables are zero is 32.20.[4]

The 5 percent critical χ^2 value for two degrees of freedom is 5.99 and the 1 percent critical value is 9.21. If the χ^2 distribution is a good approximation to the actual distribution of the "χ^2" values, the two variables are highly significant and thus the NAIRU dynamics strongly rejected. If, however, equation 4.4 is in fact the way the

---

4. Note that there is a large change in the estimate of the coefficient of the time trend when π_{t-1} and p_{t-1} are added. The time trend is serving a similar role in equation 4.5 as the constant term is in equation 4.4.

price data are generated, the χ^2 distribution may not be a good approximation for the test.[5] To check this, the actual distribution was computed using the following procedure.

First, estimate equation 4.4, and record the coefficient estimates and the estimated variance of the error term. Call this the "base" equation. Assume that the error term is normally distributed with mean zero and variance equal to the estimated variance. Then:

1. Draw a value of the error term for each quarter. Add these error terms to the base equation and solve it dynamically to generate new data for p. Given the new data for p and the data for u and pm (which have not changed), compute the χ^2 value as in Table 4.1. Record this value.

2. Do step 1 1,000 times, which gives 1,000 χ^2 values. This gives a distribution of 1,000 values.

3. Sort the χ^2 values by size, choose the value above which 5 percent of the values lie and the value above which 1 percent of the values lie. These are the 5 percent and 1 percent critical values, respectively.

These calculations were done, and the 5 percent critical value was 19.29 and the 1 percent critical value was 23.32. These values are considerably larger than the critical values from the actual χ^2 distribution (5.99 and 9.21), but they are still smaller than the computed value of 32.20. The two price variables are thus significant at the 99 percent confidence level even using the alternative critical values.

The above procedure treats u and pm as exogenous, and it may be that the estimated critical values are sensitive to this treatment. To check for this, the following two equations were postulated for u and pm:

$$pm_t = a_1 + a_2 t + a_3 pm_{t-1} + a_4 pm_{t-2} + a_5 pm_{t-3} + a_6 pm_{t-4} + v_t, \qquad (4.6)$$

$$u_t = b_1 + b_2 t + b_3 u_{t-1} + b_4 u_{t-2} + b_5 u_{t-3} + b_6 u_{t-4} + b_7 pm_{t-1} \\ + b_8 pm_{t-2} + b_9 pm_{t-3} + b_{10} pm_{t-4} + \eta_t. \qquad (4.7)$$

These two equations along with equation 4.4 were taken to be the "model," and they were estimated by ordinary least squares along with equation 4.4 to get the "base" model. The error terms ϵ_t, v_t, and η_t were then assumed to be multivariate normal with mean zero and covariance matrix equal to the estimated covariance matrix (obtained from the estimated residuals). Each trial then consisted of draws of the three error terms for each quarter and a dynamic simulation of the model to generate new data for p, pm, and u, from which the χ^2 value was computed. The computed critical values were not very sensitive to this treatment of pm and u, and they actually fell slightly. The 5 percent value was 15.49, which compares to 19.29 above, and the 1 percent value was 21.43, which compares to 23.32 above.

---

5. If the χ^2 distribution is not a good approximation, then the t-distribution will not be either, and so standard tests using the t-statistics in Table 4.1 will not be reliable. The following analysis focuses on correcting the χ^2 critical values, and no use of the t-statistics is made.

The U.S. data thus reject the dynamics implied by the NAIRU specification: π_{t-1} and p_{t-1} are significant when added to equation 4.4. This rejection may help explain two results in the literature. Staiger, Stock, and Watson (1997b), using a standard NAIRU specification, estimate variances of NAIRU estimates and find them to be very large. This is not surprising if the NAIRU specification is misspecified. Similarly, Eisner (1997) finds the results of estimating NAIRU equations sensitive to various assumptions, particularly assumptions about whether the behavior of inflation is symmetric for unemployment rates above and below the assumed NAIRU. Again, this sensitivity is not surprising if the basic equations used are misspecified.

4.3.1   Recursive RMSE Tests

An alternative way to examine equations 4.4 and 4.5 is to consider how well they predict outside sample. To do this, the following root mean squared error (RMSE) test was performed. Each equation was first estimated for the period ending in 1969:4 (all estimation periods begin in 1955:3), and a dynamic eight-quarter-ahead prediction was made beginning in 1970:1. The predicted values were recorded. The equation was then estimated through 1970:1, and a dynamic eight-quarter-ahead prediction was made beginning in 1970:2. This process was repeated through the estimation period ending in 2002:2. Since observations were available through 2002:3, this procedure generated 131 one-quarter-ahead predictions, 130 two-quarter-ahead predictions, through 124 eight-quarter-ahead predictions, where all the predictions are outside sample. RMSEs were computed using these predictions and the actual values.

The actual values of u and *pm* were used for all these predictions, which would not have been known at the time of the predictions. The aim here is not to generate predictions that could have in principle been made in real time, but to see how good the dynamic predictions from each equation are conditional on the actual values of u and *pm*.

The RMSEs are presented in the first two rows of Table 4.2 for the four- and eight-quarter-ahead predictions for p, π, and $\Delta\pi$. If the two rows are compared (equation 4.4 versus 4.5), it can be seen that the RMSEs for $\Delta\pi$ are similar, but they are much smaller for p and π for equation 4.5. The NAIRU restrictions clearly lead to a loss of predictive power for the price level and the rate of inflation. It is thus the case that the addition of π_{t-1} and p_{t-1} to the NAIRU equation 4.4 has considerably increased the accuracy of the predictions, and so these variables are not only statistically significant but also important in a predictive sense.

Equation 4.5 is not the equation that determines the price level in the US model. The price level is determined by equation 10, and this equation includes the wage rate as an explanatory variable. Equation 10 also includes the unemployment rate, the price of imports, the lagged price level, the time trend, and the constant term. The wage rate is determined by equation 16, and this equation includes the price level and the lagged price level as explanatory variables. Equation 16 also includes the lagged wage rate, the time trend, and the constant term. As discussed in Chapter 2, a restriction,

Table 4.2
Recursive RMSEs

	RMSEs (quarters ahead)					
	p		π		$\Delta\pi$	
	4	8	4	8	4	8
Eq. 4.4	2.11	4.98	2.87	3.68	2.08	2.08
Eq. 4.5	1.76	3.51	2.35	2.47	2.08	2.10
Eqs. 10 and 16	1.24	2.28	1.83	1.70	1.88	1.85

Notes:
- p = log of the price level; $\pi = \Delta p$.
- Prediction period: 1970:1–2002:3.
- RMSEs are in percentage points.

equation 2.23, is imposed on the coefficients in the wage rate equation to ensure that the properties of the implied real wage equation are sensible. The two equations are estimated by 2SLS.

An interesting question is how accurate equations 10 and 16 are relative to equation 4.5 in terms of predicting p, π, and $\Delta\pi$. In terms of the present notation equations 10 and 16 are:

$$p_t = \beta_0 + \beta_1 p_{t-1} + \beta_2 w_t + \beta_3 pm_t + \beta_4 u_t + \beta_5 t + \epsilon_t, \tag{10}$$

$$w_t = \gamma_0 + \gamma_1 w_{t-1} + \gamma_2 p_t + \gamma_3 p_{t-1} + \gamma_5 t + \mu_t, \tag{16}$$

where

$$\gamma_3 = [\beta_1/(1 - \beta_2)](1 - \gamma_2) - \gamma_1.$$

In terms of the notation in the US model $w = \log(WF/LAM)$. The estimates of equations 10 and 16 are in Tables A10 and A16 in Appendix A.

The basic procedure followed for computing the RMSEs for equations 10 and 16 was the same as that followed for equation 4.4 and equation 4.5. The beginning estimation quarter was 1954.1, and the first end estimation quarter was 1969.4. Each of the 131 sets of estimates used the 2SLS technique with the coefficient restriction imposed, where the values used for β_1 and β_2 in the restriction were the estimated values from equation 10. The same first-stage regressors were used for these estimates as were used in the basic estimation of the equations. The predictions of p and w from equations 10 and 16 were generated using the actual values of u and pm, just as was done for equations 4.4 and 4.5.

The RMSEs are presented in the third row in Table 4.2. The results show that the RMSEs using equations 10 and 16 are noticeably smaller than those using even equation 4.5. For the eight-quarter-ahead prediction, for example, the RMSE for p is 2.28 versus 3.51 for equation 4.5, and the RMSE for π is 1.70 versus 2.47 for equation 4.5. Even for $\Delta\pi$ the RMSE using equations 10 and 16 is smaller: 1.85 versus 2.10 for

Table 4.3
Results for Equations 4.4 and 4.5 for the ROW Countries

	Coeff. Est. (*t*-statistics)		Estimated Critical			RMSEs (quarters ahead)					
						p		π		$\Delta\pi$	
	π_{-1}	p_{-1}	χ^2	$\chi^2_{.05}$	$\chi^2_{.01}$	4	8	4	8	4	8
Quarterly											
CA	−0.209	−0.005	4.84	17.02	21.38	2.38	5.30	3.48	4.35	2.51	2.43
	(−2.12)	(−0.56)				2.74	6.14	3.87	4.54	2.59	2.46
JA	−0.679	−0.016	36.93	22.65	29.29	3.06	8.88	4.39	7.46	2.53	2.64
	(−5.85)	(−1.52)				1.98	4.58	2.64	3.52	2.39	2.49
AU	−1.169	−0.031	16.54	18.55	23.79	1.55	3.97	2.59	3.73	3.58	4.04
	(−3.61)	(−1.53)				1.41	3.04	2.61	3.13	3.77	4.31
FR	−0.414	−0.020	9.51	16.82	23.85	1.97	5.17	2.84	4.22	2.06	1.92
	(−3.07)	(−2.13)				1.92	4.85	2.62	3.92	2.17	1.93
GE	−0.775	−0.000	10.45	19.14	24.23	1.44	3.38	2.34	3.14	3.20	4.32
	(−2.89)	(−0.01)				1.35	2.82	2.27	3.02	3.29	4.44
IT	−1.039	−0.052	31.14	20.91	25.49	3.75	9.27	5.37	7.48	3.60	3.69
	(−5.56)	(−4.40)				2.79	4.73	4.00	3.81	3.91	3.85
NE	−0.455	−0.207	28.52	20.00	26.67	1.53	4.20	2.35	3.54	2.26	1.92
	(−1.66)	(−3.07)				1.34	2.06	2.01	1.58	2.59	2.04
ST	−0.355	−0.020	18.21	20.58	28.32	1.74	4.81	2.77	3.98	1.04	1.45
	(−3.13)	(−3.27)				1.81	4.75	2.86	3.52	1.07	1.26
UK	−0.643	−0.030	26.74	22.64	29.44	4.14	13.99	6.42	12.84	4.05	3.97
	(−4.87)	(−2.09)				3.36	8.13	4.77	5.82	3.67	3.35
FI	−2.190	−0.025	39.58	20.83	27.80	3.58	8.95	5.21	7.24	5.02	4.99
	(−6.26)	(−2.60)				2.79	6.44	4.37	4.89	5.04	4.76
AS	−0.569	−0.018	9.08	16.25	21.85	2.85	7.89	4.24	6.47	4.21	3.83
	(−2.64)	(−0.84)				2.44	5.83	3.76	4.63	4.48	4.16
KO	−0.711	−0.054	23.86	20.39	26.72	4.60	11.31	6.70	9.20	6.25	5.68
	(−3.56)	(−2.61)				3.35	5.99	4.95	4.78	6.08	5.48

equation 4.5. The structural price and wage equations clearly do better than even the price equation with the NAIRU restrictions relaxed.

In the early 1980s there began a movement away from the estimation of structural price and wage equations to the estimation of reduced-form price equations like equation 4.4.[6] The current results call this practice into question, given that considerable predictive accuracy seems to be lost when it is carried out.

---

6. See, for example, Gordon (1980) and Gordon and King (1982).

Table 4.3
(continued)

	Coeff. Est. (*t*-statistics)		Estimated Critical			RMSEs (years ahead)					
						p		π		$\Delta\pi$	
	π_{-1}	p_{-1}	χ^2	$\chi^2_{.05}$	$\chi^2_{.01}$	2	3	2	3	2	3
Annual											
BE	−0.474	−0.131	12.72	24.41	35.85	4.91	9.51	3.22	4.73	1.93	2.11
	(−2.77)	(−2.04)				4.67	8.15	2.97	3.71	1.77	1.71
DE	−0.688	−0.172	29.65	18.26	27.15	7.52	16.84	5.31	9.36	3.38	4.34
	(−4.93)	(−3.75)				4.15	7.69	2.63	3.74	1.64	1.83
NO	−0.684	−0.291	19.91	15.57	20.38	10.75	17.32	6.96	8.48	4.57	4.61
	(−2.52)	(−2.12)				8.31	11.34	5.10	5.28	4.22	4.35
SW	−0.234	−0.126	9.16	17.59	26.66	4.03	6.74	2.49	3.05	1.84	1.79
	(−1.35)	(−2.65)				4.39	6.78	2.65	2.89	2.18	2.13
GR	−1.126	0.040	16.49	22.06	28.08	11.37	22.71	7.35	11.56	4.67	5.58
	(−3.90)	(0.28)				10.38	21.04	6.61	10.86	4.76	5.59
IR	−0.496	−0.206	8.32	22.81	34.16	9.16	16.20	5.88	7.86	4.12	3.82
	(−2.13)	(−1.89)				11.77	18.02	6.75	8.94	5.51	6.03
PO	−0.786	−0.201	14.34	18.54	25.91	13.09	23.73	8.51	11.28	5.28	5.74
	(−3.71)	(−2.91)				11.48	15.14	6.51	6.40	5.62	6.70
SP	−0.109	−0.121	9.09	21.39	33.97	8.79	17.30	5.86	8.86	3.73	3.89
	(−0.97)	(−2.50)				6.32	11.33	4.08	5.43	2.81	2.61
NZ	−0.752	−0.225	27.84	21.95	32.37	11.16	20.34	7.27	9.70	4.46	4.46
	(−3.89)	(−3.17)				9.32	13.88	5.48	5.51	3.21	3.67
CO	−1.440	−0.263	15.41	24.71	34.01	18.08	27.72	10.70	11.68	9.85	9.69
	(−3.47)	(−1.45)				11.83	14.87	7.66	7.84	10.40	10.58
MA	−1.608	−0.404	29.36	23.27	32.06	16.21	30.42	9.93	15.04	7.77	9.79
	(−5.40)	(−2.15)				11.59	18.57	6.91	8.91	8.39	9.06
PA	−0.421	−0.216	7.45	17.75	26.53	11.39	16.09	7.45	8.13	8.27	8.65
	(−1.36)	(−1.32)				14.40	20.18	8.63	8.62	7.97	8.54
TH	−1.106	−0.505	45.36	22.00	31.54	7.97	9.36	4.56	4.27	3.62	3.58
	(−6.37)	(−3.15)				8.21	14.94	5.24	7.89	4.27	4.84

Notes:
- p = log of the price level; $\pi = \Delta p$.
- Five percent χ^2 critical value = 5.99; 1 percent χ^2 critical value = 9.21.
- For the RMSE results the first row for each country contains the RMSEs for equation 4.4 and the second row contains the RMSEs for equation 4.5.

4.4 Tests for the ROW Countries

Test results for the ROW countries are reported in this section. All the results are in Table 4.3. For each country the results of adding π_{t-1} and p_{t-1} are presented first, and then the RMSE results are presented. For the RMSE results the first row for each country contains the RMSEs for equation 4.4 and the second row contains the RMSEs for equation 4.5. The procedure used to compute the χ^2 critical values is the same as that used for the United States. All critical values were computed using equations 4.6 and 4.7. For the annual countries the maximum lag length in each equation was 2, not 4. With three exceptions, a country was included in Table 4.3 if equation 5 for it in Table B5 included a demand pressure variable. The three exceptions are CH, CE, and ME. The first two were excluded because the basic estimation period was too short, and ME was excluded because of poor data in the early part of the estimation period. Results for 25 countries are presented in Table 4.3, 12 quarterly countries and 13 annual countries.

The estimation period for a country was the same as that in Table B5 except when the beginning quarter or year had to be increased to account for lags. The exceptions are reported in the current footnote.[7] For the recursive RMSEs, the first estimation period ended in 1979:3 for the quarterly countries and in 1978 for the annual countries with a few exceptions. The exceptions are reported in the current footnote.[8]

The computed critical values in Table 4.3 (denoted $\chi^2_{.05}$ and $\chi^2_{.01}$) are considerably larger than the χ^2 critical values of 5.99 for 5 percent and 9.21 for 1 percent. Using the χ^2 critical values, the two added variables are jointly significant (that is, the NAIRU restrictions are rejected) at the 5 percent level in all but 1 of the 25 cases and at the 1 percent level in all but 6 of the 25 cases. On the other hand, using the computed critical values the two added variables are jointly significant at the 5 percent level in only 11 of the 25 cases and at the 1 percent level in only 6 of the 25 cases. The results thus depend importantly on which critical values are used.

The RMSE results, however, are less mixed. Consider the eight-quarter-ahead RMSEs for the quarterly countries. For all the countries except CA the RMSEs are smaller for p and π for equation 4.5, the equation without the NAIRU restrictions imposed. In many cases they are not only smaller but considerably smaller. In other words, in many cases the RMSEs using equation 4.4 are very large: the NAIRU equation has poor predictive properties regarding p and π. This is not true for $\Delta\pi$, where the RMSEs are generally similar for the two equations.

Equation 4.5 also dominates for the annual countries. For the three-year-ahead results the RMSEs for equation 4.5 are smaller in 9 of the 13 cases for p and in 10 of the 13 cases for π. Again, some of the RMSEs using equation 4.4 are very large. For $\Delta\pi$ the RMSEs are generally similar, as is the case for the quarterly countries.

The ROW results thus show that while the χ^2 tests are not nearly as negative regarding the NAIRU equation as are the U.S. results, the RMSE tests are. In general the NAIRU equations do not predict well; they have poor dynamic properties in this sense.

---

7. The changed beginning quarters are: 1972:3 for FR; 1970:3 for GE; 1972:3 for IT; 1979:3 for NE; and 1977:3 for FI. The changed beginning years are: 1964 for BE, NO, GR, PO, SP, NZ, and TH; 1973 for CO; 1975 for MA; and 1977 for PA.

8. 1989:3 for NE, ST, FI, and KO; 1989 for CO, MA, and PA.

4.5 Properties

This section examines, using the U.S. coefficient estimates, the dynamic properties of various equations. No tests are performed; this section is just an analysis of properties. The question considered is the following: if the unemployment rate were permanently lowered by one percentage point, what would the price consequences of this be?

To answer this question, the following experiment was performed for each equation. A dynamic simulation was run beginning in 2002:4 using the actual values of all the variables from 2002:3 back. The values u and of pm from 2002:4 on were taken to be the actual value for 2002:3. Call this simulation the "base" simulation. A second dynamic simulation was then run where the only change was that the unemployment rate was decreased permanently by one percentage point from 2002:4 on. The difference between the predicted value of p from this simulation and that from the base simulation for a given quarter is the estimated effect of the change in u on p.[9]

The results for four equations are presented in Table 4.4. The equations are (1) equation 4.4, (2) equation 4.4 with π_{t-1} added, (3) equation 4.5, which is equation 4.4 with both π_{t-1} and p_{t-1} added, and (4) equations 10 and 16 together. When equation 4.4 is estimated with π_{t-1} added, the summation (second-derivative) restriction is broken but the first-derivative restriction is not. For this estimated equation the δ_i coefficients summed to 0.836.[10]

Before discussing results, I should stress that these experiments are not meant to be realistic. For example, it is unlikely that the Fed would allow a permanent fall in u to take place as p rose. The experiments are simply meant to help illustrate how the equations differ in a particular dimension.

Consider the very long run properties in Table 4.4 first. For equation 4.4, the new price level grows without bounds relative to the base price level and the new inflation rate grows without bounds relative to the base inflation rate. For equation 4.4 with π_{t-1} added, the new price level grows without bounds relative to the base, but the inflation rate does not. It is 1.89 percentage points higher in the long run. For equation 4.5 (which again is equation 4.4 with both π_{t-1} and p_{t-1} added), the new price level is higher by 2.98 percent in the limit and the new inflation rate is back to the base. For equations 10

---

9. Because the equations are linear, it does not matter what values are used for pm as long as the same values are used for both simulations. Similarly, it does not matter what values are used for u as long as each value for the second simulation is one percentage point higher than the corresponding value for the base simulation.

10. When π_{t-1} is added to equation 4.4, the χ^2 value is 5.46 with computed 5 and 1 percent critical values of 9.14 and 14.58, respectively. π_{t-1} is thus not significant at even the 5 percent level when added to equation 4.4 even though the sum of .836 seems substantially less than one. (When p_{t-1} is added to the equation with π_{t-1} already added, the χ^2 value is 25.93 with computed 5 and 1 percent critical values of 13.31 and 18.20, respectively. The variable p_{t-1} is thus highly significant when added to the equation with π_{t-1} already added.) Recursive RMSE results as in Table 4.2 were also obtained for the equation with only π_{t-1} added. The six RMSEs corresponding to those in Table 4.2 are 1.93, 4.09, 2.53, 2.87, 2.09, and 2.09. These values are in between those for equation 4.4 and equation 4.5.

Table 4.4
Effects of a One-Percentage-Point Fall in u

	Equation 4.4		Equation 4.4 (π_{t-1} added)		Equation 4.5		Eqs. 10, 16	
Quar.	$P^{new} \div P^{base}$	$\pi^{new} -\pi^{base}$	$P^{new} \div P^{base}$	$\pi^{new} -\pi^{base}$	$P^{new} \div P^{base}$	$\pi^{new} -\pi^{base}$	$P^{new} \div P^{base}$	$\pi^{new} -\pi^{base}$
1	1.0019	0.75	1.0015	0.61	1.0013	0.51	1.0018	0.74
2	1.0047	1.15	1.0041	1.02	1.0031	0.73	1.0035	0.67
3	1.0066	0.73	1.0055	0.57	1.0047	0.64	1.0051	0.62
4	1.0086	0.81	1.0070	0.62	1.0062	0.62	1.0065	0.56
5	1.0110	0.97	1.0089	0.74	1.0078	0.63	1.0078	0.51
6	1.0134	0.97	1.0107	0.73	1.0192	0.56	1.0089	0.47
7	1.0160	1.01	1.0126	0.73	1.0106	0.55	1.0100	0.43
8	1.0189	1.19	1.0147	0.87	1.0120	0.58	1.0110	0.39
9	1.0221	1.27	1.0170	0.91	1.0135	0.57	1.0119	0.36
10	1.0254	1.29	1.0193	0.90	1.0148	0.53	1.0127	0.33
11	1.0285	1.28	1.0214	0.86	1.0159	0.44	1.0134	0.30
12	1.0320	1.39	1.0237	0.91	1.0170	0.49	1.0141	0.27
40	1.2196	3.80	1.1184	1.59	1.0304	0.01	1.0206	0.02
∞	∞	∞	∞	1.89	1.0298	0.00	1.0211	0.00

Note:
• P = price level; $\pi = \Delta \log P$.

and 16, the new price level is higher by 2.11 percent in the limit and the new inflation rate is back to the base.

The long-run properties are thus vastly different, as is, of course, obvious from the specifications. What is interesting, however, is that the effects are fairly close for the first few quarters. One would be hard pressed to choose among the equations on the basis of which short-run implications (say the results out to eight quarters) seem more "reasonable." Instead, tests like the ones in this chapter are needed to try to choose.

4.6 Nonlinearities

If the NAIRU specification is rejected, this changes the way one thinks about the relationship between inflation and unemployment. One should not think that there is some unemployment rate below which the price level forever accelerates and above which it forever decelerates. It is not the case, however, that equation 4.5 (or equations 10 and 16) is a sensible alternative regarding long-run properties. Equation 4.5 implies that a lowering of the unemployment rate has only a modest long-run effect on the price level regardless of how low the initial value of the unemployment rate is. For example, the results in Table 4.4 for equation 4.5 are independent of the initial value of the unemployment rate.

A key weakness of equation 4.5 is (in my view) the linearity assumption regarding the effects of u on p. It seems likely that there is a nonlinear relationship between the price level and the unemployment rate at low levels of the unemployment rate. One possible specification, for example, would be to replace u in equation 4.5 with $1/(u - .02)$. In this case as u approaches .02, the estimated effects on p become larger and larger. I have experimented with a variety of functional forms like this in estimating price equations like equation 10 in the US model and equations 5 in the ROW model to see if the data can pick up a nonlinear relationship. Unfortunately, there are so few observations of very low unemployment rates that the data do not appear capable of discriminating among functional forms. A variety of functional forms, including the linear form, lead to very similar results. In the end I simply chose the linear form for lack of a better alternative for both the US equation 10 and the ROW equations 5. This does not mean, however, that the true functional form is linear, only that the data are insufficient for estimating the true functional form. It does mean, however, that one should not run experiments using the MC model in which unemployment rates or output gaps are driven to historically low levels. The price equations are unlikely to be reliable in these cases.

The argument here about the relationship between inflation and the unemployment rate can thus be summarized by the following two points. First, the NAIRU dynamics, namely the first- and second-derivative restrictions, are not accurate. Second, the relationship between the price level and the unemployment rate is nonlinear at low values of the unemployment rate. The results in this chapter generally support the first point, but they have nothing to say about the second point.

Conditional on this argument, the main message for policymakers is that they should not think there is some value of the unemployment rate below which the price level accelerates and above which it decelerates. They should think instead that the price level is a negative function of the unemployment rate (or other measure of demand slack), where at some point the function begins to become nonlinear. How bold a policymaker is in pushing the unemployment rate into uncharted waters will depend on how fast he or she thinks the nonlinearity becomes severe.

5

U.S. Wealth Effects

5.1 Introduction

The results in this chapter are important for understanding the results in the next chapter. The purpose of this chapter is to give a general idea of the size of the wealth effect in the US model. When stock prices change, this changes the wealth of the household sector, which is turn affects household consumption expenditures. The experiment in section 5.3 shows the size of this effect. The effect of a sustained increase in wealth on consumption expenditures is estimated to be about 3 percent per year, ignoring feedback effects. The variables that are referenced in this chapter are listed in Table 5.1.

5.2 The Effects of *CG*

The variable AH in the US model is the nominal value of net financial assets of the household sector. It is determined by the identity 66 in Table A.3:

$$AH = AH_{-1} + SH - \Delta MH + CG - DISH, \tag{66}$$

where SH is the financial saving of the household sector, MH is its holdings of demand deposits and currency, CG is the value of capital gains $(+)$ or losses $(-)$ on the financial assets held by the household sector (almost all of which is the change in the market value corporate stocks held by the household sector), and $DISH$ is a discrepancy term.

A change in the stock market affects AH through CG. The variable CG is constructed from data from the U.S. Flow of Funds accounts. It is highly correlated with the change in the S&P 500 stock price index. When $CG/(PX_{-1}YS_{-1})$ is regressed on $(SP - SP_{-1})/(PX_{-1}YS_{-1})$, where SP is the value of the S&P 500 index at the end

Table 5.1
Variables Referenced in Chapter 5

AA	Total net wealth of the household sector, real
AH	Net financial assets of the household sector, nominal
CD	Consumer expenditures for durables, real
CDA	Peak to peak interpolation of *CD/POP*
CG	Capital gains (+) or losses (−) on the financial assets of the household sector, nominal
CN	Consumer expenditures for nondurable goods, real
CS	Consumer expenditures for services, real
DELD	Physical depreciation rate of the stock of durable goods
DISH	Discrepancy for the household sector, nominal
KD	Stock of durable goods, real
KH	Stock of housing, real
MH	Demand deposits and currency of the household sector, nominal
PH	Price deflator for consumer expenditures and residential investment
PIH	Price deflator for residential investment
POP	Noninstitutional population 16 and over, millions
PX	Price deflator for total sales of the firm sector
RB	Bond rate
RMA	After-tax mortgage rate
RSA	After-tax three-month Treasury bill rate
SH	Saving of the household sector, nominal
SP	S&P 500 stock price index
YD	Disposable income of the household sector, nominal
YS	Potential output of the firm sector, real
Π	After-tax profits, nominal

of the quarter and $PX_{-1}YS_{-1}$ is the value of potential nominal output in the previous quarter, the results are:

$$\frac{CG}{PX_{-1}YS_{-1}} = \underset{(5.12)}{0.0534} + \underset{(32.16)}{9.88} \frac{SP - SP_{-1}}{PX_{-1}YS_{-1}}, \tag{5.1}$$

$$R^2 = .841, \ 1954.1\text{--}2002.3.$$

$PX_{-1}YS_{-1}$ is used for scale purposes in this regression to lessen the chances of heteroskedasticity. The fit of this equation is very good, reflecting the high correlation of *CG* and the change in the S&P 500 index. A coefficient of 9.88 means that a 100-point change in the S&P 500 index results in a $988 billion dollar change in the value of stocks held by the household sector.

CG is determined by equation 25, which is repeated here:

$$\frac{CG}{PX_{-1}YS_{-1}} = \underset{(4.10)}{0.121} - \underset{(-1.73)}{0.209}\ \Delta RB + \underset{(0.28)}{3.56}\ \frac{\Delta\Pi}{PX_{-1}YS_{-1}}, \tag{25}$$

$$R^2 = .023,\ 1954.1 - 2002.3.$$

If $SP - SP_{-1}$ is used in place of *CG*, the results are:

$$\frac{SP - SP_{-1}}{PX_{-1}YS_{-1}} = \underset{(2.42)}{0.00661} - \underset{(-2.32)}{0.0260}\ \Delta RB + \underset{(0.52)}{0.623}\ \frac{\Delta\Pi}{PX_{-1}YS_{-1}}, \tag{5.2}$$

$$R^2 = .026,\ 1954.1 - 2002.3.$$

It is clear that equation 25 and equation 5.2 are telling the same story. The change in the bond rate (ΔRB) has a negative effect on the change in stock prices and the change in profits ($\Delta\Pi$) has a positive effect. The profit effect is not statistically significant, whereas the bond rate effect is or is close to being significant. There is thus at least some link from interest rates to stock prices estimated in the model.

Equation 66 above shows that when *CG* changes, *AH* changes. The wealth variable in the household expenditure equations is *AA*, which is determined by identity 89:

$$AA = (AH + MH)/PH + (PIH \cdot KH)/PH, \tag{89}$$

where *PH* is a price deflator for the household sector. *AA* appears as an explanatory variable in stochastic equations 1, 2, and 3, and these are repeated in Table 5.2. *AA* has positive effects on the three consumption expenditure variables. The wealth variable, $\log(AA/POP)_{-1}$ or $(AA/POP)_{-1}$, has *t*-statistics of 3.50, 4.78, and 1.53, respectively.

5.3   Changing *AA* by 1,000

How much do consumer expenditures change when *AA* changes? The size of this wealth effect depends on what is held constant. If the complete MC model is used, then an increase in *AA* increases U.S. household consumption expenditures, which then leads to a multiplier effect on output and at least some increase in inflation. Given the estimated interest rate rule in the model, the Fed responds to the expansion by raising interest rates, which slows down the expansion, and so on. The rest of the world also responds to what the United States is doing, which then feeds back on the United States. The size of the wealth effect with nothing held constant thus depends on many features of the MC model, not just the properties of the U.S. household consumption expenditure equations.

One can focus solely on the properties of the household consumption expenditure equations by taking income and interest rates to be exogenous. The following experi-

Table 5.2
The Three U.S. Household Consumption Expenditure
Equations (from Tables A1, A2, and A3)

	1 $\log \frac{CS}{POP}$	2 $\log \frac{CN}{POP}$	3 $\Delta \frac{CD}{POP}$
LDV	0.787	0.782	0.329
	(19.31)	(21.69)	(5.42)
$\log \frac{YD}{POP}$ or $\frac{YD}{POP}$	0.106	0.097	0.108
	(3.06)	(4.28)	(4.65)
RSA or *RMA* or *RMA · CDA*	−0.00123	−0.00174	−0.00514
	(−5.75)	(−4.24)	(−3.23)
$\frac{KD}{POP}_{-1}$	—	—	−0.024
			(−3.92)
$\log \frac{AA}{POP}_{-1}$ or $\frac{AA}{POP}_{-1}$	0.0171	0.0507	0.0003
	(3.50)	(4.78)	(1.53)

Notes:
- *LDV* = Lagged dependent variable. For equation 3 the *LDV* is $DELD(KD/POP)_{-1} - (CD/POP)_{-1}$.
- Estimation period: 1954:1–2002:3.
- Estimation technique: 2SLS.
- Not presented in the table: estimates of the constant terms; coefficient estimates of age variables; coefficient estimate of the lagged change in the dependent variable in equation 2; coefficient estimate of the time trend in equation 1.

ment was performed. The variables $YD/(POP \cdot PH)$, *RSA*, *RMA*, and *AA* were taken to be exogenous, which isolates equations 1, 2, and 3 from the rest of the model. The estimated residuals were then added to the stochastic equations and taken to be exogenous. This means that when the model is solved using the actual values of all the exogenous variables, a perfect tracking solution is obtained. The actual values are thus the base values. *AA* was then increased by $1,000 billion from the base case, and the model was solved for the 1995:1–2002:3 period. The difference for a given quarter between the predicted value of a variable and the actual value is the estimated effect of the *AA* change on that variable for that quarter.

The effects on total consumption expenditures $(CS + CN + CD)$ by quarters are presented in Table 5.3. After four quarters, expenditures have risen $18.6 billion, and after eight quarters they have risen $27.7 billion. The increases then level off at slightly less than $30 billion. The effect of a sustained increase in wealth on consumption expenditures is thus estimated to be slightly less than 3 percent per year, ignoring any feedback effects.

This roughly 3 percent estimate is consistent with results from other approaches. A recent study estimating the size of the wealth effect is discussed in Ludvigson and Steindel (1999). They conclude (p. 30) that "a dollar increase in wealth likely leads to a three- to four-cent increase in consumption in today's economy," although they argue

Table 5.3
Effects on $CS + CN + CD$ of a Change in AA of 1,000

Quarter	Year							
	1995	1996	1997	1998	1999	2000	2001	2002
1	0.0	22.0	28.5	29.3	28.8	27.8	27.3	29.1
2	7.6	24.6	29.1	29.1	28.6	27.4	27.6	29.3
3	13.9	26.3	29.4	28.8	28.3	27.2	27.9	29.8
4	18.6	27.7	29.3	28.9	28.3	27.1	28.6	

Note:
• Units are billions of 1996 dollars.

that there is considerable uncertainty regarding this estimate. Their approach is simpler and less structural than the present one, but the size of their estimate is similar. Starr-McCluer (1998) uses survey data to examine the wealth effect, and she concludes that her results are broadly consistent with a modest wealth effect.

6

Testing for a New Economy in the 1990s

6.1   Introduction

There was much talk in the United States in the last half of the 1990s about the existence of a new economy or a "new age."[1] Was this talk just media hype or were there in fact large structural changes in the 1990s? One change that seems obvious is the huge increase in stock prices relative to earnings beginning in 1995. This can be seen in Figure 6.1, where the price-earnings (PE) ratio for the S&P 500 index is plotted. The increase in the PE ratio beginning in 1995 is quite large. The mean of the PE ratio is 14.0 for the 1948.1–1994.4 period and 27.0 for the 1995.1–2002.3 period. This increase appears to be a major structural change, and an important question is whether there were other such changes.

The end-of-sample stability test of Andrews (2003) was used in Chapter 2 to test the 30 stochastic equations of the US model for structural change beginning in 1995. The hypothesis of stability was rejected for only three equations, the main equation being equation 25, explaining *CG*. The rejection for the *CG* equation is, of course, not surprising given Figure 6.1. It may be surprising, however, that there were no other major rejections, since a number of macroeconomic variables have large changes beginning about 1995. Four such variables are plotted in Figures 6.2–6.5. They are (1) the personal saving rate (lower after 1995), (2) the U.S. current account as a fraction of GDP (lower after 1995), (3) the ratio of nonresidential fixed investment to output (higher after 1995), and (4) the federal government budget surplus as a percentage of GDP (higher after 1995). The results reported in this chapter suggest that all four of these unusual changes are because of the stock market boom and not because of structural changes in the stochastic equations

The fact that the stability hypothesis is not rejected for the three U.S. consumption equations means that conditional on wealth the behavior of consumption does not seem unusual. The wealth effect on consumption also explains the low U.S. current account

---

1. The results in this chapter are the same as those in Fair (2004a).

Figure 6.1
S&P Price-Earnings Ratio, 1948:1–2002:3

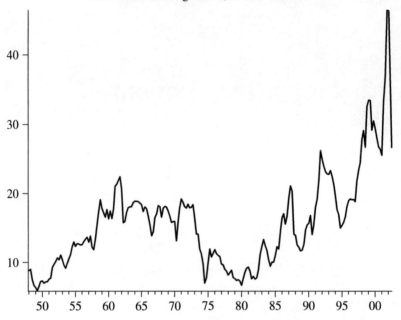

Figure 6.2
NIPA Personal Saving Rate, 1948:1–2002:3

Figure 6.3
Ratio of U.S. Current Account to GDP, 1948:1–2002:3

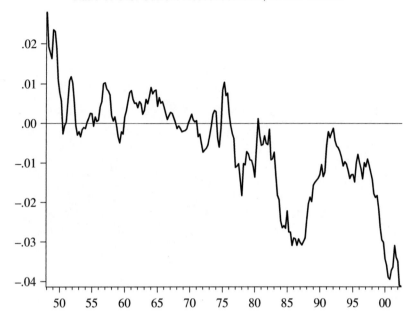

Figure 6.4
Investment-Output Ratio, 1948:1–2002:3

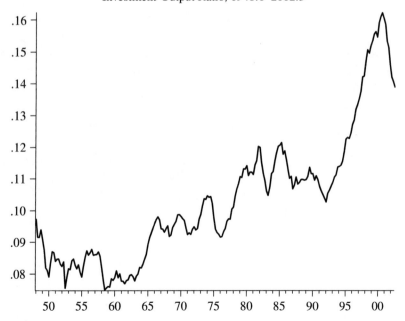

Figure 6.5
Ratio of Federal Government Surplus to GDP, 1948:1–2002:3

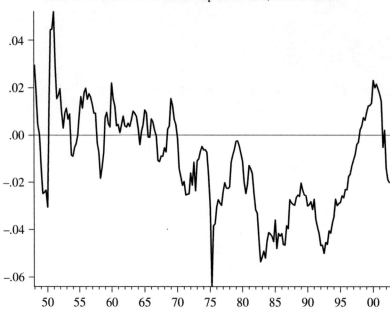

because some of any increased consumption is increased consumption of imports. Similarly, conditional on the low cost of capital caused by the stock market boom, the behavior of investment does not seem unusual according to the stability test of the investment equation. Finally, the rise in the federal government budget surplus is explained by the robust economy fueled by consumption and investment spending.

To examine the effects of the stock market boom, a counterfactual experiment is performed in this chapter using the MC model. The experiment is one in which the stock market boom is eliminated. The results show (in section 6.3) that had there been no stock market boom, the behavior of the four variables in Figures 6.2–6.5 would not have been unusual.

The overall story is thus quite simple: the only main structural change in the last half of the 1990s was the stock market boom. All other unusual changes can be explained by it. What is not simple, however, is finding a reason for the stock market boom in the first place. The possibility that the degree of risk aversion of the average investor fell in the last half of the 1990s is tested in Fair (2003c), using data on companies that have been in the S&P 500 index since 1957. The evidence suggests that risk aversion has not fallen: there is no evidence that more risky companies have had larger increases in their price-earnings ratios since 1995 than less risky companies.

If earnings growth had been unusually high in the last half of the 1990s, this might have led investors to expect unusually high growth in the future, which would have driven up stock prices relative to current earnings. Figures 6.6 and 6.7, however, show that there was nothing unusual about earnings in the last half of the 1990s. Figure 6.6

Figure 6.6
Fourth-Quarter Growth Rate of S&P 500 Earnings, 1948:1–2002:3

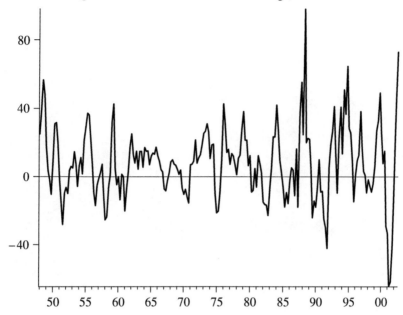

Figure 6.7
Ratio of NIPA Profits to GDP, 1948:1–2002:3

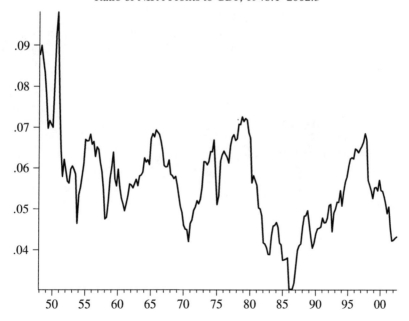

plots the four-quarter growth rate of S&P 500 earnings, and Figure 6.7 plots the ratio of NIPA after-tax profits to GDP.

Much of the new economy talk has been about productivity growth, which section 6.4 examines. It will be seen that using 1995 as the base year to measure productivity growth, which is commonly done, is misleading because 1995 is a cyclically low productivity year. If 1992 is used instead, the growth rate in the last half of the 1990s for the total economy less general government is only slightly higher than earlier (from 1.49 percent to 1.82 percent per year). There is thus nothing in the productivity data that would suggest a huge increase in stock prices relative to earnings. The huge increase in PE ratios beginning in 1995 thus appears to be a puzzle. This chapter is not an attempt to explain this puzzle. Rather, it shows that conditional on the stock market boom, the rest of the economy does not seem unusual.

6.2   End-of-Sample Stability Tests

For the end-of-sample stability tests in Chapter 2 the sample period was 1954:1–2002:3, with the potential break at 1995:1. For this chapter, tests have also been performed for the sample period 1954:1–2000:4, with again the potential break at 1995:1. In other words, the second test does not include what happened in 2001 and 2002.

The p-values for the 30 equations are presented in Table 6.1.[2] The results for the period ending in 2000:4 are very similar to the other results. There are still only three equations for which the hypothesis of stability was rejected—the interest payments equation 19, the demand for currency equation 26, and the *CG* equation 25. Overall, the results in Table 6.1 are strongly supportive of the view that there were no major structural changes beginning in 1995:1 except for the stock market boom. The next section estimates what the economy would have been like had there been no stock market boom.

6.3   No Stock Market Boom: Counterfactual

For the 10-year period prior to 1995 (1985:1–1994:4) the sum of the quarterly values of *CG*, which is the total capital gain on household financial assets for this period, was $5.248 trillion. This is an average of $131.2 billion per quarter. The sum for the next 5 years (1995:1–1999:4) was $13.560 trillion, an average of $678.0 billion per quarter. During the next 11 quarters (2000:1–2002:3) the sum was −$7.040 trillion, an average of −$640.0 billion per quarter. The total capital gain over the entire 1995:1–2002:3 period was thus $6.520 trillion, an average of $210.3 billion per quarter.

The counterfactual experiment assumes that the capital gain for each quarter of the 1995:1–2002:3 period was $131.2 billion, which is the average for the prior 10-year period. This gives a total capital gain of $4.067 trillion, which is about $2.5 trillion less

---

2. Remember from the discussion of the stability tests in section 1.5 that the coefficient estimates of the dummy variables are taken as fixed when performing the tests.

Table 6.1
End-of-Sample Test Results for the United States

Eq.	Dependent Variable	End 2002:3 p-value	End 2000:4 p-value
1	Service consumption	1.000	1.000
2	Nondurable consumption	.858	.957
3	Durable consumption	.119	.504
4	Residential investment	.716	.844
5	Labor force, men 25-54	.567	.482
6	Labor force, women 25-54	.866	.929
7	Labor force, all others 16+	.440	.766
8	Moonlighters	1.000	1.000
9	Demand for money, h	.112	.106
10	Price level	1.000	.972
11	Inventory investment	.881	.943
12	Nonresidential fixed investment	.261	.206
13	Workers	.649	.610
14	Hours per worker	.739	.624
15	Overtime hours	.976	1.000
16	Wage rate	.507	.390
17	Demand for money, f	.440	.369
18	Dividends	.500	.447
19	Interest payments, f	.000	.000
20	Inventory valuation adjustment	.134	.149
21	Depreciation, f	.500	.475
22	Bank borrowing from the Fed	.806	.667
23	AAA bond rate	.396	.362
24	Mortgage rate	.410	.340
25	Capital gains or losses	.000	.000
26	Demand for currency	.000	.000
27	Imports	.933	1.000
28	Unemployment benefits	.955	1.000
29	Interest payments, g	.784	1.000
30	Fed interest rate rule	.903	.993

Notes:
- h = household sector; f = firm sector; g = federal government sector.
- First overall sample period: 1954:1–2002:3 except 1956:1–2002:3 for equation 15.
- Second overall sample period: 1954:1–2000:4 except 1956:1–2000:4 equation 15.
- Break point tested: 1995:1.
- Estimation technique: 2SLS.

than the actual value of $6.520 trillion. The timing, of course, is quite different from what actually happened, since the experiment does not have the huge boom up to 2000 and then the large correction after that.

The entire MC model is used for the experiment, which is for the 1995:1–2002:3 period. The estimated residuals are first added to all the stochastic equations, including the trade share equations, and then taken to be exogenous. This means that when

Figure 6.8
NIPA Personal Saving Rate, 1995:1–2002:3

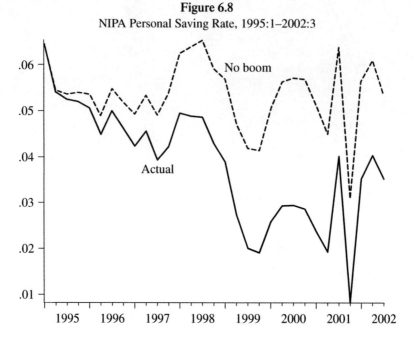

the model is solved using the actual values of all the exogenous variables, a perfect tracking solution is obtained. The actual values are thus the base values. Equation 25 is then dropped from the model, and the value of *CG* in each quarter is taken to be $131.2 billion. The model is then solved. The difference between the solution value and the actual value for each endogenous variable for each quarter is the effect of the *CG* change. The solution values will be called values in the "no boom" case.[3]

Figures 6.8–6.15 plot some of the results. Each figure presents the actual values of the variable and the solution values. Figure 6.8 shows that the personal saving rate is considerably higher in the no boom case. No longer are the values outside the range of historical experience in 1999 and 2000. This is the wealth effect on consumption at work. With no stock market boom, households are predicted to consume less. Figure 6.9 shows that the current account deficit through 2000 is not as bad in the no boom case: imports are lower because of the lower consumption. Figure 6.10 shows that there is a much smaller rise in the investment-output ratio in the no boom case. Investment is not as high because the cost of capital is not as low and because output is lower. Figure 6.11

---

3. At the time this experiment was performed, all the data for the United States were available through 2002:3, but not for the other countries. When necessary, extrapolated values of the exogenous variables for the other countries were used. This has little effect on the final results because the same values are used for both the base case and the no boom case.

Figure 6.9
Ratio of U.S. Current Account to GDP, 1995:1–2002:3

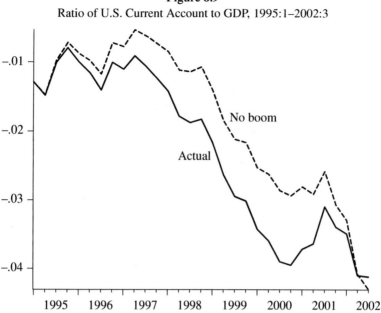

shows that the federal government budget is not as good, which is due to the less robust economy.

Figure 6.12 plots the percentage change in real GDP, and Figure 6.13 plots the unemployment rate. Both show, not surprisingly, that the real side of the economy is worse in the no boom case, especially through 2000. In the fourth quarter of 1999, for example, the unemployment rate in the no boom case is 5.5 percent, which compares to the actual value of 4.1 percent. Figure 6.14 plots the percentage change in the private nonfarm price deflator, *PF*. It shows that the rate of inflation is lower in the no boom case (because of the higher unemployment rate), although in neither case would one consider inflation to be a problem.

Figure 6.15 plots the three-month Treasury bill rate, *RS*, which is the rate determined by equation 30, the estimated interest rate rule of the Fed. The figure shows that the bill rate is lower in the no boom case. The Fed is predicted to respond to the more sluggish economy by lowering rates. In the fourth quarter of 1999, the bill rate is 3.3 percent in the no boom case, which compares to the actual value of 5.0 percent. It is interesting to note that this amount of easing of the Fed is not enough to prevent the unemployment rate from rising, as was seen in Figure 6.13. Note from Figure 6.12, however, that by the end of 2000 the growth rate is higher in the no boom case. This is partly due to the lower interest rates in the no boom case.

It is thus clear from the figures in this section that according to the MC model, the U.S. economic boom in the last half of the 1990s was fueled by the wealth effect and cost-of-capital effect from the stock market boom. Had it not been for the stock market boom, the economy would have looked more or less normal.

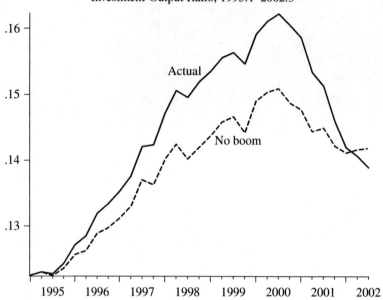

Figure 6.10
Investment-Output Ratio, 1995:1–2002:3

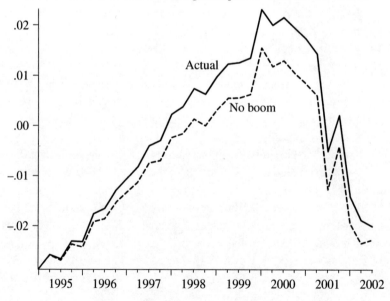

Figure 6.11
Ratio of Federal Government Budget Surplus to GDP, 1995:1–2002:3

Figure 6.12
Four-Quarter Growth Rate of Real GDP, 1995:1–2002:3

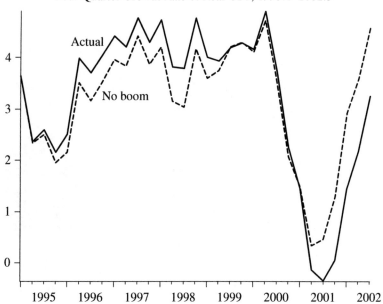

Figure 6.13
Unemployment Rate, 1995:1–2002:3

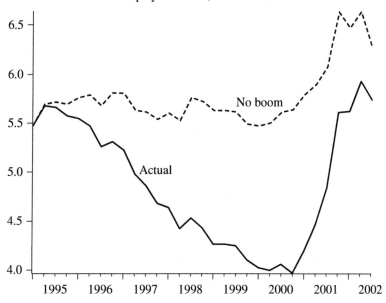

Figure 6.14
Four-Quarter Percentage Change in PF, 1995:1–2002:3

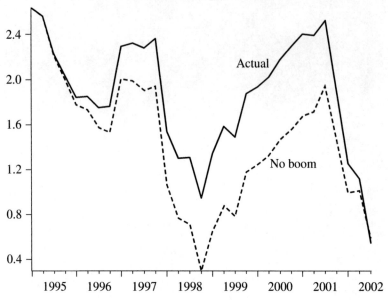

Figure 6.15
Three-Month Treasury Bill Rate, 1995:1–2002:3

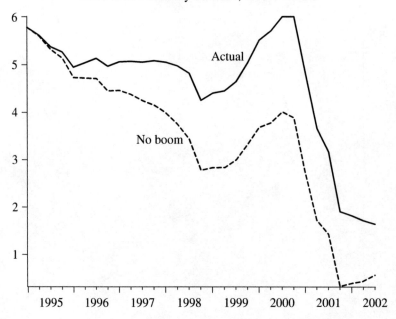

6.4 Aggregate Productivity

As noted in the introduction, much of the new economy talk has been about productivity growth. For the above experiment long-run productivity growth is exogenous: the MC model does not explain long-run productivity growth. This issue will now be addressed.

Figure 6.16a plots the log of output per worker hour for the total economy less general government for 1948:1–2002:3. Also plotted in the figure is a peak-to-peak interpolation line, with peaks in 1950:3, 1966:1, 1973:1, 1992:4, and 2002:3.[4] The annual growth rates between the peaks are 3.27, 2.72, 1.49, and 1.82 percent, respectively. Figure 6.16b is an enlarged version of Figure 6.16a for the period from 1985:1 on.

An interesting feature of Figure 6.16a is the modest increase in the peak-to-peak productivity growth rate after 1992:4: from 1.49 to 1.82 percent. This difference of 0.33 percentage points is certainly not large enough to classify as a movement into a new age.

It can be seen in Figure 6.16b why some were so optimistic about productivity growth in the last half of the 1990s. Between 1995:3 and 2000:2 productivity grew at an annual rate of 2.49 percent, which is a noticeable improvement from the 1.49 percent rate between 1973:1 and 1992:4. What this overlooks, however, is that productivity grew at an annual rate of only 0.27 percent between 1992:4 and 1995:3, so 1995 is a low year to use as a base. Under the assumption that the interpolation line measures cyclically adjusted productivity, the 2.49 percent growth rate between 1995:3 and 2000:2 is composed of 1.82 percent long-run growth and 0.67 percent cyclical growth.

Productivity data are also available for the nonfarm business sector, and it is of interest to see if the above productivity growth estimates are sensitive to the level of aggregation. In 2001 real GDP less general government output accounted for 89.4 percent real GDP and nonfarm business output accounted for 83.8 percent. (Nonfarm business output excludes output from farms, households, and nonprofit institutions in addition to output from general government.) Figures 6.17a and 6.17b are for the nonfarm business sector.

There is only a modest change in moving from Figures 6.16a and 6.16b to Figures 6.17a and 6.17b. The increase in long-run productivity growth beginning in 1992:4 is now 0.50 percentage points (from 1.43 percent to 1.93 percent) rather than 0.33 (from 1.49 percent to 1.82 percent). The actual growth rate from 1992:4 to 1995:3 is now 0.39 percent rather than 0.27 percent, and the actual growth rate from 1995:3 to 2000:2 is now 2.50 percent rather than 2.49 percent. Again, under the assumption that the interpolation line measures cyclically adjusted productivity, the 2.50 percent growth rate between 1995:3 and 2000:2 is composed of 1.93 percent long-run growth and 0.57 percent cyclical growth for the nonfarm business sector.

---

4. Although the data for the US model begin in 1952:1, the data used in this section go back to 1948:1. The same peaks in Figure 16.6a are used to construct *LAM* in the US model except that 1955:2 is used instead of 1950:3. See *LAM* in Table A.7.

Figure 6.16a

Log of Output per Worker Hour, 1948:1–2002:3: Total Economy Less General Government

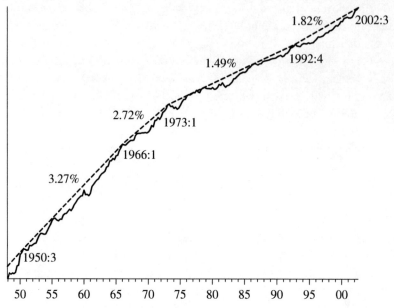

Figure 6.16b

Log of Output per Worker Hour, 1985:1–2002:3: Total Economy Less General Government

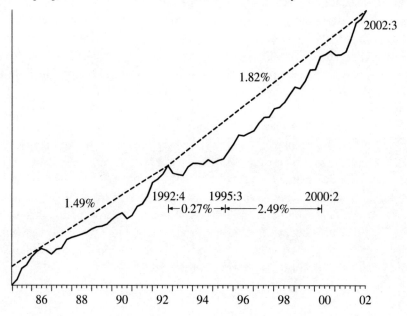

Figure 6.17a
Log of Output per Worker Hour, 1948:1–2002:3: Nonfarm Business

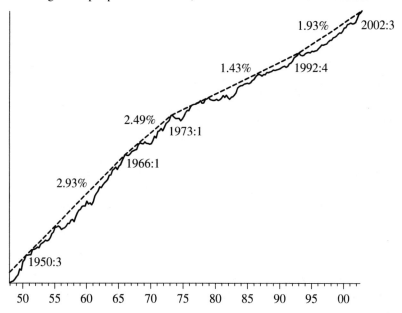

Figure 6.17b
Log of Output per Worker Hour, 1985:1–2002:3: Nonfarm Business

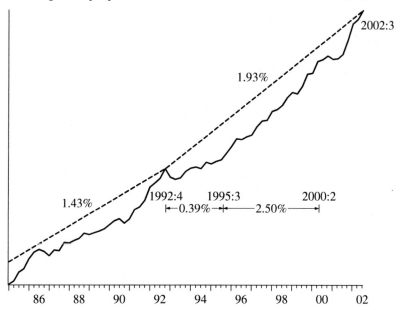

Regarding other studies of productivity growth in the 1990s, Blinder and Yellen (2001) test for a break in productivity growth beginning in 1995:4, and they find a significant break once their regression equation is estimated through 1998:3. From Figures 6.16b and 6.17b this is not surprising, given the rapid productivity growth between 1995:4 and 1998:3. Again, however, 1995:4 is a misleading base to use. Oliner and Sichel (2000) compare productivity growth in 1990–1995 to that in 1996–1999 and do not adjust for cyclical growth. This is also true in Nordhaus (2000), who compares productivity growth in 1990–1995 to that in 1996–1998.

Gordon (2000a,b) argues that some of the actual productivity growth after 1995 is cyclical. He estimates in Gordon (2000b, p. 219) that of the actual 2.82 percent productivity growth in the nonfarm business sector between 1995:4 and 1999:4, 0.54 is cyclical and 2.28 is long-run. This estimate of 0.54, which is backed out of a regression, is remarkably close to the 0.57 figure estimated above for the 1995:3–2000:2 period using the interpolation line in Figure 6.17b. Gordon's actual number of 2.82 percent is larger than the actual number of 2.50 percent in Figure 6.17b. This difference is primarily due to the fact that Figure 6.17b uses revised data. The data revisions that occurred after Gordon's work had the effect of lowering the estimates of productivity growth.

Gordon's results and the results from Figure 6.17b are thus supportive of each other. Although Gordon estimates long-run productivity growth to be 2.28 percent, Figure 6.17b suggests that this number is less than 2 percent on the basis of the revised data. The message of Figures 6.16b and 6.17b is thus that productivity growth has increased in the last half of the 1990s, but only by about 0.4 to 0.5 percentage points.

6.5   Conclusion

The results in this chapter are consistent with the simple story that the only major structural change in the last half of the 1990s was the huge increase in stock prices relative to earnings. The only major U.S. macroeconometric equation in the MC model for which the hypothesis of end-of-sample stability is rejected is the stock price equation. The counterfactual experiment using the MC model in which the stock market boom is turned off shows that were it not for the boom the behavior of variables like the saving rate, the U.S. current account, the investment-output ratio, and the federal government budget would not have been historically unusual. Nor do the data on aggregate productivity show a large increase in trend productivity growth in the last half of the 1990s: there is no evidence in the data of a new age of productivity growth.

None of the results here provide any hint as to why the stock market began to boom in 1995. In fact, they deepen the puzzle, since there appear to be no major structural changes in the economy (except the stock market) and there is no evidence of a new age of productivity growth. In addition, Figures 16.6 and 16.7 show no unusual behavior of earnings in the last half of the 1990s, and the results in Fair (2003c) suggest that the risk aversion of the average investor has not decreased. In short, there is no obvious fundamental reason for the stock market boom.

7

A "Modern" View of Macroeconomics

7.1 Introduction

Although macroeconomics has been in a state of flux at least since Lucas's (1976) critique, there has recently emerged a view that some see as a convergence.[1] Taylor (2000, p. 90), for example, states:

> At the practical level, a common view of macroeconomics is now pervasive in policy-research projects at universities and central banks around the world. This view evolved gradually since the rational-expectations revolution of the 1970's and has solidified during the 1990's. It differs from past views, and it explains the growth and fluctuations of the modern economy; it can thus be said to represent a modern view of macroeconomics.

This view is nicely summarized in Clarida, Galí, and Gertler (1999), and it is used in Clarida, Galí, and Gertler (2000) to examine monetary policy rules. Taylor (2000, p. 91) points out that virtually all the papers in Taylor (1999a) use this view and that the view is widely used for policy evaluation in many central banks. In both the backward-looking model and the forward-looking model in Svensson (2003) aggregate demand depends negatively on the real interest rate, as in the aggregate demand equation below. Romer (2000) proposes a way of teaching this modern view at the introductory level.

This view is based on three equations:

1. **Interest rate rule.** The Fed adjusts the nominal interest rate in response to inflation and the output gap (deviation of output from potential).[2] The nominal interest rate responds positively to inflation and the output gap. The coefficient on inflation is greater than one, and so the real interest rate rises when inflation rises.

---

1. The results in this chapter are updates of those in Fair (2002).

2. In empirical work the lagged interest rate is often included as an explanatory variable in the interest rate rule. This picks up possible smoothing of the interest rate by the Fed.

2. **Price equation.** Inflation depends on the output gap, cost shocks, and expected future inflation.

3. **Aggregate demand equation.** Aggregate demand (real) depends on the real interest rate, expected future demand, and exogenous shocks. The real interest rate effect is negative.

This basic model is, of course, a highly simplified view of the way the macroeconomy works, as everyone would admit. Many details have been left out. If, however, the model captures the broad features of the economy in a fairly accurate way, the lack of detail is not likely to be serious for many purposes; the details can be filled in when needed. The "modern" view of macroeconomics is that the broad features of the economy have been adequately captured by this model.

Regarding the effects of an inflation shock in the modern-view model, the aggregate demand equation implies that an increase in inflation with the nominal interest rate held constant is expansionary (because the real interest rate falls). The model is in fact not stable in this case because an increase in output increases inflation through the price equation, which further increases output through the aggregate demand equation, and so on. In order for the model to be stable, the nominal interest rate must rise more than inflation, which means that the coefficient on inflation in the interest rate rule must be greater than one. Because of this feature, some have criticized Fed behavior in the 1960s and 1970s as in effect following a rule with a coefficient on inflation less than one—see, for example, Clarida, Galí, and Gertler (1999) and Taylor (1999c).

It will be seen in the next section that in the MC model a positive inflation shock with the nominal interest rate held constant is contractionary, not expansionary as implied by the modern-view model. There are three main reasons for this difference. First, except for the US investment equation 12, nominal interest rates rather than real interest rates are used in the consumption and investment equations. The results in Chapter 3 strongly support the use of nominal over real interest rates. Second, in the MC model the percentage increase in nominal household wealth from a positive inflation shock is less than the percentage increase in the price level, and so there is a fall in real household wealth from a positive inflation shock. This has, other things being equal, a negative effect on real household expenditures. Third, in the MC model nominal wages lag prices, and so a positive inflation shock results in an initial fall in real wage rates and thus in real labor income. A fall in real labor income has, other things being equal, a negative effect on real household expenditures.

If these three features are true, they imply that a positive inflation shock has a negative effect on aggregate demand even if the nominal interest rate is held constant. The fall in real wealth and real labor income is contractionary, and there is no offsetting rise in demand from the fall in the real interest rate. Not only does the Fed not have to increase the nominal interest rate more than the increase in inflation for there to be a contraction, it does not have to increase the nominal rate at all! The inflation shock itself will contract the economy through the real wealth and real income effects.

The omission of wages from the modern-view model can be traced back to the late 1970s, where, as discussed in Chapter 4 (see note 5), there began a movement away from the estimation of structural price and wage equations to the estimation of reduced-form price equations (that is, price equations that do not include wage rates as explanatory variables). This line of research evolved to the estimation of NAIRU equations, which represent the modern view.

7.2 Estimated Effects of a Positive Inflation Shock

A simple experiment is performed in this section that shows that in the MC model a positive inflation shock is contractionary. The period used is 1994:1–1998:4, 20 quarters. The first step, as for the experiment in section 6.3, is to add the estimated residuals to the stochastic equations and take them to be exogenous. Again, this means that when the model is solved using the actual values of all the exogenous variables, a perfect tracking solution results. The base path for the experiment is thus just the historical path. Then the constant term in the US price equation 10 is increased by 0.005 (0.50 percentage points) from its estimated value.[3] The estimated interest rate rule for the Fed, equation 30, is dropped, and the nominal short-term interest rate, *RS*, is also taken to be exogenous for the United States. The model is then solved. The difference between the predicted value of each variable and each period from this solution and its base (actual) value is the estimated effect of the price-equation shock. Remember that this is an experiment in which there is no change in the U.S. short-term nominal interest rate because the US interest rate rule is dropped. There is also no effect on U.S. long-term nominal interest rates because they depend only on current and past U.S. short-term nominal interest rates.

Selected results from this experiment are presented in Table 7.1. The main point for present purposes is in row 1, which shows that real GDP falls: the inflation shock is contractionary. The rest of this section is simply a discussion of some of the details.

Row 2 shows the effects of the change in the constant term in the price equation on the price level. The price level is 0.52 percent higher than its base value in the first quarter, 1.00 percent higher in the second quarter, and so on through the twentieth quarter, where it is 4.68 percent higher. (The shock to the price equation accumulates over time because of the lagged dependent variable in the equation.) Row 3 versus row 2 shows that the nominal wage rate rises less than the price level, and so there is a fall in the real wage rate, WF/PF. Row 4 shows that real disposable income falls. (Although

---

3. Note that this is a shock to the price equation, not to the wage equation. It is similar to an increase in the price of oil. In the MC model an increase in the price of oil (which is exogenous) increases the U.S. price of imports, which is an explanatory variable in the US price equation. Either an increase in the constant term in the price equation or an increase in the price of oil leads to an initial fall in the real wage, because wages lag prices. If the shock were instead to the wage equation, there would be an initial rise in the real wage, which would have much different effects.

Table 7.1
Effects of a Positive Shock to US Price Equation 10:
Nominal Interest Rate, *RS*, Unchanged from Base Values

Variable	Changes from Base Values (quarters ahead)							
	1	2	3	4	8	12	16	20
1 Real GDP (*GDPR*)	−0.05	−0.14	−0.24	−0.36	−0.80	−1.16	−1.44	−1.70
2 Price level (*PF*)	0.52	1.00	1.43	1.82	3.04	3.83	4.34	4.68
3 Wage rate (*WF*)	0.43	0.81	1.16	1.48	2.25	3.07	3.47	3.74
4 Real DPI (*YD/PH*)	−0.21	−0.42	−0.62	−0.82	−1.55	−2.11	−2.56	−2.97
5 Change in profits (ΔΠ)	3.0	1.7	1.5	1.4	1.4	1.0	0.7	1.3
6 Capital gains (*CG*)	10.5	5.5	7.9	6.4	20.8	37.4	27.2	110.7
7 Real wealth (*AA*)	−0.29	−0.57	−0.81	−1.04	−1.70	−2.12	−2.28	−2.44
8 Service consumption (*CS*)	−0.02	−0.07	−0.13	−0.20	−0.56	−0.91	−1.21	−1.47
9 Nondurable consumption (*CN*)	−0.02	−0.07	−0.15	−0.25	−0.71	−1.14	−1.46	−1.73
10 Durable consumption (*CD*)	−0.20	−0.52	−0.93	−1.37	−3.25	−4.72	−5.61	−6.18
11 Residential inv. (*IHH*)	−0.54	−0.92	−1.34	−1.82	−3.77	−5.02	−6.05	−6.51
12 Nonresidential fixed inv. (*IKF*)	−0.11	−0.32	−0.52	−0.70	−1.50	−2.48	−3.34	−4.01
13 yen/$ rate (E_{JA})	−0.03	−0.07	−0.14	−0.22	−0.63	−1.11	−1.58	−2.00
14 DM/$ rate (E_{GE})	−0.04	−0.12	−0.23	−0.35	−0.95	−1.53	−1.94	−2.20
15 Price of imports (*PIM*)	0.12	0.18	0.24	0.30	0.72	1.02	1.20	1.21
16 Price of exports (*PEX*)	0.47	0.89	1.28	1.62	2.71	3.44	3.92	4.26
17 Real imports (*IM*)	−0.05	−0.16	−0.34	−0.58	−1.79	−3.02	−4.04	−4.88
18 Real exports (*EX*)	−0.05	−0.10	−0.16	−0.23	−0.55	−0.88	−1.29	−1.64
19 Current account	0.04	0.09	0.14	0.20	0.38	0.55	0.68	0.78

Notes:
- All variables but 13 and 14 are for the United States.
- DPI = disposable personal income.
- ΔΠ = change in nominal after-tax corporate profits. (In the notation in Table A.2, Π = *PIEF* − *TFG* − *TFS* + *PX* · *PIEB* − *TBG* − *TBS*.)
- Current account = U.S. nominal current account as a percentage of nominal GDP. The U.S. current account is *PX* · *EX* − *PIM* · *IM*.
- Changes are in percentage points except for ΔΠ and *CG*, which are in billions of dollars.
- Simulation period is 1994:1–1998:4.

not shown, nominal disposable income increases.) Real disposable income falls because of the fall in the real wage rate and because some nonlabor nominal income, such as interest income, rises less in percentage terms than the price level.

The change in nominal corporate after-tax profits is higher (row 5), and this in turn leads to a small increase in capital gains (*CG*) for the household sector (row 6). (This is US equation 25 at work.) For example, the increase in capital gains in the first quarter is $10.5 billion. (*CG* is not affected by any nominal interest rate changes because there are none.) The increase in *CG* leads to an increase in nominal household wealth (not shown), but row 7 shows that real household wealth is lower. This means that the percentage increase in nominal household wealth is smaller than the percentage increase in the price level. Put another way, US equation 25 does not lead to a large enough increase in *CG* to have real household wealth rise.

The fall in real income and real wealth leads to a fall in the four categories of household expenditures (rows 8–11). Nonresidential fixed investment is lower (row 12), which is a response to the lower values of output, although this is partly offset by the fall in the real interest rate. (Remember that US equation 12 is the one demand equation in the model that uses the real interest rate.)

Rows 13 and 14 present the Japanese and German nominal exchange rates relative to the U.S. dollar. (An increase in a rate is a depreciation of the currency.) The two currencies appreciate relative to the dollar. This is because the U.S. price level rises relative to the Japanese and German price levels, which leads, other things being equal, to an appreciation of the yen and DM through the estimated equations for the two exchange rates (see Table B9 in Appendix B).

Row 15 shows that the U.S. import price level rises, which is due to the depreciation of the dollar, and row 16 shows that the U.S. export price level rises, which is due to the increase in the overall U.S. price level.

The real value of imports in the model responds positively to a decrease in the import price level relative to the domestic price level and negatively to a decrease in real income. Row 17 shows that the real income effect dominates. The negative effect from the fall in real income dominates the positive effect from the fall in the price of imports relative to the domestic price level. The real value of U.S. exports is lower (row 18), which is due to a higher relative U.S. export price level. (The export price level increases more than the dollar depreciates, and so U.S. export prices in other countries' currencies increase.) Even though the real value of U.S. exports is lower, there is an improvement in the nominal U.S. current account (row 19). This improvement is initially due to the higher U.S. export price level (a J-curve type of effect) and later to the fact that the real value of U.S. imports falls more than does the real value of U.S. exports. In other words, the contractionary U.S. economy helps improve the U.S. current account because of the fall in imports.

Regarding long-run effects, the present experiment is somewhat artificial because of the dropping of the estimated interest rate rule of the Fed. The rule has the property that, other things being equal, the Fed will lower the nominal interest rate when the U.S. economy contracts. This will then help bring the economy out of the contraction.

The present experiment is merely meant to show what would be the case if the rule were dropped. In practice, of course, the Fed would react.

It is interesting to note that the result obtained here from analyzing the MC model—that an increase in inflation is contractionary even when the nominal interest rate is held constant—is also reached in Giordani (2003) from analyzing VAR models. The results from these two quite different approaches both cast doubt on a key property of modern-view models.

7.3   The FRB/US Model

The FRB/US model—Federal Reserve Board (2000)—is sometimes cited as a macroeconometric model that is consistent with the modern view (see, for example, Taylor 2000, p. 91). This model has strong real interest rate effects. In fact, if government spending is increased in the FRB/US model with the nominal interest rate held constant, real output eventually expands so much that the model will no longer solve.[4] The increase in government spending raises inflation, which with nominal interest rates held constant lowers real interest rates, which leads to an unlimited expansion. The model is not stable unless there is a nominal interest rate rule that leads to an increase in the real interest rate when inflation increases.

It may seem puzzling that two macroeconometric models could have such different properties. Given the empirical results in Chapter 3, how can it be that the FRB/US model finds such strong real interest rate effects? The answer is that many restrictions have been imposed on the model that have the effect of imposing large real interest rate effects. In most of the expenditure equations real interest rate effects are imposed rather than estimated. Direct tests of nominal versus real interest rates like the one used in Chapter 3 are not done, and so there is no way of knowing what the data actually support in the FRB/US expenditure equations.

Large stock market effects are also imposed in the FRB/US model. Contrary to the estimate of US equation 25, which shows fairly small effects of nominal interest rates and nominal earnings on CG, the FRB/US model has extremely large effects. A one-percentage-point decrease in the real interest rate leads to a 20 percent increase in the value of corporate equity (Reifschneider, Tetlow, and Williams (1999), p. 5). At the end of 1999 the value of corporate equity was about $20 trillion (using data from the U.S. Flow of Funds accounts), and 20 percent of this is $4 trillion. There is thus a huge increase in nominal household wealth for even a one-percentage-point decrease in the real interest rate. A positive inflation shock with the nominal interest rate held constant, which lowers the real interest rate, thus results in a large increase in both nominal and real wealth in the model. The increase in real wealth then leads through the wealth effect in the household expenditure equations to a large increase in real expenditures. This channel is an important contributor to the model's not being stable when there is an increase in inflation greater than the nominal interest rate. Again, this stock price

---

4. Personal correspondence with Andrew Levin and David Reifschneider.

effect is imposed rather than estimated, and so it is not necessarily the case that the data are consistent with this restriction.

There is thus no puzzle about the vastly different properties of the two models. It is simply that important real interest rate restrictions have been imposed in the FRB/US model and not in the MC model.

7.4 Conclusion

If a positive inflation shock with the nominal interest rate held constant is in fact contractionary, this has important implications for monetary policy. The coefficient on inflation in the nominal interest rate rule need not be greater than one for the economy to be stable. Also, if one is concerned with optimal policies, the optimal response by the Fed to an inflation shock is likely to be much smaller if inflation shocks are contractionary than if they are expansionary. The use of modern-view models for monetary policy is thus risky. If they are wrong about the effects of inflation shocks, they may lead to poor monetary policy recommendations. Optimal policies using the MC model are discussed in Chapter 11.

8

Estimated European Inflation Costs

8.1   Introduction

If macroeconomic policies had lowered European unemployment in the 1980s, what would have been the inflation costs?[1] Under the NAIRU model discussed in Chapter 4, this is not an interesting question. In that model there is a value of the unemployment rate (the NAIRU) below which the price level accelerates and above which the price level decelerates. This view of the inflation process is echoed, for example, in *Unemployment: Choices for Europe*, where Alogoskoufis et al. (1995, p. 124) state, "We would not want to dissent from the view that there is no long-run trade-off between activity and inflation, so that macroeconomic policies by themselves can do little to secure a lasting reduction in unemployment." Under this view it is not sensible to talk about long-run trade-offs between unemployment and inflation.

Since the results in Chapter 4 call into question the NAIRU dynamics, it is of interest to see what an alternative model would say about the European inflation cost question. This chapter uses the MC model to estimate what would have happened to European unemployment and inflation in the 1982:1–1990:4 period had the Bundesbank followed an easier monetary policy than it in fact did.

If the true relationship between the price level and unemployment is highly nonlinear at low values of the unemployment rate, a view put forth in section 4.6, it is problematic to consider policy experiments in which unemployment rates are pushed to very low values. Because there are few observations at low unemployment rates, it is not possible to pin down the point at which the relationship becomes highly nonlinear (if it does), and so the estimated price equations are not reliable at low values of the unemployment rate. For present purposes, however, this is not likely to be a problem because the experiment is over a period in which unemployment was generally quite high.

---

1. The results in this chapter are updates of those in Fair (1999).

8.2   The Experiment

8.2.1   The Setup

The experiment is a decrease in the German short-term interest rate between 1982:1 and 1990:4. To perform this experiment the interest rate rule of the Bundesbank was dropped, and the German short-term interest rate was taken to be exogenous. The interest rate rules for all the other countries in the model were retained, which means, for example, that the fall in the German rate directly affects the interest rates of the countries whose rules have the German rate as an explanatory variable. The German interest rate was lowered by 1.0 percentage point for 1982:1–1983:4, by 0.75 percentage points for 1984:1–1985:4, by 0.5 percentage points for 1986:1–1987:4, and by 0.25 percentage points for 1988:1–1990:4.

As in the experiments in the last two chapters, the first step is to add the estimated residuals to the model and take them to be exogenous. Doing this and then solving the model using the actual values of all the exogenous variables results in a perfect tracking solution. The German interest rate is then lowered and the model is solved. The difference between the predicted value for each variable for each period from this solution and its actual value is the estimated effect of the monetary-policy change on the variable. Selected results of this experiment are presented in Table 8.1 for six countries: Germany, France, Italy, the United Kingdom, the United States, and Japan. Each fourth-quarter value is presented in the table.

The second column in Table 8.1, labeled *UR*, gives the actual value of the unemployment rate in percentage points, and the third column, labeled π, gives the actual value of the inflation rate (percentage change in the GDP price deflator at an annual rate) in percentage points. These values are provided for reference purposes. The values in the remaining columns are either absolute or percentage changes from the base values (remember that the base values are the actual values). Absolute changes are given for the interest rate, the unemployment rate, the inflation rate, and the current account as a fraction of GDP, while percentage changes are given for the other variables. All the values are in percentage points.

8.2.2   Qualitative Discussion

Before discussing the numbers, it will be useful to review qualitatively what is likely to happen in the model in response to the decrease in the German interest rate.[2] Consider first the effects of an interest rate decrease in a particular country. A decrease in the short-term rate in a country leads to a decrease in the long-term rate through the term structure equation. A decrease in the short-term rate also leads to a depreciation of the country's currency (assuming that the interest rate decrease is relative to other

---

2. It may also be useful to review the qualitative discussion in section 2.3 regarding the effects of a depreciation and an interest rate decrease in the MC model. Some of the discussion here repeats this earlier discussion.

Table 8.1

Effects of a Decrease in the German Interest Rate in 1982:1–1990:4

Qtr. ah.	Actual Values		Deviations from Base Values										
	UR	π	RS	E	Y	UR	PY	π	PM	PX	IM	EX	S*
GE													
4	7.34	6.66	−1.00	1.43	0.38	−0.09	0.02	0.05	0.73	0.23	0.01	0.10	−0.12
8	8.13	6.46	−1.00	2.50	0.79	−0.31	0.14	0.19	1.17	0.48	0.05	0.26	−0.16
12	8.08	6.46	−0.75	2.98	1.10	−0.59	0.41	0.35	1.43	0.76	0.14	0.44	−0.12
16	7.97	5.96	−0.75	3.48	1.37	−0.86	0.84	0.51	1.79	1.15	0.25	0.56	−0.17
20	7.56	4.64	−0.50	3.67	1.49	−1.09	1.41	0.63	2.01	1.64	0.42	0.67	−0.04
24	7.66	4.78	−0.50	4.03	1.55	−1.24	2.07	0.71	2.46	2.26	0.59	0.64	−0.02
28	7.47	5.15	−0.25	4.13	1.43	−1.31	2.79	0.74	2.83	2.88	0.76	0.59	0.00
32	6.73	5.09	−0.25	4.42	1.26	−1.29	3.50	0.71	3.34	3.52	0.92	0.50	−0.05
36	5.87	1.46	−0.25	4.80	1.03	−1.20	4.16	0.61	3.86	4.14	1.04	0.36	−0.11
FR													
4	7.80	9.30	−0.57	1.44	0.09	−0.05	0.04	0.08	0.69	0.26	−0.10	0.10	−0.07
8	8.30	9.82	−0.73	2.51	0.26	−0.17	0.15	0.14	1.12	0.50	−0.23	0.24	−0.07
12	9.69	3.80	−0.62	2.95	0.44	−0.31	0.30	0.17	1.29	0.68	−0.28	0.40	−0.04
16	9.80	3.35	−0.58	3.31	0.61	−0.46	0.49	0.21	1.50	0.86	−0.28	0.51	−0.06
20	10.10	3.29	−0.42	3.25	0.74	−0.59	0.68	0.20	1.53	1.00	−0.18	0.63	0.00
24	9.90	4.28	−0.36	3.25	0.83	−0.68	0.87	0.19	1.65	1.17	0.00	0.64	0.00
28	9.40	4.59	−0.20	2.91	0.86	−0.75	1.04	0.17	1.61	1.27	0.20	0.72	0.00
32	8.90	5.02	−0.16	2.71	0.84	−0.76	1.19	0.14	1.61	1.37	0.42	0.67	−0.03
36	8.60	1.61	−0.15	2.58	0.79	−0.74	1.31	0.10	1.58	1.44	0.62	0.65	−0.06
IT													
4	9.98	15.06	0.03	1.43	0.02	−0.01	0.06	0.11	0.74	0.37	−0.10	0.09	−0.07
8	10.99	15.50	0.11	2.51	0.08	−0.03	0.21	0.19	1.17	0.69	−0.25	0.21	−0.03
12	11.30	4.74	0.18	3.00	0.14	−0.08	0.40	0.22	1.41	0.93	−0.35	0.37	0.00
16	12.00	6.93	0.27	3.47	0.19	−0.14	0.67	0.31	1.83	1.20	−0.45	0.54	−0.05
20	12.96	4.82	0.31	3.60	0.20	−0.19	0.92	0.27	1.97	1.43	−0.48	0.67	0.03
24	13.58	7.95	0.32	3.83	0.21	−0.22	1.14	0.25	2.32	1.71	−0.49	0.75	0.06
28	12.98	8.95	0.34	3.74	0.24	−0.26	1.36	0.24	2.53	1.91	−0.52	0.94	0.09
32	12.63	7.35	0.37	3.79	0.27	−0.30	1.59	0.25	2.80	2.14	−0.54	1.00	0.09
36	12.26	6.40	0.39	3.89	0.30	−0.35	1.83	0.24	3.04	2.36	−0.56	1.11	0.11
UK													
4	12.32	8.92	−0.01	0.75	0.00	0.00	−0.01	0.00	0.03	0.03	0.00	0.01	0.00
8	12.58	5.55	−0.02	1.24	0.01	0.00	−0.04	−0.05	−0.19	0.01	0.03	0.04	0.08
12	12.86	6.22	−0.02	1.37	0.05	−0.02	−0.11	−0.08	−0.41	−0.05	0.08	0.14	0.17
16	12.98	5.10	0.03	1.49	0.12	−0.05	−0.15	−0.05	−0.47	−0.12	0.15	0.34	0.12
20	12.79	5.38	0.11	1.41	0.17	−0.09	−0.12	0.08	−0.30	−0.10	0.25	0.39	0.06
24	10.26	4.64	0.17	1.39	0.18	−0.12	−0.02	0.13	−0.17	0.00	0.33	0.44	0.06
28	8.26	9.58	0.22	1.23	0.19	−0.15	0.15	0.19	−0.04	0.14	0.38	0.55	0.06
32	6.83	9.18	0.25	1.21	0.19	−0.16	0.35	0.22	0.11	0.32	0.39	0.58	0.09
36	7.56	2.42	0.25	1.24	0.17	−0.16	0.56	0.22	0.27	0.51	0.37	0.58	0.11
US													
4	10.68	4.29	−0.01		0.01	0.00	−0.05	−0.06	−0.42	−0.10	0.18	−0.08	0.02
8	8.54	3.56	−0.02		0.05	−0.02	−0.14	−0.09	−0.81	−0.22	0.44	−0.12	0.03
12	7.28	2.92	−0.01		0.10	−0.05	−0.23	−0.08	−1.00	−0.32	0.73	−0.11	0.02
16	7.05	2.97	0.00		0.13	−0.06	−0.27	0.00	−1.21	−0.37	0.76	−0.01	0.00
20	6.84	2.71	0.04		0.15	−0.08	−0.31	0.01	−1.06	−0.40	0.80	0.07	−0.01
24	5.87	3.48	0.05		0.16	−0.07	−0.32	0.00	−0.90	−0.40	0.85	0.17	0.00
28	5.35	3.08	0.05		0.15	−0.06	−0.31	0.02	−0.70	−0.37	0.77	0.24	−0.01
32	5.37	3.02	0.06		0.14	−0.05	−0.28	0.03	−0.58	−0.33	0.66	0.33	−0.01
36	6.11	3.53	0.05		0.13	−0.03	−0.26	0.02	−0.50	−0.30	0.59	0.38	0.00

Table 8.1
(*continued*)

Qtr.	Actual Values		Deviations from Base Values										
ah.	UR	π	RS	E	Y	UR	PY	π	PM	PX	IM	EX	S*
JA													
4	2.47	−0.69	−0.01	0.00	0.00	0.00	−0.01	−0.01	−0.19	−0.37	0.03	0.00	−0.03
8	2.65	1.23	−0.02	0.01	0.00	0.00	−0.03	−0.02	−0.39	−0.66	0.09	0.05	−0.05
12	2.69	5.11	−0.02	0.04	0.02	0.00	−0.04	−0.02	−0.47	−0.75	0.15	0.16	−0.05
16	2.79	1.77	−0.01	0.09	0.04	−0.01	−0.05	0.00	−0.56	−0.84	0.17	0.33	−0.06
20	2.81	−0.10	0.01	0.14	0.04	−0.02	−0.06	0.00	−0.56	−0.76	0.22	0.36	−0.04
24	2.71	−0.08	0.03	0.19	0.03	−0.02	−0.06	0.00	−0.49	−0.67	0.26	0.36	−0.02
28	2.43	2.40	0.04	0.22	0.02	−0.02	−0.06	0.00	−0.34	−0.48	0.25	0.27	−0.02
32	2.21	2.73	0.04	0.24	0.00	−0.02	−0.06	0.00	−0.23	−0.36	0.21	0.31	−0.01
36	2.11	2.84	0.04	0.24	−0.01	−0.01	−0.06	0.00	−0.18	−0.29	0.17	0.28	−0.01

Notes:
- E = exchange rate, local currency per \$.
- EX = real level of exports.
- IM = real level of imports.
- PM = import price deflator.
- PX = export price index.
- PY = GDP price deflator.
- π = percentage change in PY.
- RS = three-month interest rate.
- S^* = current account as a percent of nominal GDP.
- UR = unemployment rate.
- Y = real GDP.

countries' interest rates). The interest rate decreases lead to an increase in consumption and investment. The depreciation of the currency leads to an increase in exports. The effect on exports works through the trade-share equations. The dollar price of the country's exports that feeds into the trade-share equations is lower because of the depreciation, and this increases the share of the other countries' total imports imported from the particular country. The effect on aggregate demand in the country from the interest rate decrease is thus positive from the increase in consumption, investment, and exports.

There are two main effects on imports, one positive and one negative. The positive effect is that consumption and investment are higher, some of which is imported. The negative effect is that the price of imports is higher because of the depreciation, which has a negative effect on the demand for imports. The net effect on imports can thus go either way.

There is also a positive effect on inflation. As just noted, the depreciation leads to an increase in the price of imports. This in turn has a positive effect on the domestic price level through the price equation. In addition, if aggregate demand increases, this increases demand pressure, which has a positive effect on the domestic price level.

There are many other effects that follow from these, including effects back on the short-term interest rate itself through the interest rate rule, but these are typically second order in nature, especially in the short run. The main effects are as just described.

The decrease in the German interest rate should thus stimulate the German economy, depreciate the DM, and lead to a rise in the German price level. How much the price level rises depends, among other things, on the size of the coefficient estimate of the demand pressure variable in the German price equation. The size of the price level increase also depends on how much the DM depreciates and on the size of the coefficient estimate of the import price variable in the price equation.

For those European countries whose interest rate rules include the German interest rate as an explanatory variable, the fall in the German rate will lead to a direct fall in their interest rates. In addition, the depreciation of the DM (relative to the dollar) will lead to a depreciation of the other European countries' currencies (relative to the dollar) because they are fairly closely tied to the DM in the short run through the exchange rate equations.

8.2.3 The Results

Turn now to the results in Table 8.1. By the end of the nine-year period the German exchange rate relative to the dollar, E, depreciated 4.80 percent, the price level, PY, was 4.16 percent higher, the inflation rate, π, was 0.61 percentage points higher, and the unemployment rate, UR, was 1.20 percentage points lower—all compared with the base case (the actual values). (An increase in E for a country is a depreciation of the country's currency relative to the dollar.) The current account as a percentage of GDP, S^*, was 0.11 percentage points lower: German imports, IM, rose more than German exports, EX, while the increases in German import prices, PM, and German export prices, PX, were similar.

The interest rate, RS, for France fell because French monetary policy is directly affected by German monetary policy. (The German interest rate is an explanatory variable in the French interest rate rule.) By the end of the period the French exchange rate had depreciated 2.58 percent, the price level was 1.31 percent higher, the inflation rate was 0.10 percentage points higher, and the unemployment rate was 0.74 percentage points lower. Note that although both the DM and the French franc depreciated relative to the dollar (4.80 and 2.58 percent, respectively), the franc depreciated less and thus appreciated relative to the DM. This is because of the smaller rise in the domestic price level in France than in Germany.

The Italian lira is closely tied to the DM through equation 9 for Italy in the model, and the lira depreciated almost as much as the DM. This led to a rise in the Italian price level, which led, through the Italian interest rate rule, to an increase in the Italian interest rate. This offset much of the stimulus from the depreciation. By the end of the period the price level was 1.83 percent higher, the inflation rate 0.24 percentage points higher, and the unemployment rate 0.35 percentage points lower.

For the United Kingdom the pound depreciated relative to the dollar, but by much less than did the DM. The pound thus appreciated relative to the DM (and other European currencies), and this appreciation was large enough to lead to a slight decrease in the overall UK import price deflator for some of the period. This in turn had a slight

Table 8.2
Changes from the Base Values after 36 Quarters

	Price Level	Inflation Rate	Unempl. Rate	Output
GE	4.16	0.61	−1.20	1.03
FR	1.31	0.10	−0.74	0.79
IT	1.83	0.24	−0.35	0.30
UK	0.56	0.22	−0.16	0.17

negative effect on the UK domestic price level for some of the period. The effects on the UK real variables were modest.

The main effect on the United States was a fall in the price of imports, caused by the appreciation of the dollar relative to the European currencies. This led to a slight fall in the U.S. domestic price level. U.S. imports increased because the price of imports fell relative to the domestic price level and because output was slightly higher. The effect on U.S. output was small. Similarly, the Japanese price of imports fell, and there was a slight fall in the Japanese domestic price level. Japanese imports also increased slightly.

8.3 Conclusion

Table 8.2 summarizes some of the results from Table 8.1. Going out 36 quarters, the cost for Germany of a 1.20 percentage point fall in the unemployment rate is a 4.16 percent rise in the price level. At the end of the period inflation is still higher than the base rate by 0.61 percentage points. For France the fall in the unemployment rate is 0.74 percentage points and the rise in inflation is 0.10 percentage points. The corresponding numbers for Italy are 0.35 and 0.24, and the corresponding numbers for the United Kingdom are 0.16 and 0.22. Whether these costs are considered worth incurring depends on one's welfare function. Given the estimated costs in Table 8.2, some would surely argue that the Bundesbank should have been more expansionary in the 1980s.

The accuracy of the present results depends, of course, on the accuracy of the price and wage equations in the MC model. The results in Chapter 4 support the MC equations' dynamics over the NAIRU dynamics, which thus provides some support for the present results. Remember that the present results are not governed by the NAIRU dynamics. It is not the case that an experiment like this will result in accelerating price levels, so there are no horrible events lurking beyond the 36-quarter horizon of the present experiment.

Finally, remember that the MC estimates of the price and wage equations do not pin down the point at which the relationship between the price level and unemployment becomes nonlinear. As noted at the end of section 8.1, this is not likely to be a problem for the experiment in this chapter because it is over a period in which unemployment was generally quite high. It would not be sensible, however, to, say, triple the size of the German interest rate decrease and examine the inflation consequences.

9

Stochastic Simulation and Bootstrapping

9.1 Stochastic Simulation

So far in this book solutions have all been deterministic: the error terms have been set to fixed values and the model solved once.[1] The use of fixed error terms is relaxed beginning with this chapter.

Stochastic simulation has a long history in macroeconomics. The seminal paper in this area is Adelman and Adelman (1959), which introduced the idea of drawing errors to analyze the properties of econometric models. In the present context stochastic simulation is as follows.

The model considered is model 1.1 in section 1.4, which is repeated here:

$$f_i(y_t, y_{t-1}, \ldots, y_{t-p}, x_t, \alpha_i) = u_{it}, \quad i = 1, \ldots, n, \quad t = 1, \ldots, T, \quad (1.1)$$

where the first m equations are stochastic. Assume that the vector of error terms, $u_t = (u_{1t}, \ldots, u_{mt})'$, is distributed as multivariate normal $N(0, \Sigma)$, where Σ is an $m \times m$ covariance matrix.[2] Given consistent estimates of α_i, denoted $\hat{\alpha}_i$, consistent estimates of u_{it}, denoted $\hat{u}_{it}$, can be computed as $f_i(y_t, y_{t-1}, \ldots, y_{t-p}, x_t, \hat{\alpha}_i)$. The covariance matrix Σ can then be estimated as $(1/T)\hat{U}\hat{U}'$, where $\hat{U}$ is the $m \times T$ matrix of the values of $\hat{u}_{it}$.

Let u_t^* denote a particular draw of the m error terms for period t from the $N(0, \hat{\Sigma})$ distribution. Given u_t^* and given $\hat{\alpha}_i$ for all i, one can solve the model for period t. This is merely a deterministic simulation for the given values of the error terms and coefficients. Call this simulation a "repetition." Another repetition can be made by drawing a new set of values of u_t^* and solving again. This can be done as many times as desired. From each repetition one obtains a prediction of each endogenous variable. Let y_{it}^j

---

1. The results in this chapter are the same as those in Fair (2003b).

2. Although normality is usually assumed in the literature, other assumptions are possible. Alternative assumptions simply change the way the error terms are drawn.

denote the value on the jth repetition of variable i for period t. For J repetitions, the stochastic simulation estimate of the expected value of variable i for period t, denoted $\tilde{\mu}_{it}$, is

$$\tilde{\mu}_{it} = \frac{1}{J} \sum_{j=1}^{J} y_{it}^j. \tag{9.1}$$

Let

$$\sigma_{it}^{2j} = (y_{it}^j - \tilde{\mu}_{it})^2. \tag{9.2}$$

The stochastic simulation estimate of the variance of variable i for period t, denoted $\tilde{\sigma}_{it}^2$, is then[3]

$$\tilde{\sigma}_{it}^2 = \frac{1}{J} \sum_{j=1}^{J} \sigma_{it}^{2j}. \tag{9.3}$$

In many applications, one is interested in predicted values more than one period ahead, that is, in predicted values from dynamic simulations. The above discussion can be easily modified to incorporate this case. One simply draws values for u_t for each period of the simulation. Each repetition is one dynamic simulation over the period of interest. For, say, an eight-quarter period, each repetition yields eight predicted values, one per quarter, for each endogenous variable.

It is also possible to draw coefficients for the repetitions. Let $\hat{\alpha}$ denote, say, the 2SLS estimate of all the coefficients in the model, and let $\hat{V}$ denote the estimate of the $k \times k$ covariance matrix of $\hat{\alpha}$. Given $\hat{V}$ and given the normality assumption, an estimate of the distribution of the coefficient estimates is $N(\hat{\alpha}, \hat{V})$. When coefficients are drawn, each repetition consists of a draw of the coefficient vector from $N(\hat{\alpha}, \hat{V})$ and draws of the error terms as above.

Early stochastic simulation that treated coefficient estimates as fixed include Nagar (1969), Evans, Klein, and Saito (1972), Fromm, Klein, and Schink (1972), Green, Leibenberg, and Hirsch (1972), Cooper and Fischer (1972), Sowey (1973), Cooper (1974), Garbade (1975), Bianchi, Calzolari, and Corsi (1976), and Calzolari and Corsi (1977). Studies that drew *both* error terms and coefficients include Schink (1971), Haitovsky and Wallace (1972), Cooper and Fischer (1974), Muench et al. (1974), Schink (1974), and Fair (1980a).

It is also possible to draw errors from estimated residuals rather than from estimated distributions, although this has rarely been done. In a theoretical paper Brown and

---

3. Given the data from the repetitions, it is also possible to compute the variances of the stochastic simulation estimates and thus to examine the precision of the estimates. The variance of $\tilde{\mu}_{it}$ is simply $\tilde{\sigma}_{it}^2 / J$. The variance of $\tilde{\sigma}_{it}^2$, denoted $\text{var}(\tilde{\sigma}_{it}^2)$, is

$$\text{var}(\tilde{\sigma}_{it}^2) = \left(\frac{1}{J}\right)^2 \sum_{j=1}^{J} (\sigma_{it}^{2j} - \tilde{\sigma}_{it}^2)^2.$$

Mariano (1984) analyzed the procedure of drawing errors from the residuals for a static nonlinear econometric model with fixed coefficient estimates. For the stochastic simulation results in Fair (1998) errors were drawn from estimated residuals for a dynamic, nonlinear, simultaneous equations model with fixed coefficient estimates, and this may have been the first time this approach was used for such models. An advantage of drawing from estimated residuals is that no assumption has to be made about the distribution of the error terms.

9.2   Bootstrapping

The bootstrap was introduced in statistics in 1979 by Efron (1979).[4] Although the bootstrap procedure is obviously related to stochastic simulation, the literature that followed Efron's paper stressed the use of the bootstrap for estimation and the evaluation of estimators, not for evaluating models' properties. Although there is by now a large literature on the use of the bootstrap in economics (as well as in statistics), most of it has focused on small time-series models. Good recent reviews are Li and Maddala (1996), Horowitz (1997), Berkowitz and Kilian (2000), and Härdle, Horowitz, and Kreiss (2001).

The main purpose of this chapter is to integrate for model 1.1 (that is, a dynamic, nonlinear, simultaneous equations model) the bootstrap approach to evaluating estimators and the stochastic simulation approach to evaluating models' properties. The procedure in section 9.4 for treating coefficient uncertainty has not been used before for these kinds of models. This chapter also contains estimates of the gain in coverage accuracy from using bootstrap confidence intervals over asymptotic intervals for the US model. It will be seen that the gain is fairly large for this model.

The paper closest to the present work is Freedman (1984), who considered the bootstrapping of the 2SLS estimator in a dynamic, linear, simultaneous equations model. Runkle (1987) used the bootstrap to examine impulse response functions in VAR models, and Kilian (1998) extended this work to correct for bias. There is also work on bootstrapping GMM estimators (see, for example, Hall and Horowitz (1996)), but this work is of limited relevance here because it does not assume knowledge of a complete model.

In his review of bootstrapping MacKinnon (2002) analyzes an example of a linear simultaneous equations model consisting of one structural equation and one reduced-form equation. He points out (p. 14) that "bootstrapping even one equation of a simultaneous equations model is a good deal more complicated than bootstrapping an equation in which all the explanatory variables are exogenous or predetermined. The problem is that the bootstrap DGP must provide a way to generate all of the endogenous variables, not just one of them." In this chapter the process generating the endogenous variables is the complete model 1.1.

---

4. See Hall (1992) for the history of resampling ideas in statistics prior to Efron's paper.

This chapter does not provide the theoretical restrictions on model 1.1 that are needed for the bootstrap procedure to be valid. Assumptions beyond *iid* errors and the existence of a consistent estimator are needed, but these have not been worked out in the literature for the model considered here. This chapter simply assumes that the model meets whatever restrictions are sufficient for the bootstrap procedure to be valid. Its contribution is to apply the procedure to model 1.1 and to estimate the gain in coverage accuracy assuming the procedure is valid. It remains to be seen what restrictions are needed beyond *iid* errors and a consistent estimator. As will be seen, however, it is the case that the bootstrap works well regarding coverage accuracy when the US model is taken to be the truth. Given this, it seems likely that the US model falls within the required conditions for validity.

Section 9.3 discusses the use of the bootstrap to evaluate coefficient estimates, and it uses the US model to estimate coverage accuracy. Section 9.4 discusses the use of the bootstrap to analyze models' properties, and section 9.5 discusses bias correction. The bootstrap procedure is applied in section 9.6 to the US model.

9.3 Distribution of the Coefficient Estimates

9.3.1 Initial Estimation

Let α denote the vector of all the unknown coefficients in the model, $\alpha = (\alpha'_1, \ldots, \alpha'_m)'$, and let u denote the vector of errors for all the available periods, $u = (u'_1, \ldots, u'_T)'$, where u_t is defined in section 9.1. It is assumed that a consistent estimate of α is available, denoted $\hat{\alpha}$. This could be, for example, the 2SLS or 3SLS estimate of α. Given this estimate and the actual data, u can be estimated. Let $\hat{u}$ denote the estimate of u after the residuals have been centered at zero.[5] Statistics of interest can be analyzed using the bootstrap procedure. These can include t-statistics of the coefficient estimates and possible χ^2 statistics for various hypotheses. For the results in section 9.6 the AP test statistic is examined. τ will be used to denote the vector of estimated statistics of interest.

9.3.2 The Bootstrap Procedure

The bootstrap procedure for evaluating estimators for model 1.1 is:

1. For a given trial j, draw u_t^{*j} from $\hat{u}$ with replacement for $t = 1, \ldots, T$. Use these errors and $\hat{\alpha}$ to solve the model dynamically for $t = 1, \ldots, T$.[6] Treat the solution values as actual values and estimate α by the consistent estimator (2SLS, 3SLS, or

---

5. Freedman (1981) has shown that the bootstrap can fail for an equation with no constant term if the residuals are not centered at zero. For all the results reported in this chapter centering has been done. >From model 1.1, $\hat{u}_{it}$, an element of $\hat{u}$, is $f_i(y_t, y_{t-1}, \ldots, y_{t-p}, x_t, \hat{\alpha}_i)$ except for the adjustment that centers the residuals at zero.

6. This is just a standard dynamic simulation, where instead of using zero values for the error terms the drawn values are used.

whatever). Let $\hat{\alpha}^{*j}$ denote this estimate. Compute also the test statistics of interest, and let τ^{*j} denote the vector of these values.

2. Repeat step 1 for $j = 1, \ldots, J$.

Step 2 gives J estimates of each element of $\hat{\alpha}^{*j}$ and τ^{*j}. Using these values, confidence intervals for the coefficient estimates can be computed (see below). Also, for the originally estimated value of any test statistic, one can see where it lies on the distribution of the J values.

Note that each trial generates a new data set. Each data set is generated using the same coefficient vector ($\hat{\alpha}$), but in general the data set has different errors for a period from those that existed historically. Note also that since the drawing is with replacement, the same error vector may be drawn more than once in a given trial, while others may not be drawn at all. All data sets are conditional on the actual values of the endogenous variables prior to period 1 and on the actual values of the exogenous variables for all periods.

9.3.3   Estimating Coverage Accuracy

Three confidence intervals are empirically examined here.[7] Let β denote a particular coefficient in α. Let $\hat{\beta}$ denote the base estimate (2SLS, 3SLS, or whatever) of β, and let $\hat{\sigma}$ denote its estimated asymptotic standard error. Let $\hat{\beta}^{*j}$ denote the estimate of β on the jth trial, and let $\hat{\sigma}^{*j}$ denote the estimated asymptotic standard error of $\hat{\beta}^{*j}$. Let t^{*j} equal the t-statistic $(\hat{\beta}^{*j} - \hat{\beta})/\hat{\sigma}^{*j}$. Assume that the J values of t^{*j} have been ranked, and let t^*_r denote the value below which r percent of the values of t^{*j} lie. Finally, let $|t^{*j}|$ denote the absolute value of t^{*j}. Assume that the J values of $|t^{*j}|$ have been ranked, and let $|t^*|_r$ denote the value below which r percent of the values of $|t^{*j}|$ lie. The first confidence interval is simply $\hat{\beta} \pm 1.96\hat{\sigma}$, which is the 95 percent confidence interval from the asymptotic normal distribution. The second is $(\hat{\beta} - t^*_{.975}\hat{\sigma},\ \hat{\beta} - t^*_{.025}\hat{\sigma})$, which is the equal-tailed percentile-t interval. The third is $\hat{\beta} \pm |t^*|_{.950}\hat{\sigma}$, which is the symmetric percentile-t interval.

The following Monte Carlo procedure is used to examine the accuracy of the three intervals. This procedure assume that the data generating process is model 1.1 with true coefficients $\hat{\alpha}$.

1. For a given repetition k, draw u^{**k}_t from $\hat{u}$ with replacement for $t = 1, \ldots, T$. Use these errors and $\hat{\alpha}$ to solve the model dynamically for $t = 1, \ldots, T$. Treat the solution values as actual values and estimate α by the consistent estimator (2SLS, 3SLS, or whatever). Let $\hat{\alpha}^{**k}$ denote this estimate. Use this estimate and the solution values from the dynamic simulation to compute the residuals, u, and center them

---

7. See Li and Maddala (1996), pp. 118–121, for a review of the number of ways confidence intervals can be computed using the bootstrap. See also Hall (1988).

at zero. Let $\hat{u}^{**k}$ denote the estimate of u after the residuals have been centered at zero.[8]

2. Perform steps 1 and 2 in section 9.3.2, where $\hat{u}^{**k}$ replaces $\hat{u}$ and $\hat{\alpha}^{**k}$ replaces $\hat{\alpha}$. Compute from these J trials the three confidence intervals discussed above, where $\hat{\beta}^{**k}$ replaces $\hat{\beta}$ and $\hat{\sigma}^{**k}$ replaces $\hat{\sigma}$. Record for each interval whether or not $\hat{\beta}$ is outside of the interval.

3. Repeat steps 1 and 2 for $k = 1, \ldots, K$.

After completion of the K repetitions, one can compute for each coefficient and each interval the percentage of the repetitions that $\hat{\beta}$ was outside the interval. For, say, a 95 percent confidence interval, the difference between the computed percentage and 5 percent is the error in coverage probability.

This procedure was used on the US model to examine coverage accuracy. For all the work in this chapter, equation 9, the demand for money equation explaining MH, has been dropped from the model and MH has been taken to be exogenous. As noted in Chapter 2, the sum of the four autoregressive coefficients in equation 9 is close to one. If the equation is retained, some of the estimates for the bootstrap calculations have a sum greater than one, and this can lead to solution problems. Remember that this is not an important equation in the model.

For the work in this section both J and K were taken to be 350, for a total of 122,500 times the model was estimated (by 2SLS). There were 847 solution failures out of the 122,500 trials, and these failures were skipped. The job took about 40 hours on a 1.7 Ghz PC, about one second per estimation. The results are summarized in Table 9.1. Rejection rates are presented for 12 of the coefficients in the model. The average for the 12 coefficients is presented as well as the average for all 164 coefficients in the model. The standard deviation for the 164 coefficients is also presented.

The average rejection rate over the 164 coefficients is .085 for the asymptotic interval, which compares to .063 and .056 for the two bootstrap intervals. The asymptotic distribution thus rejects too often, and the bootstrap distributions are fairly accurate. Although not shown in Table 9.1, the results are similar if 90 percent confidence intervals are used. In this case the asymptotic rejection rate averaged across the 164 coefficients is .145 (standard deviation of .055). The corresponding values for the two bootstrap intervals are .113 (standard deviation of 030) and .107 (standard deviation of .029). As noted in section 9.1, given the good bootstrap results it seems likely that the US model falls within the required conditions for validity of the bootstrap.

It is interesting to note that although the bootstrap intervals outperform the asymptotic intervals, the asymptotic results are not terrible. One rejects too often using the asymptotic intervals, but the use of the asymptotic intervals does not seem likely to be highly misleading in practice.

---

8. From model 1.1, $\hat{u}_{it}^{**k}$, an element of $\hat{u}^{**k}$, is $f_i(y_t^{**k}, y_{t-1}^{**k}, \ldots, y_{t-p}^{**k}, x_t, \hat{\alpha}_i^{**k})$ except for the adjustment that centers the residuals at zero, where y_{t-h}^{**k} is the solution value of y_{t-h} from the dynamic simulation ($h = 0, 1, \ldots, p$).

Table 9.1
Estimated Coverage Accuracy for the US Model

	Percentage of rejections using 95 percent confidence intervals		
	Asymptotic confidence interval	Bootstrap equal-tailed percentile-t interval	Bootstrap symmetric percentile-t interval
Equation 1: Consumption of services (*CS*)			
ldv	.140	.066	.066
income	.100	.049	.057
Equation 2: Consumption of nondurables (*CN*)			
ldv	.123	.066	.066
income	.126	.063	.043
Equation 3: Consumption of durables (*CD*)			
ldv	.143	.051	.066
income	.131	.086	.071
Equation 10: Price deflator for the firm sector (*PF*)			
ldv	.074	.057	.049
import price deflator	.069	.040	.040
unemployment rate	.043	.037	.040
Equation 30: Three-month Treasury bill rate (*RS*)			
ldv	.074	.080	.066
inflation	.089	.077	.069
unemployment rate	.051	.057	.051
Average (12)	.097	.061	.057
Average (164)	.085	.063	.056
SD (164)	.045	.022	.020

Notes:
- Average (12) = average for the 12 coefficients.
- Average (164) = average for all 164 coefficients.
- SD (164) = standard deviation for all 164 coefficients.
- ldv: lagged dependent variable.

9.4 Analysis of Models' Properties

The bootstrap procedure is extended in this section to evaluating properties of models like model 1.1. The errors are drawn from the estimated residuals, which is contrary to what has been done in the previous literature except for Fair (1998). Also, as in section 9.3.2, the coefficients are estimated on each trial. In the previous literature the coefficient estimates either have been taken to be fixed or have been drawn from estimated distributions.

When examining the properties of models, one is usually interested in a period smaller than the estimation period. Assume that the period of interest is *s* through S, where $s \geq 1$ and $S \leq T$. The bootstrap procedure for analyzing properties is:

1. For a given trial j, draw u_t^{*j} from $\hat{u}$ with replacement for $t = 1, \ldots, T$. Use these errors and $\hat{\alpha}$ to solve model 1.1 dynamically for $t = 1, \ldots, T$. Treat the solution values as actual values and estimate α by the consistent estimator (2SLS, 3SLS, or whatever). Let $\hat{\alpha}^{*j}$ denote this estimate. Discard the solution values; they are not used again.

2. Draw u_t^{*j} from $\hat{u}$ with replacement for $t = s, \ldots, S$.[9] Use these errors and $\hat{\alpha}^{*j}$ to solve model 1.1 dynamically for $t = s, \ldots, S$. Record the solution value of each endogenous variable for each period. This simulation and the next one use the actual (historical) values of the variables prior to period s, not the values used in computing $\hat{\alpha}^{*j}$.

3. Multiplier experiments can be performed. The solution from step 2 is the base path. For a multiplier experiment one or more exogenous variables are changed and the model is solved again. The difference between the second solution value and the base value for a given endogenous variable and period is the model's estimated effect of the change. Record these differences.

4. Repeat steps 1, 2, and 3 for $j = 1, \ldots, J$.

5. Step 4 gives J values of each endogenous variable for each period. It also gives J values of each difference for each period if a multiplier experiment has been performed.

A distribution of J predicted values of each endogenous variable for each period is now available to examine. One can compute, for example, various measures of dispersion, which are estimates of the accuracy of the model. Probabilities of specific events happening can also be computed. If, say, one is interested in the event of two or more consecutive periods of negative growth in real output in the s through S period, one can compute the number of times this happened in the J trials. If a multiplier experiment has been performed, a distribution of J differences for each endogenous variable for each period is also available to examine. This allows the uncertainty of policy effects in the model to be examined.[10]

If the coefficient estimates are taken to be fixed, then step 1 above is skipped. The same coefficient vector ($\hat{\alpha}$) is used for all the solutions. Although in much of the stochastic simulation literature coefficient estimates have been taken to be fixed, this is not in the spirit of the bootstrap literature. From a bootstrapping perspective, the obvious

---

9. If desired, these errors can be the same errors drawn in step 1 for the s through S period. With a large enough number of trials, whether one does this or instead draws new errors makes a trivial difference. It is assumed here that new errors are drawn.

10. The use of stochastic simulation to estimate event probabilities was first discussed in Fair (1993a), where the coefficient estimates were taken to be fixed and errors were drawn from estimated distributions. Estimating the uncertainty of multiplier or policy effects in nonlinear models was first discussed in Fair (1980b), where both errors and coefficients were drawn from estimated distributions.

procedure to follow after the errors have been drawn is to first estimate the model and then examine its properties, which is what the above procedure does. For estimating event probabilities, however, one may want to take the coefficient estimates to be fixed. In this case step 1 above is skipped. If step 1 is skipped, the question being asked is: conditional on the model, including the coefficient estimates, what is the probability that the particular event will occur?

9.5   Bias Correction

Since 2SLS and 3SLS estimates are biased, it may be useful to use the bootstrap procedure to correct for bias. This is especially true for estimates of lagged dependent variable coefficients. It has been known since the work of Orcutt (1948) and Hurwicz (1950) that least squares estimates of these coefficients are biased downward even when there are no right-hand-side endogenous variables.

In the present context a bias-correction procedure using the bootstrap is as follows.

1. From step 2 in section 9.3.2 there are J values of each coefficient available. Compute the mean value for each coefficient, and let $\bar{\alpha}$ denote the vector of the mean values. Let $\gamma = \bar{\alpha} - \hat{\alpha}$, the estimated bias. Compute the coefficient vector $\hat{\alpha} - \gamma$ and use the coefficients in this vector to adjust the constant term in each equation so that the mean of the error terms is zero. Let $\tilde{\alpha}$ denote $\hat{\alpha} - \gamma$ except for the constant terms, which are as adjusted. $\tilde{\alpha}$ is then taken to be the unbiased estimate of α. Let θ denote the vector of estimated biases: $\theta = \hat{\alpha} - \tilde{\alpha}$.

2. Using $\tilde{\alpha}$ and the actual data, compute the errors. Denote the error vector as $\tilde{u}$. ($\tilde{u}$ is centered at zero because of the constant term adjustment in step 1.)

3. The steps in section 9.4 can now be performed, where $\tilde{\alpha}$ replaces $\hat{\alpha}$ and $\tilde{u}$ replaces $\hat{u}$. The only difference is that after the coefficient vector is estimated by 2SLS, 3SLS, or whatever, it has θ subtracted from it to correct for bias. In other words, subtract θ from $\hat{\alpha}^{*j}$ on each trial.[11]

The example in section 9.6 examines the sensitivity of some of the results to the bias correction.

9.6   An Example Using the US Model

In this section the overall bootstrap procedure is applied to the US model, where the estimation period is 1954:1–2002:3 and the estimation method is 2SLS.

---

11. One could for each trial do a bootstrap to estimate the bias—a bootstrap within a bootstrap. The base coefficients would be $\hat{\alpha}^{*j}$ and the base data would be the generated data on trial j. This is expensive, and an approximation is simply to use θ on each trial. This is the procedure used by Kilian (1998) in estimating confidence intervals for impulse responses in VAR models. Kilian (1998) also does, when necessary, a stationary correction to the bias correction to avoid pushing stationary impulse response estimates into the nonstationary region. This type of adjustment is not pursued here.

The calculations were run in one large batch job. The main steps were:

1. Estimate the 29 equations[12] by 2SLS for 1954:1–2002:3. Compute standard errors of the coefficient estimates, and perform the Andrews-Ploberger (1994) (AP) test on selected equations. Using the 2SLS estimates and zero values for the errors, solve the model dynamically for 2000:4–2002:3 (the last eight quarters of the overall period) and perform a multiplier experiment for this period. Using the actual data and the 2SLS estimates, compute the 29-dimensional error vectors for 1954:1–2002:3 (195 vectors).

2. Do the following 2,000 times: (1) draw with replacement 195 error vectors from the residual vectors for 1954:1–2002:3; (2) using the drawn errors and the 2SLS estimates from step 1, solve the model dynamically for 1954:1–2002:3 to get new data; (3) using the new data, estimate the model by 2SLS, compute t-statistics for the coefficient estimates, and perform the AP tests; (4) reset the data prior to 2000:4 to the actual data; (5) draw with replacement eight error vectors from the residual vectors for 2000:4–2002:3; (6) using the new 2SLS estimates and the drawn errors, solve the model dynamically for 2000:4–2002:3 and perform the multiplier experiment for this period.

3. Step 2 gives for each equation 2,000 values of each coefficient estimate, t-statistic, and AP statistic. It also gives 2,000 predicted values of each endogenous variable for each quarter within 2000:4–2002:3 and 2,000 differences for each endogenous variable and each quarter from the multiplier experiment. These values can be analyzed as desired. Some examples are given below. Steps 4–6 that follow are the bias-correction calculations.

4. From the 2,000 values for each coefficient, compute the mean and then subtract the mean from twice the 2SLS coefficient estimate from step 1. Use these values to adjust the constant term in each equation so that the mean of the error terms is zero. Using these coefficients (including the adjusted constant terms), record the differences between the 2SLS coefficient estimates from step 1 and these coefficients. Call the vector of these values the "bias-correction vector." Using the new coefficients and zero values for the errors, solve the model dynamically for 2000:4–2002:3 and perform the multiplier experiment for this period. Using the actual data and the new coefficients, compute the 29-dimensional error vectors for 1954:1–2002:3 (195 vectors).

5. Do the following 2,000 times: (1) draw with replacement 195 error vectors from the residual vectors from step 4 for 1954:1–2002:3; (2) using the drawn errors and the coefficients from step 4, solve the model dynamically for 1954:1–2002:3 to get new data; (3) using the new data, estimate the model by 2SLS and adjust the estimates for bias using the bias-correction vector from step 4; (4) reset the data prior to 2000:4 to the actual data; (5) draw with replacement eight error vectors from the residual

---

12. Remember from section 9.3 that equation 9 is dropped from the model for the work in this chapter.

vectors from step 4 for 2000:4–2002:3; (6) using the new coefficient estimates and the drawn errors, solve the model dynamically for 2000:4–2002:3 and perform the multiplier experiment for this period.

6. Step 5 gives 2,000 predicted values of each endogenous variable for each quarter within 2000:4–2002:3 and 2,000 differences for each endogenous variable and each quarter from the multiplier experiment.

The same sequence of random numbers was used for the regular calculations (steps 1–3) as was used for the bias-correction calculations (steps 4–6). This lessens stochastic simulation error in comparisons between the two sets of results. If the model failed to solve for a given trial (either for the 1954:1–2002:3 period or the 2000:4–2002:3 period), the trial was skipped. No failures occurred for the regular calculations, but there were 5 failures out of the 2,000 trials for the bias-correction calculations. Each trial takes about one second on a 1.7 GHz PC using the Fair-Parke (1995) program.

Table 9.2 presents some results from step 2 for the coefficient estimates. Results for 12 coefficients from 5 equations are presented. The 5 equations are the three consumption equations 1–3, the price equation 5, and the interest rate rule 30. The coefficients are for the lagged dependent variable in each equation, for income in each consumption equation, for the price of imports and the unemployment rate in the price equation, and for inflation and the unemployment rate in the interest rate rule. These are some of the main coefficients in the model. The first three columns show the 2SLS estimate, the mean from the 2,000 trials, and the ratio of the two. As expected, the mean is smaller than the 2SLS estimate for all the lagged dependent variable coefficients: the 2SLS estimates of these coefficients are biased downward. The smallest ratio is 0.966, a bias of 3.4 percent.

Column 4 gives the asymptotic confidence intervals; column 5 gives the confidence intervals using the equal-tailed percentile-t interval; and column 6 gives the symmetric percentile-t interval using the absolute values of the t-statistics. These columns show that the asymptotic intervals tend to be narrower than the bootstrap intervals. In 19 of the 24 cases the left value for the asymptotic interval is larger than the left value for the bootstrap interval, and in 19 of the 24 cases the right value for the asymptotic interval is smaller than the right value for the bootstrap interval. The asymptotic intervals will thus tend to reject more often than the bootstrap intervals. It was seen in section 9.3.3 that the asymptotic interval rejects too often.

Table 9.3 presents results for the AP test for five equations: the three consumption equations, the residential investment equation, and the price equation.[13] The overall sample period is 1954:1–2002:3, and the period for a possible break was taken to be 1970:1–1979:4. These are the same periods as were used in Chapter 2 for the results in Table A.4 in Appendix A. Table 9.3 gives for each equation the computed AP value,

---

13. The test was not performed for the interest rate rule because the equation is already estimated under the assumption of a change in Fed behavior in the 1979:4–1982:3 period.

Table 9.2
Confidence Intervals for Selected Coefficients

	(1) $\hat{\beta}$	(2) $\bar{\beta}$	(3) (2)/(1)	(4) $\hat{\beta} - 1.96\hat{\sigma}$ $\hat{\beta} + 1.96\hat{\sigma}$	(5) $\hat{\beta} - t^*_{.975}\hat{\sigma}$ $\hat{\beta} - t^*_{.025}\hat{\sigma}$	(6) $\hat{\beta} - |t^*|_{.950}\hat{\sigma}$ $\hat{\beta} + |t^*|_{.950}\hat{\sigma}$
Equation 1: Consumption of services (CS)						
ldv	0.7873	0.7609	0.966	0.7215	0.7449	0.7031
				0.8531	0.8827	0.8716
income	0.1058	0.1163	1.099	0.0613	0.0458	0.0516
				0.1504	0.1415	0.1601
Equation 2: Consumption of nondurables (CN)						
ldv	0.7823	0.7565	0.967	0.7219	0.7442	0.7026
				0.8427	0.8718	0.8621
income	0.0973	0.1134	1.165	0.0575	0.0393	0.0461
				0.1372	0.1241	0.1486
Equation 3: Consumption of durables (CD)						
ldv	0.3294	0.3720	1.129	0.2226	0.1755	0.1913
				0.4362	0.3979	0.4675
income	0.1077	0.1218	1.131	0.0701	0.0532	0.0591
				0.1453	0.1291	0.1564
Equation 10: Price deflator for the firm sector (PF)						
ldv	0.8806	0.8715	0.990	0.8487	0.8580	0.8426
				0.9125	0.9246	0.9186
PIM	0.0480	0.0477	0.994	0.0440	0.0442	0.0438
				0.0520	0.0525	0.0522
UR	−0.1780	−0.1787	1.004	−0.2238	−0.2239	−0.2266
				−0.1322	−0.1280	−0.1293
Equation 30: Three-month Treasury bill rate (RS)						
ldv	0.9092	0.9026	0.993	0.8834	0.8870	0.8812
				0.9349	0.9398	0.9371
inflation	0.0803	0.0848	1.057	0.0549	0.0520	0.0538
				0.1056	0.1023	0.1067
$100 \cdot UR$	−0.1128	−0.1123	0.995	−0.1699	−0.1716	−0.1713
				−0.0558	−0.0545	−0.0543

Notes:
- $\hat{\beta}$ = 2SLS estimate; $\hat{\sigma}$ = estimated asymptotic standard error of $\hat{\beta}$.
- $\bar{\beta}$ = mean of the values of $\hat{\beta}^{*j}$, where $\hat{\beta}^{*j}$ is the estimate of β on the jth trial.
- t^*_r = value below which r percent of the values of t^{*j} lie, where $t^{*j} = (\hat{\beta}^{*j} - \hat{\beta})/\hat{\sigma}^{*j}$, where $\hat{\sigma}^{*j}$ is the estimated asymptotic standard error of $\hat{\beta}^{*j}$.
- $|t^*|_r$ = value below which r percent of the values of $|t^{*j}|$ lie.
- ldv: lagged dependent variable.
- *PIM* = price of imports; *UR* = unemployment rate.

Table 9.3
Results for the AP Tests

Equation		No. of coeffs.	AP	Bootstrap			Asymptotic		
				1%	5%	10%	1%	5%	10%
1	CS	9	21.18	17.47	13.84	12.15	11.16	8.96	7.77
2	CN	9	14.67	14.50	12.16	10.64	11.16	8.96	7.77
3	CD	9	12.76	16.48	12.76	11.23	11.16	8.96	7.77
4	IHH	7	7.17	13.25	10.62	9.35	9.50	7.31	6.28
10	PF	6	12.77	10.72	8.07	6.85	8.70	6.51	5.58

Notes:
• Sample period: 1954:1–2002:3.
• Period for possible break: 1970:1–1979:4.
• Value of $\lambda = 2.29$.
• Asymptotic values from Andrews and Ploberger (1994), table I.
• *CS* = consumption of services; *CN* = consumption of nondurables; *CD* = consumption of durables; *IHH* = residential investment; *PF* = price deflator for the firm sector.

the bootstrap confidence values, and the asymptotic confidence values. The asymptotic confidence values are taken from Table 1 in Andrews and Ploberger (1994). The value of λ in the AP notation for the present results is 2.29. The bootstrap confidence values for an equation are computed using the 2,000 values of the AP statistic. The 5 percent value, for example, is the value above which 100 of the AP values lie.

There is a clear pattern in Table 9.3, which is that the asymptotic confidence values are too low. They lead to rejection of the null hypothesis of stability too often. Relying on the asymptotic values for the AP test thus appears to be too harsh.

Table 9.4 presents results for the simulations for 2000:4–2002:3. Results for four variables are presented: the log of real GDP, the log of the GDP price deflator, the unemployment rate, and the three-month Treasury bill rate. Four sets of results are presented: with and without coefficient uncertainty and with and without bias correction.[14] Consider the first set of results (upper left corner) in Table 9.4. The first column gives the deterministic prediction (based on setting the error terms to zero and solving once), and the second gives the median value of the 2,000 predictions. These two values are close to each other, which means there is little bias in the deterministic prediction. The third column gives the difference between the median predicted value and the predicted value below which 15.87 percent of the values lie, and the fourth column gives the difference between the predicted value above which 15.87 percent of the values lie and the

---

14. The results without coefficient uncertainty were obtained in a separate batch job. This batch job differed from the one outlined at the beginning of this section in that in part (6) of step 2 the 2SLS estimates from step 1 are used, not the new 2SLS estimates. Also, in part (6) of step 5 the coefficients from step 4 are used, not the new coefficient estimates. For this job there were no solution failures for the regular calculations and three failures for the bias-correction calculations.

Table 9.4
Simulation Results for 2000:4–2002:3

Variables	h	$\hat{Y}$	$Y_{.5}$	left	right	$Y_{.5}$	left	right
			Coefficient Uncertainty			No Coefficient Uncertainty		
			No bias correction					
log *GDPR*	1	7.746	7.745	0.562	0.569	7.746	0.506	0.486
	4	7.748	7.746	1.423	1.434	7.748	1.248	1.240
	8	7.778	7.774	1.719	1.712	7.777	1.445	1.522
log $100 \cdot GDPD$	1	4.681	4.681	0.275	0.322	4.681	0.277	0.291
	4	4.700	4.700	0.591	0.621	4.700	0.513	0.589
	8	4.718	4.717	0.886	0.931	4.717	0.734	0.786
$100 \cdot UR$	1	4.146	4.152	0.365	0.344	4.167	0.363	0.369
	4	4.445	4.488	0.745	0.757	4.491	0.687	0.651
	8	4.642	4.748	0.863	0.956	4.683	0.819	0.821
RS	1	5.970	5.974	0.545	0.538	5.987	0.584	0.485
	4	5.155	5.068	1.196	1.200	5.102	1.112	1.162
	8	5.002	4.829	1.428	1.455	4.969	1.327	1.359
			Bias correction					
log *GDPR*	1	7.746	7.746	0.539	0.571	7.746	0.516	0.515
	4	7.750	7.750	1.542	1.512	7.750	1.283	1.366
	8	7.781	7.782	2.020	2.105	7.781	1.658	1.709
log $100 \cdot GDPD$	1	4.681	4.681	0.270	0.324	4.681	0.281	0.303
	4	4.699	4.699	0.609	0.630	4.699	0.513	0.585
	8	4.718	4.717	0.972	0.986	4.717	0.742	0.804
$100 \cdot UR$	1	4.173	4.224	0.384	0.358	4.195	0.347	0.346
	4	4.482	4.600	0.858	0.815	4.540	0.717	0.667
	8	4.602	4.774	1.122	1.100	4.664	0.910	0.885
RS	1	5.942	5.905	0.538	0.551	5.948	0.538	0.503
	4	5.162	5.060	1.228	1.298	5.114	1.125	1.181
	8	5.086	4.997	1.628	1.567	5.077	1.425	1.395

Notes:
- h = number of quarters ahead.
- $\hat{Y}$ = predicted value from deterministic simulation.
- Y_r = value below which r percent of the values of Y^j lie, where Y^j is the predicted value on the jth trial.
- left = $Y_{.5} - Y_{.1587}$, right = $Y_{.8413} - Y_{.5}$: units are percentage points.
- *GDPR* = real GDP; *GDPD* − GDP deflator; *UR* − unemployment rate; *RS* = three month Treasury bill rate.

Table 9.5
Multiplier Results for 2000:4–2002:3

	h	$\hat{d}$	$d_{.5}$	left	right	$\hat{d}$	$d_{.5}$	left	right
Variables		**No bias correction**				**Bias correction**			
log *GDPR*	1	1.010	1.035	0.069	0.081	0.984	0.979	0.065	0.078
	4	1.571	1.613	0.075	0.088	1.530	1.530	0.067	0.078
	8	1.361	1.394	0.080	0.088	1.325	1.325	0.079	0.083
log 100 · *GDPD*	1	0.036	0.034	0.008	0.009	0.039	0.039	0.008	0.008
	4	0.282	0.279	0.045	0.048	0.284	0.279	0.044	0.046
	8	0.569	0.578	0.078	0.081	0.558	0.514	0.067	0.075
100 · *UR*	1	−0.280	−0.279	0.037	0.037	−0.281	−0.278	0.039	0.035
	4	−0.747	−0.753	0.072	0.063	−0.742	−0.742	0.074	0.061
	8	−0.560	−0.587	0.072	0.076	−0.536	−0.546	0.074	0.079
RS	1	0.258	0.261	0.046	0.054	0.255	0.251	0.044	0.052
	4	0.753	0.759	0.108	0.109	0.750	0.747	0.106	0.105
	8	0.678	0.664	0.113	0.117	0.647	0.650	0.116	0.124

Notes:
- h = number of quarters ahead.
- $\hat{Y}^a$ = predicted value from deterministic simulation, no policy change.
- $\hat{Y}^b$ = predicted value from deterministic simulation, policy change.
- $\hat{d} = \hat{Y}^b - \hat{Y}^a$.
- Y^{aj} = predicted value on the jth trial, no policy change.
- Y^{bj} = predicted value on the jth trial, policy change.
- $d^j = Y^{bj} - Y^{aj}$.
- d_r = value below which r percent of the values of d^j lie.
- left = $d_{.5} - d_{.1587}$, right = $d_{.8413} - d_{.5}$: units are percentage points.
- *GDPR* = real GDP; *GDPD* = GDP deflator; *UR* = unemployment rate; *RS* = three-month Treasury bill rate.

median value. For a normal distribution these two differences are the same and equal one standard error. Computing these differences is one possible way of measuring predictive uncertainty in the model. The same differences are presented for the other three sets of results in Table 9.4.

Three conclusions can be drawn from the results in Table 9.4. First, the left and right differences are fairly close to each other. Second, the differences with no coefficient uncertainty are only slightly smaller than those with coefficient uncertainty, and so most of the predictive uncertainty is due to the additive errors. Third, the bias-correction results are fairly similar to the non–bias-correction ones, which suggests that bias is not a major problem in the model. In most cases the uncertainty estimates are larger for the bias-correction results.

Table 9.5 presents results for the multiplier experiment. The experiment was an increase in real government purchases of goods of 1 percent of real GDP for 2000:4–2002:3. The format of Table 9.5 is similar to that of Table 9.4, where the values are multipliers[15] rather than predicted values. The first column gives the multiplier computed from deterministic simulations, and the second gives the median value of the 2,000 multipliers. As in Table 9.3, these two values are close to each other. The third column gives the difference between the median multiplier and the multiplier below which 15.87 percent of the values lie, and the fourth column gives the difference between the multiplier above which 15.87 percent of the values lie and the median multiplier. These two columns are measures of the uncertainty of the government spending effect in the model.

Three conclusions can be drawn from the results in Table 9.5. First, the left and right differences are fairly close to each other. Second, the differences are fairly small relative to the size of the multipliers, and so the estimated policy uncertainty is fairly small for a government spending change. Third, the bias-correction results are similar to the non–bias-correction ones, which again suggests that bias is not a major problem in the model.

9.7 Conclusion

This chapter has outlined a bootstrapping approach to the estimation and analysis of dynamic, nonlinear, simultaneous equations models. It draws on the bootstrapping literature initiated by Efron (1979) and the stochastic simulation literature initiated by Adelman and Adelman (1959). The procedure in section 9.4 has not been used before for these models. The procedure is distribution free, and it allows a wide range of questions to be considered, including estimation, prediction, and policy analysis.

The results in section 9.6 are suggestive of the usefulness of the bootstrapping procedure for models like model 1.1. Computations like those in Table 9.3 can be done for many different statistics. Computations like those in Table 9.4 can be used to compare different models, where various measures of dispersion can be considered. These measures account for uncertainty from both the additive error terms and the coefficient estimates, which puts models on an equal footing if they have similar sets of exogenous variables. Computations like those in Table 9.5 can be done for a wide variety of policy experiments. Finally, the results in Table 9.1 show that the bootstrap works well for the US model regarding coverage accuracy.

---

15. The word "multiplier" is used here to refer to the difference between the predicted value of a variable after the policy change and the predicted value of the variable before the change. This difference is not, strictly speaking, a multiplier, because it is not divided by the government spending change.

10

Certainty Equivalence

10.1   Introduction

In section 1.7 a procedure for solving optimal control problems for models like model 1.1 was outlined. This method is based on the assumption of certainty equivalence (CE), which is strictly valid only for a linear model and a quadratic objective function. The advantage of using CE is that if the error terms are set to their expected values (usually zero), the computational work is simply to solve an unconstrained non-linear optimization problem, and there are many algorithms available for doing this. This chapter examines in specific cases how much is lost when using CE for nonlinear models. The model used is the US model.

The results are quite encouraging regarding the CE assumption. They show that little accuracy is lost using the CE assumption when solving optimal control problems.

10.2   Analytic Results

It is difficult to find in the literature analytic comparisons of truly optimal and CE solutions. One example is in Binder, Pesaran, and Samiei (2000), who examine the finite horizon life cycle model of consumption under uncertainty. They consider the simple case of a negative exponential utility function, a constant rate of interest, and labor income following an arithmetic random walk. In this case it is possible to compute both the truly optimal and the CE solutions analytically.

Using these authors' solution code,[1] I computed for different horizons both the truly optimal and the certainty equivalence solutions. These computations are based on the following values: interest rate = .04; discount factor = .98; negative exponential utility parameter = .01; initial and terminal values of wealth = 500; initial value of income = 200; standard deviation of random walk error = 5.

---

1. I am indebted to Michael Binder for providing me with the code.

Let c_1^* denote the truly optimal first-period value of consumption, and let c_1^{**} denote the value computed under the assumption of certainty equivalence. For a life cycle horizon of 12 years, c_1^* was 0.30 percent below c_1^{**}. For 24 years it was 0.60 percent below; for 36 years it was 0.87 percent below; and for 48 years it was 1.09 percent below. Although these differences seem modest, it is not clear how much they can be generalized, given the specialized nature of the model. This chapter provides results in a more general framework.

10.3 Relaxing the CE Assumption

Recall from section 1.7 that the control problem is to maximize the expected value of W with respect to the $S - s + 1$ control values, subject to the model 1.1. The equation for W is repeated here:

$$W = \sum_{t=s}^{S} g_t(y_t, x_t) \tag{10.1}$$

The vector of control variables is denoted z_t, where z_t is a subset of x_t, and z is the vector of all the control values: $z = (z_s, \ldots, z_S)$. The problem under CE is to choose z to maximize W subject to model 1.1 with the error terms for $t = s, \ldots, S$ set to zero. For each value of z a value of W can be computed, which is all an optimization algorithm like DFP needs.

If the model is nonlinear or the function g_t is not quadratic, the computed value of W for a given value of z and zero error terms is not equal to the expected value. The optimum, therefore, does not correspond to the expected value of W being maximized other than in the linear/quadratic case.

It is possible, however, to compute the expected value of W for a given value of z using stochastic simulation. For a given value of z one can compute, say, J values of W, where each value is based on a draw of the error terms for periods s through S. An estimate of the expected value of W is then the average of the J values.

As in the last chapter, let the model be 1.1, let $\hat{\alpha}$ denote the vector of coefficient estimates, and let $\hat{u}$ denote the vector of estimated residuals. For the purposes of this chapter $\hat{\alpha}$ is taken to be fixed. In other words, the maximization is conditional on the model *and* on the coefficient estimates. The steps for maximizing the expected value of W are as follows:

1. Begin with an optimization algorithm like DFP that requires for a given value of z a value of the objective function.

2. For a given trial j, draw u_t^{*j} from $\hat{u}$ with replacement for $t = s, \ldots, S$. For the given value of z from the optimization algorithm, use these errors and $\hat{\alpha}$ to solve model 1.1 dynamically for $t = s, \ldots, S$ and compute the value of W. Let W^j denote the computed value of W on trial j.

3. Repeat step 2 for $j = 1, \ldots, J$.

4. From the J values of W^j, compute the mean: $\bar{W} = \frac{1}{J} \sum_{j=1}^{J} W^j$. Feed back to the optimization algorithm $\bar{W}$ as the value of the objective function for the given value of z. Let the optimization algorithm then find the value of z that minimizes $\bar{W}$. This solution will be called the "truly optimal" solution.

This means that the model is solved J times for periods s through S for each evaluation of the objective function (that is, each value of $\bar{W}$). In the CE case there is only one solution—the solution using zero errors.

In practice, after the solution is found, z_s^* would be implemented. Then after period s passes and the values for period s are known, the whole process would be repeated beginning in period $s + 1$. The main interest for comparison purposes is thus to compare z_s^* to the optimum value that is computed using CE, denoted, say, z_s^{**}. It is not necessary to compare solution values beyond s because these are never implemented.

10.4 Results Using the US Model

10.4.1 The Loss Function

Consider the loss function (W now measures loss rather than gain)

$$W = \sum_{t=s}^{S}[(Y_t - Y_t^*)/Y_t^*]^2 + (\dot{PF}_t - \dot{PF}_t^*)^2, \tag{10.2}$$

where Y is output (variable Y in the US model) and $\dot{PF}$ is the rate of inflation (percentage change at an annual rate in variable PF in the US model). The superscript $*$ denotes the actual (historical) value of the variable. Consider the case in which the estimated residuals are added to the equations and taken to be exogenous. This means that when the model is solved using the actual values of the exogenous variables, a perfect tracking solution results—the predicted values are just the actual values. For the rest of this chapter it will be assumed that the estimated residuals have been added to the equations and taken to be exogenous. If in this case W in equation 10.2 is minimized using CE for some given set of control variables, the optimal z values are just the actual z values. The optimal value of W is zero, which occurs when the control values equal the actual values.

In the non-CE case steps 2 and 3 in the previous section can be used to compute the expected value of W, where in the present setup the drawn errors are added to the equations with the estimated residuals already added. For any given value of z, $\bar{W}$ is, of course, not zero because Y and PF are stochastic. The optimization algorithm can be used to find the value of z that minimizes $\bar{W}$.

The advantage of this setup is that one can compare the CE and non-CE cases by simply comparing the "truly optimal" control value to the actual value, since the actual value is the solution value in the CE case. One thus needs to compute only the truly optimal value.

10.4.2 Results

As noted above, the US model is used for the present results. The control period is 1994:1–1998:4, which is 20 quarters. The DFP algorithm was used, and the number of trials, J, per function evaluation was taken to be 1,000. Two experiments were performed, one using COG, federal government purchases of goods, as the control variable, and one using RS, the three-month Treasury bill rate, as the control variable. The estimated residuals from which the draws were made were computed using coefficient estimates obtained for the 1954:1–2002:3 period (195 observations). There were thus 195 vectors of estimated residuals to draw from.

For the first experiment the optimal value of COG for the first quarter was 59.1879, which compares to the actual value of 59.1500. This difference of 0.06 percent is quite small, and so the truly optimal solution is quite close to the CE solution. (Remember that the actual value is the optimal value under CE.) The results for the second experiment were similar. The optimal value of RS for the first quarter was 3.2681, which compares to the actual value of 3.2500. These results thus suggest that there is little loss from using CE for models like 1.1. This is, of course, encouraging regarding computer time. Each experiment took about 6.5 hours on a 1.7 Ghz PC, whereas in the CE case the time would be about one one-thousandth of this.

The value of $\bar{W}$ at the optimum was 0.0100 for the first experiment and 0.0117 for the second. To get a sense of magnitudes, if the absolute value of $(Y - Y^*)/Y^*$ were 0.016 per quarter and the absolute value of $\dot{PF} - \dot{PF}^*$ were also 0.016 per quarter, the value of $\bar{W}$ would be 0.0102 ($= 20 \times 2 \times 0.016^2$). The average quarterly deviation (brought about by the stochastic simulation) is thus fairly large—on the order of 1.6 percent. What the present results show is that even though this deviation is fairly large, little is lost by ignoring it and using CE when solving optimal control problems.

Evaluating Policy Rules

11.1 Introduction

This chapter examines various interest rate rules, as well as policies derived by solving optimal control problems, for their ability to dampen economic fluctuations caused by random shocks.[1] A tax rate rule is also considered. The MC and US models are used for the experiments. The results differ sharply from those obtained using modern-view models that were discussed in Chapter 7, where the coefficient on inflation in the nominal interest rate rule must be greater than one in order for the economy to be stable.

Section 11.2 discusses a simple experiment in which the interest rate rule of the Fed (equation 30) is dropped from the model and RS is decreased by one percentage point. It will be seen that although there are substantial real output effects from this change, the effects are much smaller than those in the FRB/US model,[2] which is a modern-view model.

Section 11.3 examines the stabilization features of four interest rate rules for the United States. The first is simply the estimated rule, equation 30, which has an estimated long-run coefficient on inflation of approximately one. The other three rules are modifications of the estimated rule, with imposed long-run coefficients on inflation of 0.0, 1.5, and 2.5 respectively. It will be seen that as the inflation coefficient increases there is a reduction in price variability at a cost of an increase in interest rate variability. Even the rule with a zero inflation coefficient is stabilizing, which is contrary to what would be obtained using modern-view models.

Section 11.4 then computes optimal rules for particular loss functions. These solutions require a combination of stochastic simulation and solving deterministic optimal control problems, and this is the first time that such solutions have been obtained for a large-scale model. It will be seen that the optimal control results are similar to those ob-

---

1. The results in this chapter are the same as those in Fair (2004b).
2. Federal Reserve Board (2000).

tained using the estimated rule mentioned above for a loss function with a much higher weight on inflation than on output.

Another feature of the results in Sections 11.3 and 11.4 is that considerable variance of the endogenous variables is left, even using the best interest rate rule. Section 11.5 then adds a fiscal policy rule—a tax rate rule—to see how much help it can be to monetary policy in trying to stabilize the economy. The results show that the tax rate rule provides some help. This is also the first time that such a rule has been analyzed using a large-scale model.

11.2 The Effects of a Decrease in *RS*

It will first be useful to review the effects of a change in the U.S. short-term interest rate, *RS*, in the MC model. To examine these effects, the following experiment was run. The period used is 1994:1–1998:4, 20 quarters. As in the experiments in Chapters 6–8, the first step is to add the estimated residuals to the stochastic equations and take them to be exogenous. This means that when the model is solved using the actual values of all the exogenous variables, a perfect tracking solution results. The base path for the experiment is thus just the historical path. Then the estimated interest rate rule for the Fed, equation 30, was dropped from the model, and *RS* was decreased by one percentage point from its historical value for each quarter. The model was then solved. The difference between the predicted value of each variable and each period from this solution and its base (actual) value is the estimated effect of the interest rate change.

Selected results from this experiment are presented in Table 11.1. Row 3 shows that real output, *Y*, increases: the nominal interest rate decrease is expansionary. The peak response is 0.55 percent after 12 quarters. Row 1 shows the exogenous fall in *RS* of one percentage point, and row 2 shows the response of the long-term bond rate, *RB*, to this change. After 12 quarters the bond rate has fallen 0.79 percentage points. This reflects the properties of the estimated term structure equation 22, where *RB* responds to current and past values of *RS*. The unemployment rate is lower (row 4), and the price level is higher (row 5). The peak unemployment response is -0.23 percentage points after 8 quarters.

The change in nominal after-tax corporate profits (row 6) is higher because of the higher level of real output and higher price level. The nominal value of household capital gains, *CG*, is larger because of the lower bond rate and higher value of profits (equation 25). An increase in *CG* is an increase in nominal household wealth, and row 8 shows that real wealth, *AA*, also increases initially. By quarter 16, however, real wealth is slightly below the base value. This means that by quarter 16 the negative effect on real wealth from the higher price level has offset the positive effect from the higher nominal wealth.

Rows 9 and 10 show that although nominal disposal personal income, *YD*, increases, real disposal personal income, *YD/PH*, decreases. An important feature of the model is that when interest rates fall, interest payments of the firm and government sectors fall, and this in turn lowers interest income of the household sector. A decrease in household

Table 11.1

Effects of a Decrease in *RS*

	Variable	Changes from Base Values (quarters ahead)							
		1	2	3	4	8	12	16	20
1	Bill rate (RS)	−1.00	−1.00	−1.00	−1.00	−1.00	−1.00	−1.00	−1.00
2	Bond rate (RB)	−0.31	−0.34	−0.41	−0.48	−0.67	−0.79	−0.87	−0.92
3	Real output (Y)	0.05	0.15	0.25	0.33	0.52	0.55	0.50	0.45
4	Unemployment rate ($100 \cdot UR$)	−0.01	−0.05	−0.09	−0.13	−0.23	−0.23	−0.18	−0.13
5	Price deflator (PF)	0.01	0.04	0.07	0.11	0.34	0.59	0.82	1.04
6	Change in profits ($\Delta\Pi$)	0.4	0.7	0.6	0.5	0.1	0.2	0.1	0.3
7	Capital gains (CG)	89.8	12.0	23.4	20.9	14.7	14.1	10.5	27.6
8	Real wealth (AA)	0.42	0.45	0.50	0.55	0.48	0.27	−0.03	−0.33
9	DPI (YD)	0.01	0.04	0.09	0.14	0.31	0.40	0.45	0.49
10	Real DPI (YD/PH)	−0.03	−0.04	−0.03	−0.03	−0.11	−0.28	−0.51	−0.71
11	Service consumption (CS)	0.10	0.18	0.24	0.30	0.40	0.38	0.29	0.18
12	Nondurable consumption (CN)	0.03	0.11	0.19	0.27	0.47	0.51	0.44	0.31
13	Durable consumption (CD)	0.08	0.22	0.35	0.46	0.66	0.49	0.08	−0.35
14	Residential inv. (IHH)	−0.09	0.54	0.89	1.02	1.50	1.34	0.89	0.33
15	Nonresidential fixed inv. (IKF)	0.09	0.30	0.63	0.96	2.15	2.59	2.60	2.37
16	JA bill rate (RS_{JA})	−0.16	−0.28	−0.38	−0.46	−0.61	−0.63	−0.60	−0.56
17	GE bill rate (RS_{GE})	−0.16	−0.29	−0.39	−0.45	−0.44	−0.21	−0.03	−0.03
18	JA exchange rate (E_{JA})	−0.27	−0.49	−0.66	−0.80	−1.17	−1.42	−1.67	−1.94
19	GE exchange rate (E_{GE})	−0.36	−0.63	−0.84	−1.01	−1.55	−2.22	−3.03	−3.71
20	Price of imports (PIM)	0.24	0.35	0.43	0.48	0.82	1.22	1.76	2.23
21	Real imports (IM)	0.08	0.29	0.54	0.76	1.38	1.49	1.21	0.78
22	Price of exports (PEX)	0.04	0.07	0.11	0.16	0.40	0.65	0.90	1.13
23	Real exports (EX)	0.02	0.04	0.06	0.09	0.21	0.40	0.66	0.96
24	Current account	−0.03	−0.06	−0.09	−0.12	−0.19	−0.21	−0.19	−0.13

Notes:
- All variables but 16–19 are for the United States.
- DPI = disposable personal income.
- $\Delta\Pi$ = change in nominal after-tax corporate profits. (In the notation in Table A.2, $\Pi = PIEF - TFG - TFS + PX \cdot PIEB - TBG - TBS$.)
- Current account = U.S. nominal current account as a percentage of nominal GDP. The U.S. current account is $PX \cdot EX - PIM \cdot IM$.
- Changes are in percentage points except for $\Delta\Pi$ and CG, which are in billions of dollars.
- Simulation period is 1994:1–1998:4.

interest income is a decrease in *YD*. The household sector is a large creditor, and this interest income effect is fairly large. The increase in *YD* is thus less than it otherwise would be, and row 10 shows that the net effect on real disposable personal income is negative. Another factor contributing to the fall in real disposable personal income is that there is a slight fall in the real wage (not shown). Wages lag prices in the model, and the initial response is for the nominal wage rate to increase less than the price level.

Rows 11–14 show that real household expenditures are larger except for a small initial decrease in *IHH* and a decrease in *CD* in quarter 20. The two positive effects on expenditures are the lower interest rates (a nominal interest rate is an explanatory variable in each of the household expenditure equations) and the higher real wealth. The negative effect is the fall in real disposable personal income. There is an additional negative effect on durable expenditures and residential investment over time, which is an increase in the stocks of durables and housing. Other things being equal, an increase in the stock of durables has a negative effect on durable expenditures and an increase in the stock of housing has a negative effect on residential investment. Row 15 shows that real plant and equipment investment, *IKF*, rises. This is because of the fall in the real bond rate and the rise in real output.

Rows 16–24 pertain to the effect of the rest of the world on the United States and vice versa. Rows 16 and 17 show that the Japanese and German interest rates, RS_{JA} and RS_{GE}, both decrease. These are the estimated interest rate rules for Japan and Germany at work. The US interest rate is an explanatory variable in each of these equations. This means that the Japanese and German monetary authorities are estimated to respond directly to U.S. monetary policy. Rows 18 and 19 show that the yen and the DM appreciate relative to the dollar. (Remember that a decrease in *E* is an appreciation of the currency.) This is because there is a fall in the U.S. interest rate relative to the Japanese and German interest rates and because there is an increase in the U.S. price level relative to the Japanese and German price levels (not shown).

The depreciation of the dollar leads to an increase in the U.S. import price level, *PIM* (row 20). This increase is one of the reasons for the increase in the U.S. price level (row 5), since the price of imports has a positive effect on the domestic price level in U.S. price equation 10. Even though the price of imports rises relative to the domestic price level, which other things being equal has a negative effect on import demand, the real value of imports, *IM*, rises (row 21). In this case the positive effect from the increase in real output dominates the negative relative price effect.

The rise in the overall U.S. price level leads to a rise in the U.S. export price level, *PEX* (row 22). The real value of U.S. exports, *EX*, rises (row 23), which is due to the depreciation of the dollar. (The U.S. export price level increases less than the dollar depreciates, and so U.S. export prices in other countries' currencies fall.)

Finally, the nominal U.S. current account falls (row 24). The positive effects on the current account are the increase in real exports and the increase in the price of exports. The negative effects are the increase in real imports and the increase in the price of imports. On net the negative effects win, which is primarily due to the increase in the price of imports.

The real output effects of 0.33 percent after four quarters and 0.52 percent after eight quarters are much lower than in the FRB/US model, where the effects are 0.6 percent after four quarters and 1.7 percent after eight quarters—Reifschneider, Tetlow, and Williams (1999), table 3. The effects are even larger after that, and the model eventually blows up if the short-term nominal interest rate is held below its base value.[3] As discussed in Chapter 7, this is a modern-view feature, where the model is unstable without an inflation coefficient in the interest rate rule greater than one. In this kind of model an experiment in which the interest rate rule is dropped and the interest rate lowered is explosive.

---

3. Personal correspondence with David Reifschneider.

11.3   Stabilization Effectiveness of Four Rules

11.3.1   The Four Rules

In the estimated interest rate rule for the Fed, equation 30, the coefficient on lagged money growth is 0.011, the coefficient on inflation is 0.080, and the coefficient on the lagged dependent variable is 0.909 (Table A30 within Table A.4 in Appendix A). If it is assumed that in the long run money growth equals the rate of inflation, then the long run-coefficient on inflation in equation 30 is 1.0 [$= (0.080 + 0.011)/(1 - 0.909)$]. As noted in section 11.1, the other three rules have imposed long-run coefficients of 0.0, 1.5, and 2.5, respectively. This was done for each rule by changing the coefficient for the rate of inflation in equation 30. The respective coefficients are $-0.011, 0.1255$, and 0.2165. None of the other coefficients in the estimated equation were changed for the three rules.[4] This process is similar to that followed for the studies in Taylor (1999a), where the five main rules tried had inflation coefficients varying from 1.2 to 3.0. No inflation coefficient less than 1.0 was tried in these studies because the models, which are modern-view models, are not stable in this case.

11.3.2   The Stochastic-Simulation Procedure

The four interest rate rules are examined using stochastic simulation. For all the work in this chapter the coefficient estimates have been taken to be fixed. The results are conditional on the model and on the coefficient estimates. The focus in this chapter, as in much of the literature, is on variances, not means. The aim of monetary policy is taken to smooth the effects of shocks. In order to examine the ability of monetary policy to do this, one needs an estimate of the likely shocks that monetary policy would need to smooth, and this can be done by means of stochastic simulation. Given an econometric model, shocks can be generated by drawing errors.

In Chapter 9 stochastic simulation was used only for the US model. In this chapter the entire MC model is used except for the optimal control work. There are 362 stochastic equations in the MC model, 191 quarterly and 171 annual. There is an estimated residual for each of these equations for each period. Although the equations do not all have the same estimation period, the period 1976–1998 is common to almost all equations.[5] There are thus available 23 vectors of annual estimated residuals and 92 vectors of quarterly estimated residuals. These vectors are taken as estimates of the economic shocks, and they are drawn in the manner discussed below. Since these vectors are vectors of the historical shocks, they pick up the historical correlations of the error terms. If, for example, shocks in two consumption equations are highly positively correlated, the error terms in the two equations will tend to be high together or low together.

---

4. Note 5 in this chapter explains why the constant term in the interest rate rule does not have to be changed when the inflation coefficient is changed.

5. For the few equations whose estimation periods began later than 1976, zero residuals were used for the missing observations.

The period used for the stabilization experiments is 1994:1–1998:4, five years or 20 quarters. Since the concern here is with stabilization around base paths and not with positions of the base paths themselves, it does not matter much which path is chosen for the base path. The choice here is simply to take as the base path the historical path. The base path is generated by adding the estimated residuals to the stochastic equations and taking them to be exogenous. In other words, for all the stochastic simulations in this chapter the estimated residuals are added to the model and the draws are around these residuals.

Each trial for the stochastic simulation is a dynamic deterministic simulation for 1994:1–1998:4 using a particular draw of the error terms. For each of the five years for a given trial an integer is drawn between 1 and 23 with probability 1/23 for each integer. This draw determines which of the 23 vectors of annual error terms is used for that year. The four vectors of quarterly error terms used are the four that correspond to that year. Each trial is thus based on drawing five integers, one for each of the five years. The solution of the model for this trial is an estimate of what the world economy would have been like had the particular drawn error terms actually occurred. (Remember that the drawn error terms are on top of the estimated residuals for 1994:1–1998:4, which are always added to the equations.) The number of trials taken is 1,000, so 1,000 world economic outcomes for 1994:1–1998:4 are available for analysis.

The estimated residuals are added to the interest rate rule, but no errors are drawn for it. Adding the estimated residuals means that when the model inclusive of the rule is solved with no errors for any equation drawn, a perfect tracking solution results.[6] Not drawing errors for the rule means that the Fed does not behave randomly but simply follows the rule.

Let y_{it}^{j} be the predicted value of endogenous variable i for quarter t on trial j, and let y_{it}^{*} be the base (actual) value. How best to summarize the $1,000 \times 20$ values of y_{it}^{j}? One possibility for a variability measure is to compute the variability of y_{it}^{j} around y_{it}^{*} for each t: $(1/J) \sum_{j=1}^{J} (y_{it}^{j} - y_{it}^{*})^2$, where J is the total number of trials.[7] The problem with this measure, however, is that there are 20 values per variable, which makes summary difficult. A more useful measure is the following. Let L_i^{j} be:

$$L_i^{j} = \frac{1}{T} \sum_{i=1}^{T} (y_{it}^{j} - y_{it}^{*})^2, \tag{11.1}$$

---

6. Each of the four rules has a different set of estimated residuals associated with it, because the predicted values from the rules differ due to the different inflation coefficients. This is why the constant term does not have to be changed in the rule when the inflation coefficient is changed. The estimated residuals are changed instead.

7. If y_{it}^{*} were the estimated mean of y_{it}, this measure would be the estimated variance of y_{it}. Given the J values of y_{it}^{j}, the estimated mean of y_{it} is $(1/J) \sum_{j=1}^{J} y_{it}^{j}$, and for a nonlinear model it is not the case that this mean equals y_{it}^{*} even as J goes to infinity. As an empirical matter, however, the difference in these two values is quite small for almost all macroeconometric models, and so it is approximately the case that the above measure of variability is the estimated variance.

where T is the length of the simulation period ($T = 20$ in the present case). Then the measure is

$$L_i = \frac{1}{J} \sum_{j=1}^{J} L_i^j. \tag{11.2}$$

L_i is a measure of the deviation of variable i from its base values over the whole period.[8]

11.3.3   The Results

The results for this section are presented in the first five rows in Table 11.2. The first row ("No rule") treats RS as exogenous. This means that the value of RS in a given quarter is the historic value for all the trials: RS does not respond to the shocks. Values of L_i are presented for real output, Y; the level of the private nonfarm price deflator, PF; the percentage change in PF, $\dot{PF}$; and RS. The following discussion will focus on Y, PF, and RS. The results for $\dot{PF}$ are generally similar to those for PF, although the differences in L_i across rules are larger for PF than for $\dot{PF}$. All the experiments for the MC model use the same error draws, that is, the same sequence of random numbers. This considerably lessens stochastic simulation error across experiments.

The results in Table 11.2 are easy to summarize. Consider row 1 versus row 3. L_i for Y falls from 2.75 for the no rule case to 2.31 for the estimated rule, and L_i for PF falls from 3.07 to 2.40. Both output and price variability are thus lowered considerably by the estimated rule. Now consider rows 2 through 5. As the long-run inflation coefficient increases from 0.0 to 2.5, the variability of PF falls, the variability of RS rises, and the variability of Y is little affected. The cost of lowering PF variability is thus an increase in RS variability, not an increase in Y variability. Which rule one thinks is best depends on the weights one attaches to PF and RS variability.

How do these results compare with those in the literature? Probably the largest difference concerns row 2, where the variability in row 2 is less than the variability in row 1. This shows that even the rule with a long-run inflation coefficient of zero lowers variability. In modern-view models the rule in row 2 would be destabilizing. Clarida, Galí, and Gertler (2000) have a clear discussion of this. They conclude that the rule used by the Fed in the pre-1979 period probably had an inflation coefficient less than one (p. 177), and they leave as an open question why the Fed followed a rule that was "clearly inferior" (p. 178) during this period. The results in Table 11.2 suggest that such a rule is not necessarily bad.

Results regarding the trade-off between output variability and price variability as coefficients in a rule change appear to be quite dependent on the model used. This is evident in tables 2 and 3 in Taylor (1999b), and McCallum and Nelson (1999, p. 43) point out that increasing the inflation or output coefficient in their rule leads to a trade-off in one of their models but a reduction in *both* output and price variability in another.

---

8. L_i is, of course, not an estimated variance. Aside from the fact that for a nonlinear model the mean of y_{it} is not y_{it}^*, L_i^j is an average across a number of quarters or years, and variances are not, in general, constant across time. L_i is just a summary measure of variability.

Table 11.2
Variability Estimates: Values of L_i

		Y	PF	$\dot{PF}$	RS
MC model					
1	No rule (*RS* exogenous)	2.75	3.07	2.00	0.00
2	Modified rule (0.0)	2.32	2.72	1.91	0.42
3	Estimated rule (1.0)—eq. 30	2.31	2.40	1.85	0.58
4	Modified rule (1.5)	2.32	2.27	1.82	0.73
5	Modified rule (2.5)	2.34	2.03	1.78	1.15
6	3 with tax rule	2.01	2.28	1.82	0.52
US(EX,PIM) model					
7	No rule (*RS* exogenous)	3.42	3.12	2.04	0.00
8	Estimated rule—eq. 30	2.94	2.60	1.94	0.55
9	Optimal ($\lambda_1 = 0.5$, $\lambda_2 = 0.5$)	2.54	3.17	2.05	0.96
10	Optimal ($\lambda_1 = 0.5$, $\lambda_2 = 1.5$)	2.67	2.83	1.97	0.78
11	Optimal ($\lambda_1 = 0.5$, $\lambda_2 = 2.5$)	2.79	2.59	1.91	0.75

Notes:
- Simulation period = 1994:1–1998:4.
- Number of trials = 1000.
- Modified rule (0.0) = estimated rule with long-run inflation coefficient = 0.0.
- Modified rule (1.5) = estimated rule with long-run inflation coefficient = 1.5.
- Modified rule (2.5) = estimated rule with long-run inflation coefficient = 2.5.
- Y = real output; PF = price deflator; $\dot{PF}$ = percentage change in PF; RS = three-month Treasury bill rate.

In Table 11.2 the trade-off is between price variability and interest rate variability as the inflation coefficient is increased. There is little trade-off between output and price variability. Because the trade-offs are so model specific, one must have confidence in the model used to have confidence in the trade-off results. The results in Table 11.2 convey useful information if the MC model is a good approximation of the economy.

11.4   Optimal Control

11.4.1   The US(EX,PIM) Model

The optimal control procedure discussed in this section is too costly in terms of computer time to be able to be used for the entire MC model, and for the work in this section a slightly expanded version of the US model has been used, denoted the "US(EX,PIM) model." The expansion relates to U.S. exports, *EX*, and the U.S. price of imports, *PIM*. These two variables change when *RS* changes—primarily because the value of the dollar changes—and the effects of *RS* on *EX* and *PIM* were approximated in the following way.

First, for given values of α_1 and α_2, $\log EX_t - \alpha_1 RS_t$ was regressed on the constant term, t, $\log EX_{t-1}$, $\log EX_{t-2}$, $\log EX_{t-3}$, and $\log EX_{t-4}$, and $\log PIM_t - \alpha_2 RS_t$ was regressed on the constant term, t, $\log PIM_{t-1}$, $\log PIM_{t-2}$, $\log PIM_{t-3}$, and $\log PIM_{t-4}$. Second, these two equations were added to the US model, and an experiment was run in which equation 30 was dropped and RS was decreased by one percentage point. This was done for different values of α_1 and α_2. The final values of α_1 and α_2 chosen were ones whose experimental results most closely matched the results for the same experiment using the complete MC model. The final values chosen were -0.0004 and -0.0007, respectively. Third, the experiment in the third row of Table 11.2 was run for the US model with the EX and PIM equations added and with the estimated residuals from these equations being used for the drawing of the errors. When an error for the EX equation was drawn, it was multiplied by β_1, and when an error for the PIM equation was drawn, it was multiplied by β_2. The experiment was run for different values of β_1 and β_2, and the final values chosen were ones that led to results similar to those in the third row of Table 11.2. The values were $\beta_1 = 0.4$ and $\beta_2 = 0.75$. The results using these values are in row 8 of Table 11.2. The chosen values of α_1, α_2, β_1, and β_2 were then used for the experiments in rows 9–11.

The US(EX,PIM) model is thus a version of the US model in which EX and PIM have been made endogenous with respect to their reactions to changes in RS. It is an attempt to approximate the overall MC model in this regard.

11.4.2   The Procedure

Much of the literature on examining rules has not been concerned with deriving rules by solving optimal control problems,[9] but optimal control techniques are obvious ones to use in this context. The following procedure has been applied to the US(EX,PIM) model.

The estimated residuals for the 1976:1–1998:4 period (92 quarters) were used for the draws. Each vector of quarterly residuals had a probability of 1/92 of being drawn. Not counting the estimated interest rate rule, there are 29 estimated equations in the US(EX,PIM) model plus the EX and PIM equations discussed above.

The optimal control methodology requires that a loss function be postulated for the Fed. In the loss function used here the Fed is assumed to care about output, inflation, and interest rate fluctuations. In particular, the loss for quarter t is assumed to be:

$$H_t = \lambda_1 100[(Y_t - Y_t^*)/Y_t^*]^2 + \lambda_2 100(\dot{P}F_t - \dot{P}F_t^*)^2 + \alpha(\Delta RS_t - \Delta RS_t^*)^2 \atop + 1.0/(RS_t - 0.999) + 1.0/(16.001 - RS_t), \tag{11.3}$$

where $*$ denotes a base value. λ_1 is the weight on output deviations, and λ_2 is the weight on inflation deviations. The last two terms in equation 11.3 ensure that the optimal values of RS will be between 1.0 and 16.0. The value of α was chosen by experimentation to yield an optimal solution, with a value of L_i for RS in Table 11.2 about the same as the value that results when the estimated rule is used. The value chosen was 9.0. The base values in equation 11.3 are the actual (historical) values. The base path for each variable is the actual path (since the estimated residuals have been

---

9. Exceptions are Feldstein and Stock (1993), Fair and Howrey (1996), and Rudebusch (1999).

added to the equations), and so the losses in equation 11.3 are deviations from the actual values.

Assume that the control period of interest is 1 through T, where in the present case 1 is 1994:1 and T is 1998:4. Although this is the control period of interest, in order not to have to assume that life ends in T, the control problem should be thought of as one of minimizing the expected value of $\sum_{t=1}^{T+n} H_t$, where n is chosen to be large enough to avoid unusual end-of-horizon effects near T. The overall control problem should thus be thought of as choosing values of RS that minimize the expected value of $\sum_{t=1}^{T+n} H_t$ subject to the model used.

If the model used is linear and the loss function quadratic, it is possible to derive analytically optimal feedback equations for the control variables.[10] In general, however, optimal feedback equations cannot be derived for nonlinear models or for loss functions with nonlinear constraints on the instruments, and a numerical procedure like the one outlined in section 1.7 must be used. The following procedure was used for the results in this section. It is based on a sequence of solutions of deterministic control problems, one sequence per trial, where certainty equivalence (CE) is used.

Recall what a trial for the stochastic simulation is. A trial is a set of draws of 20 vectors of error terms, one vector per quarter. Given this set, the model is solved dynamically for the 20 quarters using an interest rate rule (or no rule). This entire procedure is then repeated 100 times (the chosen number of trials), at which time the summary statistics are computed. As will now be discussed, each trial for the optimal control procedure requires that 20 deterministic control problems be solved, and so with 100 trials, 2,000 optimal control problems have to be solved.

For purposes of solving the control problems, the Fed is assumed to know the model (its structure and coefficient estimates) and the exogenous variables, both past and future. The Fed is assumed *not* to know the future values of any endogenous variable or any error draw when solving the control problems.[11] The Fed is assumed to know the error draws for the first quarter for each solution. This is consistent with the use of the above rules, where the error draws for the quarter are used when solving the model with the rule.

The procedure for solving the overall control problem is as follows.

1. Draw a vector of errors for quarter 1, and add these errors to the equations. Take the errors for quarters 2 through k to be zero (that is, no draws, but remember that the estimated residuals are always added), where k is defined shortly. Choose values of RS for quarters 1 through k that minimize $\sum_{t=1}^{k} H_t$ subject to the model as just described. This is just a deterministic optimal control problem, which can be solved, for example, by the procedure outlined in section 1.7.[12] Let RS_1^{**} denote the optimal

---

10. See, for example, Chow (1981).

11. The main exogenous variables in the US(EX,PIM) model are fiscal policy variables. Remember that since the base is the perfect tracking solution, the estimated residuals are always added to the stochastic equations and treated as exogenous. The error draws are on top of these residuals.

12. Almost all the computer time for the overall procedure in this section is spent solving these optimization problems. The total computer time taken to solve the 2,000 optimization problems was about three hours on a computer with a 1.7 GHz Pentium chip.

value of *RS* for quarter 1 that results from this solution. The value of k should be chosen to be large enough so that making it larger has a negligible effect on RS_1^{**}. (This value can be chosen ahead of time by experimentation.) RS_1^{**} is computed at the beginning of quarter 1 under the assumptions that (1) the model is known, (2) the exogenous variable values are known, and (3) the error draws for quarter 1 are known.

2. Record the solution values from the model for quarter 1 using RS_1^{**} and the error draws. These solution values are what the model estimates would have occurred in quarter 1 had the Fed chosen RS_1^{**} and had the error terms been as drawn.

3. Repeat steps 1 and 2 for the control problem beginning in quarter 2, then for the control problem beginning in quarter 3, and so on through the control problem beginning in quarter T. For an arbitrary beginning quarter s, use the solution values of all endogenous variables for quarters $s - 1$ and back, as well as the values of RS_{s-1}^{**} and back.

4. Steps 1 through 3 constitute one trial, that is, one set of T drawn vectors of errors. Do these steps again for another set of T drawn vectors. Keep doing this until the specified number of trials has been completed.

The solution values of the endogenous variables carried along for a given trial from quarter to quarter in the above procedure are estimates of what the economy would have been like had the Fed chosen $RS_1^{**}, \ldots, RS_T^{**}$ and the error terms been as drawn.[13]

By "optimal rule" in this chapter is meant the entire procedure just discussed. There is obviously no analytic rule computed, just a numerical value of RS^{**} for each period.

11.4.3   The Results

The results are presented in rows 7–11 in Table 11.2. The experiments in these rows use the same error draws, that is, the same sequence of random numbers, to lessen stochastic simulation error across experiments, although these error draws are different from those used for the experiments in rows 1–6. Rows 7 and 8 are equivalent to rows 1 and 3: no rule and estimated rule, respectively. The same pattern holds for both the MC model and the US model results, namely that the estimated rule substantially lowers the variability of both Y and *PF*.

Row 9 presents the results for the optimal solution with equal weights (that is, $\lambda_1 = 0.5$ and $\lambda_2 = 0.5$) on output and inflation in the loss function. Rows 7 and 9 show that the optimal control procedure lowered the variability of Y substantially and had

---

13. The optimal control procedure just outlined differs from the procedure used in Fair and Howrey (1996, pp. 178–179). In Fair and Howrey (1996) the Fed is assumed not to know the exogenous variable values, but instead to use estimated autoregressive equations to predict these values for the current and future quarters. Also, the estimated residuals are not added to the equations, and no stochastic simulation is done. Instead, one optimal control problem is solved, where the target values are the historical means and the solution uses for the error draws for a given quarter the estimated residuals for that quarter. The Fed is assumed not to know the error draw for the current quarter.

little effect on the variability of *PF*. This is quite different from the estimated rule (row 8). The estimated rule lowered the variability of *both Y* and *PF*, although the fall in the variability of *Y* was much less than it was for the optimal control procedure.

For rows 10 and 11 the weight on inflation in the loss function is increased. This, not surprisingly, increases the variability of *Y* and lowers the variability of *PF*. Row 11, which has a weight of 2.5 on inflation, gives similar results to those in row 8, which uses the estimated rule. In this sense the estimated rule is consistent with the Fed minimizing the loss function with weights $\lambda_1 = 0.5$ and $\lambda_2 = 2.5$ in equation 11.3.

Again, how do these results compare to those in the literature? A common result in the Taylor (1999a) volume is that simple rules perform nearly as well as optimal rules or more complicated rules. See Taylor (1999b, p. 10), Rotemberg and Woodford (1999, p. 109), Rudebusch and Svensson (1999, p. 238), and Levin, Wieland, and Williams (1999, p. 294). The results in rows 8 and 11 are consistent with this theme, where the estimated rule performs nearly as well as the optimal control procedure. The optimal control procedure in this case is one in which the Fed puts a considerably higher weight on inflation than on output in the loss function.

11.5   Adding a Tax Rate Rule

It is clear from the results in Table 11.2 that considerable overall variability is left in rows 2–5. In this section a tax rate rule is analyzed to see how much help it can be to monetary policy in stabilizing the economy. The idea is that a particular tax rate or set of rates would be automatically adjusted each quarter as a function of the state of the economy. Congress would vote on the parameters of the tax rate rule as it was voting on the general budget plan, and the tax rate or set of rates would then become an added automatic stabilizer.

Consider, for example, the federal gasoline tax rate. If the short-run demand for gasoline is fairly price inelastic, a change in the after-tax price at the pump will have only a small effect on the number of gallons purchased. In this case a change in the gasoline tax rate is like a change in after-tax income. Another possibility would be a national sales tax if such a tax existed. If the sales tax were broad enough, a change in the sales tax rate would also be like a change in after-tax income.

For the results in this section *D3G* is used as the tax rate for the tax rate rule. It is the constructed federal indirect business tax rate in the US model—see Tables A.2 and A.7. In practice a specific tax rate or rates, such as the gasoline tax rate, would have to be used, and this would be decided by the political process. In the regular version of the US model *D3G* is exogenous.

The following equation is used for the tax rate rule:

$$D3G_t = D3G_t^* + 0.125[.5((Y_{t-1} - Y_{t-1}^*)/Y_{t-1}^*) + .5((Y_{t-2} - Y_{t-2}^*)/Y_{t-2}^*)]$$
$$+ 0.125[.5(\dot{PF}_{t-1} - \dot{PF}_{t-1}^*) + .5(\dot{PF}_{t-2} - \dot{PF}_{t-2}^*)], \tag{11.4}$$

where, as before, * denotes a base value. It is not realistic to have tax rates respond contemporaneously to the economy, and so lags have been used in equation 11.4. Lags of both one and two quarters have been used to smooth tax rate changes somewhat. The rule says that the tax rate exceeds its base value as output and the inflation rate exceed their base values. Note that unlike the basic interest rate rule, equation 30, the rule 11.4 has not been estimated. It would not make sense to try to estimate such a rule, since it is clear that the government has never followed a tax rule policy.

Results using this rule along with the estimated interest rate rule are reported in row 6 in Table 11.2. (The overall MC model is used for these calculations, not the US(EX,PIM) model.) The use of the rule lowers L_i for Y from 2.31 when only the estimated interest rate rule is used to 2.01 when both rules are used. The respective numbers for *PF* are 2.40 and 2.28. The tax rate rule is thus of some help in lowering output and price variability, with a little more effect on output variability than on price variability. The variability of *RS* falls slightly when the tax rate rule is added, since there is less for monetary policy to do when fiscal policy is helping.

11.6   Conclusion

The main conclusions about monetary policy from the results in Table 11.2 are the following:

1. The estimated rule explaining Fed behavior, equation 30, substantially reduces output and price variability (row 3 versus row 1).

2. Variability is reduced even when the long-run coefficient on inflation in the interest rate rule is set to zero (row 2 versus row 1). This is contrary to what would be the case in modern-view models, where such a rule would be destabilizing.

3. Increasing the long-run coefficient on inflation in the interest rate rule lowers price variability, but it comes at a cost of increased interest rate variability (for example, row 5 versus row 3).

4. A tax rate rule is a noticeable help to monetary policy in its stabilization effort (row 6 versus row 3).

5. The optimal control procedure with $\lambda_1 = 0.5$ and $\lambda_2 = 2.5$, which means a higher weight on inflation than on output in the loss function, gives results that are similar to the use of the estimated rule (row 11 versus row 8). The fact that the estimated rule does about as well as the optimal control procedure is consistent with many results in the literature, where simple rules tend to do fairly well.

6. Even when both the estimated interest rate rule and the tax rate rule are used, the values of L_i in Table 11.2 are not close to zero (row 6). Monetary policy even with the help of a fiscal policy rule does not come close to eliminating the effects of typical historical shocks.

12

EMU Stabilization Costs

12.1 Introduction

When different countries adopt a common currency, each gives up its own monetary policy.[1] In the common-currency regime, monetary policy responds to a shock in a particular country only to the extent that the common monetary authority responds to the shock. If this response is less than the response that the country's own monetary authority would have made in the pre–common-currency regime, there are stabilization costs of moving to a common currency. This chapter uses the MC model and stochastic simulation to estimate the stabilization costs to Germany, France, Italy, and the Netherlands from having joined the European Monetary Union (EMU). Costs to the United Kingdom from joining are also estimated. Variability estimates are computed for the non-EMU and EMU regimes.[2] The results show that Germany is hurt the most in terms of stabilization costs from joining the EMU.

The question that this chapter attempts to answer is a huge one, and the results should be interpreted with considerable caution. In order to answer this question one needs (1) an estimate of how the world economy operates in the non-EMU regime, (2) an estimate of how it operates in the EMU regime, and (3) an estimate of the likely shocks to the world economy. Each of these estimates in this chapter is obviously only an approximation.

Prior to the beginning of the EMU in 1999, there was a large literature analyzing the economic consequences of a common European currency. Wyplosz (1997) provides a useful review. Much of this literature is in the Mundell (1961), McKinnon (1963), and Kenen (1969) framework and asks whether Europe meets the standards for an optimum currency area. The questions asked include how open the countries are, how correlated individual shocks are across countries, and the degree of labor mobility. There was also work examining real exchange rate variances. The smaller are these variances,

---

1. The results in this chapter are updates of those in Fair (1998).

2. For other results using stochastic simulation to examine the EMU, see Hallett, Minford, and Rastogi (1993), Masson and Symansky (1992), and Masson and Turtelboom (1997).

the smaller are the likely costs of moving to a common currency. Von Hagen and Neumann (1994) compared variances of price levels within West German regions with variances of real exchange rates between the regions and other European countries.

The MC model contains estimates of how open countries are, in that there are estimated import demand equations and estimated trade-share equations in the model. The model also contains estimates of the correlation of individual shocks across countries through the estimated residuals in the individual stochastic equations. Real exchange rates are endogenous because there are estimated equations for nominal exchange rates and individual country price levels. The MC model thus has imbedded in it estimates of a number of the features of the world economy that are needed to analyze optimum-currency-area questions. The degree of labor mobility among countries, however, is not estimated: the specification of the model is based on the assumption of no labor mobility among countries. To the extent that there is labor mobility, the present stabilization-cost estimates are likely to be too high.

A key feature of the MC model for present purposes is that there are estimated monetary-policy rules for each of the European countries prior to 1999:1. These are the estimated interest rate rules—equation 7 for a given country in the ROW model. In the EMU regime these rules for the joining European countries are replaced with one rule— one interest rate rule for the EMU. There are also estimated exchange rate equations for each of the European countries in the model—equation 9 for a given country in the ROW model. In the EMU regime these equations for the joining European countries are replaced with one equation—the exchange rate equation for the euro. Finally, there are estimated term structure equations for each of the European countries—equation 8 for a given country in the ROW model. In the EMU regime these equations for the joining European countries are replaced with one term structure equation.

To get a sense of interest rate effects in the model, it may be useful to review the discussion at the end of Chapter 2 and the experiment in Chapter 8 where the German interest rate was decreased.

12.2   The Stochastic-Simulation Procedure

The procedure used here is the same as the one used in section 11.3.2. The simulation period is the same (1994:1–1998:4), and the period for the estimated residuals is the same (1976–1998). The number of trials is 1,000, and the values of L_i are computed as in equation 11.2. Again, the coefficient estimates are taken as fixed for purposes of the stochastic simulations.

There are 16 European countries in the model, eight quarterly and eight annual. The first experiment pertains to four of these: Germany, France, Italy, and the Netherlands. For the second experiment the United Kingdom is added.

12.3   Results for the non-EMU Regime

Since the simulation period considered in this chapter is before 1999:1, the non-EMU regime is simply the actual regime. Results for this experiment are presented

Table 12.1
Values of L_i for Four Experiments

	Real Output				Price Level				Short-Term Interest Rate			
	Experiment				Experiment				Experiment			
	1	2	3	4	1	2	3	4	1	2	3	4
GE	5.09	2.29	4.53	5.56	3.76	2.08	2.73	3.02	0.00	4.27	2.19	2.26
FR	2.46	2.85	2.03	1.87	3.36	3.45	2.58	2.60	0.00	1.80	2.19	2.26
IT	8.23	7.34	7.76	7.58	18.75	15.22	14.23	13.86	0.00	6.44	2.19	2.26
NE	10.86	9.15	10.57	10.01	1.63	1.38	1.37	1.36	0.00	3.87	2.19	2.26
UK	7.10	5.86	5.74	6.20	23.32	15.91	16.57	15.46	0.00	2.61	2.65	2.26
US	2.38	2.40	2.38	2.37	1.78	2.03	2.04	2.01	0.54	0.55	0.56	0.57

Notes:
- 1 = interest rate rules for GE, FR, IT, NE, and UK dropped.
- 2 = interest rate rules for GE, FR, IT, NE, and UK used.
- 3 = EMU regime consisting of GE, FR, IT, and NE.
- 4 = EMU regime consisting of GE, FR, IT, NE, and UK.

as experiments 1 and 2 in Table 12.1. Values of L_i are presented for six countries, GE, FR, IT, NE, UK, and US, and for three variables, real GDP, Y, the GDP deflator, PY, and the short-term interest rate, RS. (For the United States, Y is real output of the firm sector and PF is the price deflator.)

Even though results for only six countries are presented in Table 12.1, the entire MC model is used for the experiments. The same draws (that is, the same sequence of random numbers) were used for each experiment in order to lessen stochastic-simulation error for the comparisons between experiments. The one difference between the experiments here and the experiments for the MC model in Table 11.2 is that for each of the six countries, drawn errors are not used for the interest rate rule, the term structure equation, or the exchange rate equation. Since moving from the current regime to the EMU regime requires changing these equations for the European countries, it seemed best for comparison purposes not to complicate matters by having to make assumptions about what errors to use in the EMU regime for these equations. The variability estimates are thus based on all types of shocks except financial ones. This difference pertains only to the six countries; for all the other countries the error draws are as in Chapter 11.[3]

For the first experiment the estimated interest rate rules for the five European countries are dropped from the model (but not the US interest rate rule), and the five short-term interest rates are taken to be exogenous. This is not meant to be a realistic case, but merely to serve as a baseline for comparison. The results are in the first column for each variable in Table 12.1. The second experiment differs from the first in that the

---

3. In Chapter 11 errors were not drawn for equation 30 for the United States, and this is true here as well. Errors were drawn for the US term structure equations 23 and 24, but in this chapter errors are not drawn for these two equations (thus treating the United States like the other five countries).

five interest rate rules are added back in. Otherwise, everything else is the same. The results are presented in the second column for each variable.

Comparing columns 1 and 2 for output shows how stabilizing the estimated interest rate rules are. For Germany L_i falls from 5.09 to 2.29, and so the German interest rate rule is quite stabilizing. L_i also falls for Italy, the Netherlands, and the United Kingdom. However, it rises for France. The estimated interest rate rule for France (see Table B7) does not have an output variable, and the inflation variable is not significant. According to the estimated rule, the Bank of France responds mostly to the German and U.S. interest rates. The rule is thus not likely to be stabilizing, which the results in Table 12.1 show is the case.

The variability for the price level also falls in Table 12.1 from column 1 to 2 for Germany, Italy, the Netherlands, and the United Kingdom, but not for France. Note for France that the variability of *RS* does not rise much from column 1 to 2, which shows that the Bank of France is not doing much in response to the shocks.

12.4   Results for the EMU Regime

The actual EMU regime began in 1999:1, and this regime is part of the MC model from 1999:1 on. For present purposes, however, an EMU regime needs to be constructed that is comparable to the non-EMU regime regarding shocks. For the results in this section the same error draws are used as were used for the results in columns 1 and 2 in Table 12.1. Given these shocks, the question is how stabilization is affected by moving to a common monetary policy.

A hypothetical EMU regime must thus be created for the 1994:1–1998:4 period. In fact two EMU regimes are considered here, one including Germany, France, Italy, and the Netherlands, and the other including these four countries plus the United Kingdom. Three changes are required to do this. Consider first the regime without the United Kingdom.

First, the interest rate rules for France, Italy, and the Netherlands were dropped, and their short-term interest rates were assumed to move one for one with the German rate. The output gap variable that is included in the estimated German rule is the German output gap, and this variable was replaced by the total output gap of the four countries. In addition, the German inflation variable was replaced by a total inflation variable for the four countries.[4] The coefficient estimates in this equation were not changed, and the U.S. interest rate, which is an explanatory variable in the equation, was retained.

---

4. For a given country k and period t, let Y_{kt} be its real output, PY_{kt} its domestic price level, and h_{kt} its exchange rate vis-à-vis the DM. Also, let h_{k95} be its exchange rate in 1995, the base year for real output. Then total nominal output for the four countries combined, denominated in DM, is $\sum_{k=1}^{4}(PY_{kt}Y_{kt})/h_{kt}$, and total real output, denominated in 1995 DM, is $\sum_{k=1}^{4} Y_{kt}/h_{k95}$. The price level for the four countries combined is the ratio of total nominal output to total real output. The total inflation variable is the percentage change in the price level for the four countries combined. Total potential output, denominated in 1995 DM, is $\sum_{k=1}^{4} YS_{kt}/h_{k95}$, where YS_{kt} is the potential output of country i for period t. The output-gap variable used is the percentage deviation of total actual output from total potential output.

The behavior of the European monetary authority is thus assumed to be the same as the historically estimated behavior of the Bundesbank, except that the response is now to the total variables for the four countries rather than just to the German variables.

Second, the term structure equations for France, Italy, and the Netherlands were dropped, and their long-term interest rates were assumed to move one for one with the German rate. The long-term German interest rate equation was retained as is. The only explanatory variables in this equation are the lagged value of the long-term rate and the current value and lagged values of the short-term rate.

Third, the exchange rate equations for France, Italy, and the Netherlands were dropped, and their exchange rates were fixed to the German rate. The German exchange rate equation has as explanatory variables the German price level relative to the U.S. price level and the German short-term interest rate relative to the U.S. short-term interest rate. This equation was used as is except that the German price level was replaced by the total price level for the four countries. (The German short-term interest rate is now, of course, the common short-term interest rate of the four countries, as discussed above.)

No other changes were made to the model. To summarize, then, in this assumed EMU regime, the two main changes are (1) the postulation of a four-country interest rate rule that responds to the four-country output gap and the four-country inflation rate and (2) the postulation of an exchange rate equation for the four-country currency that responds to the four-country price level relative to the U.S. price level and the four-country short-term interest rate relative to the U.S. short-term interest rate.

The results for this regime are presented in column 3 in Table 12.1. The output variability results are quite interesting. The big loser is Germany, where L_i rises from 2.29 to 4.53. Italy and the Netherlands are also hurt, but not by as much (from 7.34 to 7.76 for Italy and from 9.15 to 10.57 for the Netherlands). France is helped, where L_i falls from 2.85 to 2.03. Column 2 versus 1 shows that the individual interest rate rule for France is not stabilizing, and column 3 versus 2 shows that France gains by being part of a stabilizing rule. If the French by themselves are not going to stabilize, they are better off joining a group that at least in part responds to French shocks. (Does this help explain why France has generally been quite supportive of the EMU?) Germany is hurt because its individual rule is quite stabilizing, and much of this is lost when Germany joins the other three.

Regarding price variability, again Germany is hurt and France is helped. In this case Italy is also helped and there is essentially no change for the Netherlands. Interest rate variability (which is the same for all four countries) is larger for France and smaller for the others.

The United Kingdom is not much affected by the four countries joining together (column 3 versus 2). Its interest rate rule is still quite stabilizing (column 3 versus 1). For the final experiment the United Kingdom was added to the four-country regime. Everything is the same in this five-country regime except that total output now includes UK output and the total price level now includes the UK price level. The UK interest rate rule, exchange rate equation, and term structure equation are dropped.

The five-country results are presented in column 4 in Table 12.1. These results are also interesting. The United Kingdom is definitely hurt regarding output variability from joining the group. L_i rises from 5.74 to 6.20, an 8 percent increase. Germany is hurt even more, and it is now the case that L_i for Germany is larger in column 4 than in column 1, where the German rule is dropped. The other three countries are helped slightly by the United Kingdom's joining.

The effects on the United States are modest for all of the cases.

12.5 Conclusion

This chapter has used a particular methodology for examining the stabilizations costs of the EMU, and Table 12.1 provides quantitative estimates of these costs for a four-country and a five-country regime. The estimated costs are large for Germany and modest for Italy and the Netherlands. France actually benefits. The costs for the United Kingdom, if it joined, would be noticeable, but not nearly as large as they are for Germany.

These estimates in Table 12.1 are conditional, of course, on particular interest rate rules for each country. The rules used in this chapter are the estimated rules. If different rules were used, say a more stabilizing individual rule for France, different results would be obtained. In general, the more stabilizing a rule is for a given country, the larger are the stabilization costs of joining the EMU likely to be. The results also depend on the choice of the EMU rule. For the work in this chapter the German rule has been used with different output and inflation variables, but other choices are clearly possible.

Because of the preliminary nature of the results, there are a number of extensions that might be interesting to pursue in future work. One issue is whether fiscal-policy rules, like the tax rate rule in the last chapter, should be considered. If a rule like this were used by a country after joining the EMU, it would likely lower the stabilization costs of joining. At times, however, such a rule might call for a tax rate cut that would violate the fiscal-policy constraints that are imposed on countries that join the EMU. If certain tax rate cuts were not allowed, this would lessen the rule's effectiveness.

There are some possible biases in the Table 12.1 estimates that are more difficult to examine. There is, for example, no labor mobility in the model, and to the extent that there is labor mobility between countries in Europe the real stabilization costs are likely to be smaller than those in Table 12.1. It would be difficult to modify the MC model to try to account for labor mobility. In addition, if the change in regimes results in the shocks across countries being more highly correlated than they were historically, this is likely to bias the current cost estimates upward. The more highly correlated the shocks, the more the common European monetary policy rule is likely to be stabilizing for the individual countries. It would be difficult to try to estimate how the historical correlations might change.

It may also be the case that the historical shocks used for the stochastic-simulation draws are too large. The shocks are estimated residuals in the stochastic equations, and they reflect both pure random shocks and possible misspecification. However, if the shocks are too large, it is not clear how the cost estimates in Table 12.1 would be affected, since using the correct smaller shocks would lower the values of L_i for all the experiments.

Another issue to consider is whether the EMU regime increases credibility. If, for example, Italian long-term interest rates are lower after Italy joins (because Italian policy is then more credible), this could have a beneficial effect on Italian growth. Level effects of this sort are not taken into account in this study, since only stabilization costs are being estimated.

13

RE Models

13.1 Introduction

The results in Chapter 10 suggest that the loss in accuracy from using the certainty equivalence assumption to solve optimal control problems is small.[1] The CE assumption was used in Chapter 11 to solve optimal control problems of the monetary authority. The stabilization analysis in Chapter 11 required both the use of stochastic simulation and the solving of optimal control problems using CE, which allowed the stabilization effectiveness of different rules to be analyzed. This chapter shows that the analysis in Chapter 11 can also be applied to rational expectations (RE) models under the CE assumption.

Almost all the recent studies that have used RE models to analyze stabilization questions have relied on small linear models. For example, only one of the studies in Taylor (1999a)—Levin, Wieland, and Williams (1999) (LWW)—uses large-scale models, and LWW do not solve optimal control problems. They use linearizations of the Federal Reserve model and the Taylor multicountry model to compute unconditional second moments of the variables in the models. In the recent study of Clarida, Galí, and Gertler (2000) a four-equation calibrated model is used. Finan and Tetlow (1999) discuss the optimal control of large models with rational expectations, but their method is limited to linear models. The results in this chapter show that the analysis of stabilization questions need not be limited to small linear models when the models have rational expectations.

The model used for the results in this chapter is the US(EX,PIM) model discussed in section 11.4.1 with the addition of rational expectations in the bond market and where households have rational expectations with respect to future values of income. This RE version of the US(EX,PIM) model is presented in section 13.8.

This chapter is based on the assumption of known coefficients. (As in Chapters 11 and 12, $\hat{\alpha}$ is taken to be fixed.) It does not consider, for example, the possibility of

---

1. The results in this chapter are updates of those in Fair (2003a).

Table 13.1

Notation in Alphabetical Order

h	Maximum lead
I	Number of DFP iterations needed for convergence
J	Number of stochastic-simulation repetitions
k	Extra periods beyond h needed for convergence
L	Number of function evaluations needed for line searching
M	Number of entire-path computations needed for convergence
N	Number of one-period passes needed for convergence
q	Number of control variables
Q	Length of simulation period
R	Length of optimal control horizon needed for first-period convergence
S	Length of stochastic-simulation period (number of control problems solved)
T	Length of optimal control period

unknown coefficients and learning. Amman and Kendrick (1999) consider this case within the context of the linear quadratic optimization problem for models with rational expectations. It would be interesting in future work to consider the case of unknown coefficients with learning in the more general setting here.

For ease of reference, Table 13.1 lists some of the notation used in this chapter.

13.2 The RE Model

The RE model was presented as model 1.2 in section 1.4, and it is repeated here:

$$f_i(y_t, y_{t-1}, \ldots, y_{t-p}, E_{t-1}y_t, E_{t-1}y_{t+1}, \ldots, E_{t-1}y_{t+h}, x_t, \alpha_i) = u_{it}$$
$$i = 1, \ldots, n, \qquad t = 1, \ldots, T, \tag{1.2}$$

where y_t is an n–dimensional vector of endogenous variables, x_t is a vector of exogenous variables, E_{t-1} is the conditional expectations operator based on the model and on information through period $t-1$, α_i is a vector of parameters, and u_{it} is an error term with mean zero that may be correlated across equations but not across time. The first m equations are assumed to be stochastic, with the remaining equations identities. The function f_i may be nonlinear in variables, parameters, and expectations.

13.3 Solution of RE Models

Consider the solution of model 1.2 for period t. Assume that estimates of α_i are available, that current and future values of the exogenous variables are available, and that all values for periods $t-1$ and back are known. If the current and future values of the u_{it} error terms are set to zero (their expected values), the solution of the model is straightforward. A popular method is the extended path (EP) method in Fair and Taylor (1983), which has been programmed into a number of computer packages. The method iterates over solution *paths*. Values of the expectations for period t through period $t + h + k + h$ are first guessed, where h is the maximum lead in the model and k is chosen as discussed below. Given these guesses, the model can be solved for periods t through $t + h + k$ in the usual ways (usually period by period using the Gauss-Seidel technique). This solution provides new values for the expectations through period $t + h + k$, namely the solution values. Given these new values, the model can be solved again for periods t through $t + h + k$, which provides new values for the expectations, and so on. Convergence is reached when the predicted values for periods t through $t + h$ from one iteration to the next are within a prescribed tolerance level of each other. (There is no guarantee of convergence, but in most applications convergence is not a problem.)

In this process the guessed values of the expectations for periods $t + h + k + 1$ through $t + h + k + h$ (the h periods beyond the last period solved) have not been changed. If the solution values for periods t through $t + h$ depend in a nontrivial way on these guesses, then overall convergence has not been achieved. To check for this, the entire process can be repeated for k one larger. If increasing k by one has a trivial effect (based on a tolerance criterion) on the solution values for t through $t + h$, then overall convergence has been achieved; otherwise k must continue to be increased until the criterion is met. In practice what is usually done is to experiment to find the value of k that is large enough to make it unlikely that further increases are necessary for any experiment that might be run and then do no further checking using larger values of k.

The solution requires values for x_t through x_{t+h+k}, the current and future values of the exogenous variables. These values are what the agents are assumed to know or expect at the beginning of period t. If agents are assumed not to have perfect foresight regarding x_t, then after convergence as described above has been achieved, one more step is needed. This step is to solve the model for period t using the computed expectations and the *actual* value of x_t, not the value that the agents expected. This is just a standard Gauss-Seidel solution for period t. To the extent that the expected value of x_t differs from the actual value, $E_{t-1}y_t$ will differ from the final solution value for y_t. The final solution value for y_t is conditional on (1) the use of zero errors, (2) the actual value of x_t, and (3) the values of x_t through x_{t+h+k} that are used by the agents.

So far only the solution for period t has been described. In many cases one is interested in a dynamic simulation over a number of periods, say the Q periods t through $t + Q - 1$. If it is assumed that all exogenous variable values are known by the agents, this simulation can be performed with just one use of the EP method, where the path is from t through $t + Q - 1 + h + k$ rather than just t through $t + h + k$. With known exogenous variables, the solution values for the expectations are the same as the overall solution values, and so if convergence is reached for the expectations for periods t through $t + Q - 1 + h$, the model has been solved for periods t through $t + Q - 1$.

If the actual values of the exogenous variables differ from those used by the agents, then Q separate uses of the EP method are required to solve for t through $t + Q - 1$. It is no longer the case, for example, that $E_{t-1}y_{t+1}$ equals $E_t y_{t+1}$, because the information sets through periods $t - 1$ and t differ. The latter includes knowledge of x_t and the former does not. For simplicity this chapter will only consider the case in which agents know the exogenous variables. It is straightforward but somewhat tedious to incorporate the case in which the exogenous variables are not known.

A useful way of estimating the computational cost of the EP method is to calculate the number of "passes" through the model that are used. A pass using the Gauss-Seidel technique is going through the equations of the model once for a given period and computing the values of the left-hand-side variables given the values of the right-hand-side variables. Let N denote the number of passes that are needed to obtain Gauss-Seidel convergence for a given period, and let M denote the number of times the entire path has to be computed to obtain overall convergence (assuming that k has been chosen large enough ahead of time). Then the total number of passes that are needed to solve the model for the Q periods t through $t + Q - 1$ is $N \cdot M \cdot (Q + h + k)$, since the path consists of $Q + h + k$ periods. If the model does not have rational expectations, the total number of passes is just $N \cdot Q$.

13.4 Optimal Control for RE Models

The optimal control procedure outlined in section 1.7 can be used for RE models under the CE assumption. The procedure simply requires that the model be capable of being solved for a given set of control values. The solution can be done using the EP method discussed above.

To set up the problem, assume that the period of interest is t through $t + T - 1$ (a horizon of length T) and that the objective is to maximize the expected value of W, where W is

$$W = \sum_{s=t}^{t+T-1} g_s(y_s, x_s). \tag{13.1}$$

Let z_t be a q-dimensional vector of control variables, where z_t is a subset of x_t, and let z be the $q \cdot (T + h + k)$–dimensional vector of all the control values: $z = (z_t, \ldots, z_{t+T+h+k-1})$, where k is taken to be large enough for solution convergence through period $t + T - 1$.[2] If all the error terms are set to zero, then for each value of z one can compute a value of W by first solving the model for $y_t, \ldots, y_{t+T-1}$ and then using these values along with the values for $x_t, \ldots, x_{t+T-1}$ to compute W in equation 13.1. The problem can then be turned over to an optimization algorithm like DFP.

Once the problem is solved, z_t^*, the optimal vector of control values for period t, is implemented. If, for example, the Fed is solving the control problem and there is one control variable—the interest rate—then the Fed would implement through open market operations the optimal value of the interest rate for period t. In the process of computing z_t^* the optimal values for periods $t + 1$ through $t + T + h + k - 1$ are also

---

2. Remember that the guessed values of the expectations for periods $t + T + h + k$ through $t + T + h + k + h - 1$ are never changed in the solution. k has to be large enough so that increasing it by one has a trivial effect on the relevant solution values.

computed. Agents are assumed to know these values when they solve the model to form their expectations. For the Fed example, one can think of the Fed implementing the period t value of the interest rate and at the same time announcing the planned future values.

After z_t^* is implemented and period t passes, the entire process can be repeated beginning in $t + 1$. In the present deterministic case, however, the optimal value of z_{t+1} chosen at the beginning of $t + 1$ would be the same as the value chosen at the beginning of t, and so there is no need to reoptimize. Reoptimization is needed in the stochastic case, which is discussed in section 13.6.

Each evaluation of W requires $N \cdot M \cdot (T + h + k)$ passes, since the path is of length $T + h + k$. Each iteration of the DFP algorithm requires $2q \cdot (T + h + k)$ evaluations of W to compute the derivatives numerically, assuming that two function evaluations are used per derivative calculation, and then a few more evaluations to do the line searching. Let L denote the number of evaluations that are needed for the line searching after the derivatives have been computed, and let I denote the total number of iterations of the DFP algorithm that are needed for convergence to the optimum. The total number of evaluations of W is thus $I \cdot (2q \cdot (T + h + k) + L)$. Since from section 13.3 the number of passes needed to solve a model for T periods is $N \cdot M \cdot (T + h + k)$, the total number of passes needed to compute z_t^* is $N \cdot M \cdot (T + h + k) \cdot I \cdot (2q \cdot (T + h + k) + L)$.

13.5   Stochastic Simulation of RE Models

Forget optimal control for now and assume that some (not necessarily optimal) control rule is postulated. The stabilization features of a rule can be examined using stochastic simulation, as in Chapter 11. One first needs an estimate of typical shocks to the economy, and as in section 11.3.2 these can be taken to be the estimated residuals.

At the risk of some repetition, it will be useful to outline the stochastic simulation procedure for the case of an RE model. Assume that the periods of interest are t through $t + S - 1$. The steps to estimate the variances of the endogenous variables for these periods under the rule are as follows:

1. Let u_t^*, an m-dimensional vector, denote a particular draw of the m error terms for period t, drawn from a set of estimated residuals. Assume that agents know this draw but use zero values of the errors for periods $t + 1$ and beyond. (This means that the certainty equivalence assumption is being used for agents for future periods.) Then solve the model (with the rule included) for period t using the EP method. Record the solution values for period t.

2. Draw a vector of error terms for period $t + 1$, u_{t+1}^*, and use these errors and the solution values for period t to solve the model for period $t + 1$ using the EP method. For this solution agents are assumed to use zero values of the errors for periods $t + 2$ and beyond. Record the solution values for period $t + 1$.

3. Repeat step 2 for periods $t + 2$ through $t + S - 1$. This set of solution values is one repetition. From this repetition one obtains a prediction of each endogenous variable for periods t through $t + S - 1$.

4. Repeat steps 1 through 3 J times for J repetitions.

5. Let y_{it}^j denote the value on the jth repetition of variable i for period t. Given J repetitions, equations 9.1–9.3 can be used to compute the mean and variance of variable i for period t. In addition, L_i can be computed using equations 11.1–11.2.

In the above steps agents are assumed to know the draw u_t^* when solving the model beginning in period t, to know the draw u_{t+1}^* when solving the model beginning in period $t + 1$, and so on. The steps could be set up so that agents do not know these draws and use zero errors instead. In this case the expectations would be computed using all zero errors, and after this the model would be solved using these computed expectations and the drawn error vector. For reasons that will be clear in the next section, the focus here is on the case where the current period draw is known.

The total number of passes that are needed for the J repetitions is $J \cdot S \cdot N \cdot M \cdot (h + k)$, since each path is of length $h + k$ and there are $J \cdot S$ paths solved.

13.6   Stochastic Simulation and Optimal Control

In the optimal control case the control rule is dropped and an optimal control problem is solved to determine the values of the control variables. The steps that are needed to estimate the variances of the endogenous variables in this case are similar to those in the previous section. The difference is that after each draw of the error vector an optimal control problem has to be solved. Continue to assume that the periods of interest are t through $t + S - 1$. The steps are:

1. Draw u_t^* as in section 13.5. Assume that both the control authority and the agents know this draw but use zero values of the errors for periods $t + 1$ and beyond. Given this draw and the zero future errors, solve the (deterministic) control problem beginning in period t as in section 13.4. This solution produces z_t^*, the optimal value of the control vector for period t, which is implemented. Record the solution values for period t.

2. Draw a vector of error terms for period $t + 1$, u_{t+1}^*, and use these errors and the solution values for period t to solve the control problem beginning in period $t + 1$. For this problem the control authority and the agents are assumed to use zero values of the errors for periods $t + 2$ and beyond. This solution produces z_{t+1}^*, the optimal value of the control vector for period $t + 1$, which is implemented. Record the solution values for period $t + 1$.

3. Repeat step 2 for periods $t + 2$ through $t + S - 1$. This set of solution values is one repetition. From this repetition one obtains the implemented optimal values, $z_t^*, \ldots, z_{t+S-1}^*$, and a prediction of each endogenous variable for periods t through $t + S - 1$ based on these values.

4. Repeat steps 1 through 3 J times for J repetitions. This produces J values of y_{it}^j, as in section 13.5. In addition, L_i can be computed using equations 11.1–11.2.

The values of L_i computed using this optimal control procedure can be compared with the values computed in section 13.5 using other rules. The steps are set up so that both procedures assume that agents know the current period draw of the error terms. In addition, any rule used in section 13.5 in effect knows the draw, as does the control authority in this section. The information sets are thus the same for the comparisons.

In step 1 a control problem is solved beginning in period t. In section 13.4 the horizon of the control authority regarding the objective function was taken to be length T, and values of the control variables were computed for periods t through $t + T + h + k - 1$. In step 1, however, it may be possible to shorten the horizon. What step 1 needs are only the solution values for period t (including z_t^*), and the horizon only needs to be taken long enough so that increasing it further has a trivial effect (based on a tolerance criterion) on the values for period t. One can initially experiment with different values of the horizon to see how large it has to be to meet the tolerance criterion. Let R denote this length. This value of R can be used in step 2 for the control problem beginning in period $t + 1$, and so on.

The overall procedure requires that S control problems be solved per repetition, and so with J repetitions there are $J \cdot S$ control problems solved, each with a horizon of length R. The total number of passes in this case is thus:

$$\text{Number of passes} = J \cdot S \cdot N \cdot M \cdot (R + h + k) \cdot I \cdot (2q \cdot (R + h + k) + L). \quad (13.2)$$

In terms of speed it is obviously important that efficient code be written for passing through the model, since most of the time is spent passing through. A practical way to proceed after the code is written is to set limits on N, M, I, and J that are small enough to make the problem computationally feasible (that is, completion within an hour or two). Once the bugs are out and the (preliminary) results seem sensible, the limits can be gradually increased to gain more accuracy. If two cases are being compared using stochastic simulation, such as a simple rule versus an optimal control procedure, the same draws of the errors should be used for both cases. This can considerably lessen stochastic-simulation error for the comparisons.

13.7   Coding

As just noted, it is important that efficient code be written to pass through the equations of a model. Let PASS(r) denote a subroutine written to pass through the model once for period r. Let SOLVE(s,Q) denote a subroutine written to solve a rational expectations model for periods s through $s + Q - 1$ using the extended path method. SOLVE(s,Q) calls PASS(r) many times for r equal to s through $s + Q - 1 + h + k$, where h is the maximum lead and k is chosen as discussed in the text. Let DFP(s,R) denote a subroutine written to solve an optimal control problem with beginning period s and necessary horizon R (as discussed in section 13.6). DFP(s,R) calls SOLVE(s,R) one time per evaluation of the objective function W. Finally, let DRAW(s) denote a subroutine written to draw a vector of error terms for period s.

The outline of the program to do stochastic simulation and optimal control as in section 13.6 is:

```
      DO 100 j = 1, J
      DO 200 s = t, t+S-1
      CALL DRAW(s)
      CALL DFP(s,R)
        Calls SOLVE(s,R) once per evaluation of W.
          Calls PASS(r) many times for r = s, s+R-1+h+k.
      Record predicted values on trial j for period s.
  200 CONTINUE
  100 CONTINUE
```

13.8   An Example: An RE Version of the US(EX,PIM) Model

A modified version of the US(EX,PIM) model that was used for the results in the second half of Table 11.2 was used for the present calculations. Five equations were changed: the three consumption equations, 1, 2, and 3, and the two term structure equations, 23 and 24. In each of the consumption equations the income variable, which enters as a current value, was replaced by the average of the values led one through four quarters. In other words, if y_t denotes the income variable, it was replaced by $(1/4)(y_{t+1} + y_{t+2} + y_{t+3} + y_{t+4})$. The three equations were not reestimated; the existing coefficient estimate for the income variable was retained. Equation 23, which determines RB, was replaced by

$$RB_t = \frac{1}{8}(RS_t + RS_{t+1} + RS_{t+2} + RS_{t+3} + RS_{t+4} + RS_{t+5} + RS_{t+6} + RS_{t+7}). \quad (23)$$

Equation 24, which determines RM, was replaced by the same equation. The expectations of the future values were assumed to be rational (model consistent). For this version the maximum lead length, h, is 7.

The problem in row 9 in Table 11.2 was solved for this version of the model. As in Chapter 11, the estimated residuals were added to the stochastic equations and taken to be exogenous. The residuals that are added for equations 1, 2, 3, 23, and 24 are the residuals computed from the new specification, so that the equations fit perfectly when the residuals are added. The estimated residuals used for the draws, however, are the residuals estimated from the original specification. The draws are thus the same as they are for the results in row 9 in Table 11.2.

The parameters for this problem are as follows. The simulation period is 1994:1–1998:4, and so S is 20. (Remember that S is the number of deterministic optimal control problems solved per trial.) k was taken to be 8, and some experimentation revealed that a value of 5 for R was adequate. The DFP iteration limit, I, was taken to be 10. The number of function evaluations needed for line searching, L, turned out to be about 10. No limits were imposed on N and M. The tolerance criterion for a Gauss-Seidel iteration was 0.1 percent, and the tolerance criterion for extended path convergence was

0.2 percent. It turned out that extended path convergence was almost always reached in 2 iterations, so M was effectively 2. The average value of N turned out to be 3.56. The number of control variables, q, is 1, where the control variable is RS. The total number of trials, J, was taken to be 100.

Using these numbers the formula 13.2 gives a value of 142,400,000 passes. The actual number of passes was 142,443,689. The example was run using the Fair-Parke (1995) program. The time taken was 15.5 hours on a 1.7 Ghz PC, which comes out to about 2,550 passes per second.

Regarding Table 11.2, it is interesting to note that the variability was less for the RE version. The value of L_i for Y was 2.03, which compares to 2.54 in row 9. The value for PF was 3.11 compared to 3.17, and the value for RS was 0.63 compared to 0.96. These differences are as expected. A given change in RS is more effective in the RE version because the long-term interest rates respond faster and consumption responds faster. More stability can thus be achieved with similar interest rate changes.

The time of 15.5 hours on a fairly standard PC shows that the procedure in this chapter is in the realm of computational feasibility even for a nonlinear model of over 100 equations with a nontrivial lead length (that is, 7). As mentioned above, a good approach is to set fairly small limits on the relevant parameters and then increase the limits to gain more accuracy after the bugs are worked out. One programming issue that is important is setting the step size for the numeric derivatives used by the DFP algorithm. The step size must be larger than the solution tolerance criteria in order for the computed derivatives to be any good. Some experimentation is usually needed to get this right.

For the non-RE version of the model, M is 1 and h and k are zero, and in this case the number of passes in the above example would be 7,120,000. This is 5 percent of the number of passes for the RE version.

13.9   Conclusion

This chapter has shown that it is computationally feasible to solve stochastic-simulation and optimal control problems for large nonlinear models with rational expectations if certainty equivalence is used. The analysis of monetary and fiscal policies need not be restricted to the use of small models or linear models. In particular, results like those in Table 11.2 can be obtained for RE models.

What is lost by the use of the open loop procedure of certainty equivalence and re-optimization in section 13.6? Agents know, when they solve the model to form their expectations, the current period values of the control variables that are implemented and the announced planned future values. They take the planned future values as deterministic rather than stochastic, and they take the future error terms to be deterministic, namely zero. Agents do not take into account the fact that everything will be redone at the beginning of each period after the error terms for that period are realized and known. The overall procedure is thus not fully optimal. In some cases this may be a serious problem, and if so, the procedure in section 13.6 is of little use.

14

Model Comparisons

14.1 Introduction

This chapter compares the US model with two other models in terms of predictive accuracy. The two other models are a vector autoregressive (VAR) model and an autoregressive components (AC) model. It will be seen that the US model dominates the others, which is consistent with previous results.[1] Two versions of the US model are used for the comparisons: the regular version and a version in which an autoregressive equation is added for each exogenous variable. This second version will be called the "US+" model.

14.2 The US+ Model

The US+ model is the US model with an additional 85 stochastic equations. Each of the additional equations explains an exogenous variable and is a fifth-order autoregressive equation with the constant term and time trend added. Equations are estimated for all the exogenous variables in the model except the price of imports, PIM, the age variables, the dummy variables, the variables created from peak-to-peak interpolations, and variables that are constants or nearly constants. All the exogenous variables in the model are listed in Table A.2. Those for which autoregressive equations are *not* estimated are: all the dummy variables, $AG1, AG2, AG3, CDA, DELD, DELH, DELK, DRS, HFS, HM, IHB, IHHA, JJP, LAM, MUH, PIM, T, TAUG, TAUS, TRGR, WLDF, WLDG,$ and $WLDS$. Excluding these variables left 85 variables for which autoregressive equations were estimated. Logs were used for some of the variables. Logs were not used for ratios, for variables that were negative or sometimes negative, or for variables that were sometimes close to zero. The estimation technique was ordinary least squares.

---

1. See Fair (1994), sections 8.6 and 8.7. Chapter 9 in Fair (1994) contains a comparison of the overall MC model with an autoregressive version, but this work has not been updated here.

PIM is a variable that changed very little in the 1950s and 1960s, had a huge increase in the 1970s, and then changed little after that. Its movements over the sample period are heavily influenced by OPEC oil-pricing decisions. It does not seem sensible to postulate a time-series equation for this variable, and so it is taken to be exogenous in the US+ model. It is also taken to be exogenous in the VAR model below.

The US+ model has no hard-to-forecast exogenous variables (except *PIM*), and in this sense it is comparable to the VAR and AC models discussed below, which have no exogenous variables other than the constant term and time trend (and *PIM* for the VAR model). On the other hand, adding autoregressive equations for the exogenous variables may bias the results against the model. McNees (1981, p. 404) argues that the method handicaps the model: "It is easy to think of exogenous variables (policy variables) whose future values can be anticipated or controlled with complete certainty even if the historical values can be represented by covariance stationary processes; to do so introduces superfluous errors into the model solution."

14.3   The VAR Model

The seven variables in the VAR model used here are (1) the log of real GDP, log *GDPR*, (2) the log of the GDP price deflator, log *GDPD*, (3) the log of the wage rate, log *WF*, (4) the log of the money supply, log *M*1, (5) the unemployment rate, *UR*, (6) the three-month Treasury bill rate, *RS*, and (7) the log of the import price deflator, log *PIM*. These are the same variables used by Sims (1980) with the exception of *RS*, which has been added.

Each of the first six variables is taken to be a function of the constant, the time trend, its first four lagged values, and the first two lagged values of each of the other six variables. There are thus 18 coefficients to estimate per each of the six equations. As noted above, no equation is postulated for log *PIM*. *PIM* is taken to be exogenous.

The results in Fair and Shiller (1990) and Fair (1994), Chapter 8, show that VAR results are not very sensitive to somewhat different choices of lags. The choice here of only two lags for the non-own variables saves degrees of freedom.

14.4   The AC Model

If one is only interested in GDP predictions, the results in Fair and Shiller (1990) suggest that "autoregressive components" (AC) models are more accurate than VAR models. An AC model is one in which each component of GDP is regressed on its own lagged values. GDP is then determined from the GDP identity, as the sum of the components. AC models do not have the problem, as VAR models do, of adding large numbers of parameters as the number of variables (components, in the AC case) is increased.

There are 17 components of *GDPR* in the US model (counting the statistical discrepancy *STATP*), and the AC model consists of estimated equations for each of these components.[2] Each of the 17 components is taken to be a function of the constant, the time trend, and its first five lagged values. The equations are in log form except for the equations for *IVF* and *STATP*.[3] The final equation of the AC model is the *GDPR* identity, where *GDPR* is the sum of the 17 components (with a minus sign for *IM*).

14.5   Outside Sample RMSEs

One- through eight-quarter-ahead outside sample RMSEs were computed for each of the four models. Consider the US model. The model was first estimated (by 2SLS) for the 1954:1–1982:4 period, and these coefficients were used in a dynamic prediction for the 1983:1–1984:4 period. These predictions were recorded. The model was then estimated for the 1954:1–1983:1 period, and these coefficients were used to predict the 1983:2-1985:1 period. This process was repeated through the end of the sample. The last estimation period was 1954:1–2002:2, and the last prediction period was 2002:3–2002:3. This gave 79 one-quarter-ahead predictions, 78 two-quarter-ahead predictions, and so on through 72 eight-quarter-ahead predictions. Root mean squared errors were then computed. The same process was repeated for the other three models. For the US+ model the 85 additional equations were treated like the 30 structural equations, namely reestimated for each sample period. (The 85 additional equations are estimated by ordinary least squares.)

The results are presented in Table 14.1 for the log of real GDP, the log of the GDP price deflator, the unemployment rate, and the bill rate. For the AC model the only relevant variable is the log of real GDP. The results are easy to summarize. For *GDPR* the AC model is more accurate than the VAR model. The US model is more accurate than the AC model, and the US+ model is as well, except for the one-quarter-ahead prediction, where there is essentially a tie.[4] For *GDPD* the VAR model is best by a slight amount for the one-quarter-ahead prediction, but by the eight-quarter-ahead prediction it is noticeably the worst. For both *UR* and *RS* the US and US+ models are better than the VAR model, except for the one-quarter-ahead prediction for *UR*, where the VAR model is slightly better than the US model. Overall, by eight quarters ahead the US and US+ models are substantially more accurate than the VAR model.

---

2. The 17 components, in alphabetical order, are *CD*, *CN*, *COG*, *COS*, *CS*, *EX*, *IHF*, *IHH*, *IKB*, *IKF*, *IKG*, *IKH*, *IM*, *IVF*, *PSI*13(*JG* · *HG* + *JM* · *HM*), *PSI*13 · *JS* · *HS*, and *STATP*. The variable *PSI*13(*JG* · *HG* + *JM* · *HM*) is federal government purchases of services, and the variable *PSI*13 · *JS* · *HS* is state and local government purchases of services.

3. For the results in sections 8.6 and 8.7 in Fair (1994), each of the equations of the AC model had the first two lagged values of *GDPR* added. As noted in note 4 below, the results are not sensitive to this choice.

4. If the first two lagged values of *GDPR* are added to the AC equations, the RMSEs are 0.51, 1.44, and 2.35 for the one-, four-, and eight-quarter-ahead predictions, respectively, which are quite close to the values in Table 14.1.

Table 14.1
Outside Sample RMSEs

	log *GDPR* (quarters ahead)			log *GDPD* (quarters ahead)			$100 \cdot UR$ (quarters ahead)			*RS* (quarters ahead)		
Model	1	4	8	1	4	8	1	4	8	1	4	8
US	0.45	1.02	1.46	0.26	0.78	1.39	0.23	0.57	0.70	0.52	1.46	1.80
US+	0.54	1.33	1.84	0.29	0.87	1.52	0.19	0.60	0.90	0.53	1.59	2.03
VAR	0.63	1.97	3.20	0.22	0.77	1.84	0.22	0.78	0.95	0.55	1.74	3.01
AC	0.53	1.43	2.25									

Notes:
- Prediction period: 1983:1–2002:3; 79 one-quarter-ahead predictions; 76 four-quarter-ahead predictions; 72 eight-quarter-ahead predictions.
- RMSEs are in percentage points.

14.6   FS Tests

The one-quarter-ahead RMSEs in Table 14.1 are based on 79 predictions. The RMSEs cannot be used to tell whether the predictions from one model have independent information from those in another model. The FS tests allow this to be done. In the present context the question is whether the VAR model, which is much smaller than the US model, contains any information useful for prediction that is not in the US model. Even though the US model generally beats the VAR model in Table 14.1, the VAR model may still have independent information. The same question can be asked of the AC model versus the US model and of the AC model versus the VAR model.

It will be useful to review the FS procedure briefly. Let $_{t-s}\hat{Y}_{1t}$ denote a prediction of Y_t made from model 1 using information available at time $t - s$, and let $_{t-s}\hat{Y}_{2t}$ denote the same thing for model 2. The parameter s is the length ahead of the prediction, $s > 0$. The test is based on the following regression equation:

$$Y_t - Y_{t-s} = \alpha + \beta(_{t-s}\hat{Y}_{1t} - Y_{t-s}) + \gamma(_{t-s}\hat{Y}_{2t} - Y_{t-s}) + v_t. \qquad (14.1)$$

If neither model 1 nor model 2 contains any information useful for s-period-ahead predictions of Y_t, then the estimates of β and γ should both be zero. In this case the estimate of the constant term α would be the average s period change in Y. If both models contain independent information for s-period-ahead predictions, then β and γ should both be nonzero. If both models contain information, but the information in, say, model 2 is completely contained in model 1 and model 1 contains further relevant information as well, then β but not γ should be nonzero.[5]

---

5. If both models contain the same information, then the predictions are perfectly correlated, and β and γ are not separately identified.

The procedure is to estimate equation 14.1 for different models' predictions and test the hypothesis H_1 that $\beta = 0$ and the hypothesis H_2 that $\gamma = 0$. H_1 is the hypothesis that model 1's predictions contain no information relevant to predicting s periods ahead not in the constant term and in model 2, and H_2 is the hypothesis that model 2's predictions contain no information not in the constant term and in model 1.

This procedure bears some relation to encompassing tests, but the setup and interests are somewhat different. For example, it does not make sense in the current setup to constrain β and γ to sum to one, as is usually the case for encompassing tests. If both models' predictions are just noise, the estimates of both β and γ should be zero. Also, say that the true process generating Y_t is $Y_t = X_t + Z_t$, where X_t and Z_t are independently distributed. Say that model 1 specifies that Y_t is a function of X_t only and that model 2 specifies that Y_t is a function of Z_t only. Both predictions should thus have coefficients of one in equation 14.1, and so in this case β and γ would sum to two. It also does not make sense in the current setup to constrain the constant term α to be zero. If, for example, both models' predictions were noise and equation 14.1 were estimated without a constant term, then the estimates of β and γ would not generally be zero when the mean of the dependent variable is nonzero.

It is also not sensible in the current setup to assume that v_t is identically distributed. It is likely that v_t is heteroskedastic. If, for example, $\alpha = 0$, $\beta = 1$, and $\gamma = 0$, v_t is simply the prediction error from model 1, and in general prediction errors are heteroskedastic. Also, if k-period-ahead predictions are considered, where $k > 1$, this introduces a $k - 1$ order moving average process to the error term in equation 14.1. Both heteroskedasticity and the moving average process can be corrected for in the estimation of the standard errors of the coefficient estimates. This can be done using the procedure given by Hansen (1982), Cumby, Huizinga, and Obstfeld (1983), and White and Domowitz (1984) for the estimation of asymptotic covariance matrices. Let $\theta = (\alpha \ \beta \ \gamma)'$. Also, define X as the $T \times 3$ matrix of variables, whose row t is $X_t = (1 \ _{t-s}\hat{Y}_{1t} - Y_{t-s} \ _{t-s}\hat{Y}_{2t} - Y_{t-s})$, and let $\hat{u}_t = Y_t - Y_{t-s} - X_t\hat{\theta}$. The covariance matrix of $\hat{\theta}$, $V(\hat{\theta})$, is

$$V(\hat{\theta}) = (X'X)^{-1}S(X'X)^{-1}, \tag{14.2}$$

where

$$S = \Omega_0 + \sum_{j=1}^{s-1}(\Omega_j + \Omega_j'), \tag{14.3}$$

$$\Omega_j = \sum_{t=j+1}^{T}(u_t u_{t-j})\hat{X}_t'\hat{X}_{t-j}, \tag{14.4}$$

where $\hat{\theta}$ is the ordinary least squares estimate of θ and s is the prediction horizon. When s equals 1, the second term on the right-hand side of 14.3 is zero, and the covariance matrix is simply White's (1980) correction for heteroskedasticity.

Table 14.2
FS Tests: Equation 14.1 Estimates

	cnst	US	US+	VAR	AC	SE
One-Quarter-Ahead Predictions						
Δ log *GDPR*						
1	−0.0004	0.827		0.102		0.00437
	(−0.30)	(6.80)		(0.99)		
2	−0.0009	0.821			0.180	0.00438
	(−0.55)	(6.24)			(0.82)	
3	0.0019		0.541	0.252		0.00518
	(1.34)		(3.31)	(2.10)		
4	0.0003		0.452		0.544	0.00520
	(0.18)		(2.36)		(1.97)	
5	0.0005			0.210	0.712	0.00530
	(0.27)			(1.52)	(2.62)	
Δ log *GDPD*						
6	0.0014	0.383		0.306		0.00176
	(2.66)	(4.64)		(3.00)		
7	0.0015		0.358	0.298		0.00185
	(2.57)		(3.44)	(2.40)		
100 · *UR*						
8	0.0031	0.605		0.349		0.00172
	(3.01)	(6.15)		(3.31)		
9	0.0025		0.721	0.234		0.00172
	(2.52)		(6.17)	(1.89)		
RS						
10	−0.494	0.835		0.245		0.476
	(−1.92)	(4.52)		(1.59)		
11	−0.472		0.838	0.251		0.482
	(−1.79)		(4.28)	(1.55)		

As an alternative to equation 14.1 the *level* of Y_t could be regressed on the predicted *levels* and the constant term. If Y_t is an integrated process, then any sensible prediction of Y_t will be cointegrated with Y_t itself. In the level regression, the sum of β and γ will thus be constrained in effect to one, and one would in effect be estimating one less parameter. If Y_t is an integrated process, running the levels regression with an additional independent variable Y_{t-1} (thereby estimating β and γ without constraining their sum to one) is essentially equivalent to the differenced regression 14.1. For variables that are not integrated, the levels version of 14.1 can be used.

The results of various regressions are presented in Table 14.2. For log *GDPR* and log *GDPD* equation 14.1 is used, and for *UR* and *RS* the equation in levels in used. One- and four-quarter-ahead predictions are analyzed. Again, the results are easy to summarize. For *GDPR* the AC model dominates the VAR model for both the

Table 14.2
(continued)

	cnst	US	US+	VAR	AC	SE
Four-Quarter-Ahead Predictions						
$\Delta \log GDPR$						
1	−0.0005	1.104		−0.146		0.00997
	(−0.08)	(6.34)		(−1.24)		
2	−0.0026	0.959			0.061	0.01020
	(−0.31)	(3.54)			(0.16)	
3	0.0040		1.158	−0.146		0.01295
	(0.45)		(3.59)	(−0.67)		
4	−0.0068		0.762		0.524	0.01265
	(−0.62)		(2.23)		(1.15)	
5	−0.0061			0.051	1.128	0.01451
	(−0.45)			(0.31)	(2.68)	
$\Delta \log GDPD$						
6	0.0056	0.476		0.212		0.00463
	(2.22)	(2.79)		(1.18)		
7	0.0058		0.441	0.227		0.00486
	(2.07)		(2.31)	(1.16)		
$100 \cdot UR$						
8	0.0180	0.887		−0.144		0.00416
	(4.23)	(7.97)		(−1.00)		
9	0.0142		0.911	−0.165		0.00536
	(2.39)		(4.34)	(−0.67)		
RS						
10	0.762	0.515		0.335		1.389
	(0.46)	(1.27)		(1.38)		
11	2.224		0.100	0.519		1.445
	(1.39)		(0.25)	(2.31)		

Note:
• Same predictions as used in Table 14.1.

one-quarter-ahead and four-quarter-ahead predictions. For this variable the US model dominates both the AC and the VAR model. The US+ model dominates the AC and VAR models for the four-quarter-ahead predictions, but for the one-quarter-ahead predictions the AC and VAR predictions appear to contain some independent information, with t-statistics of 1.97 and 2.10, respectively.

For *GDPD* the VAR one-quarter-ahead predictions have independent information relative to the US and US+ models, but not the four-quarter-ahead predictions. The same is true for *UR*. For *RS* the US and US+ models dominate the VAR model for the one-quarter-ahead predictions. For the four-quarter-ahead predictions, however, the VAR model dominates the US+ model and the VAR and US predictions are too collinear to

Table 14.3
Sources of Uncertainty: US Model

Model	log *GDPR* (quarters ahead)			log *GDPD* (quarters ahead)			$100 \cdot UR$ (quarters ahead)			*RS* (quarters ahead)		
	1	4	8	1	4	8	1	4	8	1	4	8
a	0.63	1.30	1.55	0.31	0.54	0.76	0.35	0.68	0.83	0.59	1.16	1.36
b	0.68	1.46	1.77	0.31	0.61	0.92	0.36	0.75	0.93	0.61	1.22	1.45
d	0.53	1.19	1.68	0.25	0.84	1.78	0.30	0.54	0.53	0.57	1.52	1.86

Notes:
• Prediction period: 2000:4–2002:3.

a: uncertainty from structural errors only.
b: uncertainty from structural errors and coefficient estimates.
d: uncertainty from structural errors, coefficient estimates, and possible misspecification of the model.

• Errors are in percentage points.

allow any conclusion to be made. Overall, the predictions from the VAR model contains at best only a small amount of information not in the predictions from the US and US+ models.

14.7   Sources of Uncertainty

The results in this section show the breakdown of the variance of a prediction into that due to the additive error terms, to the coefficient estimates, and to the possible misspecification of the model. The breakdown between the first two of these has already been presented in Table 9.4. The measures of variability in Table 9.4 are ranges, and in this section the measures used are the square roots of the variances (standard deviations) as computed by equation 9.2.

The results in Table 9.4 are based on 2,000 trials, and the same data used for the no-bias-correction calculations in this table are used for the *a* and *b* rows in Table 14.3. Standard deviations for the one-, four-, and eight-quarter-ahead predictions are presented for the log of real GDP, the log of the GDP deflator, the unemployment rate, and the bill rate. For the *a* row the coefficients are not reestimated on each trial, whereas they are for the *b* row. Comparing rows *a* and *b* shows that much more of the variance of a prediction is due to the additive error terms than to the coefficient estimates.

To account for the possible misspecification of the model requires more work. The following is a brief outline of a method for doing this.[6] Let $\tilde{\sigma}^2_{itk}$ denote the stochastic-

---

6. The method outlined here was first presented in Fair (1980a). It is also discussed in Fair (1984), Chapter 8, and Fair (1994), Chapter 7. The new feature here is that for the stochastic simulations the coefficients are estimated on each trial, as in Chapter 9, rather than being drawn from estimated distributions.

simulation estimate of the variance of the prediction error for a k period ahead prediction of variable i from a simulation beginning in period t. This estimate is as presented in equation 9.3, except that a k subscript has been added to denote the length ahead of the prediction.

Let the prediction period begin one period after the end of the estimation period, and call this period s. From a stochastic simulation beginning in period s one obtains an estimate of the variance of the prediction error, $\tilde{\sigma}_{isk}^2$, in equation 9.3, where again k refers to the length ahead of the prediction. From this simulation one also obtains an estimate of the expected value of the k period ahead prediction of variable i, $\tilde{\mu}_{isk}$, in equation 9.1. The difference between this estimate and the actual value, y_{is+k-1}, is the mean prediction error, denoted $\hat{\epsilon}_{isk}$:

$$\hat{\epsilon}_{isk} = y_{is+k-1} - \tilde{\mu}_{isk}. \tag{14.5}$$

If it is assumed that $\tilde{\mu}_{isk}$ exactly equals the true expected value, then $\hat{\epsilon}_{isk}$ in equation 14.5 is a sample draw from a distribution with a known mean of zero and variance σ_{isk}^2, where σ_{isk}^2 is the true variance. The square of this error, $\hat{\epsilon}_{isk}^2$, is thus under this assumption an unbiased estimate of σ_{isk}^2. One therefore has two estimates of σ_{isk}^2, one computed from the mean prediction error and one computed by stochastic simulation. Let d_{isk} denote the difference between these two estimates:

$$d_{isk} = \hat{\epsilon}_{isk}^2 - \tilde{\sigma}_{isk}^2. \tag{14.6}$$

If it is further assumed that $\tilde{\sigma}_{isk}^2$ exactly equals the true value (that is, $\tilde{\sigma}_{isk}^2 = \sigma_{isk}^2$), then d_{isk} is the difference between the estimated variance based on the mean prediction error and the true variance. Therefore, under the two assumptions of no error in the stochastic-simulation estimates, the expected value of d_{isk} is zero for a correctly specified model.

If a model is misspecified, it is not in general true that the expected value of d_{isk} is zero. If the model is misspecified, the estimated residuals that are used for the draws are inconsistent estimates of the true errors and the coefficient estimates obtained on each trial are inconsistent estimates of the true coefficients. The effect of misspecification on d_{isk} is ambiguous, although if data mining has occurred in that the estimated residuals are on average too small in absolute value, the mean of d_{isk} is likely to be positive. In other words, if data mining has occurred, the stochastic-simulation estimates of the variances are likely to be too small because they are based on draws from estimated residuals that are too small in absolute value. In addition, if the model is misspecified, the outside sample prediction errors are likely to be large on average, which suggests a positive mean for the d_{isk} values.

The procedure described so far uses only one estimation period and one prediction period, where the estimation period ends in period $s - 1$ and the prediction period begins in period s. It results in one value of d_{isk} for each variable i and each length ahead k. Since one observation is obviously not adequate for estimating the mean of d_{isk}, more observations must be generated. This can be done by using successively new estimation periods and new prediction periods. Assume, for example, that one has data from period 1 through period 150. The model can be estimated through, say, period 100, with the prediction beginning with period 101. Stochastic simulation for the prediction period will yield for each i and k a value of $d_{i\,101k}$ in equation 14.6. The model can then be reestimated through period 101, with the prediction period now beginning with period 102. Stochastic simulation for this prediction period will yield for each i and k a value of $d_{i\,102k}$. This process can be repeated through the estimation period ending with period 149. For the one-period-ahead prediction ($k = 1$) the procedure will yield for each variable i 50 values of d_{is1} ($s = 101, \ldots, 150$); for the two-period-ahead prediction ($k = 2$) it will yield 49 values of d_{is2}, ($s = 101, \ldots, 149$); and so on.

The final step in the process is to make an assumption about the mean of d_{isk} that allows the computed values of d_{isk} to be used to estimate the mean. A variety of assumptions, discussed in Fair (1984), Chapter 8, are possible. The assumption made for the work in this section is that the mean is constant across time. In other words, misspecification is assumed to affect the mean in the same way for all s. Given this assumption, the mean, denoted as $\bar{d}_{ik}$, can be estimated by merely averaging the computed values of d_{isk}.

Given $\bar{d}_{ik}$, an estimate of the total variance of the prediction error, denoted $\hat{\sigma}^2_{itk}$, is:

$$\hat{\sigma}^2_{itk} = \tilde{\sigma}^2_{itk} + \bar{d}_{ik}. \qquad (14.7)$$

Values of the square root of $\hat{\sigma}^2_{itk}$ are presented in the d row in Table 11.3. In calculating the values of d_{isk}, the first estimation period ended in 1982:4, the second in 1983:1, and the 79th in 2002:2. This gave 79 values of d_{is1}, 78 values of d_{is2}, and so on through 72 values of d_{is8}. $\bar{d}_{1k}$ is thus the mean of 79 values, $\bar{d}_{2k}$ is the mean of 78 values, and so on. Each value in the d row is the square root of the sum of the square of the value in the b row and $\bar{d}_{ik}$. The number of trials for each of the 79 stochastic simulations was 100. (As noted above, the number of trials used to get the a row values was 2,000, and likewise for the b row values.) Remember that each trial consists of a new set of coefficient estimates (except for the a row values).

Table 14.3 shows that the differences between the d and b rows are generally fairly small. This suggests that the US model is not seriously misspecified. The largest difference is for the eight-quarter-ahead prediction of *GDPD*, where the standard deviation is 0.92 in the b row and 1.78 in the d row. For real GDP the eight-quarter-ahead b and d row values are 1.77 and 1.68, respectively. For the unemployment rate the two values are 0.93 and 0.53, and for the bill rate the values are 1.45 and 1.86.

14.8 Conclusion

As noted in the Introduction, the results in this chapter are consistent with previous results. The US model generally does well against time-series models. There is little information in predictions from times-series models that is not in predictions from the US model.

15

Conclusion

The main empirical results in this book are as follows.

The U.S. Economy in the 1990s

Chapter 5 shows that there is a standard wealth effect in the US model. The end-of-sample tests for the US equations in Chapters 2 and 6 accept the hypothesis of stability for all the main equations except the stock price equation. The experiment in Chapter 6 shows that had there been no stock market boom in the last half of the 1990s the U.S. economy would not have looked historically unusual. The unusual features were driven by the wealth effect and cost-of-capital effect from the stock market boom. Nothing in the profit and productivity data that are discussed in Chapter 6 suggests that there should have been a stock market boom, and so the stock market boom appears to be a puzzle.

Price Equations

The tests in Chapter 4 generally reject the NAIRU dynamics. They also show that there is some loss in the movement away from the estimation of structural price and wage equations to the estimation of reduced-form price equations. The rejection of the NAIRU dynamics has important implications for long-run properties, since the NAIRU dynamics imply that the price level accelerates if the unemployment rate is held below the NAIRU. This is not true of the dynamics of the price and wage equations of the MC model. It is argued in Chapter 4, however, that the linear specification of all these equations is not likely to be accurate for low values of the unemployment rate. It seems likely that as the unemployment rate falls there is some value below which a further fall leads to a nonlinear response of prices. Unfortunately, it is not possible to estimate this nonlinearity, because there are too few observations of very low unemployment rates. This means that models like the MC model should not be pushed into areas of very low unemployment rates.

The estimates in Chapter 8 of European inflation costs in the 1980s from a more expansionary monetary policy are not likely to be affected by the nonlinearity issue, because the experiment is over a period of fairly high unemployment rates. The estimates show that going out nine years, the unemployment rate in Germany could have been lowered by over one percentage point with an inflation cost of about 0.6 percentage points. This is a trade-off that many people probably would have accepted at the time, had they believed that a trade-off was possible. Anyone who accepted the NAIRU dynamics (see the beginning of section 8.1) would not, of course, have believed that there was any trade-off.

Monetary Policy

Many of the results in this book pertain to monetary policy. Interest rate rules are estimated in Chapter 2 for each of the main countries. The first version of the US rule, equation 30, was estimated in 1978. The tests of this rule accept the hypothesis of coefficient stability both before and after the early Volcker regime, 1979:4–1982:3, when the Fed announced that it was targeting monetary aggregates rather than interest rates. The long-run inflation coefficient in the estimated rule is almost exactly one. The U.S. interest rate appears as an explanatory variable in many of the interest rate rules of the other countries, and the German interest rate appears as an explanatory variable in many of the interest rate rules of the other European countries (before 1999:1).

The effects of nominal versus real interest rates in consumption and investment equations are tested in Chapter 3, and the results strongly support the use of nominal interest rates. Nominal interest rates are used in the MC model except for the US investment equation 12. The experiment in Chapter 7 shows that a positive U.S. inflation shock with the nominal interest rate held constant is contractionary in the MC model. This is opposite to the property of modern-view models, where the shock is expansionary. The shock is expansionary in modern-view models because the real interest rate falls and demand responds positively to real interest rate decreases. The shock is contractionary in the MC model, because real income and real wealth fall, which contracts demand, and because there is no positive effect from the fall in the real interest rate except for the US investment equation.

This difference between the MC model and modern-view models has important implications for interest rate rules. In modern-view models the coefficient on inflation in the interest rate rule must be greater than one for the model to be stable, whereas in the MC model the coefficient can even be zero and the model stable. The results in Chapter 11 show that a rule with a coefficient of zero is stabilizing. The monetary-policy implications of modern-view models are thus sensitive to their use of the real interest rate and their lack of real income and real wealth effects. If the models are not adequately specified in this regard, their monetary-policy implications may not be trustworthy.

EMU Stabilization Costs

Chapter 12 probably pushes the MC model about as far as it should be pushed. Conditional on the estimated interest rate rules for Germany, France, Italy, the Netherlands, and the United Kingdom, it estimates the stabilization costs of the first four countries joining a common-currency area and then all five. Germany is by far the most hurt, but Italy, the Netherlands, and the United Kingdom are also hurt. France is helped. The estimated interest rate rule for France is not stabilizing (the Bank of France mostly just followed what Germany did), and France actually gains when it is part of a larger rule that is stabilizing. Germany is hurt a great deal because its individual interest rate rule is quite stabilizing. Although the results in Chapter 12 are preliminary, the analysis shows that stochastic simulation and the MC model can be used to try to answer a quite broad stabilization question.

Bootstrapping

The results in Chapter 9 show that the bootstrap appears to work well for the US model. They also show that in general the use of asymptotic distributions does not appear to be highly misleading. The asymptotic intervals are slightly too narrow, and the use of the AP asymptotic distribution rejects the hypothesis of stability somewhat too often. The one area where the asymptotic distributions are not very accurate is in testing the NAIRU dynamics in Chapter 4. A Monte Carlo technique is needed in this case.

For all the stochastic simulations in this book the error draws have been from estimated residuals rather than from estimated distributions. In addition, if coefficient estimate uncertainty is taken into account, this has been done by reestimating the model on each trial rather than by drawing from estimated distributions of the coefficient estimates. This is a change from the stochastic simulation work in Fair (1984, 1994), and it is in spirit of the bootstrap methodology discussed in Chapter 9.

Certainty Equivalence and Optimal Control

The results in Chapter 10 show that little is lost in using the certainty equivalence assumption in the solution of optimal control problems for nonlinear models like the US model. This is an important practical result, since it allows optimal control problems to be solved in Chapters 11 and 13 that would otherwise not be computationally feasible.

The optimal control experiments in Chapter 11 show that the estimated rule, equation 30, gives results that are similar to the Fed's minimizing a loss function in output and inflation in which the weight on inflation deviations is about five times the weight on output deviations. The results in Chapter 11 also show that a tax-rate rule would be of help in stabilizing the economy.

Rational Expectations

The single-equations tests of the rational expectations hypothesis generally reject the hypothesis. If expectations are not rational, the Lucas critique is not likely to be a problem, and one can have more confidence in the policy properties of the MC model, which does not impose rational expectations, than otherwise. If, however, one wants to impose rational expectations on a model, the results in Chapter 13 show that it is computationally feasible to analyze even large-scale versions of these models, including the use of stochastic simulation and the solution of optimal control problems.

Testing Equations and Models

The single-equation tests are generally supportive of the specifications, although there are obviously some weak equations, especially for the smaller countries. The complete-model tests in Chapter 14 show that the US model dominates time-series models, results that are consistent with earlier work. There are two approaches in future work that can be taken to try to improve accuracy. One is to work within the general framework of the MC model, testing alternative individual-equation specifications as more data become available. Alternative estimation techniques can also be tried. The other approach is to begin with a different framework, say one that relies heavily on the assumption of rational expectations or one that has features of the modern-view model discussed in Chapter 7, and develop and test a completely different model. If this is done, tests like those in Chapter 14 can be used to compare different models.

The currently popular approach in macroeconomics of working with calibrated models does not focus on either single-equation tests or complete-model tests, which leaves the field somewhat in limbo. Calibrated models are unlikely to do well in the tests stressed in this book simply because they are not designed to explain aggregate time-series data well. If in the long run the aim is to explain how the macroeconomy works, these models will need to become empirical enough to be tested, both equation by equation and against time-series models and structural models like the MC model.

Appendixes

References

Index

APPENDIX A

The US Model

A.1   About Tables A.1–A.10

The tables that pertain to the US model are presented in this appendix. Table A.1 presents the six sectors in the US model: household (h), firm (f), financial (b), foreign (r), federal government (g), and state and local government (s). In order to account for the flow of funds among these sectors and for their balance-sheet constraints, the U.S. Flow of Funds Accounts (FFA) and the U.S. National Income and Product Accounts (NIPA) must be linked. Many of the identities in the US model are concerned with this linkage. Table A.1 shows how the six sectors in the US model are related to the sectors in the FFA. The notation on the right side of this table (H1, FA, etc.) is used in Table A.5 in the description of the FFA data.

Table A.2 lists all the variables in the US model in alphabetical order, and Table A.3 lists all the stochastic equations and identities. The functional forms of the stochastic equations are given in Table A.3, but not the coefficient estimates. The coefficient estimates are presented in Table A.4, where within this table the coefficient estimates and tests for equation 1 are presented in Table A1, for equation 2 in Table A2, and so on. The results in Table A.4 are discussed in the text in section 2.3.

The remaining tables provide more detailed information about the model. Tables A.5–A.7 show how the variables were constructed from the raw data. Table A.8 shows how the model is solved under various assumptions about monetary policy. Table A.9 lists the first-stage regressors per equation that were used for the 2SLS estimates. Finally, Table A.10 shows which variables appear in which equations.

The rest of this appendix discusses the collection of the data and the construction of some of the variables.

A.2   The Raw Data

The NIPA Data

The variables from the NIPA are presented first in Table A.5, in the order in which they appear in the *Survey of Current Business*. The Bureau of Economic Analysis (BEA) is now emphasizing "chain-type weights" in the construction of real magnitudes, and the data based on these weights have been used here.[1] Because of the use of chain-type weights, real GDP is not the sum of its real components. To handle this, a discrepancy variable, denoted *STATP*, was created, which is the difference between real GDP and the sum of its real components. (*STATP* is constructed using equation 83 in Table A.3.) *STATP* is small in magnitude, and it is taken to be exogenous in the model.

The Other Data

The variables from the FFA are presented next in Table A.5, ordered by their code numbers. Some of these variables are NIPA variables that are not published in the *Survey of Current Business* but that are needed to link the two accounts. Interest rate variables are presented next in the table, followed by employment and population variables. The source for the interest rate data is the website of the Board of Governors of the Federal Reserve System (BOG). The source for the employment and population data is the website of the Bureau of Labor Statistics (BLS). Some of the employment data are unpublished data from the BLS, and these are indicated as such in the table. Data on the armed forces are not published by the BLS, and these data were computed from population data from the U.S. Census Bureau.

Adjustments that were made to the raw data are presented next in Table A.5. These are explained beginning in the next paragraph. Finally, all the raw data variables are presented at the end of Table A.5 in alphabetical order along with their numbers. This allows one to find a raw data variable quickly. All the raw data variables are numbered with an "R" in front of the number to distinguish them from the variables in the model.

The adjustments that were made to the raw data are as follows. The quarterly social insurance variables R249–R254 were constructed from the annual variables R78–R83 and the quarterly variables R40, R60, and R71. Only annual data are available on the breakdown of social insurance contributions between the federal and the state and local governments with respect to the categories "personal," "government employer," and "other employer." It is thus necessary to construct the quarterly variables using the annual data. It is implicitly assumed in this construction that as employers, state and local governments do not contribute to the federal government and vice versa.

The constructed tax variables R255 and R256 pertain to the breakdown of corporate profit taxes of the financial sector between federal and state and local. Data on this breakdown do not exist. It is implicitly assumed in this construction that the breakdown is the same as it is for the total corporate sector.

---

1. See Young (1992) and Triplett (1992) for good discussions of chain-type weights.

The quarterly variable R257, INTPRI, which is the level of net interest payments of sole proprietorships and partnerships, is constructed from the annual variable R86, INTPRIA, and the quarterly and annual data on PII, personal interest income, R53. Quarterly data on net interest payments of sole proprietorships and partnerships do not exist. It is implicitly assumed in the construction of the quarterly data that the quarterly pattern of the level of interest payments of sole proprietorships and partnerships is the same as the quarterly pattern of personal interest income.

The quarterly variable R258, INTROW, which is the level of net interest payments of the rest of the world, is constructed from the annual variable R87, INTROWA, and the quarterly and annual data on PII, personal interest income, R53. Quarterly data on net interest payments of the rest of the world do not exist. It is implicitly assumed in the construction of the quarterly data that the quarterly pattern of the level of interest payments of the rest of the world is the same as the quarterly pattern of personal interest income.

The tax variables R57 and R62 were adjusted to account for the tax surcharge of 1968:3–1970:3 and the tax rebate of 1975:2. The tax surcharge and the tax rebate were taken out of personal income taxes (TPG) and put into personal transfer payments (TRGH). The tax surcharge numbers were taken from Okun (1971), table 1, p. 171. The tax rebate was 7.8 billion dollars at a quarterly rate.

The employment and population data from the BLS are rebenchmarked from time to time, and the past data are not adjusted to the new benchmarks. Presented next in Table A.5 are the adjustments that were made to obtain consistent series. These adjustments take the form of various "multiplication factors" for the old data. For the period in question and for a particular variable the old data are multiplied by the relevant multiplication factor to create data for use in the model. The variables TPOP90 and TPOP99 listed in Table A.5 are used to phase out multiplication factors.

Table A.6 presents the balance-sheet constraints that the data satisfy. The variables in this table are raw data variables. The equations in the table provide the main checks on the collection of the data. If any of the checks is not met, one or more errors have been made in the collection process. Although the checks in the table may look easy, considerable work is involved in meeting them. All the receipts from sector i to sector j must be determined for all i and j (i and j run from 1 through 6).

A.3 Variable Construction

Table A.7 presents the construction of the variables in the model (that is, the variables in Table A.2) from the raw data variables (that is, the variables in Table A.5). With a few exceptions, the variables in the model are either constructed in terms of the raw data variables in Table A.5 or are constructed by identities. If the variable is constructed by an identity, the notation "Def., Eq." appears, where the equation number is the identity in Table A.3 that constructs the variable. In a few cases the identity that constructs an endogenous variable is not the equation that determines it in the model. For example, equation 85 constructs LM, whereas stochastic equation 8 determines LM in the model.

Equation 85 instead determines E, E being constructed directly from raw data variables. Also, some of the identities construct exogenous variables. For example, the exogenous variable $D2G$ is constructed by equation 49. In the model equation 49 determines TFG, TFG being constructed directly from raw data variables. If a variable in the model is the same as a raw data variable, the same notation is used for both except that variables in the model are in italics and raw data variables are not. For example, consumption expenditures on durable goods is CD as a raw data variable and CD as a variable in the model.

The financial stock variables in the model that are constructed from flow identities need a base quarter and a base quarter starting value. The base quarter values are indicated in Table A.7. The base quarter was taken to be 1971:4, and the stock values for this quarter were taken from the FFA stock values.

There are also a few internal checks on the data in Table A.7 (aside from the balance-sheet checks in Table A.6). The variables for which there are both raw data and an identity available are GDP, MB, $PIEF$, PUG, and PUS. In addition, the saving variables in Table A.6 (SH, SF, and so on) must match the saving variables of the same name in Table A.7. There is also one redundant equation in the model, equation 80, which the variables must satisfy.

There are a few variables in Table A.7 whose construction needs some explanation.

HFS: Peak-to-Peak Interpolation of *HF*

HFS is a peak-to-peak interpolation of *HF*, hours per job. The peaks are listed in Table A.7. "Flat end" in the table means that the interpolation line was taken to be horizontal from the last peak listed on. The deviation of HF from HFS, which is variable HFF in the model, is used in equation 15, which explains overtime hours. *HFS* is also used in equations 13 and 14.

HO: Overtime Hours

Data are not available for HO, overtime hours, for the first 16 quarters of the sample period (1952:1–1955:4). The equation that explains HO in the model has log HO on the left-hand side and the constant term, HFF, and HFF lagged once on the right-hand side. The equation is also estimated under the assumption of a first-order autoregressive error term. The missing data for HO were constructed by estimating the log HO equation for the 1956:1–2002:3 period and using the predicted values from this regression for the (outside sample) 1952:3–1955:4 period as the actual data. The values for 1952:1 and 1952:2 were taken to be the 1952:3 predicted value.

TAUS: Progressivity Tax Parameter—s

TAUS is the progressivity tax parameter in the personal income tax equation for state and local governments (equation 48). It was obtained as follows. The sample period 1952:1–2002:3 was divided into four subperiods, 1952:1–1970:4, 1971:1–1971:4, 1972:1–2001:4, and 2002:1–2002:3. These were judged from a plot of THS/YT, the ratio of state and local personal income taxes (*THS*) to taxable income (*YT*), to be periods of no large tax law changes. Two assumptions were then made about the relationship between *THS* and *YT*. The first is that within a subperiod *THS/POP* equals $[D1 + TAUS(YT/POP)](YT/POP)$ plus a random error term, where *D1* and *TAUS* are constants. The second is that changes in the tax laws affect *D1* but not *TAUS*. These two assumptions led to the estimation of an equation with *THS/POP* on the left-hand side and the constant term, $DUM1(YT/POP)$, $DUM2(YT/POP)$, $DUM3(YT/POP)$, $DUM4(YT/POP)$, and $(YT/POP)^2$ on the right-hand side, where *DUMi* is a dummy variable that takes on a value of one in subperiod *i* and zero otherwise. (The estimation period was 1952:1–2002:3 excluding 1987:2. The observation for 1987:2 was excluded because it corresponded to a large outlier.) The estimate of the coefficient of $DUMi(YT/POP)$ is an estimate of *D1* for subperiod *i*. The estimate of the coefficient of $(YT/POP)^2$ is the estimate of *TAUS*. The estimate of *TAUS* was .00153, with a *t*-statistic of 31.76. This procedure is, of course, crude, but at least it provides a rough estimate of the progressivity of the state and local personal income tax system.

Given *TAUS*, *D1S* is defined to be $THS/YT - (TAUS \cdot YT)/POP$ (see Table A.7). In the model *D1S* is taken to be exogenous, and *THS* is explained by equation 48 as $[D1S + (TAUS \cdot YT)/POP]YT$. This treatment allows a state and local marginal tax rate to be defined in equation 91: $D1SM = D1S + (2 \cdot TAUS \cdot YT)/POP$.

TAUG: Progressivity Tax Parameter—g

TAUG is the progressivity tax parameter in the personal income tax equation for the federal government (equation 47). The estimation procedure for *TAUG* was similar to that followed above for *TAUS*, where 37 subperiods where chosen. The 37 subperiods are: 1952:1–1953:4, 1954:1–1963:4, 1964:1–1964:4, 1965:1–1965:4, 1966:1–1967:4, 1968:1–1970:4, 1971:1–1971:4, 1972:1–1972:4, 1973:1–1973:4, 1974:1–1975:1, 1975:2–1976:4, 1977:1–1977:1, 1977:2–1978:2, 1978:3–1981:3, 1981:4–1982:2, 1982:3–1983:2, 1983:3–1984:4, 1985:1–1985:1, 1985:2–1985:2, 1985:3–1987:1, 1987:2–1987:2, 1987:3–1987:4, 1988:1–1988:4, 1989:1–1989:4, 1990:1–1990:4, 1991:1–1993:4, 1994:1–1996:1, 1996:2–1996:2, 1996:3–1997:2, 1997:3–1997:4, 1998:1–1999:4, 2000:1–2001:2, 2001:3–2001:3, 2001:4–2001:4, 2002:1–2002:1, 2002:2–2002:2, and 2002:3–2002:3. The estimate of *TAUG* was .00811, with a *t*-statistic of 9.02. Again, this procedure is crude, but it provides a rough estimate of the progressivity of the federal personal income tax system.

Given *TAUG*, *D1G* is defined to be $THG/YT - (TAUG \cdot YT)/POP$ (see Table A.7). In the model *D1G* is taken to be exogenous, and *THG* is explained by equation 47 as $[D1G + (TAUG \cdot YT)/POP]YT$. This treatment allows a federal marginal tax rate to be defined in equation 90: $D1GM = D1G + (2 \cdot TAUG \cdot YT)/POP$.

KD: Stock of Durable Goods

KD is an estimate of the stock of durable goods. It is defined by equation 58:

$$KD = (1 - DELD)KD_{-1} + CD. \qquad (58)$$

Given quarterly observations for *CD*, which are available from the NIPA, quarterly observations for *KD* can be constructed once a base-quarter value and values for the depreciation rate *DELD* are chosen. End-of-year estimates of the stock of durable goods are available from 1929 through 2001 from the BEA. Estimates for 1991–2001 are in table 15, p. 37, of the *Survey of Current Business*, September 2002. Estimates for earlier years are available from the BEA website. These numbers are in 1996 dollars. Given the value of *KD* at the end of 1952 and given quarterly values of *CD* for 1953:1–1953:4, a value of *DELD* can be computed such that the predicted value from equation 58 for 1953:4 matches within a prescribed tolerance level the published BEA value for the end of 1953. This value of *DELD* can then be used to compute quarterly values of *KD* for 1953:1, 1953:2, and 1953:3. This process can be repeated for each year, which results in a quarterly series for *KD*. (The value of *DELD* computed between 2000 and 2001 was used to create values of *KD* for 2002:1, 2002:2, and 2002:3.)

KH: Stock of Housing

KH is an estimate of the stock of housing of the household sector. It is defined by equation 59:

$$KH = (1 - DELH)KH_{-1} + IHH. \tag{59}$$

The same procedure was followed for estimating *DELH* as was followed for estimating *DELD*. The housing stock data are available from the above BEA references for the durable goods stock data. The BEA residential stock data is for total residential investment, which in the model is *IHH* + *IHK* + *IHB*, whereas equation 59 pertains only to the residential investment of the household sector (*IHH*). The procedure that was used for dealing with this difference is as follows. First, the values for *DELH* were chosen using total residential investment as the investment series, since this series matched the published stock data. Second, once the values of *DELH* were chosen, *KH* was constructed using *IHH* (not total residential investment). A base-quarter value of *KH* of 1729.4 in 1952:1 was used. This value is .806 times the computed value for total residential investment for 1952:1. The value .806 is the average of *IHH*/(*IHH* + *IHK* + *IHB*) over the sample period.

KK: Stock of Capital

KK is an estimate of the stock of capital of the firm sector. It is determined by equation 92:

$$KK = (1 - DELK)KK_{-1} + IKF. \tag{92}$$

The same procedure was followed for estimating *DELK* as was followed for estimating *DELD* and *DELH*. The capital stock data are available from the above BEA references for the other stock data. The BEA capital stock data is for total fixed nonresidential investment, which in the model is *IKF* + *IKH* + *IKB* + *IKG*, whereas equation 59 pertains only to the fixed nonresidential investment of the firm sector (*IKF*). The procedure for dealing with this was similar to that followed above for residential investment. First, the values for *DELK* were chosen using total fixed nonresidential investment as the investment series, since this series matched the published stock data. Second, once the values of *DELK* were chosen, *KK* was constructed using *IKF* (not total fixed nonresidential investment). A base-quarter value of *KK* of 1803.8 in 1952:1 was used. This value is .887 times the computed value for total fixed nonresidential investment for 1952:1. The value .887 is the average of $IKF/(IKF + IKH + IKB + IKG)$ over the sample period.

V: Stock of Inventories

V is the stock of inventories of the firm sector (that is, the nonfarm stock). By definition, inventory investment (*IVF*) is equal to the change in the stock, which is equation 117:

$$IVF = V - V_{-1}. \tag{117}$$

Both data on *V* and *IVF* are published in the *Survey of Current Business*, the data on *V* in Table 5.13. For present purposes *V* was constructed from the formula $V = V_{-1} + IVF$ using the IVF series and base-quarter value of 1251.9 in 1996:4. This is the value in Table 5.13 in the National Income and Product Accounts.

Excess Labor and Excess Capital

In the theoretical model the amounts of excess labor and excess capital on hand affect the decisions of firms. In order to test for this in the empirical work, one needs to estimate the amounts of excess labor and capital on hand in each period. This in turn requires an estimate of the technology of the firm sector.

The measurement of the capital stock *KK* is discussed above. The production function of the firm sector for empirical purposes is postulated to be

$$Y = \min[LAM(JF \cdot HF^a), MU(KK \cdot HK^a)], \tag{A.1}$$

where *Y* is production, *JF* is the number of workers employed, HF^a is the number of hours worked per worker, *KK* is the capital stock discussed above, HK^a is the number of hours each unit of *KK* is utilized, and *LAM* and *MU* are coefficients that may change over time due to technical progress. The variables *Y*, *JF*, and *KK* are observed; the others are not. For example, data on the number of hours paid for per worker, *HF* in the model, exist, but not on the number of hours actually worked per worker, HF^a.

Equation 92 for *KK* and the production function A.1 are not consistent with the putty-clay technology of the theoretical model. To be precise with this technology one has to keep track of the purchase date of each machine and its technological coefficients. This kind of detail is not possible with aggregate data, and one must resort to simpler specifications.

Given the production function A.1, excess labor is measured as follows. The log of output per paid-for worker hour, $\log[Y/(JF \cdot HF)]$, is first plotted for the 1952:1–2002:3 period. The peaks of this series are then assumed to correspond to cases in which the capital constraint in the production function A.1 is not binding and in which the number of hours worked equals the number of hours paid for. This implies that the values of *LAM* are observed at the peaks. The values of log *LAM* other than those at the peaks are assumed to lie on straight lines between the peaks. This allows *LAM* to be computed for each quarter.

Since *LAM* is a measure of potential productivity, an interesting question is how it grows over time. This is discussed in section 6.4, where the plot of $\log[Y/(JF \cdot HF)]$ is presented in Figure 6.16a. This plot shows that *LAM* grew more rapidly in the 1950s and 1960s than it has since. It also shows that the growth rate after 1995 was only slightly larger than before.

Coming back to the measurement of excess labor, given an estimate of *LAM* for a particular quarter and given equation A.1, the estimate of the number of worker hours required to produce the output of the quarter, denoted *JHMIN* in the model, is simply Y/LAM. This is equation 94 in Table A.3. The actual number of worker hours paid for, $JF \cdot HF$, can be compared with *JHMIN* to measure the amount of excess labor on hand. The peaks that were used for the interpolations are listed in Table A.7 in the description of *LAM*.

For the measurement of excess capital there are no data on hours paid for or worked per unit of *KK*, and thus one must be content with plotting Y/KK. This is, from the production function A.1, a plot of $MU \cdot HK^a$, where HK^a is the average number of hours that each machine is utilized. If it is assumed that at each peak of this series the labor constraint in the production function A.1 is not binding and that HK^a is equal to the same constant, say $\bar{H}$, then one observes at the peaks $MU \cdot \bar{H}$. Interpolation between peaks can then produce a complete series on $MU \cdot \bar{H}$. If, finally, $\bar{H}$ is assumed to be the maximum number of hours per quarter that each unit of *KK* can be utilized, then $Y/(MU \cdot \bar{H})$ is the minimum amount of capital required to produce Y, denoted *KKMIN*. In the model, $MU \cdot \bar{H}$ is denoted *MUH*, and the equation determining *KKMIN* is equation 93 in Table A.4. The actual capital stock (*KK*) can be compared with *KKMIN* to measure the amount of excess capital on hand. The peaks that were used for the interpolations are listed in Table A.7 in the description of *MUH*. "Flat beginning" in the table means that the interpolation line was taken to be horizontal from the beginning of the period to the first peak listed. As noted above, "flat end" means that the interpolation line was taken to be horizontal from the last peak listed on.

YS: Potential Output of the Firm Sector

YS, a measure of the potential output of the firm sector, is defined by equation 98:

$$YS = LAM(JJP \cdot POP - JG \cdot HG - JM \cdot HM - JS \cdot HS). \qquad (98)$$

JJP is the peak or potential ratio of worker hours to population. It is constructed from a peak-to-peak interpolation of *JJ*, where *JJ* is the actual ratio of the total number of worker hours paid for in the economy to the total population aged 16 and over (equation 95). $JJP \cdot POP$ is thus the potential number of worker hours. The terms that are subtracted from $JJP \cdot POP$ in equation 98 are, in order, the number of federal civilian worker hours, the number of federal military worker hours, and the number of state and local government worker hours. The entire number in parentheses is thus the potential number of worker hours in the firm sector. *LAM* is the coefficient *LAM* in the production function A.1. Since *YS* in equation 98 is *LAM* times the potential number of workers in the firm sector, it can be interpreted as the potential output of the firm sector unless the capital input is insufficient to produce *YS*. This construction of *YS* is thus based on the assumption that there is always sufficient capital on hand to produce *YS*.

A.4   The Identities

The identities in Table A.3 are of two types. One type simply defines one variable in terms of others. These identities are equations 31, 33, 34, 43, 55, 56, 58–87, and 89–131. The other type defines one variable as a rate or ratio multiplied by another variable or set of variables, where the rate or ratio has been constructed to have the identity hold. These identities are equations 32, 35–42, 44–54, and 57. Consider, for example, equation 50:

$$TFS = D2S \cdot PIEF, \tag{50}$$

where *TFS* is the amount of corporate profit taxes paid from firms (sector f) to the state and local government sector (sector s), *PIEF* is the level of corporate profits of the firm sector, and *D2S* is the "tax rate." Data exist for *TFS* and *PIEF*, and *D2S* was constructed as *TFS/PIEF*. The variable *D2S* is then interpreted as a tax rate and is taken to be exogenous. This rate, of course, varies over time as tax laws and other things that affect the relationship between *TFS* and *PIEF* change, but no attempt has been made to explain these changes. This general procedure was followed for the other identities involving tax rates.

A similar procedure was followed to handle relative price changes. Consider equation 38:

$$PIH = PSI5 \cdot PD, \tag{38}$$

where *PIH* is the price deflator for residential investment, *PD* is the price deflator for total domestic sales, and *PSI5* is a ratio. Data exist for *PIH* and *PD*, and *PSI5* was constructed as *PIH/PD*. *PSI5*, which varies over time as the relationship between *PIH* and *PD* changes, is taken to be exogenous. This procedure was followed for the other identities involving prices and wages. This treatment means that relative prices and relative wages are exogenous in the model. (Prices relative to wages are not exogenous, however.) It is beyond the scope of the model to explain relative prices and wages, and the foregoing treatment is a simple way of handling these changes.

Another identity of the second type is equation 57:

$$BR = -G1 \cdot MB, \tag{57}$$

where *BR* is the level of bank reserves, *MB* is the net value of demand deposits of the financial sector, and *G1* is a "reserve requirement ratio." Data on *BR* and *MB* exist, and

$G1$ were constructed as $-BR/MB$. (MB is negative, since the financial sector is a net debtor with respect to demand deposits, and so the minus sign makes $G1$ positive.) $G1$ is taken to be exogenous. It varies over time as actual reserve requirements and other features that affect the relationship between BR and MB change.

Many of the identities of the first type are concerned with linking the FFA data to the NIPA data. An identity like equation 66,

$$0 = SH - \Delta AH - \Delta MH + CG - DISH, \tag{66}$$

is concerned with this linkage. SH is from the NIPA, and the other variables are from the FFA. The discrepancy variable, $DISH$, which is from the FFA, reconciles the two data sets. Equation 66 states that any nonzero value of saving of the household sector must result in a change in AH or MH. There are equations like 66 for each of the other five sectors: equation 70 for the firm sector, 73 for the financial sector, 75 for the foreign sector, 77 for the federal government sector, and 79 for the state and local government sector. Equation 77, for example, is the budget constraint of the federal government sector. Note also from Table A.3 that the saving of each sector (SH, SF, etc.) is determined by an identity. The sum of the saving variables across the six sectors is zero, which is the reason that equation 80 is redundant.

Table A.1

The Six Sectors of the US Model

Sector	Corresponding Sector(s) in the U.S. Flow of Funds Accounts
1 Household (h)	1 Households and Nonprofit Organizations (H)
2 Firm (f)	2a Nonfarm Nonfinancial Corporate Business (F1) 2b Nonfarm Noncorporate Business (NN) 2c Farm Business (FA)

3 Financial (b)	3a Commercial Banking (B1):
	    (1) U.S.-Chartered Commercial Banks
	    (2) Foreign Banking Offices in U.S.
	    (3) Bank Holding Companies
	    (4) Banks in U.S.-Affiliated Areas
	3b Private Nonbank Financial Institutions (B2):
	    (1) Savings Institutions
	    (2) Credit Unions
	    (3) Bank Personal Trusts and Estates
	    (4) Life Insurance Companies
	    (5) Other Insurance Companies
	    (6) Private Pension Funds
	    (7) State and Local Government Employee Retirement Funds
	    (8) Money Market Mutual Funds
	    (9) Mutual Funds
	    (10) Closed-End Funds
	    (11) Issuers of Asset-Backed Securities
	    (12) Finance Companies
	    (13) Mortgage Companies
	    (14) Real Estate Investment Trusts
	    (15) Security Brokers and Dealers
	    (16) Funding Corporations

4 Foreign (r)	4 Rest of the World (R)
5 Fed. Gov. (g)	5a Federal Government (US) 5b Government-Sponsored Enterprises (CA) 5c Federally Related Mortgage Pools 5d Monetary Authority (MA)
6 S & L Gov. (s)	6 State and Local Governments (S)

Notes:
- The abbreviations h, f, b, r, g, and s are used throughout the book.
- The abbreviations H, F1, NN, FA, B1, B2, R, US, CA, MA, and S are used in Table A.5 in the description of the flow of funds data.

Table A.2
The Variables in the US Model in Alphabetical Order

Variable	Eq.	Description
AA	89	Total net wealth, h, B96$.
AB	73	Net financial assets, b, B$.
AF	70	Net financial assets, f, B$.
AG	77	Net financial assets, g, B$.
AG1	exog	Percent of 16+ population 26–55 minus percent 16–25.
AG2	exog	Percent of 16+ population 56–65 minus percent 16–25.
AG3	exog	Percent of 16+ population 66+ minus percent 16–25.
AH	66	Net financial assets, h, B$.
AR	75	Net financial assets, r, B$.
AS	79	Net financial assets, s, B$.
BO	22	Bank borrowing from the Fed, B$.
BR	57	Total bank reserves, B$.
CCB	exog	Capital consumption, b, B96$.
CCF	21	Capital consumption, f, B$.
CCG	exog	Capital consumption, g, B$.
CCH	exog	Capital consumption, h, B$.
CCS	exog	Capital consumption, s, B$.
CD	3	Consumer expenditures for durable goods, B96$.
CDA	exog	Peak-to-peak interpolation of CD/POP.
CF	68	Cash flow, f, B$.
CG	25	Capital gains(+) or losses(−) on the financial assets of h, B$.
CN	2	Consumer expenditures for nondurable goods, B96$.
COG	exog	Purchases of consumption and investment goods, g, B96$.
COS	exog	Purchases of consumption and investment goods, s, B96$.
CS	1	Consumer expenditures for services, B96$.
CUR	26	Currency held outside banks, B$.
D1G	exog	Personal income tax parameter, g.
D1GM	90	Marginal personal income tax rate, g.
D1S	exog	Personal income tax parameter, s.
D1SM	91	Marginal personal income tax rate, s.
D2G	exog	Profit tax rate, g.
D2S	exog	Profit tax rate, s.
D3G	exog	Indirect business tax rate, g.
D3S	exog	Indirect business tax rate, s.
D4G	exog	Employee social security tax rate, g.
D5G	exog	Employer social security tax rate, g.
D593	exog	1 in 1959:3; 0 otherwise.
D594	exog	1 in 1959:4; 0 otherwise.
D601	exog	1 in 1960:1; 0 otherwise.
D621	exog	1 in 1962:1; 0 otherwise.
D692	exog	1 in 1969:2; 0 otherwise.
D714	exog	1 in 1971:4; 0 otherwise.
D721	exog	1 in 1972:1; 0 otherwise.
D722	exog	1 in 1972:2; 0 otherwise.
D723	exog	1 in 1972:3; 0 otherwise.
D794823	exog	1 in 1979:4–1982:3; 0 otherwise.
D923	exog	1 in 1992:3; 0 otherwise.
D924	exog	1 in 1992:4; 0 otherwise.
D941	exog	1 in 1994:1; 0 otherwise.
D942	exog	1 in 1994:2; 0 otherwise.
D981	exog	1 in 1998:1; 0 otherwise.
D013	exog	1 in 2001:3; 0 otherwise.
D014	exog	1 in 2001:4; 0 otherwise.
DB	exog	Dividends paid, b, B$.

Table A.2
(continued)

Variable	Eq.	Description
DELD	exog	Physical depreciation rate of the stock of durable goods, rate per quarter.
DELH	exog	Physical depreciation rate of the stock of housing, rate per quarter.
DELK	exog	Physical depreciation rate of the stock of capital, rate per quarter.
DF	18	Dividends paid, f, B$.
DISB	exog	Discrepancy for b, B$.
DISBA	exog	Discrepancy between NIPA and FFA data on capital consumption, nonfinancial corporate business, B$.
DISF	exog	Discrepancy for f, B$.
DISG	exog	Discrepancy for g, B$.
DISH	exog	Discrepancy for h, B$.
DISR	exog	Discrepancy for r, B$.
DISS	exog	Discrepancy for s, B$.
DRS	exog	Dividends received by s, B$.
E	85	Total employment, civilian and military, millions.
EX	exog	Exports, B96$.
EXPG	106	Total expenditures, g, B$.
EXPS	113	Total expenditures, s, B$.
FA	exog	Farm gross product, B96$.
FIROW	exog	Payments of factor income to the rest of the world, B$.
FIROWD	exog	FIROW price deflator.
FIUS	exog	Receipts of factor income from the rest of the world, B$.
FIUSD	exog	FIUS price deflator.
G1	exog	Reserve requirement ratio.
GDP	82	Gross domestic product, B$.
GDPD	84	GDP price deflator.
GDPR	83	Gross domestic product, B96$.
GNP	129	Gross national product, B$.
GNPD	131	GNP price deflator.
GNPR	130	Gross national product, B96$.
HF	14	Average number of hours paid per job, f, hours per quarter.
HFF	100	Deviation of HF from its peak to peak interpolation.
HFS	exog	Peak-to-peak interpolation of HF.
HG	exog	Average number of hours paid per civilian job, g, hours per quarter.
HM	exog	Average number of hours paid per military job, g, hours per quarter.
HN	62	Average number of nonovertime hours paid per job, f, hours per quarter.
HO	15	Average number of overtime hours paid per job, f, hours per quarter.
HS	exog	Average number of hours paid per job, s, hours per quarter.
IBTG	51	Indirect business taxes, g, B$.
IBTS	52	Indirect business taxes, s, B$.
IGZ	exog	Gross investment, g, B$.
IHB	exog	Residential investment, b, B96$.
IHF	exog	Residential investment, f, B96$.
IHH	4	Residential investment, h, B96$.
IHHA	exog	Peak-to-peak interpolation of IHH/POP.
IKB	exog	Nonresidential fixed investment, b, B96$.
IKF	92	Nonresidential fixed investment, f, B96$.
IKG	exog	Nonresidential fixed investment, g, B96$.
IKH	exog	Nonresidential fixed investment, h, B96$.
IM	27	Imports, B96$.
INS	exog	Insurance and pension reserves to h from g, B$.
INTF	19	Net interest payments, f, B$.
INTG	29	Net interest payments, g, B$.
INTOTH	exog	Net interest payments, other private business, B$.
INTROW	exog	Net interest payments, r, B$.

Table A.2
(continued)

Variable	Eq.	Description
INTS	exog	Net interest payments, s, B$.
ISZ	exog	Gross investment, s, B$.
IVA	20	Inventory valuation adjustment, B$.
IVF	117	Inventory investment, f, B96$.
JF	13	Number of jobs, f, millions.
JG	exog	Number of civilian jobs, g, millions.
JHMIN	94	Number of worker hours required to produce Y, millions.
JJ	95	Ratio of the total number of worker hours paid for to the total population 16 and over.
JJP	exog	Potential value of JJ.
JM	exog	Number of military jobs, g, millions.
JS	exog	Number of jobs, s, millions.
KD	58	Stock of durable goods, B96$.
KH	59	Stock of housing, h, B96$.
KK	12	Stock of capital, f, B96$.
KKMIN	93	Amount of capital required to produce Y, B96$.
L1	5	Labor force of men 25–54, millions.
L2	6	Labor force of women 25–54, millions.
L3	7	Labor force of all others, 16+, millions.
LAM	exog	Amount of output capable of being produced per worker hour.
LM	8	Number of "moonlighters": difference between the total number of jobs (establishment data) and the total number of people employed (household survey data), millions.
*M*1	81	Money supply, end of quarter, B$.
MB	71	Net demand deposits and currency, b, B$.
MDIF	exog	Net increase in demand deposits and currency of banks in U.S. possessions plus change in demand deposits and currency of private nonbank financial institutions plus change in demand deposits and currency of federally sponsored credit agencies and mortgage pools minus mail float, U.S. government, B$.
MF	17	Demand deposits and currency, f, B$.
MG	exog	Demand deposits and currency, g, B$.
MH	9	Demand deposits and currency, h, B$.
MR	exog	Demand deposits and currency, r, B$.
MS	exog	Demand deposits and currency, s, B$.
MUH	exog	Amount of output capable of being produced per unit of capital.
PCD	37	Price deflator for CD.
PCGDPD	122	Percentage change in GDPD, annual rate, percentage points.
PCGDPR	123	Percentage change in GDPR, annual rate, percentage points.
*PCM*1	124	Percentage change in M1, annual rate, percentage points.
PCN	36	Price deflator for CN.
PCS	35	Price deflator for CS.
PD	33	Price deflator for $X - EX + IM$ (domestic sales).
PEX	32	Price deflator for EX.
PF	10	Price deflator for $X - FA$.
PFA	exog	Price deflator for FA.
PG	40	Price deflator for COG.
PH	34	Price deflator for $CS + CN + CD + IHH$ inclusive of indirect business taxes.
PIEB	exog	Before-tax profits, b, B96$.
PIEF	67	Before-tax profits, f, B$.
PIH	38	Price deflator for residential investment.
PIK	39	Price deflator for nonresidential fixed investment.
PIM	exog	Price deflator for IM.
PIV	42	Price deflator for inventory investment, adjusted.
POP	120	Noninstitutional population 16+, millions.

Table A.2

(continued)

Variable	Eq.	Description
POP1	exog	Noninstitutional population of men 25–54, millions.
POP2	exog	Noninstitutional population of women 25–54, millions.
POP3	exog	Noninstitutional population of all others, 16+, millions.
PROD	118	Output per paid for worker hour ("productivity").
PS	41	Price deflator for COS.
PSI1	exog	Ratio of PEX to PX.
PSI2	exog	Ratio of PCS to (1 + D3G + D3S)PD.
PSI3	exog	Ratio of PCN to (1 + D3G + D3S)PD.
PSI4	exog	Ratio of PCD to (1 + D3G + D3S)PD.
PSI5	exog	Ratio of PIH to PD.
PSI6	exog	Ratio of PIK to PD.
PSI7	exog	Ratio of PG to PD.
PSI8	exog	Ratio of PS to PD.
PSI9	exog	Ratio of PIV to PD.
PSI10	exog	Ratio of WG to WF.
PSI11	exog	Ratio of WM to WF.
PSI12	exog	Ratio of WS to WF.
PSI13	exog	Ratio of gross product of g and s to total employee hours of g and s.
PUG	104	Purchases of goods and services, g, B$.
PUS	110	Purchases of goods and services, s, B$.
PX	31	Price deflator for X.
Q	exog	Gold and foreign exchange, g, B$.
RB	23	Bond rate, percentage points.
RD	exog	Discount rate, percentage points.
RECG	105	Total receipts, g, B$.
RECS	112	Total receipts, s, B$.
RM	24	Mortgage rate, percentage points.
RMA	128	After-tax mortgage rate, percentage points.
RNT	exog	Rental income, h, B$.
RS	30	Three-month Treasury bill rate, percentage points.
RSA	130	After-tax bill rate, percentage points.
SB	72	Saving, b, B$.
SF	69	Saving, f, B$.
SG	76	Saving, g, B$.
SGP	107	NIPA surplus (+) or deficit (−), g, B$.
SH	65	Saving, h, B$.
SHRPIE	121	Ratio of after-tax profits to the wage bill net of employer social security taxes.
SIFG	54	Employer social insurance contributions, f to g, B$.
SIFS	exog	Employer social insurance contributions, f to s, B$.
SIG	103	Total employer and employee social insurance contributions to g, B$.
SIGG	exog	Employer social insurance contributions, g to g, B$.
SIHG	53	Employee social insurance contributions, h to g, B$.
SIHS	exog	Employee social insurance contributions, h to s, B$.
SIS	109	Total employer and employee social insurance contributions to s, B$.
SISS	exog	Employer social insurance contributions, s to s, B$.
SR	74	Saving, r, B$.
SRZ	116	Saving rate, h.
SS	78	Saving, s, B$.
SSP	114	NIPA surplus (+) or deficit (−), s, B$.
STAT	exog	Statistical discrepancy, B$.
STATP	exog	Statistical discrepancy relating to the use of chain-type price indices, B96$.
SUBG	exog	Subsidies less current surplus of government enterprises, g, B$.
SUBS	exog	Subsidies less current surplus of government enterprises, s, B$.
T	exog	1 in 1952:1, 2 in 1952:2, etc.

Table A.2
(continued)

Variable	Eq.	Description
TAUG	exog	Progressivity tax parameter in personal income tax equation for g.
TAUS	exog	Progressivity tax parameter in personal income tax equation for s.
TBG	exog	Corporate profit taxes, b to g, B$.
TBS	exog	Corporate profit taxes, b to s, B$.
TCG	102	Corporate profit tax receipts, g, B$.
TCS	108	Corporate profit tax receipts, s, B$.
TFG	49	Corporate profit taxes, f to g, B$.
TFS	50	Corporate profit taxes, f to s, B$.
THG	47	Personal income taxes, h to g, B$.
THS	48	Personal income taxes, h to s, B$.
TPG	101	Personal income tax receipts, g, B$.
TRFH	exog	Transfer payments, f to h, B$.
TRFR	exog	Transfer payments, f to r, B$.
TRGH	exog	Transfer payments, g to h, B$.
TRGR	exog	Transfer payments, g to r, B$.
TRGS	exog	Transfer payments, g to s, B$.
TRHR	exog	Transfer payments, h to r, B$.
TRRSH	111	Total transfer payments, s to h, B$.
TRSH	exog	Transfer payments, s to h, excluding unemployment insurance benefits, B$.
U	86	Number of people unemployed, millions.
UB	28	Unemployment insurance benefits, B$.
UBR	128	Unborrowed reserves, B$.
UR	87	Civilian unemployment rate.
V	63	Stock of inventories, f, B96$.
WA	126	After-tax wage rate. (Includes supplements to wages and salaries except employer contributions for social insurance.)
WF	16	Average hourly earnings excluding overtime of workers in f (Includes supplements to wages and salaries except employer contributions for social insurance.)
WG	44	Average hourly earnings of civilian workers in g. (Includes supplements to wages and salaries including employer contributions for social insurance.)
WH	43	Average hourly earnings excluding overtime of all workers. (Includes supplements to wages and salaries except employer contributions for social insurance.)
WLDF	exog	Wage accruals less disbursements, f, B$.
WLDG	exog	Wage accruals less disbursements, g, B$.
WLDS	exog	Wage accruals less disbursements, s, B$.
WM	45	Average hourly earnings of military workers. (Includes supplements to wages and salaries including employer contributions for social insurance.)
WR	119	Real wage rate of workers in f. (Includes supplements to wages and salaries except employer contributions for social insurance.)
WS	46	Average hourly earnings of workers in s. (Includes supplements to wages and salaries including employer contributions for social insurance.)
X	60	Total sales f, B96$.
XX	61	Total sales, f, B$.
Y	11	Production, f, B96$.
YD	115	Disposable income, h, B$.
YNL	99	After-tax nonlabor income, h, B$.
YS	98	Potential output of the firm sector.
YT	64	Taxable income, h, B$.

Notes:
- B$ = billions of dollars.
- B96$ = billions of 1996 dollars.

Table A.3

The Equations of the US Model

Eq.	LHS Variable	Explanatory Variables

STOCHASTIC EQUATIONS

Household sector

1   $\log(CS/POP)$ cnst, $AG1$, $AG2$, $AG3$, $\log(CS/POP)_{-1}$, $\log[YD/(POP \cdot PH)]$, RSA, $\log(AA/POP)_{-1}$, T
[Consumer expenditures: services]

2   $\log(CN/POP)$ cnst, $AG1$, $AG2$, $AG3$, $\log(CN/POP)_{-1}$, $\Delta \log(CN/POP)_{-1}$, $\log(AA/POP)_{-1}$, $\log[YD/(POP \cdot PH)]$, RMA
[Consumer expenditures: nondurables]

3   $\Delta CD/POP$ cnst, $AG1$, $AG2$, $AG3$, $DELD(KD/POP)_{-1} - (CD/POP)_{-1}$, $(KD/POP)_{-1}$, $YD/(POP \cdot PH)$, $RMA \cdot CDA$, $(AA/POP)_{-1}$
[Consumer expenditures: durables]

4   $\Delta IHH/POP$ cnst, $DELH(KH/POP)_{-1} - (IHH/POP)_{-1}$, $(KH/POP)_{-1}$, $(AA/POP)_{-1}$, $YD/(POP \cdot PH)$, $RMA_{-1}IHHA$, $RHO = 2$
[Residential investment–h]

5   $\log(L1/POP1)$ cnst, $\log(L1/POP1)_{-1}$, $\log(AA/POP)_{-1}$, UR
[Labor force—men 25–54]

6   $\log(L2/POP2)$ cnst, $\log(L2/POP2)_{-1}$, $\log(WA/PH)$, $\log(AA/POP)_{-1}$
[Labor force—women 25–54]

7   $\log(L3/POP3)$ cnst, $\log(L3/POP1)_{-1})$, $\log(WA/PH)$, $\log(AA/POP)_{-1}$, UR
[Labor force—all others 16+]

8   $\log(LM/POP)$ cnst, $\log(LM/POP)_{-1}$, $\log(WA/PH)$, UR
[Number of moonlighters]

9   $\log[MH/(POP \cdot PH)]$ cnst, $\log[MH_{-1}/(POP_{-1}PH)]$, $\log[YD/(POP \cdot PH)]$, RSA, T, $D981$, $RHO = 4$
[Demand deposits and currency–h]

Firm sector

10   $\log PF$ $\log PF_{-1}$, $\log[WF(1 + D5G)] - \log LAM$, cnst, $\log PIM$, UR, T
[Price deflator for $X - FA$]

11   $\log Y$ cnst, $\log Y_{-1}$, $\log X$, $\log V_{-1}$, $D593$, $D594$, $D601$, $RHO = 3$
[Production–f]

12   $\Delta \log KK$ $\log(KK/KKMIN)_{-1}$, $\Delta \log KK_{-1}$, $\Delta \log Y$, $\Delta \log Y_{-1}$, $\Delta \log Y_{-2}$, $\Delta \log Y_{-3}$, $\Delta \log Y_{-4}$, $\Delta \log Y_{-5}$, $RB_{-2}(1 - D2G_{-2} - D2S_{-2}) - 100(PD_{-2}/PD_{-6}) - 1)$, $(CG_{-2} + CG_{-3} + CG_{-4})/(PX_{-2}YS_{-2} + PX_{-3}YS_{-3} + PX_{-4}YS_{-4})$
[Stock of capital–f]

13   $\Delta \log JF$ cnst, $\log[JF/(JHMIN/HFS)]_{-1}$, $\Delta \log JF_{-1}$, $\Delta \log Y$, $D593$
[Number of jobs–f]

14   $\Delta \log HF$ cnst, $\log(HF/HFS)_{-1}$, $\log[JF/(JHMIN/HFS)]_{-1}$, $\Delta \log Y$
[Average number of hours paid per job–f]

15   $\log HO$ cnst, HFF, HFF_{-1}, $RHO = 1$
[Average number of overtime hours paid per job–f]

16   $\log WF - \log LAM$ $\log WF_{-1} - \log LAM_{-1}$, $\log PF$, cnst, T, $\log PF_{-1}$
[Average hourly earnings excluding overtime–f]

17   $\log(MF/PF)$ cnst, T, $\log(MF_{-1}/PF)$, $\log(X - FA)$, $RS(1 - D2G - D2S)_{-1}$, $D981$
[Demand deposits and currency–f]

18   $\Delta \log DF$ $\log[(PIEF - TFG - TFS)/DF_{-1}]$
[Dividends paid–f]

19   $\Delta[INTF/(-AF + 40)]$ cnst, $[INTF/(-AF + 40)]_{-1}$, $.75(1/400)[.3RS + .7(1/8)(RB + RB_{-1} + RB_{-2} + RB_{-3} + RB_{-4} + RB_{-5} + RB_{-6} + RB_{-7})]$, $RHO = 1$
[Interest payments–f]

20   IVA $(PX - PX_{-1})V_{-1}$, $RHO = 1$
[Inventory valuation adjustment]

21   $\Delta \log CCF$ $\log[(PIK \cdot IKF)/CCF_{-1}]$, cnst, $D621$, $D722$, $D723$, $D923$, $D924$, $D941$, $D942$, $D013$, $D014$, $RHO = 1$
[Capital consumption–f]

Table A.3
(continued)

Eq.	LHS Variable	Explanatory Variables

Financial sector

22   BO/BR cnst, $(BO/BR)_{-1}$, RS, RD
[Bank borrowing from the Fed]

23    $RB - RS_{-2}$ cnst, $RB_{-1} - RS_{-2}$, $RS - RS_{-2}$, $RS_{-1} - RS_{-2}$, $RHO = 1$
[Bond rate]

24    $RM - RS_{-2}$ cnst, $RM_{-1} - RS_{-2}$, $RS - RS_{-2}$, $RS_{-1} - RS_{-2}$
[Mortgage rate]

25    $CG/(PX_{-1} \cdot YS_{-1})$ cnst, ΔRB, $[\Delta(PIEF - TFG - TFS + PX \cdot PIEB - TBG - TBS)]/(PX_{-1} \cdot YS_{-1})$
[Capital gains or losses on the financial assets of h]

26    $\log[CUR/(POP \cdot PF)]$

       cnst, $\log[CUR_{-1}/(POP_{-1}PF)]$, $\log[(X - FA)/POP]$, RSA, $RHO = 1$
[Currency held outside banks]

Import equation

27    $\log(IM/POP)$ cnst, $\log(IM/POP)_{-1}$, $\log[(CS + CN + CD + IHH + IKF + IHB + IHF + IKB + IKH)/POP]$, $\log(PF/PIM)$, $D691$, $D692$, $D714$, $D721$, $RHO = 2$
[Imports]

Government sectors

28    $\log UB$ cnst, $\log UB_{-1}$, $\log U$, $\log WF$, $RHO = 1$
[Unemployment insurance benefits]

29    $\Delta[INTG/(-AG)]$ cnst, $[INTG/(-AG)]_{-1}$, $.75(1/400)[.3RS + .7(1/8)(RB + RB_{-1} + RB_{-2} + RB_{-3} + RB_{-4} + RB_{-5} + RB_{-6} + RB_{-7})]$

30   RS cnst, RS_{-1}, $100[(PD/PD_{-1})^4 - 1]$, UR, ΔUR, $PCM1_{-1}$, $D794823 \cdot PCM1_{-1}$, ΔRS_{-1}, ΔRS_{-2}
[Three-month Treasury bill rate]

IDENTITIES

31    $PX =$ $[PF(X - FA) + PFA \cdot FA]/X$
[Price deflator for X]

32    $PEX =$ $PSI1 \cdot PX$
[Price deflator for EX]

33    $PD =$ $(PX \cdot X - PEX \cdot EX + PIM \cdot IM)/(X - EX + IM)$
[Price deflator for domestic sales]

34    $PH =$ $(PCS \cdot CS + PCN \cdot CN + PCD \cdot CD + PIH \cdot IHH + IBTG + IBTS)/(CS + CN + CD + IHH)$
[Price deflator for $(CS + CN + CD + IHH)$ inclusive of indirect business taxes]

35    $PCS =$ $PSI2(1 + D3G + D3S)PD$
[Price deflator for CS]

36    $PCN =$ $PSI3(1 + D3G + D3S)PD$
[Price deflator for CN]

37    $PCD =$ $PSI4(1 + D3G + D3S)PD$
[Price deflator for CD]

38    $PIH =$ $PSI5 \cdot PD$
[Price deflator for residential investment]

39    $PIK =$ $PSI6 \cdot PD$
[Price deflator for nonresidential fixed investment]

40    $PG =$ $PSI7 \cdot PD$
[Price deflator for COG]

41    $PS =$ $PSI8 \cdot PD$
[Price deflator for COS]

42    $PIV =$ $PSI9 \cdot PD$
[Price deflator for inventory investment]

Table A.3

(continued)

Eq.	LHS Variable	Explanatory Variables

IDENTITIES *(continued)*

43    $WH =$ $100[(WF \cdot JF(HN + 1.5HO) + WG \cdot JG \cdot HG + WM \cdot JM \cdot HM + WS \cdot JS \cdot$
$HS - SIGG - SISS)/(JF(HN + 1.5HO) + JG \cdot HG + JM \cdot HM + JS \cdot HS)]$
[Average hourly earnings excluding overtime of all workers]

44    $WG =$ $PSI10 \cdot WF$
[Average hourly earnings of civilian workers–g]

45    $WM =$ $PSI11 \cdot WF$
[Average hourly earnings of military workers]

46    $WS =$ $PSI12 \cdot WF$
[Average hourly earnings of workers–s]

47    $THG =$ $[D1G + ((TAUG \cdot YT)/POP)]YT$
[Personal income taxes–h to g]

48    $THS =$ $[D1S + ((TAUS \cdot YT)/POP)]YT$
[Personal income taxes–h to s]

49    $TFG =$ $D2G(PIEF - TFS)$
[Corporate profits taxes–f to g]

50    $TFS =$ $D2S \cdot PIEF$
[Corporate profits taxes–f to s]

51    $IBTG =$ $[D3G/(1 + D3G)](PCS \cdot CS + PCN \cdot CN + PCD \cdot CD - IBTS)$
[Indirect business taxes–g]

52    $IBTS =$ $[D3S/(1 + D3S)](PCS \cdot CS + PCN \cdot CN + PCD \cdot CD - IBTG)$
[Indirect business taxes–s]

53    $SIHG =$ $D4G[WF \cdot JF(HN + 1.5HO)]$
[Employee social insurance contributions–h to g]

54    $SIFG =$ $D5G[WF \cdot JF(HN + 1.5HO)]$
[Employer social insurance contributions–f to g]

55   none

56   none

57    $BR =$ $-G1 \cdot MB$
[Total bank reserves]

58    $KD =$ $(1 - DELD)KD_{-1} + CD$
[Stock of durable goods]

59    $KH =$ $(1 - DELH)KH_{-1} + IHH$
[Stock of housing–h]

60    $X =$ $CS + CN + CD + IHH + IKF + EX - IM + COG + COS + IKH + IKB +$
$IKG + IHF + IHB - PIEB - CCB$
[Total sales–f]

61    $XX =$ $PCS \cdot CS + PCN \cdot CN + PCD \cdot CD + PIH \cdot IHH + PIK \cdot IKF + PEX \cdot$
$EX - PIM \cdot IM + PG \cdot COG + PS \cdot COS + PIK(IKH + IKB + IKG) +$
$PIH(IHF + IHB) - PX(PIEB + CCB) - IBTG - IBTS$
[Total nominal sales–f]

62    $HN =$ $HF - HO$
[Average number of non overtime hours paid per job–f]

63    $V =$ $V_{-1} + Y - X$
[Stock of inventories f]

64    $YT =$ $WF \cdot JF(HN + 1.5HO) + WG \cdot JG \cdot HG + WM \cdot JM \cdot HM + WS \cdot JS \cdot HS +$
$DF + DB - DRS + INTF + INTG + INTS + INTOTH + INTROW +$
$RNT + TRFH - SIGG - SISS$
[Taxable income–h]

65    $SH =$ $YT + CCH - PCS \cdot CS - PCN \cdot CN - PCD \cdot CD - PIH \cdot IHH - PIK \cdot IKH -$
$TRHR - THG - SIHG + TRGH - THS - SIHS + TRSH + UB + INS -$
$WLDF$
[Saving–h]

Table A.3
(continued)

Eq.	LHS Variable	Explanatory Variables

IDENTITIES *(continued)*

66    $0 =$

$SH - \Delta AH - \Delta MH + CG - DISH$

[Budget constraint–h (determines AH)]

67    $PIEF =$

$XX + PIV(V - V_{-1}) - WF \cdot JF(HN + 1.5HO) - RNT - TRFH - TRFR - CCH + SUBG + SUBS - INTF - INTOTH - INTROW - CCF - IVA - STAT - SIFG - SIFS + FIUS - FIROW - CCG - CCS + WLDG + WLDS + DISBA$

[Before-tax profits–f]

68    $CF =$

$XX - WF \cdot JF(HN + 1.5HO) - RNT - TRFH - TRFR - CCH + SUBG + SUBS - INTF - INTOTH - INTROW - PIK \cdot IKF - PIH \cdot IHF - SIFG - SIFS + FIUS - FIROW - CCG - CCS + WLDF$

[Cash flow–f]

69    $SF =$

$CF - TFG - TFS - DF$

[Saving–f]

70    $0 =$

$SF - \Delta AF - \Delta MF - DISF - STAT - WLDF + WLDG + WLDS + DISBA$

[Budget constraint–f (determines AF)]

71    $0 =$

$\Delta MB + \Delta MH + \Delta MF + \Delta MR + \Delta MG + \Delta MS - \Delta CUR$

[Demand deposit identity (determines MB)]

72    $SB =$

$PX(PIEB + CCB) - PIK \cdot IKB - PIH \cdot IHB - DB - TBG - TBS$

[Saving–b]

73    $0 =$

$SB - \Delta AB - \Delta MB - \Delta(BR - BO) - DISB$

[Budget constraint–b (determines AB)]

74    $SR =$

$PIM \cdot IM + TRHR + TRGR + TRFR - PEX \cdot EX + FIROW - FIUS$

[Saving–r]

75    $0 =$

$SR - \Delta AR - \Delta MR + \Delta Q - DISR$

[Budget constraint–r (determines AR)]

76    $SG =$

$THG + IBTG + TFG + TBG + SIHG + SIFG - PG \cdot COG - WG \cdot JG \cdot HG - WM \cdot JM \cdot HM - INTG - TRGR - TRGH - TRGS - SUBG - INS + SIGG - PIK \cdot IKG + CCG$

[Saving–g]

77    $0 =$

$SG - \Delta AG - \Delta MG + \Delta CUR + \Delta(BR - BO) - \Delta Q - DISG$

[Budget constraint–g (determines AG unless AG is exogenous)]

78    $SS =$

$THS + IBTS + TFS + TBS + SIHS + SIFS + TRGS + DRS - PS \cdot COS - WS \cdot JS \cdot HS - INTS - SUBS - TRSH - UB + SISS + CCS$

[Saving–s]

79    $0 =$

$SS - \Delta AS - \Delta MS - DISS$

[Budget constraint–s (determines AS)]

80    $0 =$

$\Delta AH + \Delta AF + \Delta AB + \Delta AG + \Delta AS + \Delta AR - CG + DISH + DISF + DISB + DISG + DISS + DISR + STAT + WLDF - WLDG - WLDS - DISBA$

[Asset identity (redundant equation)]

81    $M1 =$

$M1_{-1} + \Delta MH + \Delta MF + \Delta MR + \Delta MS + MDIF$

[Money supply]

82    $GDP =$

$XX + PIV(V - V_{-1}) + IBTG + IBTS + WG \cdot JG \cdot HG + WM \cdot JM \cdot HM + WS \cdot JS \cdot HS + WLDG + WLDS + PX(PIEB + CCB)$

[Nominal GDP]

83    $GDPR =$

$Y + PIEB + CCB + PSI13(JG \cdot HG + JM \cdot HM + JS \cdot HS) + STATP$

[Real GDP]

84    $GDPD =$

$GDP/GDPR$

[GDP price deflator]

85    $E =$

$JF + JG + JM + JS - LM$

[Total employment, civilian and military]

86    $U =$

$L1 + L2 + L3 - E$

[Number of people unemployed]

Table A.3
(continued)

Eq.	LHS Variable	Explanatory Variables

IDENTITIES *(continued)*

Eq.	LHS Variable	Explanatory Variables
87	$UR =$	$U/(L1 + L2 + L3 - JM)$ [Civilian unemployment rate]
88	none	
89	$AA =$	$(AH + MH)/PH + (PIH \cdot KH)/PH$ [Total net wealth–h]
90	$D1GM =$	$D1G + (2TAUG \cdot YT)/POP$ [Marginal personal income tax rate–g]
91	$D1SM =$	$D1S + (2TAUS \cdot YT)/POP$ [Marginal personal income tax rate–s]
92	$IKF =$	$KK - (1 - DELK)KK_{-1}$ [Nonresidential fixed investment–f]
93	$KKMIN =$	Y/MUH [Amount of capital required to produce Y]
94	$JHMIN =$	Y/LAM [Number of worker hours required to produce Y]
95	$JJ =$	$(JF \cdot HF + JG \cdot HG + JM \cdot HM + JS \cdot HS)/POP$ [Ratio of the total number of worker hours paid for to the total population 16 and over]
96	none	
97	none	
98	$YS =$	$LAM(JJP \cdot POP - JG \cdot HG - JM \cdot HM - JS \cdot HS)$ [Potential output of the firm sector]
99	$YNL =$	$[1 - D1G - D1S - (TAUG + TAUS)(YT/POP)](RNT + DF + DB - DRS + INTF + INTG + INTS + INTOTH + INTROW + TRFH) + TRGH + TRSH + UB$ [After-tax nonlabor income–h]
100	$HFF =$	$HF - HFS$ [Deviation of HF from its peak to peak interpolation]
101	$TPG =$	THG [Personal income tax receipts–g]
102	$TCG =$	$TFG + TBG$ [Corporate profit tax receipts–g]
103	$SIG =$	$SIHG + SIFG + SIGG$ [Total social insurance contributions to g]
104	$PUG =$	$PG \cdot COG + WG \cdot JG \cdot HG + WM \cdot JM \cdot HM + WLDG$ [Purchases of goods and services–g]
105	$RECG =$	$TPG + TCG + IBTG + SIG$ [Total receipts–g]
106	$EXPG =$	$PUG + TRGH + TRGR + TRGS + INTG + SUBG - WLDG - IGZ$ [Total expenditures–g]
107	$SGP =$	$RECG - EXPG$ [NIPA surplus or deficit–g]
108	$TCS =$	$TFS + TBS$ [Corporate profit tax receipts–s]
109	$SIS =$	$SIHS + SIFS + SISS$ [Total social insurance contributions to s]
110	$PUS =$	$PS \cdot COS + WS \cdot JS \cdot HS + WLDS$ [Purchases of goods and services–s]
111	$TRRSH =$	$TRSH + UB$ [Total transfer payments–s to h]
112	$RECS =$	$THS + TCS + IBTS + SIS + TRGS$ [Total receipts–s]

Table A.3
(continued)

Eq.	LHS Variable	Explanatory Variables

IDENTITIES *(continued)*

113    $EXPS =$ $PUS + TRRSH + INTS - DRS + SUBS - WLDS - ISZ$
[Total expenditures–s]

114    $SSP =$ $RECS - EXPS$
[NIPA surplus or deficit–s]

115    $YD =$ $WF \cdot JF(HN + 1.5HO) + WG \cdot JG \cdot HG + WM \cdot JM \cdot HM + WS \cdot JS \cdot$
$HS + RNT + DF + DB - DRS + INTF + INTG + INTS + INTOTH +$
$INTROW + TRFH + TRGH + TRSH + UB - SIHG - SIHS - THG -$
$THS - TRHR - SIGG - SISS$
[Disposable income–h]

116    $SRZ =$ $(YD - PCS \cdot CS - PCN \cdot CN - PCD \cdot CD)/YD$
[Saving rate–h]

117    $IVF =$ $V - V_{-1}$
[Inventory investment–f]

118    $PROD =$ $Y/(JF \cdot HF)$
[Output per paid for worker hour: "productivity"]

119    $WR =$ WF/PF
[Real wage rate of workers in f]

120   POP $= POP1 + POP2 + POP3$
[Noninstitutional population 16 and over]

121    $SHRPIE =$ $[(1 - D2G - D2S)PIEF]/[WF \cdot JF(HN + 1.5HO)]$
[Ratio of after-tax profits to the wage bill net of employer social security taxes]

122    $PCGDPR =$ $100[(GDPR/GDPR_{-1})^4 - 1]$
[Percentage change in GDPR]

123    $PCGDPD =$ $100[(GDPD/GDPD_{-1})^4 - 1]$
[Percentage change in GDPD]

124    $PCM1 =$ $100[(M1/M1_{-1})^4 - 1]$
[Percentage change in M1]

125    $UBR =$ $BR - BO$
[Unborrowed reserves]

126    $WA =$ $100[(1 - D1GM - D1SM - D4G)[WF \cdot JF(HN + 1.5HO)] + (1 - D1GM -$
$D1SM)(WG \cdot JG \cdot HG + WM \cdot JM \cdot HM + WS \cdot JS \cdot HS - SIGG -$
$SISS)]/[JF(HN + 1.5HO) + JG \cdot HG + JM \cdot HM + JS \cdot HS]$
[After-tax wage rate]

127    $RSA =$ $RS(1 - D1GM - D1SM)$
[After-tax three-month Treasury bill rate]

128    $RMA =$ $RM(1 - D1GM - D1SM)$
[After-tax mortgage rate]

129    $GNP =$ $GDP + FIUS - FIROW$
[Nominal GNP]

130    $GNPR =$ $GDPR + FIUS/FIUSD - FIROW/FIROWD$
[Real GNP]

131    $GNPD =$ $GNP/GNPR$
[GNP price deflator]

Table A.4
Coefficient Estimates and Test Results
for the US Equations

- See Chapter 1 for discussion of the tests.
- See Chapter 2 for discussion of the equations.
- * = significant at the 99 percent level.
- The estimation period is 1954.1–2002.3 unless otherwise specified.

Table A1
Equation 1: LHS Variable is $\log(CS/POP)$

Equation			χ^2 Tests			
RHS variable	Coeff.	t-stat.	Test	χ^2	df	p-value
cnst	0.05716	1.48	Lags	0.42	4	.9804
$AG1$	−0.32687	−4.40	RHO	3.71	4	.4471
$AG2$	−0.39071	−2.91	Leads +1	4.47	1	.0345
$AG3$	0.76866	4.89	Leads +4	8.91	4	.0633
$\log(CS/POP)_{-1}$	0.78732	19.31	Leads +8	8.47	2	.0145
$\log[YD/(POP \cdot PH)]$	0.10582	3.06				
RSA	−0.00123	−5.75				
$\log(AA/POP)_{-1}$	0.01717	3.50				
T	0.00042	4.42				

SE   0.00394
R^2 .999
DW   1.95
overid (df = 13, p-value = .0602)
χ^2 (AGE) = 36.92 (df = 3, p-value = .0000)

Stability Test					End Test	
AP	T_1	T_2	λ	Break	p-value	End
21.18*	1970.1	1979.4	2.29	1977.3	1.0000	1995.1
21.09*	1975.1	1984.4	2.26	1977.3		
16.06*	1980.1	1989.4	2.41	1980.1		

Table A2
Equation 2: LHS Variable is $\log(CN/POP)$

	Equation			χ^2 Tests		
RHS variable	Coeff.	t-stat.	Test	χ^2	df	p-value
cnst	−0.21384	−2.85	Lags	14.45	4	.0060
$AG1$	−0.06221	−0.63	RHO	16.55	4	.0024
$AG2$	0.29558	1.62	T	0.23	1	.6355
$AG3$	−0.16048	−1.06	Leads +1	4.30	1	.0382
$\log(CN/POP)_{-1}$	0.78233	21.69	Leads +4	4.66	4	.3243
$\Delta \log(CN/POP)_{-1}$	0.14449	2.30	Leads +8	3.24	2	.1976
$\log(AA/POP)_{-1}$	0.05068	4.78				
$\log[YD/(POP \cdot PH)]$	0.09733	4.28				
RMA	−0.00174	−4.24				

SE   0.00609
R^2 .999
DW   1.93
overid (df = 13, p-value = .1974)
χ^2 (AGE) = 8.22 (df = 3, p-value = .0417)

	Stability Test				End Test	
AP	T_1	T_2	λ	Break	p-value	End
14.67*	1970.1	1979.4	2.29	1975.1	.8582	1995.1
15.33*	1975.1	1984.4	2.26	1975.1		
14.94*	1980.1	1989.4	2.41	1981.1		

Table A3
Equation 3: LHS Variable is $CD/POP - (CD/POP)_{-1}$

	Equation			χ^2 Tests		
RHS variable	Coeff.	t-stat.	Test	χ^2	df	p-value
cnst	−0.16647	−1.20	Lags	2.37	5	.7957
$AG1$	−0.04158	−0.18	RHO	11.44	4	.0220
$AG2$	3.04707	4.97	T	4.00	1	.0454
$AG3$	−2.17926	−4.31	Leads +1	5.88	1	.0153
[a]	0.32939	5.42	Leads +4	6.08	4	.1932
$(KD/POP)_{-1}$	−0.02388	−3.92	Leads +8	11.93	2	.0026
$YD/(POP \cdot PH)$	0.10772	4.65				
$RMA \cdot CDA$	−0.00514	−3.23				
$(AA/POP)_{-1}$	0.00027	1.53				

SE   0.01446
R^2 .208
DW   2.07
overid (df = 9, p-value = .0711)
χ^2 (AGE) = 26.18 (df = 3, p-value = .0000)

	Stability Test				End Test	
AP	T_1	T_2	λ	Break	p-value	End
12.76*	1970.1	1979.4	2.29	1975.3	.1194	1995.1
16.42*	1975.1	1984.4	2.26	1980.3		
17.08*	1980.1	1989.4	2.41	1980.3		

Note:
a. Variable is $DELD(KD/POP)_{-1} - (CD/POP)_{-1}$.

Table A4

Equation 4: LHS Variable is $IHH/POP - (IHH/POP)_{-1}$

	Equation			χ^2 Tests		
RHS variable	Coeff.	t-stat.	Test	χ^2	df	p-value
cnst	0.34134	4.23	Lags	3.20	4	.5242
a	0.53807	7.87	RHO	0.92	2	.6316
$(KH/POP)_{-1}$	−0.03322	−3.51	T	4.41	1	.0357
$YD/(POP \cdot PH)$	0.14273	3.85	Leads +1	0.19	1	.6636
$RMA_{-1}IHHA$	−0.02955	−6.17	Leads +4	3.09	4	.5429
RHO1	0.61928	7.82	Leads +8	3.52	2	.1721
RHO2	0.23469	3.19				

SE   0.00975
R^2 .358
DW   1.97
overid (df = 17, p-value = .2892)
χ^2 (AGE) = 2.70 (df = 3, p-value = .4405)

	Stability Test				End Test	
AP	T_1	T_2	λ	Break	p-value	End
7.17	1970.1	1979.4	2.29	1971.1	.7164	1995.1
5.57	1975.1	1984.4	2.26	1975.1		
2.77	1980.1	1989.4	2.41	1989.4		

Note:
a. Variable is $DELH(KH/POP)_{-1} - (IHH/POP)_{-1}$.

Table A5

Equation 5: LHS Variable is $\log(L1/POP1)$

	Equation			χ^2 Tests		
RHS variable	Coeff.	t-stat.	Test	χ^2	df	p-value
cnst	0.02063	2.58	Lags	3.65	3	.3018
$\log(L1/POP1)_{-1}$	0.92306	31.26	RHO	43.94	4	.0000
$\log(AA/POP)_{-1}$	−0.00551	−2.66	T	4.75	1	.0294
UR	−0.02532	−1.69				

SE   0.00210
R^2 .989
DW   2.23
overid (df = 9, p-value = .0621)

	Stability Test				End Test	
AP	T_1	T_2	λ	Break	p-value	End
7.39*	1970.1	1979.4	2.29	1970.2	.5672	1995.1
0.40	1975.1	1984.4	2.26	1975.4		
1.03	1980.1	1989.4	2.41	1989.4		

Table A6
Equation 6: LHS Variable is $\log(L2/POP2)$

Equation			χ^2 Tests			
RHS variable	Coeff.	t-stat.	Test	χ^2	df	p-value
cnst	0.03455	2.22	Lags	1.94	3	.5841
$\log(L2/POP2)_{-1}$	0.99334	181.18	RHO	8.58	4	.0725
$\log(WA/PH)$	0.01732	2.69	T	0.02	1	.8817
$\log(AA/POP)_{-1}$	−0.00838	−2.64	Leads +1	0.20	1	.6579
			Leads +4	9.07	4	.0593
			Leads +8	2.22	2	.3293
			$\log PH$	0.01	1	.9437

SE   0.00576
R^2 .999
DW   2.15
overid (df = 14, p-value = .4262)

Stability Test					End Test	
AP	T_1	T_2	λ	Break	p-value	End
6.48	1970.1	1979.4	2.29	1973.1	.8657	1995.1
2.61	1975.1	1984.4	2.26	1976.1		
1.98	1980.1	1989.4	2.41	1985.1		

Table A7
Equation 7: LHS Variable is $\log(L3/POP3)$

Equation			χ^2 Tests			
RHS variable	Coeff.	t-stat.	Test	χ^2	df	p-value
cnst	0.01646	1.17	Lags	5.40	4	.2486
$\log(L3/POP3)_{-1}$	0.97777	57.64	RHO	2.97	4	.5625
$\log(WA/PH)$	0.00812	1.32	T	0.85	1	.3572
$\log(AA/POP)_{-1}$	−0.00618	−1.32	Leads +1	0.07	1	.7842
UR	−0.12585	−3.41	Leads +8	0.90	2	.6367
			$\log PH$	0.53	1	.4663

SE   0.00545
R^2 .985
DW   2.06
overid (df = 8, p-value = .3146)

Stability Test					End Test	
AP	T_1	T_2	λ	Break	p-value	End
6.56	1970.1	1979.4	2.29	1970.1	.4403	1995.1
5.85	1975.1	1984.4	2.26	1979.2		
8.28*	1980.1	1989.4	2.41	1989.4		

Table A8
Equation 8: LHS Variable is $\log(LM/POP)$

Equation			χ^2 Tests			
RHS variable	Coeff.	*t*-stat.	Test	χ^2	df	*p*-value
cnst	−0.22173	−3.43	Lags	9.01	3	.0291
$\log(LM/POP)_{-1}$	0.90339	42.10	RHO	4.74	4	.3155
$\log(WA/PH)$	0.13751	3.95	T	9.33	1	.0023
UR	−2.34060	−5.18	Leads +1	1.13	1	.2880
			Leads +4	0.65	4	.9578
			Leads +8	1.95	2	.3776
			$\log PH$	7.43	1	.0064

SE   0.06446
R^2 .956
DW   1.98
overid (df = 15, *p*-value = .0783)

	Stability Test				End Test	
AP	T_1	T_2	λ	Break	*p*-value	End
9.35*	1970.1	1979.4	2.29	1979.2	1.0000	1995.1
9.68*	1975.1	1984.4	2.26	1980.1		
9.91*	1980.1	1989.4	2.41	1989.4		

Table A9
Equation 9: LHS Variable is $\log[MH/(POP \cdot PH)]$

Equation			χ^2 Tests			
RHS variable	Coeff.	*t*-stat.	Test	χ^2	df	*p*-value
cnst	0.97229	0.19	a	0.92	1	.3372
$\log[MH_{-1}/(POP_{-1}PH)]$	0.71984	11.34	Lags	6.03	3	.1103
$\log[YD/(POP \cdot PH)]$	0.37538	1.55				
RSA	−0.01235	−4.02				
T	−0.00628	−0.45				
D981	−0.12341	−4.42				
RHO1	0.13763	1.65				
RHO2	0.32188	4.62				
RHO3	0.10284	1.46				
RHO4	0.42014	5.87				

SE   0.03184
R^2 .967
DW   2.01
overid (df = 30, *p*-value = .2173)
χ^2 (AGE) = 3.69 (df = 3, *p*-value = .2971)

	Stability Test				End Test	
AP	T_1	T_2	λ	Break	*p*-value	End
15.69*	1970.1	1979.4	2.29	1979.1	.1119	1995.1
21.15*	1975.1	1984.4	2.26	1984.1		
24.12*	1980.1	1989.4	2.41	1986.1		

Note:
a. Variable is $\log[(MH/(POP \cdot PH)]_{-1}$.

Table A10
Equation 10: LHS Variable is log PF

RHS variable	Coeff.	t-stat.	Test	χ^2	df	p-value
log PF_{-1}	0.88061	78.10	Lags	4.14	4	.3874
a	0.04411	3.24	RHO	5.64	4	.2273
cnst	−0.02368	−2.21	Leads +1	2.70	1	.1005
log PIM	0.04800	20.84	Leads +4	2.94	4	.5676
UR	−0.17797	−7.52	Leads +8	2.67	2	.2638
T	0.00030	9.80	b	0.06	1	.8140
			$(YS - Y)/YS$	0.02	1	.8881

SE   0.00333
R^2 .999
DW   1.78
overid (df = 8, p-value = .3194)

	Stability Test				End Test	
AP	T_1	T_2	λ	Break	p-value	End
12.77*	1970.1	1979.4	2.29	1972.2	1.0000	1995.1
8.70	1975.1	1984.4	2.26	1978.2		
7.96	1980.1	1989.4	2.41	1981.3		

Notes:
a. Variable is log$[WF(1 + D5G)]$ − log LAM.
b. Variable is log$[(YS - Y)/YS + .04]$.

Table A11
Equation 11: LHS Variable is log Y

RHS variable	Coeff.	t-stat.	Test	χ^2	df	p-value
cnst	0.26380	4.46	Lags	4.31	2	.1161
log Y_{-1}	0.31679	6.83	RHO	2.19	1	.1386
log X	0.88008	17.26	T	0.18	1	.6726
log V_{-1}	−0.24086	−8.32	Leads +1	2.40	1	.1212
$D593$	−0.01157	−3.11	Leads +4	2.13	4	.7123
$D594$	−0.00412	−1.11	Leads +8	1.27	2	.5291
$D601$	0.00870	2.36				
RHO1	0.41167	5.22				
RHO2	0.31158	4.18				
RHO3	0.18878	2.56				

SE   0.00403
R^2 .999
DW   2.02
overid (df = 20, p-value = .0887)

	Stability Test				End Test	
AP	T_1	T_2	λ	Break	p-value	End
6.96	1970.1	1979.4	2.29	1973.4	.8806	1995.1
6.55	1975.1	1984.4	2.26	1979.4		
5.58	1980.1	1989.4	2.41	1980.2		

Table A12
Equation 12: LHS Variable is $\Delta \log KK$

Equation			χ^2 Tests			
RHS variable	Coeff.	*t*-stat.	Test	χ^2	df	*p*-value
cnst	0.00002	0.15	Lags	5.14	5	.3990
$\log(KK/KKMIN)_{-1}$	−0.00679	−2.56	RHO	0.60	4	.9632
$\Delta \log KK_{-1}$	0.93839	57.81	T	1.13	1	.2889
$\Delta \log Y$	0.04076	4.09	Leads +1	0.00	1	.9470
$\Delta \log Y_{-1}$	0.00549	1.14	Leads +4	2.27	4	.6859
$\Delta \log Y_{-2}$	0.00477	1.12	Leads +8	3.13	2	.2094
$\Delta \log Y_{-3}$	0.00769	1.88				
$\Delta \log Y_{-4}$	0.00580	1.47				
$RBA_{-2} - p^e_{4-2}$	−0.00004	−2.45				
a	0.00048	2.19				

SE 0.00044
R^2 .970
DW 2.04
overid (df = 8, *p*-value = .5796)

Stability Test					End Test	
AP	T_1	T_2	λ	Break	*p*-value	End
5.44	1970.1	1979.4	2.29	1975.1	.2612	1995.1
6.20	1975.1	1984.4	2.26	1982.1		
6.47	1980.1	1989.4	2.41	1986.1		

Note:
a. Variable is $(CG_{-2} + CG_{-3} + CG_{-4})/(PX_{-2}YS_{-2} + PX_{-3}YS_{-3} + PX_{-4}YS_{-4})$.

Table A13
Equation 13: LHS Variable is $\Delta \log JF$

Equation			χ^2 Tests			
RHS variable	Coeff.	*t*-stat.	Test	χ^2	df	*p*-value
cnst	0.00210	3.20	Lags	4.33	3	.2280
$\log JF/(JHMIN/HFS)_{-1}$	−0.10464	−5.85	RHO	3.45	4	.4858
$\Delta \log JF_{-1}$	0.45463	10.71	T	2.13	1	.1442
$\Delta \log Y$	0.32722	9.16	Leads +1	0.14	1	.7123
D593	−0.01461	−4.74	Leads +4	5.14	4	.2728
			Leads +8	0.29	2	.8657

SE 0.00297
R^2 .771
DW 1.98
overid (df = 16, *p*-value = .5774)

Stability Test					End Test	
AP	T_1	T_2	λ	Break	*p*-value	End
3.55	1970.1	1979.4	2.29	1975.2	.6493	1995.1
3.57	1975.1	1984.4	2.26	1975.2		
2.31	1980.1	1989.4	2.41	1980.3		

Table A14
Equation 14: LHS Variable is $\Delta \log HF$

Equation			χ^2 Tests			
RHS variable	Coeff.	t-stat.	Test	χ^2	df	p-value
cnst	−0.00312	−5.08	Lags	5.87	3	.1181
$\log(HF/HFS)_{-1}$	−0.21595	−5.38	RHO	5.97	4	.2013
$\log JF/(JHMIN/HFS)_{-1}$	−0.04107	−2.49	T	0.04	1	.8350
$\Delta \log Y$	0.19529	4.81	Leads +1	0.81	1	.3671
			Leads +4	2.93	4	.5694
			Leads +8	0.80	2	.6707

SE   0.00276
R^2 .321
DW   2.06
overid (df = 6, p-value = .3277)

	Stability Test				End Test	
AP	T_1	T_2	λ	Break	p-value	End
10.13*	1970.1	1979.4	2.29	1976.2	.7388	1995.1
10.93*	1975.1	1984.4	2.26	1982.2		
11.21*	1980.1	1989.4	2.41	1988.4		

Table A15
Equation 15: LHS Variable is $\log HO$

Equation			χ^2 Tests			
RHS variable	Coeff.	t-stat.	Test	χ^2	df	p-value
cnst	3.98030	26.68	Lags	2.38	2	.3044
HFF	0.01905	8.47	RHO	4.68	3	.1972
HFF_{-1}	0.01132	5.03	T	7.06	1	.0079
RHO1	0.97503	53.83				

SE   0.04524
R^2 .956
DW   1.77

	Stability Test				End Test	
AP	T_1	T_2	λ	Break	p-value	End
2.74	1970.1	1979.4	2.41	1975.2	.9762	1995.1
4.81	1975.1	1984.4	2.33	1984.4		
5.34	1980.1	1989.4	2.47	1985.3		

Note:
• Estimation period is 1956.1–2002.3.

Table A16
Equation 16: LHS Variable is log WF − log LAM

Equation			χ^2 Tests			
RHS variable	Coeff.	t-stat.	Test	χ^2	df	p-value
log WF_{-1} − log LAM_{-1}	0.92726	39.24	RealWage Res.[b]	0.01	1	.9427
log PF	0.81226	16.23	Lags	3.00	1	.0834
cnst	−0.05848	−4.26	RHO	2.95	4	.5658
T	0.00011	2.64	UR	0.07	1	.7977
log PF_{-1}[a]	−0.75430	—				
SE	0.00696					
R^2	.887					
DW	1.72					
overid (df = 13, p-value = .1540)						

	Stability Test				End Test	
AP	T_1	T_2	λ	Break	p-value	End
3.91	1970.1	1979.4	2.29	1970.3	.5075	1995.1
2.96	1975.1	1984.4	2.26	1977.3		
2.26	1980.1	1989.4	2.41	1981.1		

Notes:
a. Coefficient constrained. See the discussion in the text.
b. Equation estimated with no restrictions on the coefficients.

Table A17
Equation 17: LHS Variable is log(MF/PF)

Equation			χ^2 Tests			
RHS variable	Coeff.	t-stat.	Test	χ^2	df	p-value
cnst	0.10232	1.75	log$(MF/PF)_{-1}$	0.05	1	.8204
log(MF_{-1}/PF)	0.94085	52.52	Lags	0.66	3	.8826
log$(X − FA)$	0.03987	4.10	RHO	2.22	4	.6961
[a]	−0.00546	−3.15	T	0.01	1	.9283
$D981$	0.13924	4.90				
SE	0.02820					
R^2	.987					
DW	2.07					
overid (df = 14, p-value = .1626)						

	Stability Test				End Test	
AP	T_1	T_2	λ	Break	p-value	End
1.68	1970.1	1979.4	2.29	1975.2	.4403	1995.1
3.27	1975.1	1984.4	2.26	1984.2		
6.14	1980.1	1989.4	2.41	1986.1		

Note:
a. Variable is $[RS(1 − D2G − D2S)]_{-1}$.

Table A18
Equation 18: LHS Variable is $\Delta \log DF$

	Equation			χ^2 Tests		
RHS variable	Coeff.	*t*-stat.	Test	χ^2	df	*p*-value
a	0.02744	12.11	Restriction[b]	1.97	1	.1601
			Lags	6.32	2	.0425
			RHO	16.20	4	.0028
			T	2.02	1	.1552
			cnst	0.55	1	.4572

SE   0.02263
R^2 .049
DW   1.66
overid (df = 7, *p*-value = .1449)

	Stability Test				End Test	
AP	T_1	T_2	λ	Break	*p*-value	End
4.41*	1970.1	1979.4	2.29	1976.1	.5000	1995.1
5.13*	1975.1	1984.4	2.26	1984.4		
6.29*	1980.1	1989.4	2.41	1986.1		

Notes:
a. Variable is $\log[(PIEF - TFG - TFS)/DF]_{-1}$.
b. $\log DF_{-1}$ added.

Table A19
Equation 19: LHS Variable is $\Delta[INTF/(-AF + 40)]$

	Equation			χ^2 Tests		
RHS variable	Coeff.	*t*-stat.	Test	χ^2	df	*p*-value
cnst	0.00016	1.84	Restriction[b]	1.13	1	.2875
a	0.02271	1.61	Lags	25.90	2	.0000
RHO1	0.45283	6.73	RHO	5.14	3	.1619
			T	10.60	1	.0011

SE   0.00065
R^2 .196
DW   2.00

	Stability Test				End Test	
AP	T_1	T_2	λ	Break	*p*-value	End
3.07	1970.1	1979.4	2.29	1977.1	.0000	1995.1
7.34*	1975.1	1984.4	2.26	1983.1		
7.57*	1980.1	1989.4	2.41	1983.1		

Notes:
a. Variable is $.75RQ - INTF_{-1}/(-AF_{-1} + 40)$.
b. $INTF_{-1}/(-AF_{-1} + 40)$ added.

Table A20
Equation 20: LHS Variable is *IVA*

	Equation			χ^2 Tests			
RHS variable	Coeff.	*t*-stat.	Test	χ^2	df	*p*-value
$(PX - PX_{-1})V_{-1}$	−0.27950	−4.70	Lags	2.22	2	.3298
RHO1	0.80731	18.14	RHO	6.44	3	.0920
			T	1.11	1	.2929
SE	1.76233					
R^2	.713					
DW	1.95					

	Stability Test				End Test	
AP	T_1	T_2	λ	Break	*p*-value	End
2.73	1970.1	1979.4	2.29	1974.4	.1343	1995.1
6.49*	1975.1	1984.4	2.26	1981.2		
7.15*	1980.1	1989.4	2.41	1989.2		

Table A21
Equation 21: LHS Variable is $\Delta \log CCF$

	Equation			χ^2 Tests			
RHS variable	Coeff.	*t*-stat.	Test	χ^2	df	*p*-value
[a]	0.06200	7.83	Restriction [b]	0.50	1	.4796
cnst	0.00278	1.24	Lags	6.40	2	.0408
*D*621	0.05796	6.36	RHO	9.34	3	.0251
*D*722	0.05332	5.60	*T*	0.53	1	.4666
*D*723	−0.04554	−4.78				
*D*923	0.07400	7.74				
*D*924	−0.07837	−8.15				
*D*941	0.07445	7.79				
*D*942	−0.05270	−5.49				
*D*013	0.04763	5.00				
*D*014	0.11290	11.84				
RHO1	0.31387	4.58				
SE	0.00954					
R^2	.748					
DW	2.07					

	Stability Test				End Test	
AP	T_1	T_2	λ	Break	*p*-value	End
4.77	1970.1	1979.4	2.29	1974.2	.5000	1995.1
3.91	1975.1	1984.4	2.26	1976.2		
2.27	1980.1	1989.4	2.41	1980.1		

Notes:
a. Variable is $\log[(PIK \cdot IKF)/CCF_{-1}]$.
b. $\log CCF_{-1}$ added.

Table A22
Equation 22: LHS Variable is BO/BR

RHS variable	Equation Coeff.	t-stat.	Test	χ^2	df	p-value
cnst	0.00119	0.38	Lags	11.12	3	.0111
$(BO/BR)_{-1}$	0.35179	5.13	RHO	30.21	4	.0000
RS	0.00460	1.39	T	6.52	1	.0107
RD	−0.00231	−0.75				

SE   0.01917
R^2 .326
DW   2.09
overid (df = 16, p-value = .0962)

AP	T_1	T_2	λ	Break	p-value	End
		Stability Test			End Test	
9.20*	1970.1	1979.4	2.29	1975.1	.8060	1995.1
9.19*	1975.1	1984.4	2.26	1975.1		
7.70*	1980.1	1989.4	2.41	1984.3		

Table A23
Equation 23: LHS Variable is $RB - RS_{-2}$

RHS variable	Equation Coeff.	t-stat.	Test	χ^2	df	p-value
cnst	0.23696	4.94	Restriction[a]	0.66	1	.4169
$RB_{-1} - RS_{-2}$	0.89059	43.85	Lags	0.44	2	.8036
$RS - RS_{-2}$	0.30766	7.07	RHO	3.62	3	.3054
$RS_{-1} - RS_{-2}$	−0.24082	−4.77	T	3.83	1	.0503
RHO1	0.25177	3.43	Leads +1	0.00	1	.9794
			Leads +8	0.66	2	.7185
			p_4^e	0.83	1	.3619
			p_8^e	1.35	1	.2445

SE   0.25897
R^2 .958
DW   2.03
overid (df = 15, p-value = .1837)

AP	T_1	T_2	λ	Break	p-value	End
		Stability Test			End Test	
3.56	1970.1	1979.4	2.29	1979.4	.3955	1995.1
5.04	1975.1	1984.4	2.26	1984.4		
5.37	1980.1	1989.4	2.41	1984.4		

Note:
a. RS_{-2} added.

Table A24
Equation 24: LHS Variable is $RM - RS_{-2}$

Equation			χ^2 Tests			
RHS variable	Coeff.	t-stat.	Test	χ^2	df	p-value
cnst	0.42974	5.65	Restriction [a]	1.12	1	.2899
$RM_{-1} - RS_{-2}$	0.85804	35.60	Lags	0.48	2	.7852
$RS - RS_{-2}$	0.25970	3.95	RHO	1.73	4	.7848
$RS_{-1} - RS_{-2}$	−0.03592	−0.42	T	0.93	1	.3352
			Leads +1	0.01	1	.9345
			Leads +4	2.99	4	.5593
			Leads +8	0.85	2	.6535
			p_4^e	0.29	1	.5886
			p_8^e	0.52	1	.4719

SE 0.35698
R^2 .892
DW 1.89
overid (df = 13, p-value = .1011)

Stability Test					End Test	
AP	T_1	T_2	λ	Break	p-value	End
3.60	1970.1	1979.4	2.29	1979.4	.4104	1995.1
11.82*	1975.1	1984.4	2.26	1984.4		
11.94*	1980.1	1989.4	2.41	1984.4		

Note:
a. RS_{-2} added.

Table A25
Equation 25: LHS Variable is $CG/(PX_{-1}YS_{-1})$

Equation			χ^2 Tests			
RHS variable	Coeff.	t-stat.	Test	χ^2	df	p-value
cnst	0.12099	4.10	Lags	0.55	3	.9087
ΔRB	−0.20871	−1.73	RHO	2.05	4	.7272
[a]	3.55665	0.28	T	0.19	1	.6616
			Leads +1	1.81	2	.4047
			Leads +4	3.15	8	.9246
			Leads +8	7.09	4	.1314
			ΔRS	2.12	1	.1455

SE 0.35444
R^2 .023
DW 1.97
overid (df = 17, p-value = .6215)

Stability Test					End Test	
AP	T_1	T_2	λ	Break	p-value	End
2.41	1970.1	1979.4	2.29	1974.4	.0000	1995.1
2.59	1975.1	1984.4	2.26	1979.1		
2.23	1980.1	1989.4	2.41	1989.4		

Note:
a. Variable is $\Delta[(PIEF - TFG - TFS + PX \cdot PIEB - TBG - TBS)]/(PX_{-1}YS_{-1})$.

Table A26
Equation 26: LHS Variable is $\log[CUR/(POP \cdot PF)]$

Equation				χ^2 Tests		
RHS variable	Coeff.	t-stat.	Test	χ^2	df	p-value
cnst	−0.05272	−7.26	a	5.86	1	.0155
$\log[CUR_{-1}/(POP_{-1}PF)]$	0.96339	129.70	Lags	5.53	3	.1366
$\log[(X - FA)/POP]$	0.04828	7.35	RHO	2.86	3	.4144
RSA	−0.00108	−2.19	T	0.25	1	.6176
RHO1	−0.31085	−4.53				
SE	0.01149					
R^2	.998					
DW	1.99					
overid (df = 17, p-value = .6669)						

Stability Test					End Test	
AP	T_1	T_2	λ	Break	p-value	End
3.33	1970.1	1979.4	2.29	1974.1	.0000	1995.1
7.40	1975.1	1984.4	2.26	1984.4		
8.73*	1980.1	1989.4	2.41	1984.4		

Note:
a. Variable is $\log[CUR/(POP \cdot PF)]_{-1}$.

Table A27
Equation 27: LHS Variable is $\log(IM/POP)$

Equation				χ^2 Tests		
RHS variable	Coeff.	t-stat.	Test	χ^2	df	p-value
cnst	−3.58632	−6.91	Lags	10.48	3	.0149
$\log(IM/POP)_{-1}$	0.21223	1.90	RHO	5.00	2	.0823
a	1.79417	6.94	T	0.58	1	.4465
$\log(PF/PIM)$	0.19470	3.58	Leads +1	2.01	1	.1561
$D691$	−0.13092	−5.43	Leads +4	3.92	4	.4171
$D692$	0.06287	2.13	Leads +8	1.71	2	.4260
$D714$	−0.07815	−3.25	$\log PF$	0.01	1	.9205
$D721$	0.05791	2.19				
RHO1	0.54484	4.46				
RHO2	0.24725	2.57				
SE	0.02666					
R^2	.998					
DW	2.03					
overid (df = 23, p-value = .2208)						

Stability Test					End Test	
AP	T_1	T_2	λ	Break	p-value	End
10.28	1973.1	1979.4	1.75	1975.1	.9328	1995.1
9.16	1975.1	1984.4	2.26	1975.1		
3.78	1980.1	1989.4	2.41	1980.3		

Note:
a. Variable is $\log[(CS + CN + CD + IHH + IKF + IKH + IKB + IHF + IHB)/POP]$.

Table A28
Equation 28: LHS Variable is log *UB*

Equation			χ^2 Tests			
RHS variable	Coeff.	*t*-stat.	Test	χ^2	df	*p*-value
cnst	1.07100	1.69	Lags	6.18	3	.1033
log UB_{-1}	0.26181	3.15	RHO	1.25	3	.7416
log U	1.15899	5.76	T	6.93	1	.0085
log WF	0.49835	4.02				
RHO1	0.92244	22.04				
SE	0.06477					
R^2	.996					
DW	2.14					
overid (df = 11, *p*-value = .0589)						

	Stability Test				End Test	
AP	T_1	T_2	λ	Break	*p*-value	End
19.29*	1970.1	1979.4	2.29	1975.2	.9552	1995.1
19.34*	1975.1	1984.4	2.26	1975.2		
18.37*	1980.1	1989.4	2.41	1980.4		

Table A29
Equation 29: LHS Variable is $\Delta[INTG/(-AG)]$

Equation			χ^2 Tests			
RHS variable	Coeff.	*t*-stat.	Test	χ^2	df	*p*-value
cnst	0.00041	3.33	Restriction [b]	23.06	1	.0000
[a]	0.06003	3.30	Lags	107.90	2	.0000
			RHO	145.33	4	.0000
			T	0.79	1	.3735
SE	0.00072					
R^2	.053					
DW	1.15					

	Stability Test				End Test	
AP	T_1	T_2	λ	Break	*p*-value	End
5.31*	1970.1	1979.4	2.29	1975.1	.7836	1995.1
17.72*	1975.1	1984.4	2.26	1982.1		
17.72*	1980.1	1989.4	2.41	1982.1		

Notes:
a. Variable is $.75RQ - [INTG/(-AG)]_{-1}$.
b. $[INTG/(-AG)]_{-1}$ added.

Table A30
Equation 30: LHS Variable is *RS*

Equation			χ^2 Tests			
RHS variable	Coeff.	t-stat.	Test	χ^2	df	p-value
cnst	0.74852	4.90	Lags	6.04	4	.1962
RS_{-1}	0.90916	46.16	RHO	5.96	4	.2021
$100[(PD/PD_{-1})^4 - 1]$	0.08027	4.50	T	0.00	1	.9957
UR	−11.28246	−3.64	Leads +1	0.75	2	.6886
ΔUR	−75.67464	−5.65	Leads +4	4.20	8	.8386
$PCM1_{-1}$	0.01100	1.88	Leads +8	2.93	4	.5699
$D794823 \cdot PCM1_{-1}$	0.21699	9.52	p_4^e	0.42	1	.5166
ΔRS_{-1}	0.22522	3.97	p_8^e	2.33	1	.1273
ΔRS_{-2}	−0.32726	−6.36				

SE   0.47591
R^2 .970
DW   1.83
overid (df = 12, p-value = .1007)
Stability Test (1954.1–1979.3 versus 1982.4–2002.3): Wald statistic is 15.32 (8 degrees of freedom, p-value = .0532).
End Test: p-value = .9030, End = 1995.1

Table A.5
The Raw Data Variables for the US Model

No.	Variable	Table	Line	Description
NIPA Data				
R1	GDP	1.1	1	Gross domestic product
R2	CDZ	1.1	3	Personal consumption expenditures, durable goods
R3	CNZ	1.1	4	Personal consumption expenditures, nondurable goods
R4	CSZ	1.1	5	Personal consumption expenditures, services
R5	IKZ	1.1	8	Nonresidential fixed investment
R6	IHZ	1.1	11	Residential fixed investment
R7	IVZ	1.1	12	Change in private inventories
R8	EXZ	1.1	14	Exports
R9	IMZ	1.1	17	Imports
R10	PURGZ	1.1	21	Consumption expenditures and gross investment, federal government
R11	PURSZ	1.1	24	Consumption expenditures and gross investment, S&L
R12	GDPR	1.2	1	Real gross domestic product
R13	CD	1.2	3	Real personal consumption expenditures, durable goods
R14	CN	1.2	4	Real personal consumption expenditures, nondurable goods
R15	*CS*	1.2	5	Real personal consumption expenditures, services
R16	IK	1.2	8	Real nonresidential fixed investment
R17	IH	1.2	11	Real residential fixed investment
R18	IV	1.2	12	Real change in private inventories
R19	EX	1.2	14	Real exports
R20	IM	1.2	17	Real imports
R21	PURG	1.2	21	Real federal government purchases
R22	PURS	1.2	24	Real state and local government purchases
R23	FAZ	1.7	6	Farm gross domestic product
R24	PROGZ	1.7	11	Federal government gross domestic product
R25	PROSZ	1.7	12	State and local government domestic gross product
R26	FA	1.8	6	Real farm gross domestic product
R27	PROG	1.8	11	Real federal government gross domestic product
R28	PROS	1.8	12	Real state and local government gross domestic product
R29	FIUS	1.9	2	Receipts of factor income from the rest of the world
R30	*FIROW*	1.9	3	Payments of factor income to the rest of the world
R31	CCT	1.9	6	Private consumption of fixed capital
R32	TRF	1.9	14	Business transfer payments
R33	STAT	1.9	15	Statistical discrepancy
R34	WLDF	1.9	21	Wage accruals less disbursements
R35	DPER	1.9	23	Personal dividend income
R36	TRFH	1.9	25	Business transfer payments to persons
R37	FIUSR	1.10	2	Real receipts of factor income from the rest of the world
R38	FIROWR	1.10	3	Real payments of factor income to the rest of the world
R39	COMPT	1.14	2	Compensation of employees
R40	SIT	1.14	7	Employer contributions for social insurance
R41	DC	1.14	25	Dividends
R42	PIECB	1.16	10	Profits before tax, corporate business
R43	DCB	1.16	13	Dividends, corporate business
R44	*IVA*	1.16	15	Inventory valuation adjustment, corporate business
R45	CCADCB	1.16	16	Capital consumption adjustment, corporate business
R46	INTF1	1.16	17	Net interest, corporate business
R47	PIECBN	1.16	28	Profits before tax, nonfinancial corporate business
R48	TCBN	1.16	29	Profits tax liability, nonfinancial corporate business

Table A.5
(continued)

No.	Variable	Table	Line	Description
NIPA Data *(continued)*				
R49	DCBN	1.16	31	Dividends, nonfinancial corporate business
R50	CCADCBN	1.16	34	Capital consumption adjustment, nonfinancial corporate business
R51	PRI	2.1	10	Proprietors' income with inventory valuation and capital consumption adjustments
R52	RNT	2.1	13	Rental income of persons with capital consumption adjustment
R53	PII	2.1	15	Personal interest income
R54	UB	2.1	18	Government unemployment insurance benefits
R55	IPP	2.1	28	Interest paid by persons
R56	TRHR	2.1	29	Personal transfer payments to rest of the world (net)
R57	TPG	3.2	2	Personal tax and nontax receipts, federal government (see below for adjustments)
R58	TCG	3.2	5	Corporate profits tax accruals, federal government
R59	IBTG	3.2	8	Indirect business tax and nontax accruals, federal government
R60	SIG	3.2	12	Contributions for social insurance, federal government
R61	CONGZ	3.2	14	Consumption expenditures, federal government
R62	TRGH	3.2	16	Transfer payments (net) to persons, federal government (see below for adjustments)
R63	TRGR	3.2	17	Transfer payments (net) to rest of the world, federal government
R64	TRGS	3.2	18	Grants in aid to state and local governments, federal government
R65	INTG	3.2	19	Net interest paid, federal government
R66	SUBG	3.2	24	Subsidies less current surplus of government enterprises, federal government
R67	WLDG	3.2	27	Wage accruals less disbursements, federal government
R68	TPS	3.3	2	Personal tax and nontax receipts, state and local government (S&L)
R69	TCS	3.3	6	Corporate profits tax accruals, S&L
R70	IBTS	3.3	7	Indirect business tax and nontax accruals, S&L
R71	SIS	3.3	11	Contributions for social insurance, S&L
R72	CONSZ	3.3	14	Consumption expenditures, S&L
R73	TRRSH	3.3	15	Transfer payments to persons, S&L
R74	INTS	3.3	16	Net interest paid, S&L
R75	SUBS	3.3	20	Subsidies less current surplus of government enterprises, S&L
R76	WLDS	3.3	23	Wage accruals less disbursements, S&L
R77	COMPMIL	3.7b	8	Compensation of employees, military, federal government
R78	SIHGA	3.14	3	Personal contributions for social insurance to the federal government, annual data only
R79	SIQGA	3.14	5	Government employer contributions for social insurance to the federal government, annual data only
R80	SIFGA	3.14	6	Other employer contributions for social insurance to the federal government, annual data only
R81	SIHSA	3.14	14	Personal contributions for social insurance to the S&L governments, annual data only
R82	SIQSA	3.14	16	Government employer contributions for social insurance to the S&L governments, annual data only
R83	SIFSA	3.14	17	Other employer contributions for social insurance to the S&L governments, annual data only
R84	IVFAZ	5.10	2	Change in farm private inventories
R85	IVFA	5.11	2	Real change in farm private inventories
R86	INTPRIA	8.20	61	Net interest, sole proprietorships and partnerships, annual data only
R87	INTROWA	8.20	63	Net interest, rest of the world, annual data only

Table A.5

(continued)

No.	Variable	Code	Description
Flow of Funds Data			
R88	CDDCF	103020000	Change in demand deposits and currency, F1
R89	NFIF	105000005	Net financial investment, F1
R90	IHFZ	105012003	Residential construction, F1
R91	ACR	105030003	Access rights from federal government
R92	PIEF	106060005	Profits before tax, F1
R93	CCNF	106300015	Depreciation charges, NIPA, F1
R94	DISF1	107005005	Discrepancy, F1
R95	CDDCNN	113020003	Change in demand deposits and currency, NN
R96	NFINN	115000005	Net financial investment, NN
R97	IHNN	115012003	Residential construction, NN
R98	CCNN	116300005	Consumption of fixed capital, NN. Also, current surplus = gross saving, NN
R99	CDDCFA	133020003	Change in demand deposits and currency, FA
R100	NFIFA	135000005	Net financial investment, FA
R101	CCFAT	136300005	Consumption of fixed capital, FA
R102	PIEFA	136060005	Corporate profits, FA
R103	CCADFA	136310103	Capital consumption adjustment, FA
R104	CDDCH1	153020005	Change in checkable deposits and currency, H
R105	MVCE,	154090005	Total financial assets of households.
R106	CCE		MVCE is the market value of the assets. CCE is the change in assets excluding capital gains and losses
R107	NFIH1	155000005	Net financial investment, H
R108	CCHFF	156300005	Total consumption of fixed capital, H
R109	CCCD	156300103	Consumption of fixed capital, consumer durables, H
R110	DISH1	157005005	Discrepancy, H
R111	IKH1	165013005	Nonresidential fixed investment, nonprofit institutions
R112	NFIS	215000005	Net financial investment, S
R113	CCS	206300003	Consumption if fixed capital, S
R114	DISS1	217005005	Discrepancy, S
R115	CDDCS	213020005	Change in demand deposits and currency, S
R116	CGLDR	263011005	Change in gold and SDR's, R
R117	CDDCR	263020005	Change in U.S. demand deposits, R
R118	CFXUS	263111005	Change in U.S. official foreign exchange and net IMF position
R119	NFIR	265000005	Net financial investment, R
R120	PIEF2	266060005	Corporate profits of foreign subsidiaries, F1
R121	DISR1	267005005	Discrepancy, R
R122	CGLDFXUS	313011005	Change in gold, SDR's, and foreign exchange, US
R123	CDDCUS	313020005	Change in demand deposits and currency, US
R124	INS	313154015	Insurance and pension reserves, US
R125	NFIUS	315000005	Net financial investment, US
R126	CCG	316300003	Consumption of fixed capital, US
R127	DISUS	317005005	Discrepancy, US
R128	CDDCCA	403020003	Change in demand deposits and currency, CA
R129	NIACA	404090005	Net increase in financial assets, CA
R130	NILCA	404190005	Net increase in liabilities, CA
R131	IKCAZ	405013005	Fixed nonresidential investment, CA
R132	GSCA	406000105	Gross saving, CA
R133	DISCA	407005005	Discrepancy, CA
R134	NIDDLB2=		Net increase in liabilities in the form of checkable deposits, B2
R135		443127005	NIDDLZ1
R136		+473127003	NIDDLZ2
R137	CBRB2	443013053	Change in reserves at Federal Reserve, B2
R138	IHBZ	645012205	Residential construction, multifamily units, Reits

Table A.5
(continued)

No.	Variable	Code	Description
Flow of Funds Data *(continued)*			
R139	CDDCB2=		Change in demand deposits and currency, B2
R140		793020005	CDDCFS
		−NIDDAB1	
		−CDDCCA	
R141	NIAB2=		Net increase in financial assets, B2
R142		444090005	NIAZ1
R143		+474090005	NIAZ2
R144		+604090005	NIAZ3
R145		+544090005	NIAZ4
R146		+514090005	NIAZ5
R147		+574090005	NIAZ6
R148		+224090005	NIAZ7
R149		+634000005	NIAZ8
R150		+654090005	NIAZ9
R151		+554090005	NIAZ10
R152		+674190005	NIAZ11
R153		+614090005	NIAZ12
R154		+623065003	NIAZ13
R155		+644090005	NIAZ14
R156		+664090005	NIAZ15
R157		+504090005	NIAZ16
R158	NILB2=		Net increase in liabilities, B2
R159		444190005	NILZ1
R160		+474190005	NILZ2
R161		+604090005	NILZ3
R162		+544190005	NILZ4
R163		+514190005	NILZ5
R164		+573150005	NILZ6
R165		+223150005	NILZ7
R166		+634000005	NILZ8
R167		+653164005	NILZ9
R168		+554090005	NILZ10
R169		+674190005	NILZ11
R170		+614190005	NILZ12
R171		+624190005	NILZ13
R172		+644190005	NILZ14
R173		+664190005	NILZ15
R174		+504190005	NILZ16
R175	IKB2Z=		Nonresidential fixed investment, B2
R176		795013005	IKFCZ
		−IKB1Z	
		−IKCAZ	
		−IKMAZ	
R177	DISB2=		Discrepancy, B2
R178		447005005	DISZ1
R179		+477005005	DISZ2
R180		+607005005	DISZ3
R181		+547005005	DISZ4
R182		+517005005	DISZ5
R183		+657005005	DISZ9
R184		+677005005	DISZ11
R185		+617005005	DISZ12
R186		+647005005	DISZ14

Table A.5
(continued)

No.	Variable	Code	Description
Flow of Funds Data *(continued)*			
R187		+667005005	DISZ15
R188	GSB2=		Gross saving, B2
R189		446000105	GSZ1
R190		+476000105	GSZ2
R191		+546000105	GSZ4
R192		+516000105	GSZ5
R193		+576330063	GSZ6
R194		+226330063	GSZ7
R195		+656006003	GSZ9
R196		+676330023	GSZ11
R197		+616000105	GSZ12
R198		+646000105	GSZ14
R199		+666000105	GSZ15
R200	CGLDFXMA	713011005	Change in gold and foreign exchange, MA
R201	CFRLMA	713068003	Change in Federal Reserve loans to domestic banks, MA
R202	NILBRMA	713113000	Change in member bank reserves, MA
R203	NIDDLRMA	713122605	Change in liabilities in the form of demand deposits and currency due to foreign of the MA
R204	NIDDLGMA	713123105	Change in liabilities in the form of demand deposits and currency due to U.S. government of the MA
R205	NILCMA	713125005	Change in liabilities in the form of currency outside banks of the MA
R206	NIAMA	714090005	Net increase in financial assets, MA
R207	NILMA	714190005	Net increase in liabilities, MA
R208	IKMAZ	715013005	Fixed nonresidential investment, MA
R209	GSMA	716000105	Gross savings, MA
R210	DISMA	717005005	Discrepancy, MA
R211	CVCBRB1	723020005	Change in vault cash and member bank reserves, U.S. chartered commercial banks
R212	NILVCMA	723025000	Change in liabilities in the form of vault cash of commercial banks of the MA
R213	NIDDAB1	743020003	Net increase in financial assets in the form of demand deposits and currency of banks in U.S. possessions
R214	CBRB1A	753013003	Change in reserves at Federal Reserve, foreign banking offices in U.S.
R215	NIDDLB1	763120005	Net increase in liabilities in the form of checkable deposits, B1
R216	NIAB1	764090005	Net increase in financial assets, B1
R217	NILB1	764190005	Net increase in liabilities, B1
R218	IKB1Z	765013005	Nonresidential fixed investment, B1
R219	GSB1	766000105	Gross saving, B1
R220	DISB1	767005005	Discrepancy, B1
R221	MAILFLT1	903023105	Mail float, U.S. government
R222	MAILFLT2	903029205	Mail float, private domestic nonfinancial
R223	CTRH	155400263	Net capital transfers, immigrants' transfers received by persons
R224	CTHG	315400153	Net capital transfers, estate and gift taxes paid by persons, federal
R225	CTHS	205400153	Net capital transfers, estate and gift taxes paid by persons, state and local
R226	CTGS	205400313	Net capital transfers, federal investment grants to state and local governments
R227	CTGR	265400313	Net capital transfers, capital transfers paid to the rest of the world, federal
R228	CTGF	105400313	Net capital transfers, investment grants to business, federal

Table A.5

(continued)

No.	Variable	Description
Interest Rate Data		
R229	RS	Three-month Treasury Bill rate (secondary market), percentage points. [BOG. Quarterly average.]
R230	RM	Conventional mortgage rate, percentage points. [BOG. Quarterly average.]
R231	RB	Moody's Aaa Corporate Bond Rate, percentage points. [BOG. Quarterly average.]
R232	RD	Discount window borrowing rate, percentage points. [BOG. Quarterly average.]
Labor Force and Population Data		
R233	CE	Civilian employment, SA in millions. [BLS. Quarterly average. See below for adjustments.]
R234	U	Unemployment, SA in millions. [BLS. Quarterly average. See below for adjustments.]
R235	CL1	Civilian labor force of males 25–54, SA in millions. [BLS. Quarterly average. See below for adjustments.]
R236	CL2	Civilian labor force of females 25–54, SA in millions. [BLS. Quarterly average. See below for adjustments.]
R237	AF	Total armed forces, millions. [Computed from population data from the U.S. Census Bureau. Quarterly average.]
R238	AF1	Armed forces of males 25–54, millions. [Computed from population data from the U.S. Census Bureau. Quarterly average.]
R239	AF2	Armed forces of females 25–54, millions. [Computed from population data from the U.S. Census Bureau. Quarterly average.]
R240	CPOP	Total civilian noninstitutional population 16 and over, millions. [BLS. Quarterly average. See below for adjustments.]
R241	CPOP1	Civilian noninstitutional population of males 25–54, millions. [BLS. Quarterly average. See below for adjustments.]
R242	CPOP2	Civilian noninstitutional population of females 25–54, millions [BLS. Quarterly average. See below for adjustments.]
R243	JF	Employment, total private sector, all persons, SA in millions. [BLS, unpublished, "Basic Industry Data for the Economy less General Government, All Persons."]
R244	HF	Average weekly hours, total private sector, all persons, SA. [BLS, unpublished, "Basic Industry Data for the Economy less General Government, All Persons."]
R245	HO	Average weekly overtime hours in manufacturing, SA. [BLS. Quarterly average.]
R246	JQ	Total government employment, SA in millions. [BLS. Quarterly average.]
R247	JG	Federal government employment, SA in millions. [BLS. Quarterly average.]
R248	JHQ	Total government employee hours, SA in millions of hours per quarter. [BLS, Table B10. Quarterly average.]

Notes:
- BLS = Website of the Bureau of Labor Statistics.
- BOG = Website of the Board of Governors of the Federal Reserve System.
- SA = Seasonally adjusted.
- For the construction of variables R249, R251, R253, R257, and R258 below, the annual observation for the year was used for each quarter of the year.

No.	Variable	Description
Adjustments to the Raw Data		
R249	SIHG =	[SIHGA/(SIHGA + SIHSA)](SIG + SIS − SIT)
		[Employee contributions for social insurance, h to g.]
R250	SIHS =	SIG + SIS − SIT − SIHG
		[Employee contributions for social insurance, h to s.]
R251	SIFG =	[SIFGA/(SIFGA + SIQGA)](SIG − SIHG)
		[Employer contributions for social insurance, f to g.]

Table A.5

(continued)

No.	Variable	Description

Adjustments to the Raw Data *(continued)*

No.	Variable	Description
R252	SIGG =	SIG − SIHG − SIFG
		[Employer contributions for social insurance, g to g.]
R253	SIFS =	[SIFSA/(SIFSA + SIQSA)](SIS − SIHS)
		[Employer contributions for social insurance, f to s.]
R254	SISS =	SIS − SIHS − SIFS
		[Employer contributions for social insurance, s to s.]
R255	TBG =	[TCG/(TCG + TCS)](TCG + TCS − TCBN)
		[Corporate profit tax accruals, b to g.]
R256	TBS =	TCG + TCS − TCBN − TBG
		[Corporate profit tax accruals, b to s.]
R257	INTPRI =	[PII/(PII annual)]INTPRIA
		[Net interest payments, sole proprietorships and partnerships.]
R258	INTROW =	[PII/(PII annual)]INTROWA
		[Net interest payments of r.]
	TPG =	TPG from raw data − TAXADJ
	TRGH =	TRGH from raw data − TAXADJ
		[TAXADJ: 1968:3 = 1.525, 1968:4 = 1.775, 1969:1 = 2.675, 1969:2 = 2.725,
		1969:3 = 1.775, 1969:4 = 1.825, 1970:1 = 1.25, 1970:2 = 1.25, 1970:3 = 0.1,
		1975:2 = −7.8.]
R259	POP =	CPOP + AF
		[Total noninstitutional population 16 and over, millions.]
R260	POP1 =	CPOP1 + AF1
		[Total noninstitutional population of males 25–54, millions.]
R261	POP2 =	CPOP2 + AF2
		[Total noninstitutional population of females 25–54, millions.]

Variable	1952:1–1971:4	1952:1–1972:4	1973:1	1952:1–1977:4	1970:1–1989:4

Adjustments to Labor Force and Population Data

Variable	1952:1–1971:4	1952:1–1972:4	1973:1	1952:1–1977:4	1970:1–1989:4
POP	1.00547	1.00009	1.00006	—	1.0058886 − .0000736075TPOP90
POP1	0.99880	1.00084	1.00056	—	1.0054512 − .00006814TPOP90
POP2	1.00251	1.00042	1.00028	—	1.00091654 − .000011457TPOP90
(CE+U)	1.00391	1.00069	1.00046	1.00239	1.0107312 − .00013414TPOP90
CL1	0.99878	1.00078	1.00052	1.00014	1.00697786 − .00008722TPOP90
CL2	1.00297	1.00107	1.00071	1.00123	—
CE	1.00375	1.00069	1.00046	1.00268	1.010617 − .00013271TPOP90

	1990:1–1998:4
POP	1.0014883 − .0000413417TPOP99
POP1	.99681716 + .000088412TPOP99
POP2	1.0045032 − .00012509TPOP99
(CE+U)	1.00041798 − .000011611TPOP99
CL1	.9967564 + .0000901TPOP99
CL2	1.004183 − .00011619TPOP99
CE	1.00042068 − .000011686TPOP99

Notes:
- TPOP90 is 79 in 1970:1, 78 in 1970:2, . . . , 1 in 1989:3, 0 in 1989:4.
- TPOP99 is 35 in 1990:1, 34 in 1990:2, . . . , 1 in 1998:3, 0 in 1998:4.

Table A.5
(continued)

The Raw Data Variables in Alphabetical Order

Var.	No.	Var.	No.	Var.	No.	Var.	No.	Var.	No.
ACR	R91	CTHG	R224	HF	R244	NIAZ11	R152	POP1	R260
AF	R237	CTHS	R225	HO	R245	NIAZ12	R153	POP2	R261
AF1	R238	CTRH	R223	IBTG	R59	NIAZ13	R154	PRI	R51
AF2	R239	CVCBRB1	R211	IBTS	R70	NIAZ14	R155	PROG	R27
CBRB1A	R214	DC	R41	IH	R17	NIAZ15	R156	PROGZ	R24
CBRB2	R137	DCB	R43	IHBZ	R138	NIAZ16	R157	PROS	R28
CCADCB	R45	DCBN	R49	IHFZ	R90	NIAZ2	R143	PROSZ	R25
CCADCBN	R50	DISB1	R220	IHNN	R97	NIAZ3	R144	PURG	R21
CCADFA	R103	DISB2	R177	IHZ	R6	NIAZ4	R145	PURGZ	R10
CCCD	R109	DISCA	R133	IK	R16	NIAZ5	R146	PURS	R22
CCE	R106	DISF1	R94	IKB1Z	R218	NIAZ6	R147	RB	R231
CCFAT	R101	DISH1	R110	IKB2Z	R175	NIAZ7	R148	RD	R232
CCG	R126	DISMA	R210	IKCAZ	R131	NIAZ8	R149	RM	R230
CCHFF	R108	DISR1	R121	IKFCZ	R176	NIAZ9	R150	RNT	R52
CCNF	R93	DISS1	R114	IKH1	R111	NIDDAB1	R213	RS	R229
CCNN	R98	DISUS	R127	IKMAZ	R208	NIDDLB1	R215	SIFG	R251
CCS	R113	DISZ1	R178	IKZ	R5	NIDDLB2	R134	SIFGA	R80
CCT	R31	DISZ11	R184	IM	R20	NIDDLGMA	R204	SIFS	R253
CD	R13	DISZ12	R185	IMZ	R9	NIDDLRMA	R203	SIFSA	R83
CDDCB2	R139	DISZ14	R186	INS	R124	NIDDLZ1	R135	SIGG	R252
CDDCCA	R128	DISZ15	R187	INTF1	R46	NIDDLZ2	R136	SIHG	R249
CDDCF	R88	DISZ2	R179	INTG	R65	NILB1	R217	SIHGA	R78
CDDCFA	R99	DISZ3	R180	INTPRI	R257	NILB2	R158	SIHS	R250
CDDCFS	R140	DISZ4	R181	INTPRIA	R86	NILBRMA	R202	SIHSA	R81
CDDCH1	R104	DISZ5	R182	INTROW	R258	NILCA	R130	SIQGA	R79
CDDCNN	R95	DISZ9	R183	INTROWA	R87	NILCMA	R205	SIQSA	R82
CDDCR	R117	DPER	R35	INTS	R74	NILMA	R207	SIS	R71
CDDCS	R115	EX	R19	IPP	R55	NILVCMA	R212	SISS	R254
CDDCUS	R123	EXZ	R8	IV	R18	NILZ1	R159	SIT	R40
CDZ	R2	FA	R26	IVA	R44	NILZ10	R168	STAT	R33
CE	R233	FAZ	R23	IVFA	R85	NILZ11	R169	SUBG	R66
CFRLMA	R201	FIROW	R30	IVZ	R7	NILZ12	R170	SUBS	R75
CFXUS	R118	FIROWR	R38	JG	R247	NILZ13	R171	TBG	R255
CGLDFXMA	R200	FIUSR	R37	JHQ	R248	NILZ14	R172	TBS	R256
CGLDFXUS	R122	GDP	R1	JQ	R246	NILZ15	R173	TCG	R58
CGLDR	R116	GDPR	R12	MAILFLT1	R221	NILZ16	R174	TCS	R69
CL1	R235	GSB1	R219	MAILFLT2	R222	NILZ2	R160	TPG	R57
CL2	R236	GSB2	R188	MVCE	R105	NILZ3	R161	TPS	R68
CN	R14	GSCA	R132	NFIF	R89	NILZ4	R162	TRF	R32
CNZ	R3	GSMA	R209	NFIFA	R100	NILZ5	R163	TRFH	R36
COMPMIL	R77	GSZ1	R189	NFIH1	R107	NILZ6	R164	TRGH	R62
COMPT	R39	GSZ11	R196	NFINN	R96	NILZ7	R165	TRGR	R63
CONGZ	R61	GSZ12	R197	NFIR	R119	NILZ8	R166	TRGS	R64
CONSZ	R72	GSZ14	R198	NFIS	R112	NILZ9	R167	TRHR	R56
CPOP	R240	GSZ15	R199	NFIUS	R125	PIECB	R42	TRRSH	R73
CPOP1	R241	GSZ2	R190	NIAB1	R216	PIECBN	R47	U	R234
CPOP2	R242	GSZ4	R191	NIAB2	R141	PIEF	R92	UB	R54
CS	R15	GSZ5	R192	NIACA	R129	PIEF2	R120	WLDF	R34
CTGF	R228	GSZ6	R193	NIAMA	R206	PIEFA	R102	WLDG	R67
CTGR	R227	GSZ7	R194	NIAZ1	R142	PII	R53	WLDS	R76
CTGS	R226	GSZ9	R195	NIAZ10	R151	POP	R259		

Table A.6
Links between the National Income and Product Accounts and the Flow of Funds Accounts

Receipts from i to j: (i,j = h, f, b, r, g, s)

fh = COMPT − PROGZ − PROSZ − (SIT − SIGG − SISS) − SUBG − SUBS + PRI + RNT
+ INTF + TRFH + DC − DRS − (DCB − DCBN) + INTOTH + INTROW
+ CCHFF − CCCD − WLDF + WLDG + WLDS

bh = DCB − DCBN

gh = PROGZ − SIGG − WLDG + TRGH + INS + INTG + SUBG

sh = PROSZ − SISS − WLDS + TRRSH + INTS + SUBS

hf = CSZ + CNZ + CDZ − IBTG − IBTS − IMZ − FIROW −[GSB1 + GSB2 + (DCB − DCBN)
+ TBG + TBS] + (IHZ − IHFZ − IHBZ − IHNN) + IKH1

bf = IHBZ + IKB1Z + IKB2Z

rf = EXZ + FIUS

gf = PURGZ − PROGZ + IKMAZ + IKCAZ − CCG

sf = PURSZ − PROSZ − CCS

hb = GSB1 + GSB2 + (DCB − DCBN) + TBG + TBS

hr = IMZ + TRHR + FIROW

fr = TRFR

gr = TRGR

hg = TPG + IBTG + SIHG

fg = TCG − TBG + SIFG

bg = TBG

gg = SIGG

hs = TPS + IBTS + SIHS

fs = TCS − TBS + SIFS + DRS

bs = TBS

gs = TRGS

ss = SISS

Saving of the Sectors

SH = fh + bh + gh + sh − (hf + hb + hr + hg + hs)

SF = hf + bf + rf + gf + sf − (fh + fg + fs + fr)

SB = hb − (bh + bf + bs + bg)

SR = hr + gr − rf + fr

SG = hg + fg + bg − (gh + gf + gr + gs)

SS = hs + fs + bs + gs − (sh + sf)

Checks

0 = SH + SF + SB + SR + SG + SS

SH = NFIH1 + DISH1 − CTRH + CTHG + CTHS

SF = NFIF + DISF1 + NFIFA + NFINN + STAT − CCADFA + ACR + WLDF − WLDG − WLDS
− DISBA − CTGF

SB = NIAB1 − NILB1 + NIAB2 − NILB2 + DISB1 + DISB2

SR = NFIR + DISR1 + CTRH − CTGR

SG = NFIUS + NIACA − NILCA + NIAMA − NILMA + DISUS + DISCA + DISMA
− GSMA − GSCA − ACR + CTGF + CTGR − CTHG + CTGS

SS = NFIS1 + DISS1 − CTHS − CTGS

0 = −NIDDLB1 + NIDDAB1 +CDDCB2 − NIDDLB2 + CDDCF + MAILFLT1 + MAILFLT2
+ CDDCUS + CDDCCA − NIDDLRMA − NIDDLGMA + CDDCH1 + CDDCFA
+ CDDCNN + CDDCR + CDDCS − NILCMA

0 = CVCBRB1 + CBRB1A + CBRB2 − NILBRMA − NILVCMA

0 = CGLDR − CFXUS + CGLDFXUS + CGLDFXMA

Note:
• See Table A.5 for the definitions of the raw data variables.

Table A.7
Construction of the Variables for the US Model

Variable	Construction
AA	Def., Eq. 89
AB	Def., Eq. 73. Base Period = 1971:4, Value = 248.176
AF	Def., Eq. 70. Base Period = 1971:4, Value = −388.975
AG	Def., Eq. 77. Base Period = 1971:4, Value = −214.587
AH	Def., Eq. 66. Base Period = 1971:4, Value = 2222.45
AR	Def., Eq. 75. Base Period = 1971:4, Value = −18.359
AS	Def., Eq. 79. Base Period = 1971:4, Value = −160.5
BO	Sum of CFRLMA. Base Period = 1971:4, Value = .039
BR	Sum of CVCBRB1. Base Period = 1971:4, Value = 35.329
CCB	[GSB1 + GSB2 − (PIECB − PIECBN) − (DCB − DCBN) − TBG − TBS]/*PX*.
CCF	CCNF + CCNN + CCFAT
CCG	CCG
CCH	CCHFF − CCCD
CCS	CCS
CD	CD
CDA	Peak-to-peak interpolation of *CD*/*POP*. Peak quarters are 1953:1, 1955:3, 1960:2, 1963:2, 1965:4, 1968:3, 1973:2, 1978:4, 1985:1, 1988:4, 1994:1, 1995:4, and 2000:3.
CF	Def., Eq. 68
CG	$MVCE - MVCE_{-1} - CCE$
CN	CN
COG	PURG − PROG
COS	PURS − PROS
CS	CS
CUR	Sum of NILCMA. Base Period = 1971:4, Value = 53.521
D1G	Def., Eq. 47
D1GM	Def., Eq. 90
D1S	Def., Eq. 48
D1SM	Def., Eq. 91
D2G	Def., Eq. 49
D2S	Def., Eq. 50
D3G	Def., Eq. 51
D3S	Def., Eq. 52
D4G	Def., Eq. 53
D5G	Def., Eq. 55
DB	DCB − DCBN
DELD	Computed using NIPA asset data
DELH	Computed using NIPA asset data
DELK	Computed using NIPA asset data
DF	DC − (DCB − DCBN)
DISB	DISB1 + DISB2
DISBA	GSB1 + GSB2 − (PIECB − PIECBN) − (DCB − DCBN) − TBG − TBS − CCT + (CCHFF − CCCD) + CCNF + CCNN + CCFAT − CCADCB
DISF	DISF1 − CCADFA + ACR − CTGF
DISG	DISUS + DISCA + DISMA − GSCA − GSMA − ACR + CTGF + CTGR − CTHG + CTGS
DISH	DISH1 − CTRH + CTHG + CTHS
DISR	DISR1 + CTRH − CTGR
DISS	DISS1 − CTHS − CTGS
DRS	DC − DPER
E	CE + AF
EX	EX
EXPG	Def., Eq. 106
EXPS	Def., Eq. 113
FA	FA

Table A.7
(continued)

Variable	Construction
FIROW	FIROW
FIROWD	FIROW/FIROWR
FIUS	FIUS
FIUSD	FIUS/FIUSR
G1	Def., Eq. 57
GDP	Def., Eq. 82, or GDP
GDPD	Def., Eq. 84
GDPR	GDPR
GNP	Def., Eq. 129
GNPD	Def., Eq. 131
GNPR	Def., Eq. 130
HF	$13 \cdot HF$
HFF	Def., Eq. 100
HFS	Peak-to-peak interpolation of *HF*. The peaks are 1952:4, 1960.3, 1966:1, 1977:2, and 1990:1. Flat end.
HG	JHQ/JQ
HM	520
HN	Def., Eq. 62
HO	$13 \cdot HO$. Constructed values for 1952:1–1955:4.
HS	JHQ/JQ
IBTG	IBTG
IBTS	IBTS
IGZ	PURGZ − CONGZ
IHB	IHBZ/(IHZ/IH)
IHF	(IHFZ + IHNN)/(IHZ/IH)
IHH	(IHZ − IHFZ − IHBZ − IHNN)/(IHZ/IH)
IHHA	Peak-to-peak interpolation of *IHH*/*POP*. Peak quarters are 1955:2, 1963:4, 1978:3, 1986:3, 1994:2, and 2000:1.
IKB	(IKB1Z + IKB2Z)/(IKZ/IK)
IKF	(IKZ − IKH1 − IKB1Z − IKB2Z)/(IKZ/IK)
IKG	((IKCAZ + IKMAZ)/(IKZ/IK)
IKH	IKH1/(IKZ/IK)
IM	IM
INS	INS
INTF	INTF1 + INTPRI
INTG	INTG
INTOTH	PII − INTF1 − INTG − INTS − IPP − INTROW − INTPRI
INTROW	INTROW
INTS	INTS
ISZ	PURSZ − CONSZ
IVA	IVA
IVF	IV
JF	JF
JG	JG
JHMIN	Def., Eq. 94
JJ	Def., Eq. 95
JJP	Peak-to-peak interpolation of *JJ*. The peaks are 1952:4, 1955:4, 1959:3, 1969:1, 1973:3, 1979:3, 1985:4, 1990:1, 1995:1, and 2000:2. Flat end.
JM	AF
JS	JQ − JG
KD	Def., Eq. 58. Base Period = 1952:1, Value = 276.24, Dep. Rate = DELD
KH	Def., Eq. 59. Base Period = 1952:1, Value = 1729.44, Dep. Rate = DELH
KK	Def., Eq. 92. Base Period = 1952:1, Value = 1803.81, Dep. Rate = DELK

Table A.7

(continued)

Variable	Construction
KKMIN	Def., Eq. 93
*L*1	CL1 + AF1
*L*2	CL2 + AF2
*L*3	Def., Eq. 86
LAM	Computed from peak-to-peak interpolation of $\log[Y/(JF \cdot HF)]$. Peak quarters are 1955:2, 1966:1, 1973:1, 1992:4, and 2002:3.
LM	Def., Eq. 85
*M*1	Def., Eq. 81. Base Period = 1971:4, Value = 250.218
MB	Def., Eq. 71. Also sum of −NIDDLB1 + CDDCFS − CDDCCA − NIDDLZ1 − NIDDLZ2. Base Period = 1971:4, Value = −191.73
MDIF	CDDCFS − MAILFLT1
MF	Sum of CDDCF + MAILFLT1 + MAILFLT2 + CDDCFA + CDDCNN, Base Period = 1971:4, Value = 84.075
MG	Sum of CDDCUS + CDDCCA − NIDDLRMA − NIDDLGMA, Base Period = 1971:4, Value = 10.526
MH	Sum of CDDCH1. Base Period = 1971:4, Value = 125.813
MR	Sum of CDDCR. Base Period = 1971:4, Value = 12.723
MS	Sum of CDDCS. Base Period = 1971:4, Value = 12.114
MUH	Peak-to-peak interpolation of Y/KK. Peak quarters are 1953:2, 1955:3, 1959:2, 1962:3, 1965:4, 1969:1, 1973:1, 1977:3, 1981:1, 1984:2, 1988:4, 1993:4, 1998:1. Flat beginning; flat end.
PCD	CDZ/CD
PCGNPD	Def., Eq. 122
PCGNPR	Def., Eq. 123
*PCM*1	Def., Eq. 124
PCN	CNZ/CN
PCS	CSZ/CS
PD	Def., Eq. 33
PEX	EXZ/EX
PF	Def., Eq. 31
PFA	FAZ/FA
PG	(PURGZ − PROGZ)/(PURG − PROG)
PH	Def., Eq. 34
PIEB	(PIECB − PIECBN)/*PX*.
PIEF	Def., Eq. 67, or PIEF1 + PIEF2 + PIEFA (for checking only)
PIH	IHZ/IH
PIK	IKZ/IK
PIM	IMZ/IM
PIV	IVZ/IV, with the following adjustments: 1954:4 = .2917, 1959:3 = .2945, 1971:4 = .3802, 1975:3 = .5694, 1975:4 = .5694, 1979:4 = .9333, 1980:2 = .7717, 1982:3 = .8860, 1983:3 = .8966, 1987:3 = .9321, 1991:3 = .9315, 1992:1 = .9177, 2000:2 = 1.0000, 2002:3 = 1.0000
POP	POP
*POP*1	POP1
*POP*2	POP2
*POP*3	POP − POP1 − POP2
PROD	Def., Eq. 118
PS	(PURSZ − PROSZ)/(PURS − PROS)
*PSI*1	Def., Eq. 32
*PSI*2	Def., Eq. 35
*PSI*3	Def., Eq. 36
*PSI*4	Def., Eq. 37
*PSI*5	Def., Eq. 38
*PSI*6	Def., Eq. 39

Table A.7
(continued)

Variable	Construction
*PSI*7	Def., Eq. 40
*PSI*8	Def., Eq. 41
*PSI*9	Def., Eq. 42
*PSI*10	Def., Eq. 44
*PSI*11	Def., Eq. 45
*PSI*12	Def., Eq. 46
*PSI*13	(PROG + PROS)/(JHQ + 520AF)
PUG	Def., Eq. 104 or PURGZ
PUS	Def., Eq. 110 or PURSZ
PX	(CDZ + CNZ + CSZ + IHZ + IKZ + PURGZ − PROGZ + PURSZ − PROSZ + EXZ − IMZ − IBTG − IBTS)/ (CD + CN + CS + IH + IK + PURG − PROG + PURS − PROS + EX − IM)
Q	Sum of CGLDFXUS + CGLDFXMA. Base Period = 1971:4, Value = 12.265
RB	RB
RD	RD
RECG	Def., Eq. 105
RECS	Def., Eq. 112
RM	RM
RMA	Def., Eq. 128
RNT	RNT
RS	RS
RSA	Def., Eq. 130
SB	Def., Eq. 72
SF	Def., Eq. 69
SG	Def., Eq. 76
SGP	Def., Eq. 107
SH	Def., Eq. 65
SHRPIE	Def., Eq. 121
SIFG	SIFG
SIFS	SIFS
SIG	SIG
SIGG	SIGG
SIHG	SIHG
SIHS	SIHS
SIS	SIS
SISS	SISS
SR	Def., Eq. 74
SRZ	Def., Eq. 116
SS	Def., Eq. 78
SSP	Def., Eq. 114
STAT	STAT
STATP	Def., Eq. 83
SUBG	SUBG
SUBS	SUBS
T	1 in 1952:1, 2 in 1952:2, etc.
TAUG	Determined from a regression. See the discussion in the text.
TAUS	Determined from a regression. See the discussion in the text.
TBG	TBG
TBS	TBS
TCG	TCG
TCS	TCS
TFG	Def., Eq. 102
TFS	Def., Eq. 108
THG	Def., Eq. 101

Table A.7
(continued)

Variable	Construction
THS	TPS
TPG	TPG
TRFH	TRFH
TRFR	TRF − TRFH
TRGH	TRGH
TRGR	TRGR
TRGS	TRGS
TRHR	TRHR
TRRSH	TRRSH
TRSH	Def., Eq. 111
U	(CE + U) − CE
UB	UB
UBR	Def., Eq. 125
UR	Def., Eq. 87
V	Def., Eq. 117. Base Period = 1996:4, Value = 1251.9
WA	Def., Eq. 126
WF	[COMPT − (PROGZ − WLDG) − (PROSZ − WLDS) − (SIT − SIGG − SISS) + PRI]/[JF(HF + .5HO)]
WG	(PROGZ − COMPMIL − WLDG)/[JG(JHQ/JQ)]
WH	Def., Eq. 43
WLDF	WLDF
WLDG	WLDG
WLDS	WLDS
WM	COMPMIL/(520AF)
WR	Def., Eq. 119
WS	(PROSZ − WLDS)/[(JQ − JG)(JHQ/JQ)]
X	Def., Eq. 60
XX	Def., Eq. 61
Y	Def., Eq. 63
YD	Def., Eq. 115
YNL	Def., Eq. 99
YS	Def., Eq. 98
YT	Def., Eq. 64

Note:
- The variables in the first column are the variables in the model. They are defined by the identities in Table A.3 or by the raw data variables in Table A.5. A right-hand-side variable in this table is a raw data variable unless it is in italics, in which case it is a variable in the model. Sometimes the same letters are used for both a variable in the model and a raw data variable.

Table A.8
Solution of the Model under Alternative Monetary Assumptions

There are five possible assumptions that can be made with respect to monetary policy in the US model. In the standard version monetary policy is endogenous; it is explained by equation 30—the interest rate rule. Under alternative assumptions, where monetary policy is exogenous, equation 30 is dropped and some of the other equations are rearranged for purposes of solving the model. For example, in the standard version equation 125 is used to solve for the level of nonborrowed reserves, *UBR*:

$$UBR = BR - BO. \qquad (125)$$

When, however, the level of nonborrowed reserves is set exogenously, the equation is rearranged and used to solve for total bank reserves, *BR*:

$$BR = UBR + BO. \qquad (125)$$

The following shows the arrangement of the equations for each of the five monetary policy assumptions. The variable listed is the one that is put on the left-hand side of the equation and "solved for."

Eq. no.	RS Eq. 30	RS exog	M1 exog	UBR exog	AG exog
9	MH	MH	RSA	RSA	RSA
30	RS	Out	Out	Out	Out
57	BR	BR	BR	MB	MB
71	MB	MB	MB	MH	MH
77	AG	AG	AG	AG	BR
81	M1	M1	MH	M1	M1
125	UBR	UBR	UBR	BR	UBR
127	RSA	RSA	RS	RS	RS

Table A.9

First-Stage Regressors for the US Model for 2SLS

Eq.	First-Stage Regressors
1	cnst, $AG1$, $AG2$, $AG3$, $\log(CS/POP)_{-1}$, $\log[YD/(POP \cdot PH)]_{-1}$, RSA_{-1}, $\log(AA/POP)_{-1}$, T, $\log(1 - D1GM - D1SM - D4G)_{-1}$, $\log(IM/POP)_{-1}$, $\log[(JG \cdot HG + JM \cdot HM + JS \cdot HS)/POP]$, $\log(PIM/PF)_{-1}$, $\log[YNL/(POP \cdot PH)]_{-1}$, $100[(PD/PD_{-1})^4 - 1]_{-1}$, $\log[(COG + COS)/POP]$, $\log[(TRGH + TRSH)/(POP \cdot PH_{-1})]$, RS_{-2}, RB_{-1}, $\log(Y/POP)_{-1}$, $\log(V/POP)_{-1}$, UR_{-1}
2	cnst, $AG1$, $AG2$, $AG3$, $\log(CN/POP)_{-1}$, $\Delta \log(CN/POP)_{-1}$, $\log(AA/POP)_{-1}$, $\log[YD/(POP \cdot PH)]_{-1}$, RMA_{-1}, $\log(1 - D1GM - D1SM - D4G)_{-1}$, $\log(IM/POP)_{-1}$, $\log(EX/POP)_{-1}$, $\log[(JG \cdot HG + JM \cdot HM + JS \cdot HS)/POP]$, $\log(PIM/PF)_{-1}$, $\log[YNL/(POP \cdot PH)]_{-1}$, $100[(PD/PD_{-1})^4 - 1]_{-1}$, $\log[(COG + COS)/POP]$, $\log[(TRGH + TRSH)/(POP \cdot PH_{-1})]$, RS_{-1}, RS_{-2}, $\log(V/POP)_{-1}$, UR_{-1}
3	cnst, $AG1$, $AG2$, $AG3$, $(KD/POP)_{-1}$, $DELD(KD/POP)_{-1} - (CD/POP)_{-1}$, $YD/(POP \cdot PH)$, $(RMA \cdot CDA)_{-1}$, $(AA/POP)_{-1}$, $\log(1 - D1GM - D1SM - D4G)_{-1}$, $\log(IM/POP)_{-1}$, $\log(EX/POP)_{-1}$, $\log(PIM/PF)_{-1}$, $\log[YNL/(POP \cdot PH)]_{-1}$, $\log[(COG + COS)/POP]$, $\log[(TRGH + TRSH)/(POP \cdot PH_{-1})]$, $\log(Y/POP)_{-1}$, $\log(V/POP)_{-1}$, UR_{-1}
4	cnst, $(KH/POP)_{-1}$, $[YD/(POP \cdot PH)]_{-1}$, $RMA_{-1}IHHA$, $[YD/(POP \cdot PH)]_{-2}$, $RMA_{-2}IHHA_{-1}$, $RMA_{-3}IHHA_{-2}$, $(KH/POP)_{-2}$, $(KH/POP)_{-3}$, $\Delta(IHH/POP)_{-1}$, $\Delta(IHH/POP)_{-2}$, $DELH(KH/POP)_{-1} - (IHH/POP)_{-1}$, $DELH_{-1}(KH/POP)_{-2} - (IHH/POP)_{-2}$, $DELH_{-2}(KH/POP)_{-3} - (IHH/POP)_{-3}$, $\log(1 - D1GM - D1SM - D4G)_{-1}$, $\log(IM/POP)_{-1}$, $\log(EX/POP)_{-1}$, $\log[(JG \cdot HG + JM \cdot HM + JS \cdot HS)/POP]$, $\log[YNL/(POP \cdot PH)]_{-1}$, $100[(PD/PD_{-1})^4 - 1]_{-1}$, $\log[(COG + COS)/POP]$, $\log[(TRGH + TRSH)/(POP \cdot PH_{-1})]$
5	cnst, $\log(L1/POP1)_{-1}$, $\log(AA/POP)_{-1}$, UR_{-1}, $\log(1 - D1GM - D1SM - D4G)_{-1}$, $\log(IM/POP)_{-1}$, $\log[(JG \cdot HG + JM \cdot HM + JS \cdot HS)/POP]$, $\log(PIM/PF)_{-1}$, $\log[YNL/(POP \cdot PH)]_{-1}$, $100[(PD/PD_{-1})^4 - 1]_{-1}$, $\log[(COG + COS)/POP]$, $\log(Y/POP)_{-1}$, $\log(V/POP)_{-1}$
6	cnst, $\log(L2/POP2)_{-1}$, $\log(WA/PH)_{-1}$, $\log(AA/POP)_{-1}$, T, $\log(1 - D1GM - D1SM - D4G)_{-1}$, $\log(IM/POP)_{-1}$, $\log(EX/POP)_{-1}$, $\log[(JG \cdot HG + JM \cdot HM + JS \cdot HS)/POP]$, $\log(PIM/PF)_{-1}$, $\log[YNL/(POP \cdot PH)]_{-1}$, $\log[(COG + COS)/POP]$, $\log[(TRGH + TRSH)/(POP \cdot PH_{-1})]$, RS_{-1}, RS_{-2}, RB_{-1}, $\log(Y/POP)_{-1}$, $\log(V/POP)_{-1}$
7	cnst, $\log(L3/POP1)_{-1}$, $\log(WA/PH)_{-1}$, $\log(AA/POP)_{-1}$, UR_{-1}, $\log(1 - D1GM - D1SM - D4G)_{-1}$, $\log(IM/POP)_{-1}$, $\log(EX/POP)_{-1}$, $\log[(JG \cdot HG + JM \cdot HM + JS \cdot HS)/POP]$, $\log(PIM/PF)_{-1}$, $100[(PD/PD_{-1})^4 - 1]_{-1}$, $\log[(TRGH + TRSH)/(POP \cdot PH_{-1})]$, $\log(Y/POP)_{-1}$
8	cnst, $\log(LM/POP)_{-1}$, $\log(WA/PH)_{-1}$, UR_{-1}, $\log(1 - D1GM - D1SM - D4G)_{-1}$, $\log(IM/POP)_{-1}$, $\log(EX/POP)_{-1}$, $\log[(JG \cdot HG + JM \cdot HM + JS \cdot HS)/POP]$, $\log(PIM/PF)_{-1}$, $\log[YNL/(POP \cdot PH)]_{-1}$, $100[(PD/PD_{-1})^4 - 1]_{-1}$, $\log[(COG + COS)/POP]$, $\log[(TRGH + TRSH)/(POP \cdot PH_{-1})]$, RS_{-1}, RS_{-2}, RB_{-1}, $\log(Y/POP)_{-1}$, $\log(V/POP)_{-1}$, $\log(AA/POP)_{-1}$
9	cnst, $\log[MH_{-1}/(POP_{-1}PH)]_{-1}$, $\log[YD/(POP \cdot PH)]_{-1}$, RSA_{-1}, T, $D981$, $\log[MH_{-1}/(POP_{-1}PH)]_{-2}$, $\log[MH_{-1}/(POP_{-1}PH)]_{-3}$, $\log[MH_{-1}/(POP_{-1}PH)]_{-4}$, $\log[YD/(POP \cdot PH)]_{-2}$, $\log[YD/(POP \cdot PH)]_{-3}$, $\log[YD/(POP \cdot PH)]_{-4}$, $\log[YD/(POP \cdot PH)]_{-5}$, RSA_{-2}, RSA_{-3}, RSA_{-4}, RSA_{-5}, $\log[MH_{-1}/(POP_{-1}PH_{-1})]$, $D981_{-1}$, $D981_{-2}$, $D981_{-3}$, $D981_{-4}$, $\log(1 - D1GM - D1SM - D4G)_{-1}$, $\log(IM/POP)_{-1}$, $\log(EX/POP)_{-1}$, $\log[(JG \cdot HG + JM \cdot HM + JS \cdot HS)/POP]$, $\log(PIM/PF)_{-1}$, $\log[YNL/(POP \cdot PH)]_{-1}$, $100[(PD/PD_{-1})^4 - 1]_{-1}$, $\log[(COG + COS)/POP]$, $\log[(TRGH + TRSH)/(POP \cdot PH_{-1})]$, RB_{-1}, UR_{-1}, $\log(Y/POP)_{-1}$, $\log(V/POP)_{-1}$, $\log(AA/POP)_{-1}$

Table A.9

(continued)

Eq.	First-Stage Regressors
10	$\log PF_{-1}$, $\log[[WF(1+D5G)] - \log LAM]_{-1}$, cnst, $\log(PIM/PF)_{-1}$, UR_{-1}, T, $\log(1 - D1GM - D1SM - D4G)_{-1}$, $\log(IM/POP)_{-1}$, $\log(EX/POP)_{-1}$, $\log[YNL/(POP \cdot PH)]_{-1}$, $\log[(COG + COS)/POP]$, $\log[(TRGH + TRSH)/(POP \cdot PH_{-1})]$, $\log(Y/POP)_{-1}$, $\log(AA/POP)_{-1}$
11	cnst, $\log Y_{-1}$, $\log V_{-1}$, $D593$, $D594$, $D601$, $\log Y_{-2}$, $\log Y_{-3}$, $\log Y_{-4}$, $\log V_{-2}$, $\log V_{-3}$, $\log V_{-4}$, $D601_{-1}$, $D601_{-2}$, $D601_{-3}$, T, $\log(1 - D1GM - D1SM - D4G)_{-1}$, $\log(IM/POP)_{-1}$, $\log(EX/POP)_{-1}$, $\log(PIM/PF)_{-1}$, $\log[YNL/(POP \cdot PH)]_{-1}$, $100[(PD/PD_{-1})^4 - 1]_{-1}$, $\log[(COG + COS)/POP]$, $\log[(TRGH + TRSH)/(POP \cdot PH_{-1})]$, RS_{-1}, RB_{-1}, UR_{-1}
12	cnst, $\log KK_{-1}$, $\log KK_{-2}$, $\log Y_{-1}$, $\log Y_{-2}$, $\log Y_{-3}$, $\log Y_{-4}$, $\log Y_{-5}$, $\log(KK/KKMIN)_{-1}$, $RB_{-2}(1 - D2G_{-2} - D2S_{-2}) - 100(PD_{-2}/PD_{-6}) - 1)$, $(CG_{-2} + CG_{-3} + CG_{-4})/(PX_{-2}YS_{-2} + PX_{-3}YS_{-3} + PX_{-4}YS_{-4})$, $\log(1 - D1GM - D1SM - D4G)_{-1}$, $\log(EX/POP)_{-1}$, $\log[(JG \cdot HG + JM \cdot HM + JS \cdot HS)/POP]$, $\log[YNL/(POP \cdot PH)]_{-1}$, $\log[(TRGH + TRSH)/(POP \cdot PH_{-1})]$, UR_{-1}, $\log(AA/POP)_{-1}$
13	cnst, $\log[JF/(JHMIN/HFS)]_{-1}$, $\Delta \log JF_{-1}$, $\Delta \log Y_{-1}$, $D593$, $\log(1 - D1GM - D1SM - D4G)_{-1}$, $\log(IM/POP)_{-1}$, $\log(EX/POP)_{-1}$, $\log[(JG \cdot HG + JM \cdot HM + JS \cdot HS)/POP]$, $\log(PIM/PF)_{-1}$, $\log[YNL/(POP \cdot PH)]_{-1}$, $100[(PD/PD_{-1})^4 - 1]_{-1}$, $\log[(COG + COS)/POP]$, $\log[(TRGH + TRSH)/(POP \cdot PH_{-1})]$, RS_{-1}, RS_{-2}, RB_{-1}, $\log(Y/POP)_{-1}$, $\log(V/POP)_{-1}$, UR_{-1}, $\log(AA/POP)_{-1}$
14	cnst, $\log(HF/HFS)_{-1}$, $\log[JF/(JHMIN/HFS)]_{-1}$, $\Delta \log Y_{-1}$, $\log[(JG \cdot HG + JM \cdot HM + JS \cdot HS)/POP]$, $\log(PIM/PF)_{-1}$, $100[(PD/PD_{-1})^4 - 1]_{-1}$, RS_{-1}, RS_{-2}, UR_{-1}
16	$\log WF_{-1} - \log LAM_{-1} - \log PF_{-1}$, cnst, T, $\log(1 - D1GM - D1SM - D4G)_{-1}$, $\log(EX/POP)_{-1}$, $\log[(JG \cdot HG + JM \cdot HM + JS \cdot HS)/POP]$, $\log(PIM/PF)_{-1}$, $\log[YNL/(POP \cdot PH)]_{-1}$, $\log[(COG + COS)/POP]$, $\log[(TRGH + TRSH)/(POP \cdot PH_{-1})]$, RS_{-1}, RS_{-2}, RB_{-1}, $\log(Y/POP)_{-1}$, $\log(V/POP)_{-1}$, UR_{-1}, $\log PF_{-1} - [\beta_1/(1 - \beta_2)] \log PF_{-2}$
17	cnst, T, $\log(MF/PF)_{-1}$, $\log(X - FA)_{-1}$, $RS(1 - D2G - D2S)_{-1}$, $D981$, T, $\log(1 - D1GM - D1SM - D4G)_{-1}$, $\log(IM/POP)_{-1}$, $\log(EX/POP)_{-1}$, $\log[(JG \cdot HG + JM \cdot HM + JS \cdot HS)/POP]$, $\log(PIM/PF)_{-1}$, $\log[YNL/(POP \cdot PH)]_{-1}$, $100[(PD/PD_{-1})^4 - 1]_{-1}$, $\log[(COG + COS)/POP]$, RS_{-2}, RB_{-1}, $\log(Y/POP)_{-1}$, $\log(V/POP)_{-1}$, UR_{-1}
18	cnst, $\log[(PIEF - TFG - TFS)/DF_{-1}]_{-1}$, $\log[(JG \cdot HG + JM \cdot HM + JS \cdot HS)/POP]$, $\log(PIM/PF)_{-1}$, $100[(PD/PD_{-1})^4 - 1]_{-1}$, RS_{-1}, RS_{-2}, UR_{-1}
22	cnst, $(BO/BR)_{-1}$, RS_{-1}, RD_{-1}, T, $\log(1 - D1GM - D1SM - D4G)_{-1}$, $\log(IM/POP)_{-1}$, $\log(EX/POP)_{-1}$, $\log[(JG \cdot HG + JM \cdot HM + JS \cdot HS)/POP]$, $\log(PIM/PF)_{-1}$, $\log[YNL/(POP \cdot PH)]_{-1}$, $100[(PD/PD_{-1})^4 - 1]_{-1}$, $\log[(COG + COS)/POP]$, $\log[(TRGH + TRSH)/(POP \cdot PH_{-1})]$, RS_{-2}, RB_{-1}, $\log(Y/POP)_{-1}$, $\log(V/POP)_{-1}$, UR_{-1}, $\log(AA/POP)_{-1}$
23	cnst, RB_{-1}, RB_{-2}, RS_{-1}, RS_{-2}, RS_{-3}, $\log(1 - D1GM - D1SM - D4G)_{-1}$, $\log(IM/POP)_{-1}$, $\log(EX/POP)_{-1}$, $\log[(JG \cdot HG + JM \cdot HM + JS \cdot HS)/POP]$, $\log(PIM/PF)_{-1}$, $\log[YNL/(POP \cdot PH)]_{-1}$, $100[(PD/PD_{-1})^4 - 1]_{-1}$, $\log[(COG + COS)/POP]$, $\log[(TRGH + TRSH)/(POP \cdot PH_{-1})]$, $\log(Y/POP)_{-1}$, $\log(V/POP)_{-1}$, $\log(AA/POP)_{-1}$, UR_{-1}
24	cnst, RM_{-1}, RS_{-1}, RS_{-2}, $\log(1 - D1GM - D1SM - D4G)_{-1}$, $\log(IM/POP)_{-1}$, $\log(EX/POP)_{-1}$, $\log[(JG \cdot HG + JM \cdot HM + JS \cdot HS)/POP]$, $\log(PIM/PF)_{-1}$, $\log[YNL/(POP \cdot PH)]_{-1}$, $100[(PD/PD_{-1})^4 - 1]_{-1}$, $\log[(COG + COS)/POP]$, $\log[(TRGH + TRSH)/(POP \cdot PH_{-1})]$, $\log(Y/POP)_{-1}$, $\log(V/POP)_{-1}$, $\log(AA/POP)_{-1}$, UR_{-1}

Table A.9
(continued)

Eq.	First-Stage Regressors

25   cnst, ΔRB_{-1}, $[[\Delta(PIEF - TFG - TFS + PX \cdot PIEB - TBG - TBS)]/(PX_{-1} \cdot YS_{-1})]_{-1}$, T, $\log(1 - D1GM - D1SM - D4G)_{-1}$, $\log(IM/POP)_{-1}$, $\log(EX/POP)_{-1}$, $\log[(JG \cdot HG + JM \cdot HM + JS \cdot HS)/POP]$, $\log(PIM/PF)_{-1}$, $\log[YNL/(POP \cdot PH)]_{-1}$, $100[(PD/PD_{-1})^4 - 1]_{-1}$, $\log[(COG + COS)/POP]$, $\log[(TRGH + TRSH)/(POP \cdot PH_{-1})]$, RS_{-1}, RS_{-2}, RB_{-1}, $\log(Y/POP)_{-1}$, $\log(V/POP)_{-1}$, UR_{-1}, $\log(AA/POP)_{-1}$

26   cnst, $\log[CUR_{-1}/(POP_{-1}PF)]_{-1}$, $\log[(X - FA)/POP]_{-1}$, RSA_{-1}, $\log[CUR_{-1}/(POP_{-1}PF_{-1})]$, T, $\log(1 - D1GM - D1SM - D4G)_{-1}$, $\log(IM/POP)_{-1}$, $\log(EX/POP)_{-1}$, $\log[(JG \cdot HG + JM \cdot HM + JS \cdot HS)/POP]$, $\log(PIM/PF)_{-1}$, $\log[YNL/(POP \cdot PH)]_{-1}$, $100[(PD/PD_{-1})^4 - 1]_{-1}$, $\log[(COG + COS)/POP]$, $\log[(TRGH + TRSH)/(POP \cdot PH_{-1})]$, RS_{-2}, RB_{-1}, $\log(Y/POP)_{-1}$, $\log(V/POP)_{-1}$, UR_{-1}, $\log(AA/POP)_{-1}$

27   cnst, $\log(IM/POP)_{-1}$, $\log[(CS + CN + CD + IHH + IKF + IHB + IHF + IKB + IKH)/POP]_{-1}$, $\log(PF/PIM)_{-1}$, $D691$, $D692$, $D714$, $D721$, $\log(IM/POP)_{-2}$, $\log(IM/POP)_{-3}$, $\log[(CS + CN + CD + IHH + IKF + IHB + IHF + IKB + IKH)/POP]_{-2}$, $\log[(CS + CN + CD + IHH + IKF + IHB + IHF + IKB + IKH)/POP]_{-3}$, $\log(PF/PIM)_{-2}$, $\log(PF/PIM)_{-3}$, $D692_{-1}$, $D692_{-2}$, $D721_{-1}$, $D721_{-2}$, $\log(1 - D1GM - D1SM - D4G)_{-1}$, $\log(EX/POP)_{-1}$, $\log[(JG \cdot HG + JM \cdot HM + JS \cdot HS)/POP]$, $\log[YNL/(POP \cdot PH)]_{-1}$, $100[(PD/PD_{-1})^4 - 1]_{-1}$, $\log[(COG + COS)/POP]$, $\log[(TRGH + TRSH)/(POP \cdot PH_{-1})]$, RS_{-1}, RB_{-1}, $\log(Y/POP)_{-1}$, $\log(V/POP)_{-1}$, UR_{-1}, $\log(AA/POP)_{-1}$

28   cnst, $\log UB_{-1}$, $\log U_{-1}$, $\log WF_{-1}$, $\log UB_{-2}$, $\log(1 - D1GM - D1SM - D4G)_{-1}$, $\log(IM/POP)_{-1}$, $\log[(JG \cdot HG + JM \cdot HM + JS \cdot HS)/POP]$, $\log(PIM/PF)_{-1}$, $\log[YNL/(POP \cdot PH)]_{-1}$, $100[(PD/PD_{-1})^4 - 1]_{-1}$, $\log[(COG + COS)/POP]$, $\log[(TRGH + TRSH)/(POP \cdot PH_{-1})]$, RS_{-1}, RS_{-2}

30   cnst, RS_{-1}, $100[(PD/PD_{-1})^4 - 1]_{-1}$, UR_{-1}, ΔUR_{-1}, $PCM1_{-1}$, $D794823 \cdot PCM1_{-1}$, ΔRS_{-1}, ΔRS_{-2}, T, $\log(1 - D1GM - D1SM - D4G)_{-1}$, $\log(IM/POP)_{-1}$, $\log(EX/POP)_{-1}$, $\log[(JG \cdot HG + JM \cdot HM + JS \cdot HS)/POP]$, $\log(PIM/PF)_{-1}$, $\log[YNL/(POP \cdot PH)]_{-1}$, $\log[(COG + COS)/POP]$, $\log[(TRGH + TRSH)/(POP \cdot PH_{-1})]$, $\log(Y/POP)_{-1}$, $\log(V/POP)_{-1}$, $\log(AA/POP)_{-1}$

Table A.10
Variables Used in Each Equation

Var.	Eq.	Used in Equation	Var.	Eq.	Used in Equation
AA	89	1, 2, 3, 4, 5, 6, 7	*D942*	exog	21
AB	73	80	*D981*	exog	9, 17
AF	70	19, 80	*D013*	exog	21
AG	77	29, 80	*D014*	exog	21
AG1	exog	1, 2, 3	*DB*	exog	64, 72, 99, 115
AG2	exog	1, 2, 3	*DELD*	exog	3, 58
AG3	exog	1, 2, 3	*DELH*	exog	4, 59
AH	66	80, 89	*DELK*	exog	92
AR	75	80	*DF*	18	64, 69, 99, 115
AS	79	80	*DISB*	exog	73, 80
BO	22	73, 77, 125	*DISBA*	exog	67, 70, 80
BR	57	22, 73, 77, 125	*DISF*	exog	70, 80
CCB	exog	60, 61, 72, 82, 83	*DISG*	exog	77, 80
CCF	21	67	*DISH*	exog	66, 80
CCG	exog	67, 68, 76	*DISR*	exog	75, 80
CCH	exog	65, 67, 68	*DISS*	exog	79, 80
CCS	exog	67, 68, 77	*DRS*	exog	64, 78, 99, 113, 115
CD	3	27, 34, 51, 52, 58, 60, 61, 65, 116	*E*	85	86
CDA	exog	3	*EX*	exog	33, 60, 61, 74
CF	68	69	*EXPG*	106	107
CG	25	12, 66, 80	*EXPS*	113	114
CN	2	27, 34, 51, 52, 60, 61, 65, 116	*FA*	exog	17, 26, 31
COG	exog	60, 61, 76, 104	*FIROW*	exog	67, 68, 74, 129, 130
COS	exog	60, 61, 78, 110	*FIROWD*	exog	130
CS	1	27, 34, 51, 52, 60, 61, 65, 116	*FIUS*	exog	67, 68, 74, 129, 130
CUR	26	71, 77	*FIUSD*	exog	130
D1G	exog	47, 90, 99	*G1*	exog	57
D1GM	90	126, 127, 128	*GDP*	82	84, 129
D1S	exog	48, 91, 99	*GDPD*	84	123
D1SM	91	126, 127, 128	*GDPR*	83	84, 122, 130
D2G	exog	12, 17, 49, 121	*GNP*	129	131
D2S	exog	12, 17, 50, 121	*GNPD*	131	-
D3G	exog	35, 36, 37, 51	*GNPR*	130	131
D3S	exog	35, 36, 37, 52	*HF*	14	62, 95, 100, 118
D4G	exog	53, 126	*HFF*	100	15
D5G	exog	10, 54	*HFS*	exog	13, 14, 100
D593	exog	11, 13	*HG*	exog	43, 64, 76, 82, 83, 95, 98, 104, 115, 126
D594	exog	11	*HM*	exog	43, 64, 76, 82, 83, 95, 98, 104, 115, 126
D601	exog	11	*HN*	62	43, 53, 54, 64, 67, 68, 115, 121, 126
D621	exog	21	*HO*	15	43, 53, 54, 62, 64, 67, 68, 115, 121, 126
D691	exog	27	*HS*	exog	43, 64, 78, 82, 83, 95, 98, 110, 115, 126
D692	exog	27	*IBTG*	51	34, 52, 61, 76, 82, 105
D714	exog	27	*IBTS*	52	34, 51, 61, 78, 82, 112
D721	exog	27	*IGZ*	exog	106
D722	exog	21	*IHB*	exog	27, 60, 61, 72
D723	exog	21	*IHF*	exog	27, 60, 61, 68
D794823	exog	30	*IHH*	4	27, 34, 59, 60, 61, 65
D923	exog	21	*IHHA*	exog	4
D924	exog	21	*IKB*	exog	27, 60, 61, 72
D941	exog	21	*IKF*	92	21, 27, 60, 61, 68

Table A.10
(continued)

Var.	Eq.	Used in Equation	Var.	Eq.	Used in Equation
IKG	exog	60, 61, 76	PIEB	exog	25, 60, 61, 72, 82, 83
IKH	exog	27, 60, 61, 65	PIEF	67	18, 49, 25, 50, 121
IM	27	33, 60, 61, 74	PIH	38	34, 61, 65, 68, 72, 89
INS	exog	65, 76	PIK	39	21, 61, 65, 68, 72, 76
INTF	19	64, 67, 68, 99, 115	PIM	exog	10, 27, 33, 61, 74
INTG	29	64, 76, 99, 106, 115	PIV	42	67, 82
INTOTH	exog	64, 67, 68, 99, 115	POP	120	1, 2, 3, 4, 5, 6, 7, 8, 9, 26, 27, 47, 48, 90, 91
INTROW	exog	64, 67, 68, 99, 115	POP1	exog	5, 120
INTS	exog	64, 78, 99, 113, 115	POP2	exog	6, 120
ISZ	exog	113	POP3	exog	7, 120
IVA	20	67	PROD	118	—
IVF	117	—	PS	41	61, 78, 110
JF	13	14, 43, 53, 54, 64, 67, 68, 85, 95, 115, 118,	PSI1	exog	32
JG	exog	43, 64, 76, 82, 83, 85, 95, 98, 104, 115, 126	PSI2	exog	35
JHMIN	94	13, 14	PSI3	exog	36
JJ	95	96, 97	PSI4	exog	37
JJP	exog	96, 97, 98	PSI5	exog	38
JM	exog	43, 64, 76, 82, 83, 85, 87, 95, 98, 104, 115	PSI6	exog	39
JS	exog	43, 64, 78, 82, 83, 85, 95, 98, 110, 115, 126	PSI7	exog	40
KD	58	3	PSI8	exog	41
KH	59	4, 89	PSI9	exog	42
KK	12	92	PSI10	exog	44
KKMIN	93	12	PSI11	exog	45
L1	5	86, 87	PSI12	exog	46
L2	6	86, 87	PSI13	exog	83
L3	7	86, 87	PUG	104	106
LAM	exog	10, 16, 94, 98	PUS	110	113
LM	8	85	PX	31	12, 20, 25, 32, 33, 61, 72, 82, 119
M1	81	124	Q	exog	75, 77
MB	71	57, 73	RB	23	12, 19, 25, 29
MDIF	exog	81	RD	exog	22
MF	17	70, 71, 81	RECG	105	107
MG	exog	71, 77	RECS	112	114
MH	9	66, 71, 81, 89	RM	24	128
MR	exog	71, 75, 81	RMA	128	2, 3, 4
MRS	exog	68, 76	RNT	exog	64, 67, 68, 99, 115
MS	exog	71, 79, 81	RS	30	17, 22, 23, 24, 29, 127
MUH	exog	93	RSA	130	1, 9, 26
PCD	37	34, 51, 52, 61, 65, 116	SB	72	73
PCGDPD	122	—	SF	69	70
PCGDPR	123	30	SG	76	77
PCM1	124	30	SGP	107	—
PCN	36	34, 51, 52, 61, 65, 116	SH	65	66
PCS	35	34, 51, 52, 61, 65, 116	SHRPIE	121	—
PD	33	12, 30, 35, 36, 37, 38, 39, 40, 41, 42	SIFG	54	67, 68, 76, 103
PEX	32	33, 61, 74	SIFS	exog	67, 68, 78, 109
PF	10	16, 17, 26, 27, 31, 119	SIG	103	105
PFA	exog	31	SIGG	exog	43, 64, 76, 103, 115, 126
PG	40	61, 76, 104	SIHG	53	65, 76, 103, 115
PH	34	1, 2, 3, 4, 6, 7, 8, 9, 89	SIHS	exog	65, 78, 109, 115

Table A.10
(continued)

Var.	Eq.	Used in Equation	Var.	Eq.	Used in Equation
SIS	109	112	*TRGS*	exog	76, 78, 106, 112
SISS	exog	43, 64, 78, 109, 115, 126	*TRHR*	exog	65, 74, 115
SR	74	75	*TRRSH*	111	113
SRZ	116	—	*TRSH*	exog	65, 78, 99, 111, 115
SS	78	79	*U*	86	28, 87
SSP	114	—	*UB*	28	65, 78, 99, 111, 115
STAT	exog	67, 70, 80	*UBR*	128	—
STATP	exog	83	*UR*	87	5, 7, 8, 10, 30
SUBG	exog	67, 68, 76, 106	*V*	63	11, 20, 67, 82, 117
SUBS	exog	67, 68, 78, 113	*WA*	126	6, 7, 8
T	exog	1, 9, 10, 16	*WF*	16	10, 28, 43, 44, 45, 46, 53, 54, 64, 67, 68, 115, 119, 126
TAUG	exog	47, 90, 99	*WG*	44	43, 64, 76, 82, 104, 115, 126
TAUS	exog	48, 91, 99	*WH*	43	—
TBG	exog	25, 72, 76, 102	*WLDF*	exog	65, 68, 70
TBS	exog	25, 72, 78, 108	*WLDG*	exog	82, 104, 106
TCG	102	105	*WLDS*	exog	82, 110, 113
TCS	108	112	*WM*	45	43, 64, 76, 82, 104, 115, 126
TFG	49	18, 25, 69, 76, 102	*WR*	119	—
TFS	50	18, 25, 49, 69, 78, 108	*WS*	46	43, 64, 78, 82, 110, 115, 126
THG	47	65, 76, 101, 115	*X*	60	11, 17, 26, 31, 33, 63
THS	48	65, 78, 112, 115	*XX*	61	67, 68, 82
TPG	101	105	*Y*	11	10, 12, 13, 14, 63, 83, 93, 94, 118
TRFH	exog	64, 67, 68, 99, 115	*YD*	115	1, 2, 3, 4, 9, 116
TRFR	exog	67, 68, 74	*YNL*	99	—
TRGH	exog	65, 76, 99, 106, 115	*YS*	98	12, 25
TRGR	exog	74, 76, 106	*YT*	64	47, 48, 65, 90, 91, 99

The ROW Model

B.1 About Tables B.1–B.6

The tables that pertain to the ROW model are presented in this appendix. Table B.1 lists the countries in the model. The 38 countries for which structural equations are estimated are Canada (CA) through Peru (PE). Countries 40 through 59 are countries for which only trade share equations are estimated. The countries that make up the EMU are listed at the bottom of Table B.1. The EMU is denoted EU in the model.

A detailed description of the variables per country is presented in Table B.2, where the variables are listed in alphabetical order. Data permitting, each of the countries has the same set of variables. Quarterly data were collected for countries 2 through 14, and annual data were collected for the others. Countries 2 through 14 will be referred to as "quarterly" countries, and the others will be referred to as "annual" countries. The way in which each variable was constructed is explained in brackets in Table B.2. All of the data with potential seasonal fluctuations have been seasonally adjusted.

Table B.3 lists the stochastic equations and the identities. The functional forms of the stochastic equations are given, but not the coefficient estimates. The coefficient estimates for all the countries are presented in Table B.4, where within this table the coefficient estimates and tests for equation 1 are presented in Table B1, for equation 2 in Table B2, and so on. The results in Table B.4 are discussed in section 2.4. Table B.3 also lists the equations that pertain to the trade and price links among the countries, and it explains how the quarterly and annual data are linked for the trade share calculations. Table B.5 lists the links between the US and ROW models, and Table B.6 explains the construction of the balance-of-payments data—data for variables S and TT.

The rest of this appendix discusses the collection of the data and the construction of some of the variables.

B.2   The Raw Data

The data sets for the countries other than the United States (that is, the countries in
the ROW model) begin in 1960. The sources of the data are the IMF and the OECD.
Data from the IMF are international financial statistics (IFS) data and direction of trade
(DOT) data. Data from the OECD are quarterly national accounts data, annual national
accounts data, quarterly labor force data, and annual labor force data. These are the
"raw" data. As noted above, the way in which each variable was constructed is explained
in brackets in Table B.2. When "IFS" precedes a number or letter in the table, this refers
to the IFS variable number or letter. Some variables were constructed directly from IFS
and OECD data (that is, directly from the raw data), and some were constructed from
other (already constructed) variables. The construction of the EU variables is listed near
the end of Table B.2.

B.3   Variable Construction

S, TT, and *A*: Balance-of-Payments Variables

One important feature of the data collection is the linking of the balance-of-payments
data to the other export and import data. The two key variables involved in this process
are S, the balance of payments on current account, and TT, the value of net transfers.
The construction of these variables and the linking of the two types of data are explained
in Table B.6. Quarterly balance-of-payments data do not generally begin as early as the
other data, and the procedure in Table B.6 allows quarterly data on S to be constructed
as far back as the beginning of the quarterly data for merchandise imports and exports
($M\$$ and $X\$$).

The variable A is the net stock of foreign security and reserve holdings. It is
constructed by summing past values of S from a base period value of zero. The
summation begins in the first quarter for which data on S exist. This means that
the A series is off by a constant amount each period (the difference between the
true value of A in the base period and zero). In the estimation work the functional
forms were chosen in such a way that this error was always absorbed in the esti-
mate of the constant term. It is important to note that A measures only the net as-
set position of the country vis-à-vis the rest of the world. Domestic wealth, such
as the domestically owned housing stock and plant and equipment stock, is not in-
cluded.

V: Stock of Inventories

Data on inventory investment, denoted $V1$ in the ROW model, are available for each
country, but not data on the stock of inventories, denoted V. By definition $V = V_{-1} + V1$. Given this equation and data for $V1$, V can be constructed once a base period and
base period value are chosen. The base period was chosen for each country to be the

quarter or year prior to the beginning of the data on $V1$. The base period value was taken to be the value of Y in the base period for the quarterly countries and the value of $.25Y$ for the annual countries.

Excess Labor

Good capital stock data are not available for countries other than the United States. If the short-run production function for a country is one of fixed proportions and if capital is never the constraint, then the production function can be written:

$$Y = LAM(J \cdot H^a), \tag{B.1}$$

where Y is production, J is the number of workers employed, and HJ^a is the number of hours worked per worker. LAM is a coefficient that may change over time due to technical progress. The notation in equation B.1 is changed slightly from that in equation A.1 for the US model. J is used in place of JF because there is no disaggregation in the ROW model between the firm sector and other sectors. Similarly, H^a is used in place of HF^a. Note also that Y refers here to the total output of the country (real GDP), not just to the output of the firm sector. Data on Y and J are available. Contrary to the case for the United States, data on the number of hours paid for per worker (denoted HF in the US model) are not available.

Given the production function B.1, excess labor is measured as follows for each country. First, $\log(Y/J)$ is plotted for the sample period. This is from equation B.1 a plot of $\log(LAM \cdot H^a)$. If it is assumed that at each peak of this plot H^a is equal to the same constant, say $\bar{H}$, then one observes at the peaks $\log(LAM \cdot \bar{H})$. Straight lines are drawn between the peaks (peak-to-peak interpolation), and $\log(LAM \cdot \bar{H})$ is assumed to lie on the lines. If, finally, $\bar{H}$ is assumed to be the maximum number of hours that each worker can work, then $Y/(LAM \cdot \bar{H})$ is the minimum number of workers required to produce Y, which is denoted $JMIN$ in the ROW model. $LAM \cdot \bar{H}$ is simply denoted LAM, and the equation determining $JMIN$ is equation I-13 in Table B.3. The actual number of workers on hand, J, can be compared to $JMIN$ to measure the amount of excess labor on hand.

Labor Market Tightness: The Z Variable

A labor market tightness variable, denoted Z, is constructed for each country as follows. First, a peak-to-peak interpolation of $JJ (= J/POP)$ is made, and JJP (the peak-to-peak interpolation series) is constructed. Z is then equal to the minimum of 0 and $1 - JJP/JJ$, which is equation I-16 in Table B.3. Z is such that when labor markets are tight (JJ close to JJP) it is zero or close to zero, and as labor markets loosen (JJ falling relative to JJP) it increases in absolute value.

YS: Potential Output

A measure of potential output, *YS*, is constructed for each country in the same manner as was done for the US model. The only difference is that here output refers to the total output of the country rather than just the output of the firm sector. The equation for *YS* is $YS = LAM \cdot JJP \cdot POP$, which is equation I-17 in Table B.3. Given *YS*, a gap variable can be constructed as $(YS - Y)/YS$, which is denoted *ZZ* in the ROW model. *ZZ* is determined by equation I-18 in Table B.3.

B.4   The Identities

The identities for each country are listed in Table B.3. There are up to 20 identities per country. (The identities are numbered I-1 through I-22, with no identities I-10 and I-11.) Equation I-1 links the non-NIPA data on imports (that is, data on *M* and *MS*) to the NIPA data (that is, data on *IM*). The variable *IMDS* in the equation picks up the discrepancy between the two data sets. It is exogenous in the model. Equation I-2 is a similar equation for exports. Equation I-3 is the income identity; equation I-4 defines inventory investment as the difference between production and sales; and equation I-5 defines the stock of inventories as the previous stock plus inventory investment.

Equation I-6 defines *S*, the current account balance. Equation I-7 defines *A*, the net stock of foreign security and reserve holdings, as equal to last period's value plus *S*. (Remember that *A* is constructed by summing past values of *S*.)

Equation I-8 links *M*, total merchandise imports in 95 lc, to *M95$A*, merchandise imports from the countries in the trade share matrix in 95$. The variable *M95$B* is the difference between total merchandise imports (in 95$) and merchandise imports (in 95$) from the countries in the trade share matrix. It is exogenous in the model.

Equation I-9 links *E*, the average exchange rate for the period, to *EE*, the end of period exchange rate. If the exchange rate changes fairly smoothly within the period, then *E* is approximately equal to $(EE + EE_{-1})/2$. A variable *PSI*1 was defined to make the equation $E = PSI1[(EE + EE_{-1})/2]$ exact, which is equation I-9. One would expect *PSI*1 to be approximately one and not to fluctuate much over time, which is generally the case in the data.

Equation I-12 defines the civilian unemployment rate, *UR*. *L*1 is the labor force of men, and *L*2 is the labor force of women. *J* is total employment, including the armed forces, and *AF* is the number of people in the armed forces. *UR* is equal to the number of people unemployed divided by the civilian labor force.

Equations I-13 through I-18 pertain to the measurement of excess labor, the labor constraint variable, and potential output. These have all been discussed above.

Equation I-19 links *PM*, the import price deflator obtained from the IFS data, to *PMP*, the import price deflator computed from the trade share calculations. The variable that links the two, *PSI*2, is taken to be exogenous.

Equation I-20 links the exchange rate relative to the U.S. dollar, *E*, to the exchange rate relative to the German Deutsche mark, *H*. This equation is used to determine

H when equation 9 determines *E*, and it is used to determine *E* when equation 9 determines *H*.

Equation I-21 determines *NW*, an estimate of the net worth of the country. Net worth is equal to last period's net worth plus investment plus net exports.

Finally, equation I-22 defines the country's export price index in terms of U.S. dollars.

B.5   The Linking Equations

The equations that pertain to the trade and price links among countries are presented next in Table B.3. All imports and exports in this part of the table are merchandise imports and exports only. The equations L-1 determine the trade share coefficients, a_{ij}. The estimation of the trade share equations is discussed in section 2.4. a_{ij} is the share of *i*'s merchandise exports to *j* out of total merchandise imports of *j*. Given a_{ij} and $M95\$A_j$, the total merchandise imports of *j*, the equations L-2 determine the level of exports from *i* to *j*, $XX95\$_{ij}$. The equations L-3 then determine the total exports of country *i* by summing $XX95\$_{ij}$ over *j*.

The equations L-4 link export prices to import prices. The price of imports of country *i*, PMP_i, is a weighted average of the export prices of other countries (except for country 59, the "all other" category, where no data on export prices were collected). The weight for country *j* in calculating the price index for country *i* is the share of country *j*'s exports imported by *i*.

The equations L-5 define a world price index for each country, which is a weighted average of the 58 countries' export prices except the prices of the oil-exporting countries. The world price index differs slightly by country because the own country's price is not included in the calculations. The weight for each country is its share of total exports of the relevant countries.

B.6   Solution of the MC Model

The way in which the US and ROW models are linked is explained in Table B.5. The two key variables that are exogenous in the US model but become endogenous in the overall MC model are exports, *EX*, and the price of imports, *PIM*. *EX* depends on $X95\$_{US}$, which is determined in Table B.3. *PIM* depends on PM_{US}, which depends on PMP_{US}, which is also determined in Table B.3.

Feeding into Table B.3 from the US model are PX_{US} and $M95\$A_{US}$. PX_{US} is determined in the same way that *PX* is determined for the other countries, namely by equation 11. In the US case $\log PX_{US} - \log PW\$_{US}$ is regressed on $\log GDPD - \log PW\$_{US}$. The equation is:

$$\log PX_{US} - \log PW\$_{US} = \lambda(\log GDPD - \log PW\$_{US}).$$

This equation is estimated under the assumption of a second-order autoregressive error for the 1962:1–2001:4 period. The estimate of λ is .925 with a *t*-statistic of

25.86. The estimates (t-statistics) of the two autoregressive coefficients are 1.48 (21.00) and $-.49$ (-6.87), respectively. The standard error is .0114. Given the predicted value of PX_{US} from this equation, PEX is determined by the identity listed in Table B.5: $PEX = DEL3 \cdot PX_{US}$. This identity replaces identity 32 in Table A.3 in the US model.

$M95\$A_{US}$, which, as just noted, feeds into Table B.3, depends on M_{US}, which depends on IM. This is shown in Table B.5. IM is determined by equation 27 in the US model. Equation 27 is thus the key equation that determines the U.S. import value that feeds into Table B.3.

Because some of the countries are annual, the overall MC model is solved a year at a time. A solution period must begin in the first quarter of the year. In the following discussion, assume that year 1 is the first year to be solved. The overall MC model is solved as follows:

1. Given values of $X95\$$, PMP, and $PW\$$ for all four quarters of year 1 for each quarterly country and for year 1 for each annual country, all the stochastic equations and identities are solved. For the annual countries "solved" means that the equations are passed through k_1 times for year 1, where k_1 is determined by experimentation (as discussed below). For the quarterly countries "solved" means that quarter 1 of year 1 is passed through k_1 times, then quarter 2 k_1 times, then quarter 3 k_1 times, and then quarter 4 k_1 times. The solution for the quarterly countries for the four quarters of year 1 is a dynamic simulation in the sense that the predicted values of the endogenous variables from previous quarters are used, when relevant, in the solution for the current quarter.

2. Given from the solution in step 1 values of E, PX, and $M95\$A$ for each country, the calculations in Table B.3 can be performed. Since all the calculations in Table B.3 are quarterly, the annual values of E, PX, and $M95\$A$ from the annual countries have to be converted to quarterly values first. This is done in the manner discussed at the bottom of Table B.3. The procedure in effect takes the distribution of the annual values into the quarterly values to be exogenous. The second task is to compute $PX\$$ using equation L-1. Given the values of $PX\$$, the third task is to compute the values of α_{ij} from the trade share equations—see equation 2.41 in Chapter 2. This solution is also dynamic in the sense that the predicted value of α_{ij} for the previous quarter feeds into the solution for the current quarter. (Remember that the lagged value of α_{ij} is an explanatory variable in the trade share equations.) The fourth task is to compute $X95\$$, PMP, and $PW\$$ for each country using equations L-2, L-3, and L-4. Finally, for the annual countries the quarterly values of these three variables are then converted to annual values by summing in the case of $X95\$$ and averaging in the case of PMP and $PW\$$.

3. Given the new values of $X95\$$, PMP, and $PW\$$ from step 2, repeat step 1 and then step 2. Keep repeating steps 1 and 2 until they have been done k_2 times. At the end of this, declare that the solution for year 1 has been obtained.

4. Repeat steps 1, 2, and 3 for year 2. If the solution is meant to be dynamic, use the predicted values for year 1 for the annual countries and the predicted values for the four quarters of year 1 for the quarterly countries, when relevant, in the solution for year 2. Continue then to year 3, and so on.

I have found that going beyond $k_1 = 10$ and $k_2 = 10$ leads to very little change in the final solution values, and these are the values of k_1 and k_2 that have been used for the results in this book.

Table B.1
The Countries and Variables in the MC Model

			Local Currency			Trade Share Equations Only
Quarterly countries						
1	US	United States	U.S. dollar (mil.)	40	TU	Turkey
2	CA	Canada	Can. dollar (mil.)	41	PD	Poland
3	JA	Japan	Yen (bil.)	42	RU	Russia
4	AU	Austria	Euro (mil.)	43	UE	Ukraine
5	FR	France	Euro (mil.)	44	EG	Egypt
6	GE	Germany	Euro (mil.)	45	IS	Israel
7	IT	Italy	Euro (mil.)	46	KE	Kenya
8	NE	Netherlands	Euro (mil.)	47	BA	Bangladesh
9	ST	Switzerland	Swiss franc (bil.)	48	HK	Hong Kong
10	UK	United Kingdom	Pound sterling (mil.)	49	SI	Singapore
11	FI	Finland	Euro (mil.)	50	VI	Vietnam
12	AS	Australia	Aust. dollar (mil.)	51	NI	Nigeria
13	SO	South Africa	Rand (mil.)	52	AL	Algeria
14	KO	Rep. of Korea	Won (bil.)	53	IA	Indonesia
Annual countries				54	IN	Iran
15	BE	Belgium	Euro (mil.)	55	IQ	Iraq
16	DE	Denmark	Den. kroner (bil.)	56	KU	Kuwait
17	NO	Norway	Nor. kroner (bil.)	57	LI	Libya
18	SW	Sweden	Swe. kroner (bil.)	58	UA	United Arab Emirates
19	GR	Greece	Euro (mil.)	59	AO	All Other
20	IR	Ireland	Euro (mil.)			
21	PO	Portugal	Euro (mil.)			
22	SP	Spain	Euro (mil.)			
23	NZ	New Zealand	N.Z. dollar (mil.)			
24	SA	Saudi Arabia	Riyal (bil.)			
25	VE	Venezuela	Bolivar (bil.)			
26	CO	Colombia	Col. peso (bil.)			
27	JO	Jordan	Jor. dinar (mil.)			
28	SY	Syria	Syr. pound (mil.)			
29	ID	India	Ind. rupee (bil.)			
30	MA	Malaysia	Ringgit (mil.)			
31	PA	Pakistan	Pak. rupee (bil.)			
32	PH	Philippines	Phil. peso (bil.)			
33	TH	Thailand	Baht (bil.)			
34	CH	China	Yuan (bil.)			
35	AR	Argentina	Arg. peso (mil.)			
36	BR	Brazil	Real (mil.)			
37	CE	Chile	Chi. peso (bil.)			
38	ME	Mexico	New peso (mil.)			
39	PE	Peru	Nuevo sole (mil.)			

Notes:
- The countries that make up the EMU, denoted EU in the model, are AU, FR, GE, IT, NE, FI, BE, IR, PO, SP, GR. (GR begins in 2001.) (Luxembourg, which is also part of the EMU, is not in the model.)
- Prior to 1999:1 the currency is schillings for AU, Fr. francs for FR, DM for GE, lira for IT, guilders for NE, markkaa for FI, Bel. francs for BE, Irish pounds for IR, escudos for PO, pesetas for SP, and drachmas for GR (prior to 2001:1). The units are in euro equivalents. For example, in 1999:1 the lira was converted to the euro at 1936.27 liras per euro, and 1936.27 was used to convert the lira to its euro equivalent for 1998:4 back.
- The NIPA base year is 1995 for all countries except CA (1997), ST (1990), and AS (1999–2000).

Table B.2

The Variables for a Given Country in Alphabetical Order

Variable	Eq. No.	Description
a_{ij}	L-1	Share of i's merchandise exports to j out of total merchandise imports of j. [See below.]
A	I-7	Net stock of foreign security and reserve holdings, end of quarter, in lc. [$A_{-1} + S$. Base value of zero used for the quarter prior to the beginning of the data.]
AF	exog	Level of the armed forces in thousands. [OECD data]
C	2	Personal consumption in constant lc. [OECD data or IFS96F/CPI]
E	9	Exchange rate, average for the period, lc per \$. [IFSRF]
EE	I-9	Exchange rate, end of period, lc per \$. [IFSAE]
EX	I-2	Total exports (NIPA) in constant lc. [OECD data or (IFS90C or IFS90N)/ PX]
$EXDS$	exog	Discrepancy between NIPA export data and other export data in constant lc. [$EX - PX95(E95 \cdot X95\$ + XS)$]
$E95$	exog	E in 1995, 95 lc per 95 \$. [IFSRF in 1995]
F	10	Three-month forward exchange rate, lc per \$. [IFSB]
G	exog	Government purchases of goods and services in constant lc. [OECD data or (IFS91F or IFS91FF)/PY] (Denoted GZ for countries CO and TH.)
H	9	Exchange rate, average for the period, lc per DM euro. [E/E_{GE}]
I	3	Gross fixed investment in constant lc. [OECD data or IFS93/PY]
IM	I-1	Total imports (NIPA) in constant lc. [OECD data or IFS98C/PM]
$IMDS$	exog	Discrepancy between NIPA import data and other import data in constant lc. [$IM - PM95(M + MS)$]
J	13	Total employment in thousands. [OECD data or IFS67 or IFS67E or IFS67EY or IFS67EYC]
JJ	I-14	Employment population ratio. [J/POP]
JJP	exog	Peak-to-peak interpolation of JJ.
JJS	I-15	Ratio of JJ to JJP. [JJ/JJP]
$JMIN$	I-13	Minimum amount of employment needed to produce Y in thousands. [Y/LAM]
LAM	exog	Computed from peak-to-peak interpolation of $\log(Y/J)$.
$L1$	14	Labor force of men in thousands. [OECD data]
$L2$	15	Labor force of women in thousands. [OECD data]
M	1	Total merchandise imports (fob) in 95 lc. [IFS71V/PM]
MS	exog	Other goods, services, and income (debit) in 95 lc, BOP data. [((IFS78AED+IFS78AHD)E)/PM]
$M95\$A$	I-8	Merchandise imports (fob) from the trade share matrix in 95 \$. [See below.]
$M95\$B$	exog	Difference between total merchandise imports and merchandise imports from the trade share matrix in 95 \$ (that is, imports from countries other than the 44 in the trade share matrix). [$M/E95 - M95\$A$]
$M1$	6	Money supply in lc. [IFS34 or IFS34A.N + IFS34B.N or IFS35L.B or IFS39MAC or IFS59MA or IFS59MC]
NW	I-21	National wealth in constant lc. [$NW_{-1} + I + V1 + EX - IM$. Base value of zero used for the quarter prior to the beginning of the data.]
PM	I-19	Import price deflator, 1995 = 1.0. [IFS75/100]
PMP	L-4	Import price index from DOT data, 1995 = 1.0. [See below.]
$PM95$	exog	PM in the NIPA base year divided by PM in 1995.
POP	exog	Population in millions. [IFS99Z]
$POP1$	exog	Population of labor-force-age men in thousands. [OECD data]
$POP2$	exog	Population of labor-force-age women in thousands. [OECD data]
$PSI1$	exog	[$(EE + EE_{-1})/2]/E$]
$PSI2$	exog	[PM/PMP]
$PW\$$	L-5	World price index, \$/95\$. [See below.]
PX	11	Export price index, 1995 = 1.0. [IFS74/100. If no IFS74 data for t, then $PX_t = PX\$_t(E_t/E95_t$, where $PX\$_t$ is defined next.]
$PX\$$	I-22	Export price index, \$/95\$, 1995 = 1.0. [$(E95 \cdot PX)/E$. If no IFS74 data at all, then $PX\$_t = PX_{USt}$ for all t. If IFS74 data only from t through $t + h$, then for $i > 0$, $PX\$_{t-i} = PX\$_t(PX_{USt-i}/PX_{USt})$ and $PX\$_{t+h+i} = PX\$_{t+h}(PX_{USt+k+i}/PX_{USt}).$]

Table B.2
(continued)

Variable	Eq. No.	Description
*PX*95	exog	*PX* in the NIPA base year divided by *PX* in 1995.
PY	5	GDP or GNP deflator, equals 1.0 in the NIPA base year. [OECD data or (IFS99B/IFS99B.P)]
RB	8	Long-term interest rate, percentage points. [IFS61]
RS	7	Three-month interest rate, percentage points. [IFS60 or IFS60B or IFS60C or IFS60L or IFS60P]
S	I-6	Total net goods, services, and transfers in lc. Current account balance. [See Table B.7.] (Denoted *SZ* for countries CO and TH.)
STAT	exog	Statistical discrepancy in constant lc. [$Y - C - I - G - EX + IM - V1$]
T	exog	Time trend. [For quarterly data, 1 in 1952.1, 2 in 1952.2, etc.; for annual data, 1 in 1952, 2 in 1953, etc.]
TT	exog	Total net transfers in lc. [See Table B.7.]
UR	I-12	Unemployment rate. [$(L1 + L2 - J)/(L1 + L2 - AF)$]
V	I-5	Stock of inventories, end of period, in constant lc. [$V_{-1} + V1$. Base value of zero was used for the period (quarter or year) prior to the beginning of the data.]
*V*1	I-4	Inventory investment in constant lc. [OECD data or IFS93I/*PY*]
W	12	Nominal wage rate. [IFS65..C or IFS65A or IFS65EY or IFS65UMC]
X	I-3	Final sales in constant lc. [$Y - V1$] (Denoted *XZ* for country PE.)
XS	exog	Other goods, services, and income (credit) in 95 lc. BOP data. [$(E(\text{IFS78ADD}+\text{IFS78AGD}))/PX$]
*X*95$	L-3	Merchandise exports from the trade share matrix in 95 $. [See below.]
*XX*95$$_{ij}$	L-2	Merchandise exports from *i* to *j* in 95 $. [See below.]
Y	4	Real GDP or GNP in constant lc. [OECD data or IFS99B.P or IFS99B.R]
YS	I-17	Potential value of *Y*. [$LAM \cdot JJP \cdot POP$]
Z	I-16	Labor constraint variable. [$\min(0, 1 - JJP/JJ)$]
ZZ	I-18	Demand pressure variable. [$(YS - Y)/YS$]

Construction of variables related to the trade share matrix

The raw data are

XX$$_{ij}$	Merchandise exports from *i* to *j* in $, $i, j = 1, \ldots, 58$ [DOT data. 0 value used if no data.]
X$$_i$	Total merchandise exports (fob) in $. $i = 1, \ldots, 39$ [IFS70/E or IFS70D]

The constructed variables are

$XX\$_{i59} =$	$X\$_i - \sum_{j=1}^{58} XX\$_{ij}, i = 1, \ldots, 39$
$XX95\$_{ij} =$	$XX\$_{ij}/PX\$_i, i = 1, \ldots, 39, j = 1, \ldots, 59$ and $i = 40, \ldots, 58, j = 1, \ldots, 58$
$M95\$A_i =$	$\sum_{j=1}^{58} XX95\$_{ji}, i = 1, \ldots, 58; M95\$A_{59} = \sum_{j=1}^{39} XX95\$_{j59}$
$a_{ij} =$	$XX95\$_{ij}/M95\$A_j, i = 1, \ldots, 39, j = 1, \ldots, 59$ and $i = 40, \ldots, 58, j = 1, \ldots, 58$
$X95\$_i =$	$\sum_{j=1}^{59} XX95\$_{ij}, i = 1, \ldots, 39; X95\$_i = \sum_{j=1}^{58} XX95\$_{ij}, i = 40, \ldots, 58$
$PMP_i =$	$(E_i/E95_i) \sum_{j=1}^{58} a_{ji} PX\$_j, i = 1, \ldots, 39$
$PW\$_i =$	$(\sum_{j=1}^{58} PX\$_j X95\$_j)/(\sum_{j=1}^{58} X95\$_j), i = 1, \ldots, 39$
	An element in this summation is skipped if $j = i$. This summation also excludes the oil-exporting countries, which are SA, VE, NI, AL, IA, IN, IQ, KU, LI, UA.

Notes:
- Variables available for trade share–only countries are *M*95$*A*, *PX*$, *X*95$.
- lc = local currency.
- IFSxxxxx = variable number xxxxx from the IFS data.

Table B.2

(continued)

Variable	Eq. No.	Description
The EU Variables		
E	9	Exchange rate, average for the period, euro per \$. [IFSRF]
PY	[ ]	GDP deflator. $[(\sum_{i=1}^{6} PY_i Y_i)/Y_{EU}$, where the summation is for $i =$ GE, AU, FR, IT, NE, FI.]
RB	8	Long-term interest rate, percentage points. [IFS61]
RS	7	Three-month interest rate, percentage points. [IFS60]
Y	[ ]	Real GDP in constant euros. $[Y_{GE} + \sum_{i=1}^{5}[Y_i/(E95_i/E95_{GE})]$, where the summation is for $i =$ AU, FR, IT, NE, FI.]
YS	[ ]	Potential value of Y_{EU}. $[YS_{GE} + \sum_{i=1}^{5}[YS_i/(E95_i/E95_{GE})]$, where the summation is for $i =$ AU, FR, IT, NE, FI.]
ZZ	I-18	Demand pressure variable. $[(YS_{EU} - Y_{EU})/YS_{EU}]$

Table B.3

The Equations for a Given Country

Eq.	LHS Variable	Explanatory Variables
Stochastic Equations		
1	$\log(IM/POP)$	cnst, $\log(IM/POP)_{-1}$, $\log(PY/PM)$, $\log[(C + I + G)/POP]$ [Total Imports (NIPA), constant lc]
2	$\log(C/POP)$	cnst, $\log(C/POP)_{-1}$, RS or RB, $\log(Y/POP)$, $[A/(PY \cdot YS)]_{-1}$ [Consumption, constant lc]
3	$\log I$	cnst, $\log I_{-1}$, $\log Y$, RS or RB [Fixed Investment, constant lc]
4	$\log Y$	$\log Y_{-1}$, $\log X$, $\log V_{-1}$ [Real GDP, constant lc]
5	$\log PY$	cnst, $\log PY_{-1}$, $\log W - \log LAM$, $\log PM$, DP, T [GDP Price Deflator, base year = 1.0]
6	$\log[M1/(POP \cdot PY)]$	cnst, $\log[M1/(POP \cdot PY)]_{-1}$ or $\log[M1_{-1}/(POP_{-1}PY)]$, RS, $\log(Y/POP)$ [Money Supply, lc]
7	RS	cnst, RS_{-1}, $100[(PY/PY_{-1})^4 - 1]$, ZZ or JJS, RS_{GE}, RS_{US} [Three-Month Interest Rate, percentage points]
8	$RB - RS_{-2}$	cnst, $RB_{-1} - RS_{-2}$, $RS - RS_{-2}$, $RS_{-1} - RS_{-2}$ [Long-Term Interest Rate, percentage points]
9	$\Delta \log E$	cnst, $\log(PY/PY_{US} - \log E_{-1}$, $.25 \log[(1 + RS/100)/(1 + RS_{US}/100)]$ [Exchange Rate, lc per \$] [For all countries but AU, FR, IT, NE, ST, UK, FI, BE, DE, NO, SW, GR, IR, PO, and SP]
9	$\Delta \log H$	cnst, $\log(PY/PY_{GE} - \log H_{-1}$, $.25 \log[(1 + RS/100)/(1 + RS_{GE}/100)]$ [Exchange Rate, lc per DM] [For countries AU, FR, IT, NE, ST, UK, FI, BE, DE, NO, SW, GR, IR, PO, and SP]
10	$\log F$	$\log EE$, $.25 \log[(1 + RS/100)/(1 + RS_{US}/100)]$ [Three-Month Forward Rate, lc per \$]
11	$\log PX - \log[PW\$(E/E95)]$	$\log PY - \log[PW\$(E/E95)]$ [Export Price Index, 1995 = 1.0]
12	$\log W - \log LAM$	cnst, $\log W_{-1} - \log LAM_{-1}$, $\log PY$, DW, T, $\log PY_{-1}$ [Nominal Wage Rate, base year = 1.0]
13	$\Delta \log J$	cnst, T, $\log(J/JMIN)_{-1}$, $\Delta \log Y$, $\Delta \log Y_{-1}$ [Employment, thousands]
14	$\log(L1/POP1)$	cnst, T, $\log(L1/POP1)_{-1}$, $\log(W/PY)$, Z [Labor Force—men, thousands]
15	$\log(L2/POP2)$	cnst, T, $\log(L2/POP2)_{-1}$, $\log(W/PY)$, Z [Labor Force—women, thousands]

Table B.3
(continued)

Eq.	LHS Variable	Explanatory Variables

Identities

I-1 $M =$ $(IM - IMDS)/PM95 - MS$
[Merchandise Imports, 95 lc]

I-2 $EX =$ $PX95(E95 \cdot X95\$ + XS) + EXDS$
[Total Exports (NIPA), constant lc]

I-3 $X =$ $C + I + G + EX - IM + STAT$
[Final Sales, constant lc]

I-4 $V1 =$ $Y - X$
[Inventory Investment, constant lc]

I-5 $V =$ $V_{-1} + V1$
[Inventory Stock, constant lc]

I-6 $S =$ $PX(E95 \cdot X95\$ + XS) - PM(M + MS) + TT$
[Current Account Balance, lc]

I-7 $A =$ $A_{-1} + S$
[Net Stock of Foreign Security and Reserve Holdings, lc]

I-8 $M95\$A =$ $M/E95 - M95\$B$
[Merchandise Imports from the Trade Share Calculations, 95 $]

I-9 $EE =$ $2PSI1 \cdot E - EE_{-1}$
[Exchange Rate, end of period, lc per $]

I-12 $UR =$ $(L1 + L2 - J)/(L1 + L2 - AF)$
[Unemployment Rate]

I-13 $JMIN =$ Y/LAM
[Minimum Required Employment, thousands]

I-14 $JJ =$ J/POP
[Employment Population Ratio]

I-15 $JJS =$ JJ/JJP
[Peak-to-Peak Interpolation of JJ]

I-16 $Z =$ $\min(0, 1 - JJP/JJ)$
[Labor Constraint Variable]

I-17 $YS =$ $LAM \cdot JJP \cdot POP$
[Potential Y]

I-18 $ZZ =$ $(YS - Y)/YS$
[Demand Pressure Variable]

I-19 $PM =$ $PSI2 \cdot PMP$
[Import Price Deflator, 1995 = 1.0]

I-20 E $E = H \cdot E_{GE}$
[Exchange Rate: lc per $] [Equation relevant for countries AU, FR, IT, NE, ST, UK, FI, BE, DE, NO, SW, GR, IR, PO, and SP only]

I-21 $NW =$ $NW_{-1} + I + V1 + EX - IM$
[National Wealth, constant lc]

I-22 $PX\$ =$ $(E95/E)PX$
[Export Price Index, $/95$]

Notes:
- From 1999:1 on for GE: $E_{GE} = E_{EU}$, $RS_{GE} = RS_{EU}$, and $RB_{GE} = RB_{EU}$. From 1999:1 on for an EU country i (except GE): $H_i = 1.0$, $RS_i = RS_{EU}$, and $RB_i = RB_{EU}$.
- In equations 5 and 12 DP and DW are demand pressure variables.
- $PX\$$ and $M95\$A$ are exogenous for trade share–only countries.

Table B.3

(continued)

Equations that Pertain to the Trade and Price Links among Countries

---

L-1 $a_{ij} =$ computed from trade share equations
                     [Trade Share Coefficients]

L-2 $XX95\$_{ij} =$ $a_{ij}M95\$A_j$, $i = 1, \ldots, 39$, $j = 1, \ldots, 59$ and $i = 40, \ldots, 58$, $j = 1, \ldots, 58$
                     [Merchandise Exports from i to j, 95\$]

L-3 $X95\$_i =$ $\sum_{j=1}^{59} XX95\$_{ij}$, $i = 1, \ldots, 39$
          $X95\$_i =$ $\sum_{j=1}^{58} XX95\$_{ij}$, $i = 40, \ldots, 58$
                     [Total Merchandise Exports, 95\$]

L-4 $PMP_i =$ $(E_i/E95_i) \sum_{j=1}^{58} a_{ji}PX\$_j$, $i = 1, \ldots, 39$
                     [Import Price Deflator, 1995 = 1.0]

L-5 $PW\$_i =$ $(\sum_{j=1}^{58} PX\$_j X95\$_j)/(\sum_{j=1}^{58} X95\$_j)$, $i = 1, \ldots, 39$
                     An element in this summation is skipped if $j = i$. This summation also excludes the
                        oil-exporting countries, which are SA, VE, NI, AL, IA, IN, IQ, KU, LI, UA.
                     [World Price Index, \$/95\$]

Linking of the Annual and Quarterly Data

• Quarterly data exist for all the trade share calculations, and all these calculations are quarterly. Feeding into these calculations from the annual models are predicted annual values of $PX\$_i$, $M95\$A_i$, and E_i. For each of these three variables the predicted value for a given quarter was taken to be the predicted annual value multiplied by the ratio of the actual quarterly value to the actual annual value. This means in effect that the distribution of an annual value into its quarterly values is taken to be exogenous.

• Once the quarterly values have been computed from the trade share calculations, the annual values of $X95\$_i$ that are needed for the annual models are taken to be the sums of the quarterly values. Similarly, the annual values of PMP_i and $PW\$_i$ are taken to be the averages of the quarterly values.

Table B.4
Coefficient Estimates and Test Results
for the ROW Equations

- See Chapter 1 for discussion of the tests.
- See Chapter 2 for discussion of the equations.
- * = significant at the 99 percent confidence level.
- ρ = first-order autoregressive coefficient of the error term.
- † = variable is lagged one period.
- Dummy variable coefficient estimates are not shown for GE and EU.
- *t*-statistics are in parentheses.

Table B1
Coefficient Estimates for Equation 1:

$$\log(IM/POP) = a_1 + a_2 \log(IM/POP)_{-1} + a_3 \log(PY/PM) + a_4 \log[(C + I + G)/POP)]$$

	a_1	a_2	a_3	a_4	ρ	SE	DW
Quarterly							
CA	−0.319	0.960	0.069	0.072	0.237	0.0296	2.02
	(−0.82)	(35.56)	(1.41)	(1.08)	(2.74)		1966.1–2001.4
JA	−0.055	0.913	0.059	0.065		0.0290	1.89
	(−0.34)	(37.33)	(5.90)	(1.72)			1966.1–2001.3
AU	−0.284	0.904	0.116	0.121		0.0360	2.36
	(−0.38)	(17.40)	(2.28)	(0.94)			1970.1–2001.3
FR	−0.654	0.927	0.077	0.138		0.0219	1.28
	(−1.51)	(29.10)	(3.76)	(1.82)			1971.1–2001.3
GE	−0.100	0.962	0.020	0.045		0.0241	2.07
	(−0.25)	(27.55)	(1.22)	(0.62)			1970.1–2001.4
IT	−1.125	0.851	0.070	0.260		0.0377	2.05
	(−2.56)	(19.89)	(3.27)	(3.02)			1971.1–2001.3
NE	−0.474	0.951	0.039	0.104		0.0183	1.83
	(−0.70)	(21.74)	(1.72)	(0.87)			1978.1–2001.4
UK	−2.258	0.767	0.033	0.480		0.0293	1.96
	(−3.82)	(13.26)	(1.64)	(3.94)			1966.1–2001.3
FI	−0.217	0.944	0.030	0.075		0.0598	2.73
	(−0.29)	(21.71)	(0.56)	(0.69)			1976.2–2001.3
AS	−3.728	0.751	0.113	0.621	0.285	0.0383	2.04
	(−3.49)	(10.15)	(2.38)	(3.48)	(2.51)		1966.1–2001.2
SO	−0.253	0.853	0.040	0.153	0.201	0.0625	2.01
	(−0.64)	(14.10)	(0.93)	(1.99)	(2.03)		1961.1–2001.3
KO	−0.174	0.813	0.167	0.186		0.0571	2.20
	(−0.35)	(16.42)	(2.82)	(1.85)			1974.1–2001.4

Table B1
Coefficient Estimates for Equation 1 *(continued)*

	a_1	a_2	a_3	a_4	ρ	SE	DW
Annual							
BE	−3.695	0.417	0.298	0.936		0.0402	1.56
	(−2.22)	(2.31)	(3.90)	(2.77)			1962–1998
DE	−3.774	0.489	0.143	1.130		0.0399	1.87
	(−3.55)	(3.82)	(1.49)	(3.81)			1967–2000
NO	−0.009	0.517	0.271	0.392		0.0495	1.44
	(−0.02)	(3.87)	(2.57)	(2.47)			1962–2000
GR	−2.301	0.743	0.258	0.468		0.0645	1.86
	(−2.10)	(7.94)	(3.04)	(2.40)			1963–2000
IR	−5.491	0.492	0.616	1.071		0.0580	1.14
	(−2.97)	(3.26)	(4.59)	(3.20)			1968–2000
PO	−3.265	0.362	0.418	0.926		0.0852	1.08
	(−3.33)	(2.21)	(4.19)	(3.74)			1962–1998
SP	−1.738	0.661	0.284	0.477		0.0709	1.13
	(−0.98)	(5.34)	(3.84)	(1.67)			1962–2000
NZ	−6.273	0.568	0.313	1.001		0.0717	1.83
	(−2.26)	(3.87)	(3.19)	(2.54)			1962–2000
SA	−0.215	0.564		0.386		0.1381	0.74
	(−0.77)	(3.66)		(2.29)			1970–2000
CO	−2.946	0.210	0.273	1.003		0.0884	1.19
	(−1.60)	(1.08)	(1.71)	(3.49)			1971–2000
SY	−4.262	0.317	0.097	1.012		0.1348	1.25
	(−3.03)	(1.98)	(1.92)	(3.86)			1965–2000
ID	−0.839	0.850		0.375		0.1108	1.80
	(−1.61)	(7.79)		(1.72)			1962–1997
MA	−2.105	0.759		0.475		0.1022	1.39
	(−2.09)	(7.23)		(2.30)			1972–2000
PA	−1.244	0.297		0.738		0.0687	1.45
	(−3.25)	(2.11)		(3.81)			1974–2000
PH	−3.833	0.531	0.184	1.471		0.1625	1.97
	(−3.17)	(4.23)	(0.97)	(3.34)			1962–2001
TH	−1.062	0.671		0.532		0.1010	1.27
	(−2.70)	(5.76)		(2.89)			1962–2000
CH	−1.091	0.449		0.761		0.1144	1.59
	(−2.59)	(2.87)		(2.76)			1984–1999
AR		0.203		0.604		0.1044	1.25
		(0.75)		(2.96)			1994–2001
BR		0.834		0.127		0.1068	2.91
		(2.03)		(0.43)			1995–2000
CE	−1.755	0.372		0.763		0.1082	0.93
	(−2.11)	(1.61)		(2.69)			1979–2001
ME	−3.105	0.852	0.332	0.440		0.1702	1.32
	(−1.73)	(9.01)	(1.81)	(1.83)			1962–2000
PE		0.508		0.392		0.0568	1.88
		(2.99)		(2.94)			1992–2000

Table B1
Test Results for Equation 1

	Lags	log *PY*	RHO	*T*	Stability			End Test		overid	
	p-val	*p*-val	*p*-val	*p*-val	AP	df	λ	*p*-val	End	*p*-val	df
Quarterly
CA	.714	.344	.192	.001	*10.05	5	6.531	.639	1998.4	.001	6
JA	.445	.747	.002	.389	6.90	4	6.405	.873	1998.3	.717	5
AU	.018	.671	.032	.006	*14.04	4	4.562	.706	1998.3	.000	5
FR	.000	.581	.000	.588	*11.42	4	4.150	.316	1998.3	.001	5
GE	.636	.339	.444	.350	*13.15	4	4.668	.330	1998.4		
IT	.585	.530	.527	.006	*7.07	4	4.150	1.000	1998.3	.000	5
NE	.368	.041	.000	.012	1.54	4	1.878	.915	1998.4		
UK	.998	.102	.002	.761	*9.29	4	6.405	.686	1998.3	.000	5
FI	.000	.233	.000	.000	*22.39	4	2.306	.909	1998.3	.000	4
AS	.163	.362	.048	.045	4.62	5	6.281	1.000	1998.2	.019	6
SO	.034	.107	.021	.162	6.69	5	9.149	.565	1998.3	.001	6
KO	.023	.517	.000	.000	*14.30	4	3.117	.103	1998.4		
Annual
BE	.382	.199	.020	.023	*10.25	4	6.370	.281	1996	.004	5
DE	.450	.088	.097	.000	*32.24	4	5.009	.724	1998	.002	5
NO	.029	.000	.000	.046	*36.13	4	7.367	.471	1998		
GR	.586	.008	.051	.001	*16.22	4	6.859	.242	1998	.012	5
IR	.178	.660	.030	.255	*12.45	4	4.592	.750	1998	.091	5
PO	.006	.002	.001	.002	*17.63	4	6.370	.867	1995	.011	5
SP	.077	.310	.000	.008	*15.73	4	7.367	.206	1998		
NZ	.676	.009	.003	.000	*14.84	4	7.367	.882	1998	.001	5
SA	.004		.000	.000	*28.98	3	3.812	.231	1998		
CO	.276	.707	.000	.866	*7.60	4	3.449	.480	1998		
SY	.258	.143	.000	.059	*10.11	4	5.898	.742	1998		
ID	.628		.494	.126	*6.63	3	5.898				
MA	.597		.096	.019	*6.23	3	3.104	.167	1998		
PA	.147		.069	.003	2.17	3	2.469	.227	1998		
PH	.009	.000	.780	.000	*19.45	4	7.893	.914	1999		
TH	.305		.002	.382	4.29	3	7.367	.000	1998		
CH	.121		.193	.999							
CE	.132		.000	.041	2.27	3	1.417				
ME	.000	.000	.000	.001	*11.62	4	7.367	.794	1998		

Table B2
Coefficient Estimates for Equation 2:
$$\log(C/POP) = a_1 + a_2 \log(C/POP)_{-1} + a_3 RS + a_4 RB + a_5 \log(Y/POP)$$
$$+ a_6 [A/(PY \cdot YS)]_{-1}$$

	a_1	a_2	a_3	a_4	a_5	a_6	ρ	SE	DW
Quarterly									
CA	−0.067	0.898		−0.0010†	0.105	0.007		0.0083	2.14
	(−1.18)	(16.41)		(−2.98)	(2.00)	(1.70)		1966.1–2001.4	
JA	0.089	0.814		−0.0012	0.158		−0.315	0.0109	2.11
	(3.62)	(19.61)		(−2.91)	(3.96)		(−3.77)	1966.1–2001.3	
AU		0.818	−0.0018		0.170			0.0173	2.46
		(18.90)	(−2.24)		(4.22)			1970.1–2001.3	
FR	0.118	0.883	−0.0004		0.096			0.0071	2.16
	(3.00)	(19.52)	(−1.41)		(2.26)			1971.1–2001.3	
GE	0.120	0.859		−0.0023	0.119	0.011	−0.356	0.0097	2.12
	(1.22)	(22.86)		(−4.26)	(2.72)	(2.47)	(−4.09)	1970.1–2001.4	
IT	−0.120	0.883	−0.0004		0.125			0.0059	0.85
	(−1.94)	(27.59)	(−3.22)		(3.38)			1971.1–2001.3	
NE	0.162	0.934		−0.0023	0.044			0.0085	2.35
	(1.65)	(28.72)		(−2.94)	(1.71)			1978.1–2001.4	
ST	0.040	0.792		−0.0031	0.152		0.698	0.0023	1.63
	(0.73)	(5.15)		(−2.14)	(1.30)		(4.16)	1983.1–2000.4	
UK	−0.424	0.848		−0.0015	0.199	0.013		0.0101	2.38
	(−4.02)	(18.20)		(−3.94)	(3.64)	(2.45)		1966.1–2001.3	
FI	0.046	0.859	−0.0004		0.125			0.0109	1.73
	(0.64)	(18.26)	(−1.21)		(2.72)			1976.2–2001.3	
AS	−0.180	0.862		−0.0003	0.153	0.007		0.0071	2.09
	(−1.79)	(23.49)		(−0.93)	(3.86)	(1.70)		1966.1–2001.2	
SO	−0.084	0.973	−0.0013†		0.038	0.004		0.0170	1.67
	(−0.80)	(32.75)	(−2.83)		(1.52)	(1.74)		1961.1–2001.3	
KO	0.148	0.835		−0.0012	0.135			0.0184	1.98
	(2.81)	(12.57)		(−2.05)	(2.20)			1974.1–2001.4	
Annual									
BE	−0.110	0.584			0.403			0.0115	1.66
	(−1.13)	(7.50)			(5.00)			1962–1998	
DE	0.472	0.339		−0.0007	0.491	0.101		0.0161	1.55
	(3.57)	(2.24)		(−0.64)	(4.07)	(2.02)		1967–2000	
NO	0.225	0.636			0.279			0.0193	1.54
	(3.37)	(5.50)			(3.03)			1962–2000	
SW	0.451	0.593			0.272			0.0160	1.14
	(3.92)	(6.29)			(4.01)			1965–2000	
GR	0.089	0.966	−0.0033		0.030			0.0233	1.47
	(0.68)	(19.99)	(−2.81)		(0.63)			1963–2000	
IR	2.003	0.561		−0.0034	0.214	0.207		0.0210	1.46
	(3.72)	(3.24)		(−1.73)	(1.90)	(3.48)		1968–2000	
PO	0.022	0.472		−0.0022	0.509	0.193		0.0322	2.05
	(−0.16)	(5.32)		(−1.83)	(6.00)	(2.55)		1962–1998	
SP	0.254	0.660	−0.0024		0.299			0.0145	1.50
	(3.13)	(5.81)	(−2.39)		(2.69)			1962–2000	
NZ	0.950	0.462		−0.0027	0.419			0.0179	1.47
	(3.05)	(3.44)		(−2.68)	(3.72)			1962–2000	
SA		0.868			0.072	0.110		0.1520	1.82
		(12.96)			(1.61)	(1.93)		1970–2000	
VE	−0.326	0.762			0.270			0.0741	1.87
	(−0.31)	(8.83)			(1.86)			1962–2000	

Table B2
Coefficient Estimates for Equation 2 *(continued)*

	a_1	a_2	a_3	a_4	a_5	a_6	ρ	SE	DW
Annual *(continued)*									
CO	1.099	0.390	−0.0012		0.442	0.263		0.0207	1.80
	(2.72)	(3.47)	(−1.85)		(4.13)	(4.06)			1971–2000
SY	0.672	0.008			0.893			0.0610	1.42
	(1.63)	(0.08)			(9.05)				1965–2000
ID	0.147	0.153	−0.0013		0.653			0.0290	1.72
	(2.47)	(1.18)	(−0.84)		(6.79)				1962–1997
MA	0.336	0.525			0.405	0.172		0.0441	1.35
	(0.76)	(2.55)			(2.70)	(1.62)			1972–2000
PA	0.150	0.589			0.311			0.0310	1.35
	(1.91)	(3.93)			(2.50)				1974–2000
PH	0.091	0.835	−0.0021		0.131			0.0278	1.92
	(0.78)	(10.18)	(−1.91)		(1.95)				1962–2001
TH	0.110	0.321			0.557			0.0227	1.75
	(4.62)	(4.13)			(8.65)				1962–2000
CH	−0.331	0.302	−0.0062		0.624			0.0256	1.83
	(−3.70)	(2.31)	(−1.65)		(5.31)				1984–1999
AR		0.180			0.772			0.0196	1.57
		(0.74)			(3.35)				1995–2000
BR		0.180			0.772			0.0196	1.57
		(0.74)			(3.35)				1995–2000
CE	0.016	0.481			0.489			0.0378	1.45
	(0.07)	(5.39)			(6.34)				1979–2001
ME	1.168	0.306			0.547			0.0229	1.05
	(5.58)	(3.84)			(8.36)				1962–2000
PE		0.627			0.360			0.0201	0.83
		(4.20)			(2.52)				1992–2000

Table B2
Test Results for Equation 2

	Lags	RHO	T	Leads	Stability			End Test		overid	
	p-val	*p*-val	*p*-val	*p*-val	AP	df	λ	*p*-val	End	*p*-val	df
Quarterly											
CA	.269	.526	.288	.130	*23.47	5	6.531	.849	1998.4	.001	3
JA	.088	.004	.734	.015	*11.41	5	6.405	.153	1998.3	.005	4
AU	.001	.000	.000	.926	*8.13	2	4.562	.980	1998.3	.000	5
FR	.124	.000	.006	.005	*27.49	4	4.150	1.000	1998.3		
GE	.039	.045	.580	.916	6.41	6	4.668	.874	1998.4	.000	6
IT	.000	.000	.000	.009	*13.92	4	4.150	.704	1998.3	.000	4
NE	.128	.076	.000	.188	*8.81	4	1.878	.901	1998.4	.004	3
ST	.045	.020	.009	.903	3.11	5	1.000	.717	1998.3	.022	4
UK	.012	.065	.037	.155	1.98	5	6.405	1.000	1998.3	.161	3
FI	.147	.275	.112	.462	*10.93	4	2.306	.805	1998.3	.000	3
AS	.481	.408	.009	.154	6.72	5	6.281	.966	1998.2	.300	3
SO	.032	.008	.001	.238	*10.34	5	9.149	.935	1998.3	.000	4
KO	.920	.648	.241	.203	5.92	4	3.117	.448	1998.4	.040	3
Annual											
BE	.483	.201	.184	.539	3.21	3	6.370	.719	1996	.220	4
DE	.404	.014	.485	.278	5.47	5	5.009	.379	1998	.022	3
NO	.118	.034	.033	.696	*7.12	3	7.367	1.000	1998	.360	4
SW	.001	.006	.039	.220	3.14	3	5.898	.613	1998	.043	4
GR	.338	.000	.000	.253	*12.76	4	6.859	.424	1998		
IR	.031	.077	.539	.338	*10.55	5	4.592	.714	1998	.003	3
PO	.952	.816	.046	.069	3.99	5	6.370	.800	1995	.229	3
SP	.069	.106	.001	.403	*23.27	4	7.367	1.000	1998	.191	3
NZ	.102	.023	.628	.228	*11.42	4	7.367	.941	1998	.345	3
SA	.496	.722	.093	.887	2.04	3	3.812	.500	1998		
VE	.958	.653	.016	.086	*11.82	3	7.367	.500	1998		
CO	.988	.030	.016	.091	0.67	5	1.000	.040	1998		
SY	.736	.003	.041	.288	5.17	3	5.898	.742	1998		
ID	.590	.012	.000	.738	*13.32	4	5.898				
MA	.022	.011	.651	.986	2.97	4	3.104	.000	1998		
PA	.172	.053	.326	.649	*17.01	3	2.469	.409	1998		
PH	.913	.842	.001	.905	*10.86	4	7.893	.771	1999		
TH	.591	.121	.322	.327	5.00	3	7.367	.000	1998		
CH	.265	.864	.058	.000							
CE	.664	.001	.000	.012	0.84	3	1.417				
ME	.006	.004	.565	.958	3.02	3	7.367	.176	1998		

Table B3
Coefficient Estimates for Equation 3:
$$\log I = a_1 + a_2 \log I_{-1} + a_3 \log Y + a_4 RS + a_5 RB$$

	a_1	a_2	a_3	a_4	a_5	SE	DW
Quarterly							
CA	−0.419	0.895	0.126		−0.0010†	0.0220	1.35
	(−2.58)	(26.40)	(3.04)		(−1.21)		1966.1–2001.4
JA	0.291	0.923	0.045		−0.0026	0.0211	1.74
	(3.01)	(34.13)	(1.51)		(−2.52)		1966.1–2001.3
AU	0.748	0.732	0.165		−0.0073	0.0377	2.27
	(3.13)	(11.91)	(3.05)		(−2.60)		1970.1–2001.3
FR	0.252	0.955	0.021		−0.0025†	0.0138	1.26
	(2.56)	(39.71)	(1.08)		(−4.76)		1971.1–2001.3
GE	0.101	0.893	0.088		−0.0027	0.0343	2.30
	(0.46)	(23.39)	(2.17)		(−1.07)		1970.1–2001.4
IT	0.318	0.914	0.051		−0.0017†	0.0149	1.49
	(2.44)	(31.16)	(2.72)		(−4.31)		1971.1–2001.3
NE	0.069	0.743	0.221		−0.0086†	0.0287	2.66
	(0.24)	(12.47)	(3.62)		(−3.32)		1978.1–2001.4
UK	−0.155	0.840	0.153		−0.0042†	0.0262	2.12
	(−1.12)	(22.03)	(3.96)		(−4.06)		1966.1–2001.3
FI	0.050	0.949	0.038			0.0445	2.10
	(0.18)	(32.02)	(1.45)				1976.2–2001.3
AS	0.071	0.904	0.080		−0.0024	0.0281	1.61
	(0.83)	(25.58)	(2.66)		(−2.69)		1966.1–2001.2
SO	−0.404	0.969	0.070		−0.0073†	0.0362	2.24
	(−2.33)	(67.07)	(3.09)		(−4.33)		1961.1–2001.3
KO		0.953	0.044			0.0475	1.54
		(29.24)	(1.03)				1974.1–2001.4
Annual							
BE	0.018	0.711	0.265		−0.0217	0.0483	1.89
	(0.06)	(7.96)	(3.23)		(−4.79)		1962–1998
DE	1.028	0.684	0.112		−0.0142	0.0685	1.79
	(1.86)	(6.45)	(1.27)		(−3.55)		1967–2000
NO	0.213	0.919	0.042	−0.0049		0.0660	1.68
	(0.99)	(9.74)	(0.67)	(−1.24)			1962–2000
SW	0.083	0.737	0.196	−0.0043		0.0567	1.11
	(0.25)	(6.15)	(2.12)	(−1.29)			1965–2000
GR	0.556	0.481	0.421	−0.0169		0.0841	1.84
	(1.03)	(3.94)	(3.63)	(−3.69)			1963–2000
IR	0.259	0.839	0.124		−0.0074	0.0845	1.55
	(0.54)	(6.19)	(0.97)		(−1.18)		1968–2000
PO	−0.766	0.524	0.495		−0.0106	0.0672	1.22
	(−2.09)	(3.88)	(3.63)		(−3.73)		1962–1998
SP	0.061	0.783	0.196	−0.0086		0.0571	1.17
	(0.15)	(8.68)	(1.88)	(−3.31)			1962–2000

Table B3
Coefficient Estimates for Equation 3 *(continued)*

	a_1	a_2	a_3	a_4	a_5	SE	DW
Annual *(continued)*							
NZ	−1.439	0.598	0.477		−0.0055	0.0758	1.15
	(−1.78)	(4.28)	(2.70)		(−1.43)		1962–2000
SA	−0.147	0.747	0.215			0.1724	1.67
	(−0.19)	(6.41)	(1.08)				1970–2000
VE	−1.834	0.604	0.541	−0.0050		0.1614	1.20
	(−1.49)	(5.24)	(2.60)	(−2.28)			1962–2000
CO	−0.735	0.634	0.375			0.1120	1.18
	(−0.77)	(3.68)	(1.75)				1971–2000
JO	−0.353	0.580	0.396			0.1402	1.28
	(−0.13)	(2.09)	(0.80)				1987–1998
SY	−0.680	0.758	0.269			0.1738	1.29
	(−0.70)	(6.57)	(1.61)				1965–2000
ID	−2.050	0.570	0.587			0.0482	1.46
	(−3.36)	(4.52)	(3.45)				1962–1997
MA	−0.898	0.638	0.406			0.1516	1.03
	(−1.03)	(4.34)	(2.10)				1972–2000
PA	0.199	0.767	0.152			0.0637	1.48
	(0.58)	(7.20)	(1.26)				1974–2000
PH	−0.541	0.770	0.289	−0.0141		0.1125	1.16
	(−1.05)	(6.92)	(1.97)	(−3.04)			1962–2001
TH	−0.332	0.771	0.242			0.1216	0.86
	(−0.66)	(5.85)	(1.40)				1962–2000
CH	−1.535	0.340	0.767	−0.0074		0.0892	0.89
	(−1.55)	(1.12)	(2.11)	(−0.55)			1984–1999
ME	−0.765	0.410	0.577			0.0979	1.14
	(−1.46)	(3.21)	(4.25)				1962–2000
PE		0.565	0.380			0.1053	1.24
		(2.78)	(2.17)				1992–2000

Table B3
Test Results for Equation 3

	Lags	RHO	*T*	Leads	Stability			End Test		overid	
	p-val	*p*-val	*p*-val	*p*-val	AP	df	λ	*p*-val	End	*p*-val	df
Quarterly											
CA	.000	.000	.010	.025	*8.51	4	6.531	1.000	1998.4	.001	4
JA	.106	.000	.000	.272	*20.85	4	6.405	.619	1998.3		
AU	.057	.002	.679	.677	*12.41	4	4.562	.853	1998.3	.059	4
FR	.000	.000	.615	.004	*10.78	4	4.150	.806	1998.3	.003	4
GE	.033	.005	.000	.138	5.82	4	4.668	1.000	1998.4		
IT	.003	.002	.051	.356	*10.75	4	4.150	.908	1998.3	.424	4
NE	.000	.000	.016	.271	2.44	4	1.878	1.000	1998.4	.031	4
UK	.264	.619	.003	.186	4.79	4	6.405	.907	1998.3	.054	4
FI	.382	.007	.000	.005	*19.17	3	2.306	.922	1998.3	.000	5
AS	.011	.000	.192	.216	5.87	4	6.281	.521	1998.2	.047	4
SO	.179	.162	.000	.369	*7.65	4	9.149	.464	1998.3	.001	4
KO	.008	.028	.000	.092	. 5.70	3	3.117	.655	1998.4	.014	5
Annual											
BE	.550	.768	.033	.638	*8.49	4	6.370	.875	1996	.305	4
DE	.317	.633	.000	.776	*12.10	4	5.009	.724	1998	.030	4
NO	.325	.254	.003	.285	4.85	4	7.367	.294	1998		
SW	.000	.000	.381	.362	*8.97	4	5.898	.516	1998	.001	4
GR	.798	.912	.170	.842	*9.94	4	6.859	.788	1998	.236	4
IR	.056	.002	.000	.998	*10.83	4	4.592	.929	1998		
PO	.000	.011	.975	.052	3.60	4	6.370	1.000	1995	.029	4
SP	.000	.000	.748	.046	*7.74	4	7.367	1.000	1998	.059	4
NZ	.000	.001	.747	.886	*11.05	4	7.367	.971	1998	.122	4
SA	.267	.394	.043	.634	1.86	3	3.812	.346	1998		
VE	.000	.004	.000	.933	*11.20	4	7.367	.353	1998		
CO	.000	.005	.000	.745	0.38	3	3.449	.000	1998		
JO	.425	.098	.813	.574							
SY	.034	.000	.000	.653	*16.77	3	5.898	.516	1998		
ID	.261	.055	.115	.841	*12.51	3	5.898				
MA	.000	.000	.000	.961	1.26	3	3.104	.000	1998		
PA	.004	.035	.003	.095	1.82	3	2.469	.136	1998		
PH	.003	.002	.000	.146	*12.07	4	7.893	.029	1999		
TH	.000	.000	.000	.006	4.22	3	7.367	.000	1998		
CH	.000	.027	.016	.017							
ME	.002	.000	.006	.689	*29.23	3	7.367	.588	1998		

Table B4
Coefficient Estimates for Equation 4:
$$\log Y = a_1 + a_2 \log Y_{-1} + a_3 \log X + a_4 \log V_{-1}$$

	a_1	a_2	a_3	a_4	ρ	λ	α	β	SE	DW
Quarterly										
JA	0.240	0.147	0.879	−0.0480	0.571	0.853	0.056	0.540	0.0034	1.98
	(7.38)	(6.41)	(37.98)	(−3.55)	(7.78)				1966.1–2001.3	
IT	−0.253	0.669	0.493	−0.1394	0.372	0.331	0.421	1.159	0.0059	2.04
	(−2.82)	(10.28)	(7.34)	(−4.63)	(3.91)				1971.1–2001.3	
NE	0.224	0.547	0.487	−0.0542		0.453	0.119	0.618	0.0061	1.80
	(2.36)	(9.90)	(8.89)	(−3.34)					1978.1–2001.4	
UK	0.528	0.221	0.816	−0.0825	0.531	0.779	0.106	0.457	0.0058	2.12
	(2.97)	(5.33)	(18.96)	(−2.95)	(6.24)				1966.1–2001.3	
AS	0.231	0.334	0.710	−0.0678	0.297	0.666	0.102	0.653	0.0063	1.96
	(2.75)	(4.92)	(10.31)	(−3.18)	(2.63)				1975.1–2001.2	
Annual										
SW	0.170	0.092	0.911	−0.0311		0.908	0.034	0.093	0.0093	1.16
	(3.34)	(1.05)	(10.78)	(−2.14)					1965–2000	
GR	0.094	0.466	0.554	−0.0307		0.534	0.058	0.642	0.0227	1.20
	(0.66)	(5.12)	(6.10)	(−3.11)					1963–2000	
SP	0.149	0.102	0.963	−0.0845		0.898	0.094	0.764	0.0041	1.75
	(5.59)	(2.34)	(25.84)	(−5.79)					1962–2000	
MA	0.144	0.026	0.981	−0.0228		0.974	0.023	0.288	0.0131	1.78
	(2.25)	(0.40)	(14.94)	(−1.56)					1972–2000	
PA	−0.177	0.111	0.941	−0.0317		0.889	0.036	1.636	0.0045	1.51
	(−2.29)	(1.96)	(18.75)	(−2.08)					1974–2000	

Implied Values See eq. 2.10 spans columns λ, α, β.

Table B4
Test Results for Equation 4

	Lags	RHO	T	Leads	Stability			End Test	
	p-val	p-val	p-val	p-val	AP	df	λ	p-val	End
Quarterly									
JA	.054	.666	.015	.117	*21.93	5	6.405	.331	1998.3
IT	.633	.315	.623	.000	*10.94	5	4.150	.714	1998.3
NE	.621	.025	.550	.592	*16.02	4	1.878	.746	1998.4
UK	.361	.165	.081	.006	*15.80	5	6.405	1.000	1998.3
AS	.351	.437	.471	.042	*12.65	5	2.616	1.000	1998.2
Annual									
SW	.004	.001	.116	.922	*15.27	4	5.898	.806	1998
GR	.000	.001	.105	.550	*9.89	4	6.859	.970	1998
SP	.243	.448	.113	.618	5.63	4	7.367	.912	1998
MA	.764	.531	.370	.111	6.09	4	3.104	.833	1998
PA	.086	.251	.727	.290	5.48	4	2.469	.364	1998

Table B5
Coefficient Estimates for Equation 5:

$$\log PY = a_1 + a_2 \log PY_{-1} + a_3(\log W - \log LAM) + a_4 \log PM + a_5 DP + a_6 T$$

	a_1	a_2	a_3	a_4	a_5	a_6	ρ	SE	DW
Quarterly									
CA	2.023	0.726	0.214	0.028	−0.16411†	0.00025	0.704	0.0055	2.13
	(2.65)	(7.01)	(2.59)	(1.18)	(−2.35)	(1.04)	(7.01)	1966.1–2001.4	
JA	−0.062	0.937		0.016	−0.08016	0.00035	0.424	0.0076	1.99
	(−2.05)	(45.73)		(2.27)	(−3.44)	(2.04)	(5.30)	1966.1–2001.3	
AU	−0.008	0.976		0.006	−0.04696	0.00007	−0.342	0.0091	2.00
	(−0.40)	(62.95)		(0.52)	(−1.64)	(0.63)	(−4.01)	1970.1–2001.3	
FR	−0.003	0.886	0.057	0.023	−0.04437†	0.00002	0.261	0.0045	1.97
	(−0.16)	(31.45)	(2.06)	(1.88)	(−1.50)	(0.23)	(2.91)	1971.1–2001.3	
GE	0.002	0.984		0.008†	−0.15020†	0.00008		0.0069	2.86
	(0.07)	(57.45)		(1.23)	(−2.29)	(0.71)		1970.1–2001.4	
IT	−0.075	0.942		0.033	−0.21032†	0.00050		0.0081	1.66
	(−3.43)	(140.46)		(7.28)	(−5.74)	(3.94)		1971.1–2001.3	
NE	−0.150	0.816		0.050	−0.05633†	0.00086		0.0056	1.71
	(−3.26)	(15.76)		(4.15)	(−1.94)	(3.35)		1978.1–2001.4	
ST	−0.003	0.974			−0.11527†	0.00006	0.621	0.0019	1.29
	(−0.19)	(53.92)			(−4.71)	(0.51)	(5.92)	1983.1–2000.4	
UK	1.301	0.829	0.136	0.063†	−0.30246†	−0.00034	0.331	0.0081	2.16
	(3.04)	(18.48)	(2.86)	(6.19)	(−4.64)	(−1.82)	(3.86)	1966.1–2001.3	
FI	0.026	0.982		0.006	−0.10955†	−0.00011		0.0077	2.33
	(1.66)	(113.06)		(0.79)	(−3.31)	(−1.16)		1976.2–2001.3	
AS	1.018	0.900	0.099	0.017	−0.17668†	−0.00035	−0.364	0.0133	2.01
	(3.25)	(27.35)	(3.05)	(1.58)	(−5.73)	(−3.36)	(−4.48)	1966.1–2001.2	
SO	−0.057	0.943		0.041†		0.00045	0.237	0.0081	2.00
	(−2.79)	(165.15)		(8.38)		(3.92)	(3.03)	1961.1–2001.3	
KO	0.283	0.790	0.140	0.052	−0.08799†	−0.00161		0.0152	2.02
	(3.01)	(17.54)	(3.97)	(2.46)	(−2.09)	(−3.00)		1974.1–2001.4	
Annual									
BE	−0.186	0.796		0.088	−0.32742†	0.00586		0.0119	0.83
	(−3.11)	(17.09)		(3.92)	(−10.10)	(3.54)		1962–1998	
DE	−0.062	0.805		0.152	−0.35198†	0.00245		0.0134	1.27
	(−1.17)	(18.93)		(5.23)	(−5.11)	(1.64)		1967–2000	
NO	−0.165	0.733		0.185	−1.81460†	0.00881		0.0288	1.37
	(−1.25)	(6.37)		(2.09)	(−3.90)	(2.46)		1962–2000	
SW	2.684	0.581	0.415	0.114	−0.32306†	−0.00411		0.0153	1.57
	(5.36)	(8.87)	(5.08)	(4.46)	(−1.83)	(−2.34)		1965–2000	
GR	0.840	0.989		0.166	−0.34198†	−0.01821		0.0316	1.71
	(2.74)	(9.07)		(2.81)	(−2.37)	(−2.25)		1963–2000	

Table B5
Coefficient Estimates for Equation 5 *(continued)*

	a_1	a_2	a_3	a_4	a_5	a_6	ρ	SE	DW
Annual *(continued)*									
IR	0.004	0.795		0.187	−0.20919†	0.00091		0.0307	1.55
	(0.03)	(9.06)		(3.14)	(−1.69)	(0.26)		1968–2000	
PO	−0.176	0.744		0.224	−0.28391†	0.00615		0.0296	1.66
	(−1.78)	(30.79)		(12.76)	(−2.10)	(2.29)		1962–1998	
SP	0.163	0.719	0.198	0.048†	−0.44613†	−0.00353		0.0123	1.83
	(2.65)	(26.53)	(17.48)	(2.96)	(−5.99)	(−2.11)		1962–2000	
NZ	0.086	0.839		0.190	−0.24694†	−0.00180		0.0324	1.48
	(0.84)	(15.18)		(5.37)	(−2.06)	(−0.64)		1962–2000	
CO	−0.880	0.724		0.164†	−0.57726	0.02787		0.0365	2.11
	(−1.16)	(8.28)		(3.69)	(−3.01)	(1.38)		1971–2000	
JO	−0.561	0.387		0.280		0.01578		0.0358	1.92
	(−1.36)	(1.94)		(3.54)		(1.41)		1987–1998	
SY	−0.153	0.888		0.097		0.00650		0.0698	1.30
	(−0.49)	(14.09)		(2.56)		(0.78)		1965–2000	
MA	−0.659	0.345		0.261	−0.22406	0.01791		0.0333	1.86
	(−4.65)	(2.82)		(4.32)	(−1.92)	(4.75)		1972–2000	
PA	−0.262	0.868			−0.71152†	0.00923		0.0306	1.42
	(−0.69)	(7.35)			(−2.41)	(0.92)		1974–2000	
PH	−0.561	0.590		0.261		0.01610		0.0511	1.63
	(−2.26)	(8.09)		(6.18)		(2.39)		1962–2001	
TH	−0.520	0.313		0.329	−0.32170	0.01354		0.0257	1.38
	(−5.16)	(3.74)		(8.19)	(−5.26)	(5.07)		1962–2000	
CH	−0.915	0.688			−0.67643	0.02532		0.0583	0.52
	(−1.19)	(2.95)			(−1.49)	(1.26)		1984–1999	
CE	0.243	0.645		0.398	−0.42155†	−0.00594		0.0485	1.68
	(0.75)	(6.17)		(3.26)	(−1.71)	(−0.68)		1979–2001	
ME	0.019	0.479		0.512	−0.21247†	0.00520		0.0451	1.08
	(0.16)	(18.69)		(22.19)	(−1.84)	(1.61)		1962–2000	

Note:
• Demand pressure variable *DP* is *UR* for GE, UK, and NO; it is *ZZ* for CA, FI, SW, PO, SP, PA, and ME; it is the deviation of output from trend for the rest.

Table B5
Test Results for Equation 5

	Lags-1	Lags-2	RHO	Leads	Stability			End Test		overid	
	p-val	*p*-val	*p*-val	*p*-val	AP	df	λ	*p*-val	End	*p*-val	df
Quarterly											
CA	.727	.705	.292	.616	6.97	7	6.531	.193	1998.4	.484	5
JA	.009	.003	.000		*58.17	6	6.405	.966	1998.3	.000	5
AU	.275	.003	.004		6.37	6	4.562	1.000	1998.3	.209	5
FR	.153	.329	.976	.023	*15.84	7	4.150	.806	1998.3	.027	6
GE	.000	.000	.000		5.69	5	4.668	.738	1998.4	.036	4
IT	.074	.064	.075		6.57	5	4.150	.520	1998.3	.228	4
NE	.059	.492	.076		*9.17	5	1.878	.915	1998.4	.001	4
ST	.001	.000	.000		2.63	5	1.000	.170	1998.3	.144	6
UK	.018	.010	.012	.009	*21.53	7	6.405	.907	1998.3	.008	7
FI	.270	.469	.222		*9.57	5	2.306	.727	1998.3	.442	4
AS	.383	.579	.745	.002	*11.35	7	6.281	.735	1998.2	.003	6
SO	.619	.000	.791		*14.31	5	9.149	.275	1998.3	.001	6
KO	.859	.981	.797	.255	4.80	6	3.117	.678	1998.4	.571	5
Annual											
BE	.000	.004	.000		*28.59	5	6.370	.906	1996		
DE	.000	.000	.020		*9.07	5	5.009	.897	1998		
NO	.004	.009	.031		*7.87	5	7.367	.000	1998		
SW	.011	.000	.150	.000	*11.06	6	5.898	.903	1998		
GR	.862	.955	.424		4.34	5	6.859	1.000	1998		
IR	.136	.676	.477		*18.37	5	4.592	.714	1998		
PO	.675	.471	.346		*12.72	5	6.370	.900	1995		
SP	.450	.041	.617	.753	*9.23	6	7.367	.588	1998		
NZ	.024	.114	.132		5.06	5	7.367	.853	1998		
CO	.980	.663	.794		4.24	5	3.449	1.000	1998		
JO	.581	.447	.958								
SY	.011	.050	.002		*16.33	4	5.898	.516	1998		
MA	.017	.000	.002		*21.10	5	3.104	.667	1998		
PA	.089	.334	.084		*7.47	4	2.469	.955	1998		
PH	.201	.030	.058		*15.73	4	7.893	.829	1999		
TH	.316	.152	.065		7.77	5	7.367	.559	1998		
CH	.000	.000	.000								
CE	.092	.348	.535		*16.69	5	1.417				
ME	.015	.075	.007		*14.65	5	7.367	.294	1998		

Table B6
Coefficient Estimates for Equation 6:

$$\log[M1/(POP \cdot PY)] = a_1 + a_2 \log[M1/(POP \cdot PY)]_{-1} + a_3 \log[M1_{-1}/(POP_{-1} \cdot PY)]$$
$$+ a_4 RS + a_5 \log(Y/POP)$$

	a_1	a_2	a_3	a_4	a_5	ρ	SE	DW
Quarterly								
CA	−0.289		0.932	−0.0043	0.102		0.0259	2.30
	(−2.52)		(54.98)	(−3.63)	(4.46)			1968.1–2001.4
FR	0.222	0.969		−0.0020†	0.007		0.0230	2.16
	(1.61)	(28.04)		(−2.84)	(0.22)			1971.1–2001.3
GE	−0.319	0.970		−0.0024	0.069		0.0181	2.06
	(−1.68)	(55.27)		(−2.96)	(1.83)			1970.1–2001.4
NE	−1.228		0.814	−0.0043	0.340		0.0185	2.18
	(−2.69)		(12.63)	(−2.95)	(2.86)			1978.1–2001.4
ST	0.116	0.904		−0.0093	0.074	−0.415	0.0277	1.76
	(0.88)	(38.50)		(−6.31)	(1.27)	(−3.71)		1983.1–2000.4
UK	0.113	0.979		−0.0030	0.005		0.0143	2.02
	(0.78)	(85.73)		(−5.90)	(0.45)			1970.1–2001.3
FI	−0.475		0.874	−0.0033	0.188		0.0393	2.22
	(−1.43)		(22.47)	(−2.11)	(2.61)			1976.2–2001.3
AS	−0.587		0.905	−0.0057	0.164		0.0218	1.82
	(−5.02)		(52.06)	(−5.49)	(5.88)			1966.1–2001.2
KO	0.169		0.842		0.114		0.0641	2.25
	(1.87)		(13.72)		(2.06)			1974.1–2001.4
Annual								
BE	2.825	0.640		−0.0070	0.034		0.0244	1.90
	(3.59)	(6.57)		(−4.13)	(1.93)			1962–1998
DE	−0.889		0.706	−0.0071	0.412		0.0530	2.37
	(−1.86)		(8.97)	(−2.15)	(2.87)			1967–1999
SW	0.765	0.585		−0.0015	0.209		0.0397	1.61
	(1.97)	(2.98)		(−0.64)	(1.62)			1971–2000
IR	−0.169		0.423	−0.0119	0.516		0.1267	1.77
	(−0.07)		(1.62)	(−0.60)	(1.37)			1983–2000
PO	−1.075	0.892		−0.0058	0.232		0.1380	1.53
	(−1.49)	(9.64)		(−1.32)	(1.61)			1962–1998
SP	0.575		0.813	−0.0022	0.113		0.0444	1.26
	(2.50)		(7.83)	(−0.88)	(1.08)			1962–2000
NZ	0.781		0.739	−0.0043	0.139		0.0758	1.21
	(0.64)		(9.18)	(−1.03)	(1.38)			1962–2000
VE	−5.312	0.607		−0.0058	1.111		0.1504	2.13
	(−2.58)	(6.59)		(−3.73)	(3.20)			1962–2000
ID	−0.863		0.538		0.494		0.0470	2.00
	(−3.76)		(4.22)		(4.17)			1962–1997
PA	−0.735		0.369	−0.0161	0.667		0.0520	1.72
	(−2.52)		(2.31)	(−2.39)	(3.53)			1974–2000
PH	−0.344		0.767	−0.0082	0.230		0.0824	2.21
	(−1.09)		(8.62)	(−2.05)	(2.16)			1962–2001

Table B6
Test Results for Equation 6

	N vs. R [a]	Lags	RHO	T	Stability			End Test		overid	
	p-val	p-val	p-val	p-val	AP	df	λ	p-val	End	p-val	df
Quarterly											
CA	.123	.202	.005	.629	*8.56	4	6.531	.622	1998.4	.228	5
FR	.359	.535	.417	.378	*7.99	4	4.150	.429	1998.3	.147	4
GE	.878	.489	.809	.009	*8.72	4	4.668	.126	1998.4	.420	4
NE	.425	.647	.550	.028	3.25	4	1.878	.000	1998.4	.519	5
ST	.903	.074	.026	.432	3.96	5	1.000	.264	1998.3	.275	5
UK	.000	.262	.601	.036	3.69	4	4.562	.314	1998.3	.203	4
FI	.268	.293	.000	.000	*16.36	4	2.306	.792	1998.3	.005	4
AS	.482	.707	.733	.943	5.59	4	6.281	.615	1998.2	.503	4
KO	.480	.114	.108	.415	2.50	3	3.117	.310	1998.4	.219	5
Annual											
BE	.102	.322	.026	.000	*10.07	4	6.370	.594	1996		
DE	.038	.392	.224	.006	*7.10	4	4.592	.933	1998		
SW	.246	.152	.019	.528	3.16	4	3.449	.720	1998		
IR	.954	.458	.548	.591	0.72	4	1.000	.615	1998		
PO	.015	.005	.144	.180	*37.72	4	6.370	.967	1995		
SP	.238	.030	.006	.001	*7.63	4	6.370	.469	1998		
NZ	.735	.073	.000	.088	*8.79	4	7.367	.500	1998		
VE	.419	.759	.507	.040	*9.03	4	7.367	1.000	1998		
ID	.552	.734	.952	.713	*15.38	3	5.898				
PA	.442	.019	.735	.353	1.96	4	2.469	.636	1998		
PH	.285	.073	.412	.219	3.29	4	7.893	.057	1999		

Note:

a. N vs. R: nominal versus real adjustment test—adding either $\log[M1/(POP \cdot PY)]_{-1}$ or $\log[M1_{-1}/(POP_{-1} \cdot PY)]$.

Table B7
Coefficient Estimates for Equation 7:
$$RS = a_1 + a_2 RS_{-1} + a_3 PCPY + a_4 ZZ + a_5 RS_{GE} + a_6 RS_{US}$$

	a_1	a_2	a_3	a_4	a_5	a_6	ρ	SE	DW
Quarterly									
EU	0.17	0.872	0.052	−36.0		0.15		0.807	1.95
	(0.71)	(22.73)	(1.30)	(−4.25)		(4.08)		1972.2–2001.3	
CA		0.813	0.028	−11.2		0.25		0.880	1.74
	(−0.01)	(18.80)	(0.96)	(−2.82)		(3.52)		1972.2–2001.4	
JA	−0.42	0.799	0.128	−3.9		0.16	0.347	0.656	2.04
	(−1.26)	(14.27)	(4.51)	(−0.45)		(2.84)	(3.13)	1972.2–2001.3	
AU	0.21	0.773	0.041		0.13	0.04		0.762	1.57
	(0.79)	(11.82)	(1.20)		(2.20)	(1.12)		1972.2–1998.4	
FR	−0.33	0.732	0.041		0.21	0.17		0.872	1.57
	(−1.17)	(17.61)	(1.45)		(4.52)	(3.61)		1972.2–1998.4	
GE	0.20	0.852	0.079	−43.7		0.17		0.878	1.98
	(0.71)	(20.36)	(1.85)	(−4.76)		(4.28)		1972.2–1998.4	
IT	1.56	0.800	0.117	−18.8			0.383	1.041	1.92
	(2.42)	(14.50)	(3.65)	(−2.06)			(3.43)	1972.2–1998.4	
NE	0.04	0.584		−23.4	0.30	0.17		0.901	1.91
	(0.14)	(6.14)		(−3.37)	(3.11)	(3.76)		1978.1–1998.4	
ST	0.30	0.929		−1.7			0.316	0.578	2.01
	(1.29)	(18.62)		(−0.25)			(2.39)	1983.1–2000.4	
UK	0.14	0.810	0.050	−14.5		0.24		0.975	1.56
	(0.45)	(18.57)	(2.60)	(−3.07)		(4.51)		1972.2–2001.3	
FI	−0.15	0.931				0.11	0.156	1.025	1.98
	(−0.35)	(23.22)				(2.10)	(1.36)	1976.2–1998.4	
AS	0.07	0.907	0.012	−10.6		0.14		1.094	1.93
	(0.21)	(27.92)	(0.54)	(−1.67)		(2.56)		1972.2–2001.2	
SO	0.89	0.902		−12.5		0.09	0.433	1.098	2.00
	(0.90)	(18.77)		(−1.80)		(1.14)	(4.12)	1972.2–2001.3	
KO	1.05	0.844	0.080	−19.9		0.11		1.612	1.62
	(1.95)	(18.71)	(3.63)	(−3.58)		(1.65)		1974.1–2001.4	
Annual									
BE	0.21	0.453			0.60			1.482	2.25
	(0.22)	(3.77)			(4.69)			1972–1998	
DE	0.52	0.647			0.50			2.448	2.19
	(0.36)	(5.03)			(2.40)			1972–2000	
NO	0.19	0.749			0.12	0.22		1.692	2.17
	(0.17)	(7.36)			(0.80)	(1.51)		1972–2000	
SW	−0.89	0.748				0.45		1.867	2.49
	(−0.72)	(7.12)				(3.18)		1972–2000	
IR	2.67		0.154		0.24	0.75		2.059	1.74
	(2.10)		(2.20)		(1.25)	(3.99)		1972–1998	
PO	−1.61	0.884	0.310	−42.0				2.855	1.94
	(−1.01)	(7.21)	(3.72)	(−1.96)				1972–1998	
SP	1.90	0.553	0.192			0.21		3.015	2.41
	(0.91)	(3.05)	(1.70)			(0.72)		1972–1998	
NZ	1.55	0.703	0.205					2.750	1.90
	(1.16)	(6.08)	(2.44)					1972–2000	
ID	2.11	0.582	0.226					2.981	1.56
	(0.76)	(3.09)	(1.54)					1972–1997	
PA	2.45	0.576	0.145					1.201	2.50
	(1.88)	(4.30)	(3.00)					1974–2000	
PH	1.73	0.677	0.160			0.23		2.814	1.42
	(0.70)	(5.77)	(2.70)			(1.04)		1972–2001	

Table B7
Test Results for Equation 7

	Lags	RHO	T	Stability			End Test		overid	
	p-val	p-val	p-val	AP	df	λ	p-val	End	p-val	df
Quarterly										
CA	.001	.087	.108	5.63	5	3.757	.926	1998.4	.001	5
JA	.698	.560	.354	4.15	6	3.662	1.000	1998.3	.134	6
AU	.318	.003	.170	6.68	5	2.696			.122	5
FR	.270	.213	.019	4.12	5	2.696			.048	5
GE	.375	.719	.183	4.14	5	2.696			.027	5
IT	.468	.228	.568	2.78	5	2.696	.404	1998.3	.024	6
NE	.428	.333	.000	*14.04	5	1.154			.003	5
ST	.252	.770	.007	4.65	4	1.000	.906	1998.3	.004	6
UK	.188	.029	.117	6.32	5	3.662	.957	1998.3	.056	5
FI	.832	.425	.481	4.09	4	1.555			.092	5
AS	.131	.776	.530	3.39	5	3.568	1.000	1998.2	.005	5
SO	.840	.905	.323	*9.79	5	3.662	.032	1998.3	.002	6
KO	.118	.001	.755	*10.97	5	3.117	1.000	1998.4	.117	5
Annual										
BE	.143	.365	.600	0.65	3	2.469				
DE	.254	.454	.047	2.87	3	3.104	.917	1998		
NO	.284	.631	.550	*7.27	4	3.104	.667	1998		
SW	.166	.126	.916	1.17	3	3.104	.958	1998		
IR	.924	.803	.088	4.99	4	2.469				
PO	.409	.936	.431	3.22	4	2.469				
SP	.377	.114	.478	1.78	4	2.469				
NZ	.811	.748	.161	*14.06	3	3.104	.708	1998		
ID	.277	.341	.746	1.49	3	2.179				
PA	.090	.025	.412	0.77	3	2.469	.818	1998		
PH	.061	.109	.203	*12.39	4	3.449	.520	1999		

Table B8
Coefficient Estimates for Equation 8:
$$RB - RS_{-2} = a_1 + a_2(RB_{-1} - RS_{-2}) + a_3(RS - RS_{-2}) + a_4(RS_{-1} - RS_{-2})$$

	a_1	a_2	a_3	a_4	ρ	SE	DW
Quarterly							
EU	0.087	0.924	0.413	−0.389		0.4378	1.85
	(1.52)	(28.98)	(3.93)	(−3.02)			1970.1–2001.4
CA	0.112	0.908	0.418	−0.375		0.4388	2.02
	(2.30)	(33.06)	(4.20)	(−3.05)			1966.1–2001.4
JA	0.023	0.913	0.447	−0.489		0.3854	2.14
	(0.58)	(23.39)	(2.72)	(−2.06)			1966.1–2001.3
AU	0.039	0.957	0.132	−0.041	0.396	0.2714	1.91
	(0.57)	(28.26)	(1.13)	(−0.48)	(4.17)		1970.1–1998.4
FR	0.075	0.871	0.346	−0.170	0.343	0.4144	1.99
	(0.97)	(13.94)	(2.58)	(−1.36)	(2.72)		1971.1–1998.4
GE	0.093	0.916	0.458	−0.435		0.4617	1.93
	(1.50)	(27.79)	(4.38)	(−3.37)			1970.1–1998.4
IT	−0.073	0.722	0.451	−0.273	0.469	0.5830	2.01
	(−0.70)	(8.38)	(3.66)	(−2.35)	(3.68)		1971.1–1998.4
NE	0.067	0.917	0.245	−0.136		0.4119	1.77
	(1.03)	(25.54)	(2.61)	(−1.51)			1978.1–1998.4
ST	0.004	0.972	0.413	−0.398		0.2658	1.95
	(0.11)	(38.91)	(4.16)	(−2.99)			1983.1–2000.4
UK	0.026	0.966	0.379	−0.399		0.4940	1.59
	(0.53)	(39.58)	(2.43)	(−2.07)			1966.1–2001.3
AS	0.094	0.906	0.483	−0.417		0.5273	1.74
	(1.66)	(24.32)	(3.97)	(−3.20)			1966.1–2001.2
SO	0.177	0.922	0.802	−1.072		0.6412	1.96
	(2.25)	(29.80)	(3.74)	(−3.63)			1961.1–2001.3
KO	0.124	0.920	0.327	−0.083		1.1602	2.07
	(0.76)	(18.38)	(1.96)	(−0.42)			1974.1–2001.4
Annual[a]							
BE	0.541	0.742	0.399			0.7780	1.47
	(1.90)	(6.57)	(5.21)				1962–1998
DE	0.311	0.747	0.434			1.3221	1.67
	(1.05)	(5.74)	(4.38)				1967–2000
NO	0.012	0.837	0.438			0.6850	1.64
	(0.11)	(8.00)	(5.58)				1962–2000
IR	0.501	0.528	0.483			1.2667	1.48
	(1.85)	(3.99)	(5.74)				1968–1998
PO	0.109	0.715	0.431			1.4529	1.71
	(0.45)	(6.38)	(4.96)				1962–1998
NZ	−0.196	0.768	0.371			1.0138	2.39
	(−0.98)	(6.99)	(5.07)				1962–2000
PA	−0.082	0.977	−0.024			0.8754	1.91
	(−0.45)	(15.42)	(0.21)				1974–2000
TH	−0.015	0.830	0.351			1.1652	2.15
	(−0.06)	(7.75)	(4.70)				1978–2000

Note:
a. For annual countries a_4 is zero and RS_{-1} rather than RS_{-2} is subtracted from the other variables.

Table B8
Test Results for Equation 8

	Restr.[a]	Lags	RHO	T	Leads	Stability			End Test		overid	
	p-val	p-val	p-val	p-val	p-val	AP	df	λ	p-val	End	p-val	df
Quarterly												
CA	.023	.053	.900	.317	.034	3.38	4	6.531	.807	1998.4	.105	5
JA	.061	.241	.503	.735	.088	1.43	4	6.405	.636	1998.3	.130	5
AU	.564	.118	.691	.011	.333	2.66	5	3.475			.028	6
FR	.377	.562	.800	.287	.382	2.87	5	3.117			.596	6
GE	.205	.014	.059	.266	.230	4.59	4	4.668	.757	1998.4	.023	5
IT	.831	.902	.806	.905	.807	5.84	5	3.117			.955	6
NE	.407	.407	.123	.649	.443	2.29	4	1.154			.074	5
ST	.007	.007	.890	.898	.017	2.54	4	1.000	.208	1998.3	.017	5
UK	.945	.503	.040	.007	.917	6.15	4	6.405	1.000	1998.3	.004	5
AS	.111	.179	.010	.169	.197	*9.62	4	6.281	.581	1998.2	.098	5
SO	.217	.020	.305	.130	.210	5.15	4	9.149	.109	1998.3	.128	5
KO	.976	.856	.621	.024		3.47	4	3.117	.563	1998.4	.038	5
Annual												
BE	.252	.080	.036	.003	.666	*6.54	3	6.370				
DE	.968	.834	.236	.010	.555	*9.44	3	5.009	1.000	1998		
NO	.077	.042	.245	.046	.841	4.44	3	7.367	.500	1998		
IR	.645	.593	.026	.001	.751	*9.11	3	3.812				
PO	.003	.001	.156	.008	.335	4.47	3	6.370				
NZ	.160	.000	.005	.572	.351	1.98	3	3.626	.588	1998		
PA	.561	.636	.829	.004	.628	*7.78	3	2.469	.409	1998		
TH	.058	.305	.644	.883	.916	3.75	3	1.417	.889	1998		

Note:
a. RS_{-2} added for the quarterly countries; RS_{-1} added for the annual countries.

Table B9
Coefficient Estimates for Equation 9:

$$\Delta \log E = a_1 + \lambda[\log(PY/PY_{US}) - \log E_{-1}]$$
$$+.25\lambda\beta \log[(1 + RS/100)/(1 + RS_{US}/100)]$$

or

$$\Delta \log H = a_1 + \lambda[\log(PY/PY_{GE}) - \log H_{-1}]$$
$$+.25\lambda\beta \log[(1 + RS/100)/(1 + RS_{GE}/100)]$$

	a_1	λ	λβ	ρ	SE	DW
Quarterly						
EU	−0.011	0.088	−1.891	0.291	0.0485	2.00
	(−1.49)	(2.12)	(−1.53)	(2.79)		1972.2–2001.4
CA	0.021	0.050	−1.323	0.314	0.0163	2.01
	(6.90)		(−2.26)	(3.52)		1972.2–2001.4
JA	−0.109	0.050	−1.318	0.316	0.0505	1.94
	(−13.30)		(−1.22)	(3.45)		1972.2–2001.3
AU	0.002	0.050		0.512	0.0045	2.19
	(2.12)			(6.25)		1972.2–1998.4

Table B9
Coefficient Estimates for Equation 9 *(continued)*

	a_1	λ	$\lambda\beta$	ρ	SE	DW
Quarterly *(continued)*						
FR	−0.003	0.195		0.221	0.0197	2.04
	(−0.75)	(3.48)		(1.94)		1972.2–1998.4
GE	−0.014	0.088	−1.749	0.303	0.0490	1.98
	(−1.74)	(2.00)	(−1.38)	(2.77)		1972.2–1998.4
IT	0.014	0.050		0.337	0.0333	1.95
	(2.94)			(3.67)		1972.2–1998.4
NE	−0.003	0.050	−0.705		0.0050	1.32
	(−5.08)		(−3.10)			1978.1–1998.4
ST	−1.528	0.233			0.0165	1.64
	(−3.15)	(3.15)				1983.1–2000.4
UK	−0.003	0.050	−0.799		0.0439	1.43
	(−0.39)		(−1.11)			1972.2–2001.3
FI	0.002	0.088	−0.496	0.419	0.0291	2.02
	(0.25)	(1.25)	(−0.42)	(3.12)		1976.2–1998.4
AS	0.024	0.053		0.246	0.0393	2.01
	(1.81)	(1.35)		(2.41)		1972.2–2001.2
SO	0.088	0.050			0.0573	1.60
	(16.65)					1972.2–2001.3
KO	0.015	0.059		0.316	0.0479	1.91
	(2.06)	(1.62)		(3.14)		1974.1–2001.4
Annual						
BE	0.003	0.168			0.0287	1.39
	(0.36)	(2.15)				1972–1998
DE	−0.327	0.071			0.0286	1.02
	(−0.52)	(0.55)				1972–2000
NO	−0.567	0.118			0.0484	1.57
	(−1.60)	(1.67)				1972–2000
SW	−1.377	0.288			0.0651	1.84
	(−2.78)	(2.86)				1972–2000
GR	0.038	0.339			0.0657	0.96
	(1.14)	(2.07)				1972–2000
IR	0.029	0.176			0.0610	0.96
	(1.73)	(1.42)				1972–1998
PO	0.095	0.286			0.0968	0.57
	(5.09)	(1.15)				1972–1998
SP	0.040	0.179			0.0720	1.27
	(2.27)	(1.23)				1972–1998
NZ	0.099	0.077	−2.601		0.1002	1.11
	(1.10)	(0.48)	(−1.32)			1972–2000
VE	−0.849	0.489			0.2324	0.96
	(−2.06)	(2.49)				1972–2000
JO	−0.152	0.445			0.1033	1.20
	(−1.72)	(2.54)				1987–1998
PH	−1.247	0.366			0.0977	1.19
	(−2.36)	(2.50)				1972–2001

Table B9
Test Results for Equation 9

	Restr. [a]	Lags	RHO	T	Stability			End Test		overid	
	p-val	p-val	p-val	p-val	AP	df	λ	p-val	End	p-val	df
Quarterly											
CA	.142	.730	.420	.060	4.13	3	3.757	.362	1998.4	.182	7
JA	.144	.853	.399	.035	3.98	3	3.662	.161	1998.3	.083	7
AU	.001	.009	.062	.000	4.57	2	2.696			.004	7
FR	.499	.574	.504	.930	1.21	3	2.696			.731	6
GE	.910	.654	.936	.854	4.58	4	2.696			.255	6
IT	.001	.919	.515	.004	4.44	2	2.696			.068	7
NE	.064	.285	.001	.000	*9.98	2	1.154			.001	7
ST	.200	.100	.216	.374	1.55	2	1.000	.604	1998.3	.226	6
UK	.000	.002	.004	.000	*5.03	2	3.662	.753	1998.3	.001	7
FI	.232	.787	.612	.317	0.44	4	1.555			.026	6
AS	.076	.616	.610	.042	1.90	3	3.568	.370	1998.2	.170	6
SO	.053	.035	.094	.024	2.00	1	3.662	.204	1998.3		
KO	.127	.415	.125	.266	2.35	3	3.117	.253	1998.4	.629	6
Annual											
BE	.800	.139	.126	.958	*25.91	2	2.469				
DE	.000	.004	.001	.000	*16.65	2	3.104	.625	1998		
NO	.779	.151	.315	.909	0.32	2	3.104	.500	1998		
SW	.517	.450	.682	.370	0.77	2	3.104	1.000	1998		
GR	.004	.002	.001	.001	*5.62	2	3.104	.125	1998		
IR	.000	.002	.000	.000	*5.36	2	2.469				
PO	.019	.000	.000	.003	*10.01	2	2.469				
SP	.003	.047	.003	.009	4.23	2	2.469	.500	1998		
NZ	.984	.000	.015	.827	3.34	3	3.104	.458	1998		
VE	.008	.072	.000	.001	*19.84	2	3.104	1.000	1998		
JO	.050	.011	.042	.831							
PH	.161	.033	.006	.192	4.63	2	3.449	.400	1999		

Note:
a. $\log E_{-1}$ or $\log H_{-1}$ added.

Table B10
Coefficient Estimates for Equation 10:
$$\log F = a_1 \log EE + a_2(.25) \log[(1 + RS/100)/(1 + RS_{US}/100)]$$

	a_1	a_2	ρ	SE	DW
Quarterly					
CA	0.9824	1.761	0.793	0.0096	2.28
	(49.23)	(3.68)	(11.64)		1972.2–1997.3
JA	1.0008	1.215	0.376	0.0091	1.82
	(1114.03)	(6.47)	(4.35)		1972.2–2001.3
AU	0.9930	1.049	0.250	0.0058	2.10
	(299.71)	(8.25)	(2.60)		1972.2–1998.4
FR	1.0076	0.644		0.0071	1.54
	(333.90)	(4.78)			1972.2–1989.3
GE	0.9960	1.198	0.720	0.0032	2.21
	(250.42)	(10.89)	(10.67)		1972.2–1998.4
IT	0.9977	0.984		0.0097	2.03
	(274.00)	(8.50)			1978.1–1998.4
NE	0.9955	1.472		0.0097	2.03
	(123.29)	(4.84)			1978.1–1990.4
ST	1.0002	1.086		0.0030	2.23
	(14732.73)	(19.78)			1983.1–2000.4
UK	1.0014	1.278	0.398	0.0061	1.95
	(367.01)	(5.52)	(2.76)		1972.2–1984.4
FI	0.9942	1.211	0.676	0.0071	2.63
	(103.38)	(4.80)	(6.79)		1976.2–1989.3
AS	1.0010	1.286		0.0052	1.97
	(491.01)	(19.97)			1976.1–2001.2

Table B11
Coefficient Estimates for Equation 11:
$$\log PX - \log[PW\$(E/E95)] = a_1 + \lambda[\log PY - \log[PW\$(E/E95)]$$

	a_1	λ	ρ_1	ρ_2	SE	DW
Quarterly						
CA		0.729	1.178	−0.190	0.0173	2.06
		(13.60)	(14.05)	(−2.27)		1966.1–2001.4
JA		0.421	1.310	−0.322	0.0139	1.93
		(14.59)	(16.39)	(−4.09)		1966.1–2001.3
AU		0.825	0.675	0.303	0.0121	2.03
		(25.20)	(7.83)	(3.57)		1970.1–2001.3
FR		0.732	1.165	−0.173	0.0091	2.01
		(27.37)	(12.85)	(−1.93)		1971.1–2001.3
GE		0.757	0.870	0.114	0.0102	2.00
		(29.97)	(9.57)	(1.27)		1970.1–2001.4
IT		0.606	0.896	0.091	0.0168	1.95
		(14.00)	(9.81)	(1.00)		1971.1–2001.3
NE		0.493	0.985	−0.010	0.0226	1.99
		(6.49)	(9.40)	(−0.10)		1978.1–2001.4
ST		0.854	0.883	0.120	0.0096	1.94
		(27.39)	(6.86)	(0.92)		1983.1–2000.4
UK		0.692	1.043	−0.050	0.0159	2.01
		(19.00)	(12.32)	(−0.59)		1966.1–2001.3
FI		0.684	0.947	0.075	0.0164	1.99
		(14.14)	(9.72)	(0.73)		1976.2–2001.3
AS		0.511	1.186	−0.202	0.0276	2.02
		(8.70)	(14.10)	(−2.42)		1966.1–2001.2
SO		0.757	0.841	0.132	0.0305	1.99
		(13.97)	(10.70)	(1.70)		1961.1–2001.3
KO		0.274	0.996	−0.042	0.0299	1.95
		(4.31)	(9.46)	(−0.40)		1974.1–2001.4
Annual						
BE		0.411	0.803	0.115	0.0217	2.06
		(7.59)	(4.68)	(0.71)		1962–1998
DE		0.588	1.093	−0.151	0.0193	1.71
		(10.85)	(6.20)	(−0.91)		1967–2000
NO		0.812	1.280	−0.327	0.0751	1.67
		(2.39)	(7.39)	(−1.96)		1962–2000
SW		0.464	1.091	−0.425	0.0326	1.70
		(5.31)	(6.63)	(−2.58)		1965–2000
GR	0.039		0.688	−0.088	0.0502	1.88
	(1.92)		(3.95)	(−0.52)		1963–2000

Table B11
Coefficient Estimates for Equation 11 *(continued)*

	a_1	λ	ρ_1	ρ_2	SE	DW
Annual *(continued)*						
IR		0.510	1.107	−0.136	0.0290	1.93
		(6.35)	(5.67)	(−0.71)		1968–2000
PO	0.081		1.126	−0.451	0.0382	2.08
	(4.19)		(7.36)	(−2.95)		1962–1998
SP		0.550	1.062	−0.101	0.0385	1.69
		(5.87)	(6.42)	(−0.64)		1962–2000
NZ		0.568	1.023	−0.112	0.0718	1.85
		(3.27)	(6.05)	(−0.69)		1962–2000
CO		0.870	1.099	−0.139	0.1331	1.98
		(3.24)	(5.49)	(−0.71)		1971–2000
JO		0.076	1.003	−0.405	0.0585	2.28
		(0.27)	(3.66)	(−1.64)		1987–1998
SY		1.000	1.205	−0.226	0.1806	2.09
			(7.19)	(−1.36)		1965–2000
ID		0.641	0.752	−0.191	0.0564	1.81
		(15.17)	(4.17)	(−1.08)		1962–1997
MA		1.000	0.858	−0.125	0.1255	1.87
			(4.49)	(−0.66)		1972–2000
PA		0.604	0.455	−0.214	0.0670	2.01
		(7.53)	(2.59)	(−1.41)		1974–2000
TH		0.471	1.058	−0.219	0.0676	1.81
		(2.04)	(6.25)	(−1.37)		1962–2000
CH	0.065		1.025	−0.318	0.0446	2.09
	(1.66)		(4.19)	(−1.34)		1984–1999
AR	0.026				0.0520	1.42
	(1.42)					1994–2001
CE	0.094		1.111	−0.423	0.0456	2.18
	(3.00)		(5.69)	(−2.14)		1979–2001
ME	0.085		1.140	−0.462	0.0379	2.08
	(4.53)		(7.58)	(−3.07)		1962–2000
PE	0.003				0.1437	1.09
	(0.07)					1992–2000

Table B11
Test Results for Equation 11

	Restr.[a]	Stability			End Test	
	p-val	AP	df	λ	p-val	End
Quarterly						
CA	.234	3.83	3	6.755	.000	1998.4
JA	.000	1.50	3	6.405	.831	1998.3
AU	.000	2.81	3	4.562	.902	1998.3
FR	.003	*18.22	3	4.150	.388	1998.3
GE	.000	5.24	3	4.668	.883	1998.4
IT	.050	*6.04	3	4.150	.959	1998.3
NE	.090	*9.53	3	1.878	.211	1998.4
ST	.054	2.62	3	1.000	.151	1998.3
UK	.371	1.77	3	6.405	.941	1998.3
FI	.171	*5.65	3	2.306	.013	1998.3
AS	.000	1.36	3	1.915	.299	1998.2
SO	.055	1.76	3	9.149	1.000	1998.3
KO	.000	4.16	3	3.117	.874	1998.4
Annual						
BE	.001	*7.81	3	6.370	.844	1996
DE	.619	1.22	3	5.009	.793	1998
NO	.000	*14.62	3	7.367	.088	1998
SW	.013	*10.93	3	5.898	.452	1998
GR	.000	4.38	3	6.859	.364	1998
IR	.724	0.64	3	4.592	.429	1998
PO	.000	3.59	3	6.370	.667	1995
SP	.005	3.17	3	7.367	.853	1998
NZ	.000	*7.39	3	7.367	.588	1998
CO	.159	1.72	3	3.449	.880	1998
JO	.006					
SY	.031	*6.14	2	5.898	.871	1998
ID	.004	1.48	3	5.898		
MA	.579	0.35	2	3.104	.583	1998
PA	.145	3.73	3	2.469	.318	1998
TH	.017	2.10	3	7.367	.618	1998
CH	.525					
CE	.323	1.48	3	1.417		
ME	.090	1.65	3	7.367	.706	1998

Note:
a. log *PY* and log *E* added.

Table B12
Coefficient Estimates for Equation 12:

$$\log W - \log LAM = a_1 + a_2(\log W_{-1} - \log LAM_{-1}) + a_3 \log PY$$
$$+ a_4 DW + a_5 T + a_6 \log PY_{-1}$$

	a_1	a_2	a_3	a_4	a_5	ρ	a_6	SE	DW
Quarterly									
CA	−1.054	0.887	1.222		−0.00018	0.225	−1.093	0.0090	2.02
	(−2.21)	(17.43)	(9.70)		(−1.81)	(2.14)		1966.1–2001.4	
FR	−0.011	0.922	1.398		0.00009		−1.296	0.0084	1.79
	(−1.01)	(22.84)	(4.84)		(1.30)			1971.1–2001.3	
UK	−1.117	0.875	0.856	−0.03818†	0.00007		−0.736	0.0106	1.87
	(−3.30)	(22.84)	(13.84)	(−1.05)	(1.66)			1966.1–2001.3	
AS	−1.263	0.867	0.751	−0.05318†	−0.00009		−0.618	0.0133	2.21
	(−2.90)	(19.10)	(3.86)	(−1.03)	(−2.69)			1966.1–2001.2	
KO	−0.473	0.828	0.860	−0.11013†	0.00275		−0.700	0.0312	2.16
	(−3.00)	(13.38)	(3.04)	(−1.46)	(3.10)			1974.1–2001.4	
Annual									
SW	−2.568	0.543	0.419	−0.31227	−0.00467		0.036	0.0237	1.80
	(−3.46)	(4.15)	(2.43)	(−2.35)	(−3.57)			1965–2000	
SP	−0.072	0.817	1.274	−0.22570†	0.00218		−1.063	0.0189	2.11
	(−1.81)	(16.79)	(9.22)	(−4.48)	(1.88)			1962–2000	

Note:
a. The demand pressure variable *DW* for all the countries is the deviation of output from trend.

Table B12
Test Results for Equation 12

	Restr.[a]	Lags	RHO	Stability			End Test		overid	
	p-val	*p*-val	*p*-val	AP	df	λ	*p*-val	End	*p*-val	df
Quarterly										
CA	.904	.029	.099	*21.26	4	6.531	.000	1998.4	.079	6
FR	.008	.077	.152	*13.92	4	4.150	.786	1998.3	.059	4
UK	.837	.529	.047	*10.04	5	6.405	.568	1998.3	.042	6
AS	.450	.015	.128	*13.37	5	6.281	1.000	1998.2	.004	4
KO	.890	.273	.476	3.01	5	3.117	.460	1998.4	.554	4
Annual										
SW	.004	.223	.622	*13.81	5	5.898	.774	1998		
SP	.714	.967	.527	*28.81	5	7.367	.706	1998		

Note:
a. $\log PY_{-1}$ added.

Table B13
Coefficient Estimates for Equation 13:
$$\Delta \log J = a_1 + a_2 T + a_3 \log(J/JMIN)_{-1} + a_4 \Delta \log Y + a_5 \Delta \log Y_{-1}$$

	a_1	a_2	a_3	a_4	a_5	ρ	SE	DW
Quarterly								
CA	0.006	−0.00002	−0.146	0.304	0.197		0.0043	1.72
	(3.58)	(−2.35)	(−4.84)	(3.02)	(3.46)		1966.1–2001.4	
JA	0.003	−0.00001	−0.070	0.126			0.0035	2.05
	(1.53)	(−0.87)	(−3.25)	(1.93)			1966.1–2001.3	
FR	−0.007	0.00004	−0.193	0.507			0.0020	1.62
	(−5.21)	(5.03)	(−4.04)	(6.21)			1979.1–2001.3	
GE	0.002	−0.00000	−0.148	0.084			0.0044	2.02
	(1.26)	(−0.29)	(−3.27)	(0.81)			1970.1–2001.4	
IT	−0.001	0.00002	−0.130	0.129			0.0052	1.99
	(−0.50)	(1.32)	(−4.36)	(1.22)			1971.1–2001.3	
ST	0.011	−0.00006	−0.205	0.375			0.0037	1.77
	(2.96)	(−2.82)	(−4.66)	(3.36)			1983.1–2000.4	
UK	0.002	0.00001	−0.166	0.098		0.533	0.0029	2.10
	(0.95)	(0.80)	(−5.41)	(2.14)		(7.31)	1966.1–2001.3	
FI	0.018	−0.00009	−0.323	0.260		0.314	0.0054	2.20
	(3.81)	(−3.09)	(−7.45)	(3.15)		(3.19)	1976.2–2001.3	
AS	0.006	−0.00001	−0.192	0.066		0.282	0.0051	2.09
	(2.96)	(−0.43)	(−4.51)	(0.88)		(3.22)	1966.1–2001.2	
Annual								
BE	−0.018	0.00045	−0.087	0.349			0.0087	1.93
	(−2.83)	(2.32)	(−0.92)	(4.01)			1962–1998	
DE	−0.000	0.00001	−0.262	0.384			0.0159	1.51
	(−0.04)	(0.03)	(−1.74)	(2.86)			1967–2000	
NO	−0.005	0.00013	−0.353	0.385			0.0120	0.94
	(−0.73)	(0.72)	(−4.06)	(3.12)			1962–2000	
SW	−0.002	−0.00014	−0.133	0.474			0.0129	0.91
	(−0.34)	(−0.66)	(−1.34)	(4.15)			1965–2000	
IR	−0.027	0.00117	−0.443	0.403			0.0166	1.82
	(−3.30)	(3.58)	(−2.98)	(4.09)			1968–2000	

Table B13
Test Results for Equation 13

	Lags	RHO	Leads	Stability			End Test		overid	
	p-val	*p*-val	*p*-val	AP	df	λ	*p*-val	End	*p*-val	df
Quarterly										
CA	.538	.250	.366	*10.29	5	6.531	1.000	1998.4	.262	5
JA	.051	.455	.434	*13.11	4	6.405	.314	1998.3	.001	6
FR	.003	.000	.102	*11.42	4	1.555	.848	1998.3	.001	6
GE	.114	.021	.192	6.94	4	4.668	.495	1998.4	.000	6
IT	.202	.313	.921	1.64	4	4.150	.816	1998.3	.797	6
ST	.584	.060	.206	6.97	4	1.000	1.000	1998.3	.008	6
UK	.003	.183	.171	*11.30	5	6.405	.644	1998.3	.004	6
FI	.000	.000	.052	*18.99	5	2.306	.818	1998.3	.004	7
AS	.000	.001	.277	6.25	5	6.281	.530	1998.2	.204	7
Annual										
BE	.247	.829	.221	5.35	4	6.370	.625	1996		
DE	.117	.052	.332	5.55	4	5.009	1.000	1998		
NO	.001	.000	.834	*22.46	4	7.367	.912	1998		
SW	.000	.000	.244	*24.74	4	5.898	.806	1998		
IR	.896	.592	.000	6.07	4	4.592	.214	1998		

Table B14
Coefficient Estimates for Equation 14:
$$\log(L1/POP1) = a_1 + a_2T + a_3\log(L1/POP1)_{-1} + a_4\log(W/PY) + a_5Z$$

	a_1	a_2	a_3	a_4	a_5	SE	DW
Quarterly							
CA	−0.003	−0.00010	0.939	0.022	0.039	0.0044	2.02
	(−0.49)	(−2.44)	(37.43)	(2.09)	(1.18)		1966.1–2001.4
JA	−0.010	−0.00004	0.938			0.0029	1.98
	(−2.22)	(−2.62)	(35.87)				1966.1–2001.3
AU	−0.063	−0.00021	0.724		0.078	0.0037	2.38
	(−3.55)	(−3.16)	(8.87)		(1.18)		1970.1–2001.3
GE	−0.023	0.00002	0.966			0.0027	1.87
	(−3.33)	(2.82)	(85.43)				1970.1–2001.4
IT	−0.019	−0.00010	0.923			0.0040	1.75
	(−2.65)	(−1.99)	(27.39)				1971.1–2001.3
ST	0.018	−0.00018	0.923		0.270	0.0041	2.07
	(2.49)	(−3.36)	(29.28)		(2.42)		1983.1–2000.4
UK	−0.007	−0.00005	0.957		0.003	0.0028	1.85
	(−1.95)	(−0.98)	(26.46)		(0.14)		1966.1–2001.3
FI	−0.015	−0.00014	0.897		0.088	0.0056	2.43
	(−2.33)	(−2.39)	(22.06)		(2.16)		1976.2–2001.3
AS	−0.012	−0.00012	0.895		0.027	0.0035	2.16
	(−3.17)	(−2.50)	(22.98)		(1.30)		1966.1–2001.2
Annual							
BE	−0.051	−0.00138	0.804		0.234	0.0056	1.98
	(−2.16)	(−1.81)	(7.94)		(3.32)		1962–1998
DE	−0.073	−0.00091	0.672		0.115	0.0085	1.76
	(−3.57)	(−2.39)	(6.53)		(1.49)		1967–2000
NO	−0.066	−0.00045	0.753		0.628	0.0066	1.33
	(−3.76)	(−1.90)	(10.42)		(5.11)		1962–2000
SW	−0.102	−0.00267	0.522	0.024	0.269	0.0065	1.21
	(−2.81)	(−3.12)	(3.24)	(1.10)	(2.25)		1965–2000
IR	−0.026	−0.00105	0.811		0.266	0.0160	2.69
	(−1.39)	(−1.01)	(5.74)		(2.50)		1968–2000

Table B14
Test Results for Equation 14

	Lags p-val	log *PY* p-val	RHO p-val	Stability AP	df	λ	End Test p-val	End	overid p-val	df
Quarterly										
CA	.846	.744	.091	5.48	5	6.531	.815	1998.4	.009	5
JA	1.000		.995	4.42	3	6.405	.559	1998.3	.013	5
AU	.006		.032	6.32	4	4.562	.951	1998.3	.419	5
GE	.438		.149	2.13	3	4.668	.650	1998.4	.192	5
IT	.145		.322	*7.78	3	4.150	.969	1998.3	.332	5
ST	.420		.085	*12.57	4	1.000	.925	1998.3	.000	5
UK	.283		.452	2.70	4	6.405	.280	1998.3	.513	4
FI	.006		.007	*18.30	4	2.306	.273	1998.3	.000	5
AS	.166		.394	*11.39	4	6.281	.846	1998.2	.097	5
Annual										
BE	.767		.565	*12.53	4	6.370	.719	1996		
DE	.357		.404	*12.35	4	5.009	.621	1998		
NO	.001		.024	3.15	4	7.367	.500	1998		
SW	.000	.016	.016	0.35	0	.000				
IR	.001		.001	*11.01	4	4.592	.500	1998		

Table B15
Coefficient Estimates for Equation 15:
$$\log(L2/POP2) = a_1 + a_2T + a_3\log(L2/POP2)_{-1} + a_4\log(W/PY) + a_5Z$$

	a_1	a_2	a_3	a_4	a_5	SE	DW
Quarterly							
CA	−0.002	−0.00007	0.976	0.037	0.029	0.0060	1.94
	(−0.14)	(−1.56)	(72.97)	(1.86)	(0.66)		1966.2–2001.4
JA	−0.033	0.00002	0.958			0.0075	2.16
	(−2.02)	(1.24)	(43.98)				1966.1–2001.3
AU	−0.083	0.00019	0.931			0.0098	2.46
	(−2.55)	(2.72)	(33.95)				1970.1–2001.3
IT	−0.295	0.00043	0.793	0.049		0.0109	2.23
	(−3.71)	(3.52)	(14.46)	(2.80)			1971.1–2001.3
ST	−0.040	0.00001	0.933		0.409	0.0048	1.84
	(−1.43)	(0.18)	(36.66)		(3.72)		1983.1–2000.4
UK	−0.025	−0.00004	0.949	0.036	0.013	0.0035	1.21
	(−1.02)	(−0.58)	(43.81)	(3.23)	(0.39)		1966.1–2001.3
FI	−0.022	−0.00005	0.944		0.107	0.0054	2.24
	(−2.00)	(−2.34)	(42.06)		(2.83)		1976.2–2001.3
AS	−0.086	0.00022	0.920		0.015	0.0082	1.92
	(−2.27)	(2.22)	(27.79)		(0.35)		1966.1–2001.2
Annual							
BE	−0.167	0.00168	0.860			0.0077	1.85
	(−1.73)	(1.86)	(11.19)				1962–1998
DE	−0.029	−0.00012	0.923		0.214	0.0157	1.62
	(−0.56)	(−0.19)	(14.80)		(1.65)		1967–2000
NO	−0.035	0.00061	0.952			0.0315	1.10
	(−0.44)	(0.44)	(15.03)				1962–2000
IR	−0.291	0.00398	0.809		0.227	0.0215	2.63
	(−2.14)	(2.83)	(8.63)		(1.29)		1968–2000

Table B15
Test Results for Equation 15

	Lags	log PY	RHO	Stability			End Test		overid	
	p-val	p-val	p-val	AP	df	λ	p-val	End	p-val	df
Quarterly										
CA	.701	.000	.821	*67.00	5	6.531	.908	1998.4	.000	5
JA	.281		.553	*12.26	3	6.405	.619	1998.3	.133	4
AU	.004		.015	2.50	3	4.562	.696	1998.3	.138	5
IT	.133	.348	.154	5.23	4	4.150	.969	1998.3	.065	5
ST	.868		.055	*9.46	4	1.000	.887	1998.3	.000	5
UK	.000	.000	.007	*27.19	5	6.405	.763	1998.3	.000	4
FI	.077		.221	6.73	4	2.306	.312	1998.3	.001	5
AS	.903		.929	5.48	4	6.281	.615	1998.2	.381	5
Annual										
BE	.678		.669	*17.69	3	6.370	.406	1996		
DE	.462		.424	*26.75	4	5.009	.966	1998		
NO	.119		.001	*17.91	3	7.367	.853	1998		
IR	.028		.039	3.47	4	4.592	.500	1998		

Table B.5

Links between the US and ROW Models

The data on the variables for the United States that are needed when the US model is imbedded in the MC model were collected as described in Table B.2. These variables are (with the US subscript dropped): *EXDS*, *IMDS*, *M*, *MS*, *M95$A*, *M95$B*, *PM*, *PMP*, *PSI2*, *PW$*, *PX* (= *PX$*), *S*, *TT*, *XS*, and *X95$*. The PX_{US} variable here is not the same as the *PX* variable for the United States in Appendix A. The variable here is denoted *USPX* in the MC model. The *PX* variable for the United States is the price deflator of total sales of the firm sector.

Variable	Determination
$X95\$_{US}$	Determined in Table B.3.
PMP_{US}	Determined in Table B.3.
$PW\$_{US}$	Determined in Table B.3.
PX_{US}	Determined by an equation that is equivalent to equation 11 for the other countries. See the discussion in section B.6.
PEX =	$DEL3 \cdot PX_{US}$. In the US model by itself, *PEX* is determined as $PSI1 \cdot PX$, which is equation 32 in Table A.2. This equation is dropped when the US model is linked to the ROW model. *DEL3* is constructed from the data as PEX/PX_{US} and is taken to be exogenous.
PM_{US} =	$PSI2_{US} \cdot PMP_{US}$. This is the same as equation I-19 for the other countries.
PIM =	$DEL4 \cdot PM_{US}$. *PIM* is an exogenous variable in the US model by itself. *DEL4* is constructed from the data as PIM/PM_{US} and is taken to be exogenous.
EX =	$(X95\$_{US} + XS_{US} + EXDS_{US})/1000$. This is the same as equation I-2 for the other countries. *EX* is an exogenous variable in the US model by itself. $EXDS_{US}$ is constructed from the data as $1000EX - X95\$_{US} - XS_{US}$ and is taken to be exogenous.
M_{US} =	$1000IM - MS_{US} - IMDS_{US}$. This is the same as equation I-1 for the other countries. $IMDS_{US}$ is constructed from the data as $1000IM - M_{US} - MS_{US}$ and is taken to be exogenous.
$M95\$A_{US}$ =	$M_{US} - M95\$B_{US}$. This is the same as equation I-8 for the other countries.
S_{US} =	$PX_{US}(X95\$_{US} + XS_{US}) - PM_{US}(M_{US} + MS_{US}) + TT_{US}$. This is the same as equation I-6 for the other countries.

Note:

- The new exogenous variables for the US model when it is linked to the ROW model are *DEL3*, *DEL4*, $EXDS_{US}$, $IMDS_{US}$, $M95\$B_{US}$, MS_{US}, $PSI2_{US}$, TT_{US}, and XS_{US}. *EX* and *PIM* are exogenous in the US model by itself, but endogenous when the US model is linked to the ROW model.

Table B.6

Construction of the Balance-of-Payments Data: Data for S and TT

The relevant raw data variables are:

$M\$'$	Goods imports (fob) in \$, BOP data. [IFS78ABD]
$M\$$	Goods imports (fob) in \$. [IFS71V/E]
$X\$'$	Goods exports (fob) in \$, BOP data. [IFS78AAD]
$X\$$	Goods exports (fob) in \$. [IFS70/E]
$MS\$$	Services and income (debit) in \$, BOP data. [IFS78AED + IFS78AHD]
$XS\$$	Services and income (credit) in \$, BOP data. [IFS78ADD + IFS78AGD]
$XT\$$	Current transfers, n.i.e., (credit) in \$, BOP data. [IFS78AJD]
$MT\$$	Current transfers, n.i.e., (debit) in \$, BOP data. [IFS78AKD]

When quarterly data on all the above variables were available, then $S\$$ and $TT\$$ were constructed as:

$$S\$ = \qquad X\$' + XS\$ - M\$' - MS\$ + XT\$ - MT\$$$
$$TT\$ = \qquad S\$ - X\$ - XS\$ + M\$ + MS\$$$

where $S\$$ is total net goods, services, and transfers in \$ (balance of payments on current account) and $TT\$$ is total net transfers in \$.

When only annual data on $M\$'$ were available and quarterly data were needed, interpolated quarterly data were constructed using $M\$$. Similarly for $MS\$$.

When only annual data on $X\$'$ were available and quarterly data were needed, interpolated quarterly data were constructed using $X\$$. Similarly for $XS\$$, $XT\$$, and $MT\$$.

When no data on $M\$'$ were available, then $M\$'$ was taken to be $\lambda M\$$, where λ is the last observed value of $M\$'/M\$$. Similarly for $MS\$$ (where λ is the last observed annual value of $MS\$/M\$$).

When no data on $X\$'$ were available, then $X\$'$ was taken to be $\lambda X\$$, where λ is the last observed value of $X\$'/X\$$. Similarly for $XS\$$ (where λ is the last observed annual value of $XS\$/X\$$), for $XT\$$ (where λ is the last observed annual value of $XT\$/X\$$), and for $MT\$$ (where λ is the last observed annual value of $MT\$/X\$$).

The above equations for $S\$$ and $TT\$$ were then used to construct quarterly data for $S\$$ and $TT\$$.

After data on $S\$$ and $TT\$$ were constructed, data on S and TT were constructed as:

$$S = \qquad E \cdot S\$$$
$$TT = \qquad E \cdot TT\$$$

Note from MS and XS in Table B.2 and from $MS\$$ and $XS\$$ above that

$$MS\$ = \qquad (PM \cdot MS)/E$$
$$XS\$ = \qquad (PX \cdot XS)/E$$

Note also from Table B.2 that

$$M\$ = \qquad (PM \cdot M)/E$$
$$X\$ = \qquad (E95 \cdot PX \cdot X95\$)/E$$

Therefore, from the above equations, the equation for S can be written

$$S = \qquad\qquad PX(E95 \cdot X95\$ + XS) - PM(M + MS) + TT,$$

which is equation I-6 in Table B.3.

References

Adelman, I., and F. L. Adelman. 1959. "The Dynamic Properties of the Klein-Goldberger Model." *Econometrica*, 27, 596–625.

Akerlof, George A., William T. Dickens, and George L. Perry. 1996. "The Macroeconomics of Low Inflation." *Brookings Papers on Economic Activity*, 1–76.

Alogoskoufis, George, Charles Bean, Giuseppe Bertola, Daniel Cohen, Juan Dolado, and Gilles Saint-Paul. 1995. *Unemployment: Choices for Europe*. London: Centre for Economic Policy Research.

Amman, Hans M., and David A. Kendrick. 1999. "Linear Quadratic Optimization for Models with Rational Expectations and Learning." *Macroeconomic Dynamics*, 3, 534–543.

Andrews, Donald W. K. 2003. "End-of-Sample Instability Tests." *Econometrica*, 71, 1661–1694.

Andrews, Donald W. K., and Ray C. Fair. 1988. "Inference in Nonlinear Econometric Models with Structural Change." *Review of Economic Studies*, 55, 615–640.

Andrews, Donald W. K., and Werner Ploberger. 1994. "Optimal Tests When a Nuisance Parameter Is Present Only under the Alternative." *Econometrica*, 62, 1383–1414.

Berkowitz, J., and L. Kilian. 2000. "Recent Developments in Bootstrapping Time Series." *Econometric Reviews*, 19, 1–48.

Bianchi, C., G. Calzolari, and P. Corsi. 1976. "Divergences in the Results of Stochastic and Deterministic Simulation of an Italian Non-Linear Econometric Model." In L. Dekker, ed., *Simulation of Systems*. Amsterdam: North-Holland.

Binder, Michael, M. Hashem Pesaran, and S. Hossein Samiei. 2000. "Solution of Nonlinear Rational Expectations Models with Applications to Finite-Horizon Life-Cycle Models of Consumption." *Computational Economics*, 15, 25–57.

Blinder, Alan S. 1981. "Retail Inventory Behavior and Business Fluctuations." *Brookings Papers on Economic Activity*, 443–505.

Blinder, Alan S., and Janet L. Yellen. 2001. *The Fabulous Decade: Macroeconomic Lessons from the 1990s*. New York: Century Foundation Press.

Brown, B. W., and R. S. Mariano. 1984. "Residual-Based Procedures for Prediction and Estimation in a Nonlinear Simultaneous System." *Econometrica*, 52, 321–343.

Calzolari, G., and P. Corsi. 1977. "Stochastic Simulation as a Validation Tool for Econometric Models." Paper presented at IIASA Seminar, September 13–15, Laxenburg, Vienna.

Chow, Gregory C. 1968. "The Acceleration Principle and the Nature of Business Cycles." *Quarterly Journal of Economics*, 82, 403–418.

———— 1981. *Econometric Analysis by Control Methods*. New York: John Wiley & Sons.

———— 1989. "Rational versus Adaptive Expectations in Present Value Models." *Review of Economics and Statistics*, 71, 376–384.

Christian, James W. 1968. "A Further Analysis of the Objectives of American Monetary Policy." *Journal of Finance*, 23, 465–477.

Clarida, Richard, Jordi Galí, and Mark Gertler. 1999. "The Science of Monetary Policy: A New Keynesian Perspective." *Journal of Economic Literature*, 37, 1661–1707.

———— 2000. "Monetary Policy Rules and Macroeconomic Stability: Evidence and Some Theory." *Quarterly Journal of Economics*, 115, 147–180.

Cooper, J. P. 1974. *Development of the Monetary Sector, Prediction, and Policy Analysis in the FRB-MIT-Penn Model*. Lexington, MA: D.C. Heath.

Cooper, J. P., and S. Fischer. 1972. "Stochastic Simulation of Monetary Rules in Two Macroeconometric Models." *Journal of the American Statistical Association*, 67, 750–760.

———— 1974. "Monetary and Fiscal Policy in the Fully Stochastic St. Louis Econometric Model." *Journal of Money, Credit and Banking*, 6, 1–22.

Cumby, Robert E., John Huizinga, and Maurice Obstfeld. 1983. "Two-Step Two-Stage Least Squares Estimation in Models with Rational Expectations." *Journal of Econometrics*, 21, 333–355.

Dewald, William G., and Harry G. Johnson. 1963. "An Objective Analysis of the Objectives of American Monetary Policy, 1952–61." In Deane Carson, ed., *Banking and Monetary Studies*, 171–189. Homewood, IL: Richard D. Irwin.

Efron, B. 1979. "Bootstrap Methods: Another Look at the Jackknife." *Annals of Statistics*, 7, 1–26.

Eisner, Robert. 1997. "A New View of the NAIRU." In P. Davidson and J. Kregel, eds., *Improving the Global Economy: Keynesianism and the Growth in Output and Employment*. Cheltenham, UK, and Brookfield, VT: Edward Algar.

Evans, George W., and Garey Ramey. 2003. "Adaptive Expectations, Underparameterization, and the Lucas Critique."

Evans, M. K., L. Klein, and M. Saito. 1972. "Short-Run Prediction and Long-Run Simulation of the Wharton Model." In B. G. Hickman, ed., *Econometric Models of Cyclical Behavior*, 949–1139. New York: Columbia University Press.

Fair, R. C. 1974a. *A Model of Macroeconomic Activity*. Vol. 1: *The Theoretical Model*. Cambridge, MA: Ballinger Publishing Co.

———— 1974b. "On the Solution of Optimal Control Problems as Maximization Problems." *Annals of Economic and Social Measurement*, 3, 135–154.

———— 1978. "The Sensitivity of Fiscal Policy Effects to Assumptions about the Behavior of the Federal Reserve." *Econometrica*, 46, 1165–1179.

———— 1980a. "Estimating the Expected Predictive Accuracy of Econometric Models." *International Economic Review*, 21, 355–378.

———— 1980b. "Estimating the Uncertainty of Policy Effects in Nonlinear Econometric Models." *Econometrica*, 48, 1381–1391.

—— 1984. *Specification, Estimation, and Analysis of Macroeconometric Models.* Cambridge, MA: Harvard University Press.

—— 1989. "The Production Smoothing Model Is Alive and Well." *Journal of Monetary Economics*, 23, 353–370.

—— 1993a. "Estimating Event Probabilities in Macroeconometric Models." In J. H. Stock and M. W. Watson, eds., *Business Cycles, Indicators, and Forecasting*, 157–176. Chicago: University of Chicago Press.

—— 1993b. "Testing the Rational Expectations Hypothesis in Macroeconometric Models." *Oxford Economic Papers*, 45, 169–190.

—— 1994. *Testing Macroeconometric Models.* Cambridge, MA: Harvard University Press.

—— 1998. "Estimated Stabilization Costs of the EMU." *National Institute Economic Review*, 164, 90–99.

—— 1999. "Estimated Inflation Costs Had European Unemployment Been Reduced in the 1980s by Macro Policies." *Journal of Macroeconomics*, 21, 1–28.

—— 2000. "Testing the NAIRU Model for the United States." *Review of Economics and Statistics*, 82, 64–71.

—— 2002. "On Modeling the Effects of Inflation Shocks," *Contributions to Macroeconomics*, vol. 2, no. 1, article 3. *http://www.bepress.com/bejm/contributions/vol2/iss1/art3.*

—— 2003a. "Optimal Control and Stochastic Simulation of Large Nonlinear Models with Rational Expectations." *Computational Economics*, 21, 245–256.

—— 2003b. "Bootstrapping Macroeconomeric Models." *Studies in Nonlinear Dynamics and Econometrics*, vol. 7, no. 4, article 1. *http://www.bepress.com/snde/vol7/iss4/art1.*

—— 2003c. "Risk Aversion and Stock Prices."

—— 2004a. "Testing for a New Economy in the 1990s." *Business Economics*, 43–53.

—— 2004b. "Estimates of the Effectiveness of Monetary Policy," *Journal of Money, Credit, and Banking*. Forthcoming.

Fair, Ray C., and Kathryn M. Dominguez. 1991. "Effects of the Changing U.S. Age Distribution on Macroeconomic Equations." *American Economic Review*, 81, 1276–1294.

Fair, Ray C., and E. Philip Howrey. 1996. "Evaluating Alternative Monetary Policy Rules." *Journal of Monetary Economics*, 38, 173–193.

Fair, Ray C., and William R. Parke. 2003. *The Fair-Parke Program for the Estimation and Analysis of Nonlinear Econometric Models.* Available at *http://fairmodel.econ.yale.edu.* (First version dated 1980.)

Fair, Ray C., and Robert J. Shiller. 1990. "Comparing information in Forecasts from Econometric Models." *American Economic Review*, 80, 375–389.

Fair, Ray C., and John B. Taylor. 1983. "Solution and Maximum Likelihood Estimation of Dynamic Rational Expectations Models." *Econometrica*, 51, 1169–1185.

—— 1990. "Full Information Estimation and Stochastic Simulation of Models with Rational Expectations." *Journal of Applied Econometrics*, 5, 381–392.

Federal Reserve Board. 2000. "FRB/US Equation Documentation for the VAR-Based Expectations Version of the Model."

Feldstein, Martin, and James H. Stock. 1993. "The Use of a Monetary Aggregate to Target Nominal GDP." NBER Working Paper no. 4304.

Finan, Frederico S., and Robert Tetlow. 1999. "Optimal Control of Large, Forward-Looking Models." Board of Governors of the Federal Reserve System.

Freedman, D. 1981. "Bootstrapping Regression Models." *Annals of Statistics*, 9, 1218–1228.

———— 1984. "On Bootstrapping Two-Stage Least-Squares Estimates in Stationary Linear Models." *Annals of Statistics*, 12, 827–842.

Fromm, G., L. R. Klein, and G. R. Schink. 1972. "Short- and Long-Term Simulations with the Brookings Model." In B. G. Hickman, ed., *Econometric Models of Cyclical Behavior*, 201–292. New York: Columbia University Press.

Fuhrer, Jeffrey C. 1995. "The Phillips Curve Is Alive and Well." *New England Economic Review*, 41–56.

Garbade, K. D. 1975. *Discretionary Control of Aggregate Economic Activity*. Lexington, MA: D. C. Heath.

Giordani, Paolo. 2003. "On Modeling the Effects of Inflation Shocks: Comments and Some Further Evidence." *Contributions to Macroeconomics*, vol. 3, no. 1, article 1. *http://www.bepress.com/bejm/contributions/vol3/iss1/art1*.

Gordon, Robert J. 1980. "Comments on George L. Perry, 'Inflation in Theory and Practice,' " *Brookings Papers on Economic Activity*, 249–257.

———— 1997. "The Time-Varying NAIRU and Its Implications for Economic Policy." *Journal of Economic Perspectives*, 11, 11–32.

———— 2000a. Comment on Dale W. Jorgenson and Kevin J. Stiroh, "Raising the Speed Limit: U.S. Economic Growth in the Information Age." *Brookings Papers on Economic Activity*, 1, 212–222.

———— 2000b. "Does the 'New Economy' Measure up to the Great Inventions of the Past?" *Journal of Economic Perspectives*, 14, 49–74.

Gordon, Robert J., and Stephen R. King. 1982. "The Output Cost of Disinflation in Traditional and Vector Autoregressive Models." *Brookings Papers on Economic Activity*, 205–242.

Green, G. R., M. Liebenberg, and A. A. Hirsch. 1972. "Short- and Long-Term Simulations of the OBE Econometric Model." In B. G. Hickman, ed., *Econometric Models of Cyclical Behavior*, 25–123. New York: Columbia University Press.

Haitovsky, Y., and N. Wallace. 1972. "A Study of Discretionary and Nondiscretionary Monetary and Fiscal Policies in the Context of Stochastic Macroeconometric Models." In V. Zarnowitz, ed., *The Business Cycle Today*. New York: Columbia University Press.

Hall, P. 1988. "Theoretical Comparison of Bootstrap Confidence Intervals." *Annals of Statistics*, 16, 927–953.

———— 1992. *The Bootstrap and Edgeworth Expansion*. New York: Springer-Verlag.

Hall, P., and J. L. Horowitz. 1996. "Bootstrap Critical Values for Tests Based on Generalized-Method-of-Moments Estimators." *Econometrica*, 64, 891–916.

Hallett, Andrew Hughes, Patrick Minford, and Anupam Rastogi. 1993. "The European Monetary System: Achievements and Survival." In Ralph C. Bryant, Peter Hooper, and Catherine L. Mann, eds., *Evaluating Policy Regimes: New Research in Empirical Macroeconomics*, 617–668. Washington, DC: Brookings Institution.

Hansen, Lars Peter. 1982. "Large Sample Properties of Generalized Method of Moments Estimators." *Econometrica*, 50, 1029–1054.

Härdle, W., J. Horowitz, and J. Kreiss. 2001. "Bootstrap Methods for Time Series."

Hendry, David F., Adrian R. Pagan, and J. Denis Sargan. 1984. "Dynamic Specifications." In Z. Griliches and M. D. Intriligator, eds., *Handbook of Econometrics*, 1023–1100. Amsterdam: North-Holland.

Horowitz, J. L. 1997. "Bootstrap Methods in Econometrics: Theory and Numerical Performance." Chapter 7 in D. M. Kreps and K. F. Wallis, *Advances in Economics and Econometrics: Theory and Applications*, vol. 3, 188–222. Cambridge: Cambridge University Press.

Hurwicz, L. 1950. "Least-Squares Bias in Time Series." In T. C. Koopmans, ed., *Statistical Inference in Dynamic Economic Models*, 365–383. Cowles Commission Monograph no. 10. New York: John Wiley & Sons.

Judd, John P., and Glen D. Rudebusch. 1998. "Taylor's Rule and the Fed: 1970–1997," *Federal Reserve Bank of San Francisco Economic Review*, 3, 3–16.

Kenen, Peter B. 1969. "The Theory of Optimum Currency Areas." In Mundell, Robert A., and Alexander A. Swoboda, eds., *Monetary Problems of the International Economy*, 41–60. Chicago: University of Chicago Press.

Khoury, Salwa S. 1990. "The Federal Reserve Reaction Function: A Specification Search." In Thomas Mayer, ed., *The Political Economy of American Monetary Policy*, 27–49. Cambridge: Cambridge University Press.

Kilian, L. 1998. "Small-Sample Confidence Intervals for Impulse Response Functions." *Review of Economics and Statistics*, 80, 218–230.

Krugman, Paul. R. 1996. "Stay on Their Backs," *New York Times Magazine*, 36–37, February 4.

Layard, Richard, Stephen Nickell, and Richard Jackman. 1991. *Unemployment*. Oxford: Oxford University Press.

Levin, Andrew, Volker Wieland, and John C. Williams. 1999. "Robustness of Simple Monetary Policy Rules under Model Uncertainty." In Taylor (1999a), 263–316.

Li, H., and G. S. Maddala. 1996. "Bootstrapping Time Series Models." *Econometric Reviews*, 15, 115–158.

Lucas, Robert E., Jr. 1976. "Econometric Policy Evaluation: A Critique." In K. Brunner and A. H. Meltzer, eds., *The Phillips Curve and Labor Markets*. Amsterdam: North-Holland.

Ludvigson, Sydney, and Charles Steindel. 1999. "How Important Is the Stock Market Effect on Consumption." *Economic Policy Review*, Federal Reserve Bank of New York, 5, 29–51.

MacKinnon, J. G. 2002. "Bootstrap Inference in Econometrics." Presidential address at the 2002 Annual Meeting of the Canadian Economics Association.

Mankiw, N. Gregory. 1994. *Macroeconomics*. 2nd ed. New York: Worth Publishers.

Masson, Paul R., and Stephen Symansky. 1992. "Evaluating the EMS and EMU Using Stochastic Simulations: Some Issues." In Ray Barrell and John Whitley, eds., *Macroeconomic Policy Coordination in Europe: The ERM and Monetary Union*, 12–34. London: Sage Publications.

Masson, Paul R., and Bart G. Turtelboom. 1997. "Characteristics of the Euro, the Demand for Reserves, and Policy Coordination under the EMU." In Paul R. Masson, Thomas H. Krueger, and Bart G. Turtelboom, *EMU and the International Monetary System*, 194–224. Washington, DC: International Monetary Fund.

McCallum, Bennett T., and Edward Nelson. 1999. "Performance of Operational Policy Rules in an Estimated Semiclassical Structural Model." In Taylor (1999a), 15–45.

McKinnon, Ronald. 1963. "Optimum Currency Areas." *American Economic Review*, 53, 717–725.

McNees, Stephen K. 1981. "The Methodology of Macroeconometric Model Comparisons." In J. Kmenta and J. B. Ramsey, eds., *Large Scale Macroeconometric Models*, 397–442. Amsterdam: North-Holland.

——— 1986. "Modeling the Fed: A Forward-Looking Monetary Policy Reaction Function." *New England Economic Review*, November/December, 3–8.

——— 1992. "A Forward-Looking Monetary Policy Reaction Function: Continuity and Change." *New England Economic Review*, November/December, 3–13.

Muench, T., A. Rolnick, N. Wallace, and W. Weiler. 1974. "Tests for Structural Change and Prediction Intervals for the Reduced Forms of the Two Structural Models of the US: The FRB-MIT and Michigan Quarterly Models." *Annals of Economic and Social Measurement*, 3, 491–519.

Mundell, Robert A. 1961. "A Theory of Optimum Currency Areas." *American Economic Review*, 50, 657–665.

Nagar, A.L. 1969. "Stochastic Simulation of the Brookings Econometric Model." In J. S. Duesenberry, G. Fromm, L. R. Klein, and E. Kuh, eds., *The Brookings Model: Some Further Results*. Chicago: Rand McNally.

Nordhaus, William D. 2000. "Productivity Growth and the New Economy." Cowles Foundation Discussion Paper no. 1284.

Okun, Arthur M. 1971. "The Personal Tax Surcharge and Consumer Demand, 1968–70." *Brookings Papers on Economic Activity*, 167–204.

Oliner, Stephen D., and Daniel E. Sichel. 2000. "The Resurgence of Growth in the Late 1990s: Is Information Technology the Story?" *Journal of Economic Perspectives*, 14, 3–22.

Orcutt, G. H. 1948. "A Study of the Autoregressive Nature of the Time Series Used for Tinbergen's Model of the Economic System of the United States, 1919–1932," *Journal of the Royal Statistical Society*, series B, 1–45.

Reifschneider, David, Robert Tetlow, and John Williams. 1999. "Aggregate Disturbances, Monetary Policy, and the Macroeconomy: The FRB/US Perspective." *Federal Reserve Bulletin*, January, 1–19.

Romer, David. 2000. "Keynesian Macroeconomics without the LM Curve." *Journal of Economic Perspectives*, 14, 149–169.

Rotemberg, Julio J., and Michael Woodford. 1999. "Interest Rate Rules in an Estimated Sticky Price Model." In Taylor (1999a), 57–119.

Rudebusch, Glenn D. 1999. "Is the Fed Too Timid? Monetary Policy in an Uncertain World."

Rudebusch, Glenn D., and Lars E. O. Svensson. 1999. "Policy Rules for Inflation Targeting." In Taylor (1999a), 203–246.

Runkle, D. E. 1987. "Vector Autoregressions and Reality." *Journal of Business and Economic Statistics*, 5, 437–442.

Schink, G. R. 1971. "Small Sample Estimates of the Variance-Covariance Matrix Forecast Error for Large Econometric Models: The Stochastic Simulation Technique." Ph.D. dissertation, University of Pennsylvania.

———— 1974. "Estimation of Small Sample Forecast Error for Nonlinear Dynamic Models: A Stochastic Simulation Approach."

Sims, Christopher A. 1980. "Macroeconomics and Reality." *Econometrica*, 48, 1–48.

Sowey, E. R. 1973. "Stochastic Simulation for Macroeconomic Models: Methodology and Interpretation." In A. A. Powell and R. W. Williams, eds., *Econometric Studies of Macro and Monetary Relations*. Amsterdam: North-Holland.

Staiger, Douglas, James Stock, and Mark Watson. 1997a. "The NAIRU, Unemployment and Monetary Policy." *Journal of Economic Perspectives*, 11, 33–49.

———— 1997b. "How Precise are Estimates of the Natural Rate of Unemployment." In Christina Romer and David Romer, eds., *Reducing Inflation: Motivation and Strategy*. Chicago: University of Chicago Press for the NBER.

Starr-McCluer, Martha. 1998. "Stock Market Wealth and Consumer Spending." Board of Governors of the Federal Reserve System.

Svensson, Lars E. O. 2003. "What Is Wrong with Taylor Rules? Using Judgement in Monetary Policy through Targeting Rules." *Journal of Economic Literature*, 41, 426–477.

Taylor, John B. 1985. "What Would Nominal GDP Targeting Do to the Business Cycle?" *Carnegie-Rochester Series on Public Policy*, 22, 61–84.

———— 1993. "Discretion versus Policy Rules in Practice." *Carnegie-Rochester Series on Public Policy*, 39, 195–214.

———— ed. 1999a. *Monetary Policy Rules*. Chicago: University of Chicago Press.

———— 1999b. "Introduction." In Taylor (1999a), 1–14.

———— 1999c. "A Historical Analysis of Monetary Policy Rules." In Taylor (1999a), 319–341.

———— 2000. "Teaching Modern Macroeconomics at the Principles Level." *American Economic Review*, 90, 90–94.

Triplett, Jack E. 1992. "Economic Theory and BEA's Alternative Quantity and Price Indexes." *Survey of Current Business*, 72, 49–52.

von Hagen, Jürgen, and Manfred J. M. Neumann. 1994. "Real Exchange Rates within and between Currency Areas: How Far Away Is the EMU?" *Review of Economics and Statistics*, 76, 236–244.

White, Halbert. 1980. "A Heteroskedasticity Consistent Covariance Matrix Estimator and a Direct test for Heteroskedasticity." *Econometrica*, 48, 817–838.

White, Halbert,and Ian Domowitz. 1984. "Nonlinear Regression with Dependent Observations." *Econometrica*, 52, 143–161.

Wooldridge, Jeffrey M. 2000. *Introductory Econometrics: A Modern Approach*. Mason, OH: South-Western College Publishing.

Wyplosz, Charles. 1997. "EMU: Why and How It Might Happen." *Journal of Economic Perspectives*, 11, 3–22.

Young, Allan H. 1992. "Alternative Measures of Change in Real Output and Prices." *Survey of Current Business*, 72, 32–48.

Index